DEBT is a Four-Letter Word
But it Need Not Be!

THE COLLEGE EXPERIENCE

By
Richard M. Gutkowski, Ph.D., P.E.

ISBN-13: 978-0-9977216-0-7

Cover Design by Jody Zorn
http://www.zornphoto.com

DEDICATION

For the long line of young people and parents
nearing or already in the red rut of student loan debt!

Table of Contents

Borrowing money is an act of getting into **DEBT**. Repaying money is the act of getting out of **DEBT**. The getting into step can occur very easily. The getting out of step is the challenge. But if either step is handled poorly, then trouble will ensue.

When the amount of one's **DEBT** feels like it's becoming hard to repay, that's worrisome. When it actually gets too hard to repay, that's concerning. If the reason you got there was borrowing the money as an act of desperation – that's scary. But **DEBT** need not be scary. The way to avoid this is to be armed with the skills necessary to wisely borrow money and effectively repay it.

THE COLLEGE EXPERIENCE is the first volume in an ongoing series of books; **DEBT is a Four-Letter word, But it Need Not Be!** The focus of the books is on individuals who are new or relatively new to debt and are hesitant, nervous or afraid of it. Each volume will cover different aspects of debt needs and issues that occur as a young person grows from about the age of 16 to the age of 35 or so. The format of each book is a set of Lessons written in a narrative style – not as a textbook. But the series is not written in the fashionable style of "Subject for Dummies" primers. It does target basic, beginner subject matter but the content is extensive and thorough.

My underlying purpose in writing this book series is to guide the reader toward avoiding excessive debt and to effectively get out of excessive debt should it happen or already exist. Collectively, the books will help you gain solid technical ability to understand and effectively use debt; not abuse or be abused by it. I will prepare you to be logical and wise in dealing with any loan from the moment you first encounter a need for it. You will learn to conceive, calculate and evaluate options for any loan and make astute, strategic choices.

In my early years, I had some naiveté, unawareness, and a degree of ignorance about formally borrowing money. I had plenty of the negative surprises that debt can and does put into one's life and its consequences to financial well-being. Little by little I learned about the ins and outs of credit cards, bank loans, auto loans, student loans (first when I was a student, later for my daughter), home mortgages and other common types of loans. I learned from my mistakes, omissions and ignorance about exactly how to prepare for and make decisions about borrowing and paying back money. When I learned to dig into and understand the details, I began to make better decisions and do it faster but effectively.

As a professor in civil engineering for almost forty years, teaching and advising young people was a large part of my heart beat. Helping them hone their technical talents and launch professional careers was my endearing commitment. Now retired, it was with that same vigor and caring that I undertook writing this book series. I dedicated myself to developing a valuable guide for young people and their parents to use in managing debt matters as they move through their college experience.

During my career as a university professor I applied for and obtained numerous education and research grants and awards. So maneuvering through the mind-taxing, sometimes befuddling language of government program and application material is in my sweet spot. I am accustomed to deciphering requirements, rules, and regulations that seem overwhelming at first glance.

I managed hundreds of budgets with bottom lines ranging from the low thousands of dollars, to six figures, and beyond. Collectively, I managed millions of dollars. Aside from that, I guided numerous college students to effectively utilize and manage portions of the budget available from my funded research projects. If they ran out of money, they would be in trouble. With proper oversight, that never happened

My evolution in budget management as a professor led me to transfer those highly developed skills into the domestic environment. Computer-based tools I honed at work found their way into managing home finances. They enabled invaluable tracking of income and expenses and producing periodic account summaries, budget status, expenditure projections and so forth. Indeed, those very tools served to produce all of the numerical content of my book series. With these tools at hand, my wife and I grew to manage finances and debt in a strongly cooperative and coordinated way.

The ***DEBT is a Four -Letter word, But it Need Not Be!!*** book series converts my lifetime of hard knocks, bad and good experiences and subsequent growth in debt management into a powerful sequence of Lessons I learned and now share with you. It reflects my incisive evolution about debt acquisition and management and my developed techniques and strategies to astutely deal with debt needs at all stages of life. It compacts my many years of development into a powerful guide to help you gain that knowledge in the time it takes you to read and learn the content. While pragmatic and detailed, I wrote it in a fun, narrative style so the reader will enjoy learning what otherwise might be unexciting financial matters.

In part, I wrote for parents who want to work with their child to develop his or her skills in borrowing money. I am a parent and worked carefully and effectively to achieve wise debt management and positive outcomes for my daughter's needs as she grew up. In doing that I strove to teach her skills along the way and motivate her to use them. I feel I achieved that to a high degree. Some of the content of ***DEBT is a Four-Letter word, But it Need Not Be!*** reflects personal parenting steps I used along the way.

The purpose of the books is to help the reader understand and control debt in technically strategic ways. The bulwark is the Situations described in each Lesson which illustrate examples of various loan events with extensive details about them (including needed calculations) based on the considerations taught in the series. While hypothetical, they realistically mimic circumstances commonly encountered in everyday life. By learning the concepts and examining the Situations described in each volume an adult of any age who desires to leapfrog to greater understanding the ins and outs of loans, expanded ability to negotiate wise loans and confidence to do so, will achieve those needs.

DEBT is a Four -Letter word, But it Need Not Be! is an enjoyable, in-depth written path for both the neophyte and the experienced budgeter to progress to higher skills and confidence about borrowing money and repaying it. The intent is to keep the cost of debt as low as possible. Hence the use of "it" instead of "It" in the sub-tile to the book series. I invite you to one of its trailheads. You can walk along at your own pace and have fun!

Open your mind, sharpen your pencil and let the LESSONS on **THE COLLEGE EXPERIENCE** begin!

A FEW WORDS ABOUT "Math"

Debt involves money and money involves numbers. I remember my Dad admonishing me (then a kid) "Be sure to know how to count money-yours and others! Getting through life is tough and costly if you cannot do it." All calculations in this Primer are applicable to savings, debt and interest paid on debt. The reader needs to be able to multiply, divide, add, and subtract as learned up to a high school level and to follow formulas.

Many realistic, hypothetical "Situations" are used and involve debt depicted in ways one can and, for many, will encounter. They are written in narrative style to tell the story needed as the main setting for learning. Any mathematics involved is presented in prose style. Calculations are first presented step by step. Once the sequence is shown, further results are summarized and/or tabulated. Formulas are written in worded form matched to words in the text. They don't look like what one sees in a math book, but rather what one might say if spoken as words. So, the need to "memorize" symbols that look like math is entirely avoided. Short, easy to do "Exercises" primarily augment Situations and focus on the reader doing pieces of the same math.

For business matters, monetary amounts are in dollars and cents, e.g. $22.64 or $1024.00. Occasionally a value is written in whole dollars, e.g. $1024, for ease and to help fit tabulated numbers into the page width. In the digital present, numerical information is often presented in printed documents (such as mortgage statements) and computer output, <u>without</u> commas. Almost always tabulated information is so presented. So $1,000.00, $100,000.00, $12,345.67 and $123,456.78 will be written as $1000.00, $100000.00, $12345.67 and $123456.78. It spins one's eyeballs for a while, but they do adjust to it. Please bear with it until you hone in.

Electronic calculators in your cell phone are adequate. Of course, some calculated numbers are extremely and overly precise. For example, 1/3 = 0.33333333 so if it is $ we "round it off" to $0.33. But some number must be precise when part of a calculation. A number like 0.02178467 might be rounded to 0.02178 or 0.021785 or might be used as is. The less it is "rounded" the more "precise" it is. Sometimes "very precise" is needed, mostly not. Don't worry! The author had to do that, not you, and mostly behind the scenes.

If you repeat a series of the author's calculations on a calculator your results can be somewhat different. Where he gets $20.61 you might get $20.63, $20.67, $20.70, or even something more different! When reading, just follow the numbers, even if you get slightly different ones if you try to confirm them. That way you avoid the weeds and see the forest. Sometimes you need to see individual trees, too. So in each Situation, read to see the flow of numbers to and look again to see the details of the trickling stream. It is not vital that you absorb every number. Watch enough to know how the water got from point A to point B to point C and onward to the faucet which gives you the results.

INTRODUCTION

What is "the college experience"?

About the age of sixteen, young people are approaching the time period wherein **DEBT** enters their world in a formal way. For many the first encounter will be with aspects of attending college. Indeed, about 80% of high school graduates choose to and do proceed to higher education. When that decision process begins the child and his or her parents embark on the period of time I term "the college experience".

The college experience is the time period of anticipating, pursuing and paying for a college education. It begins before ever stepping foot on a campus. It starts with a child's heartfelt desire to be accepted into an academic program at a college that best fits his or her career endeavor and the family's financial means. It ends when all the costs of that education have been paid. It is my belief that to effectively finance a college education the parents and child must team in the development of and use of the resources necessary to complete the experience.

At the outset, the opportunity to fulfill the heartfelt desire is hanging in the balance. College entrance examinations are taken and results are awaited. Applications are made to a slew of institutions fitting one's academic goals. Most students have a top choice in mind, the one college they most desire to attend. Uncertainty of acceptance leads to several desirable alternatives. A pile of applications get submitted. Outcomes are awaited.

Atop the anxiety-filled application and selection process involved in admission to a college of one's choice are the high costs involved. Be it a two-year vocational or community college option or a full blown four-year program of study at a major university or options in between, it costs lots of money to attend college. The cost of multiple application fees alone can accumulate to a noticeable amount of money. Tuition, fees, book costs, living expenses, transportation, and social life are the primary demands on financial resources. In many, maybe most, cases the worrisome first need to have a young person obtain and use a credit and/or debit card aggravates the anxiety.

Parents weigh the possible extent of financial commitment needed. One thing is certain; the total cost involved will be substantial. Financial aid in the form of scholarships and means based grants may come along. But relatively few students manage the full costs that way. Usually, parents have to infill the residual costs. Mostly, parents cannot sustain even those remaining costs "out of pocket". Borrowing money is on their radar. "Student loans" are in sight.

Uncertainty of parental capacity to finance the costs of the college experience adds to the "hanging in the balance" scale involved in their child proceeding to a reachable college of choice. So the cost component must be faced; mutually between parents and the student. Assembling complete information on the cost of potential academic programs, likely student loan needs, and comparisons of costs of different loan options move front and center. To reach the goal of affording the resulting costs for that reachable college of choice, strategically planning the acceptance of loans and their eventual repayment is essential.

How this book will help you

THE COLLEGE EXPERIENCE volume provides my focused insight and effective strategies about the managing debt aspects faced in preparing for and completing college studies. Narratively, the reader is sequentially placed within settings that typically occur as the college experience moves along. Monetarily, detailed procedures and tactics are offered for numerically assessing and handling the financial challenges that arise in each setting. Learning the overall content will significantly help young people and parents aiming to strategically finance a college education. Moreover, you will be well armed to complete the college experience on good financial terms.

This volume begins with the topic of credit card debt. Credit (or debit) cards enter a student's zone early in the college experience. Indeed, high schoolers tend to want such cards as soon as possible. Not all parents want to let them have them. College students will need one for ongoing normal daily expenses. If you are a student reader, maybe credit and debit cards scare you. I would bet my mortgage most parent readers are wary and extremely cautious about your emerging need for a credit card. Some student readers may already have one, have actually fallen into too much debt and need to get out of it. Perhaps some parent readers face the same hurdles and value advice themselves. Both will learn how credit card debt works and how it can become unpayable, if uniformed about how that can occur. If so, you will learn how to dig out of the hole. Then you will learn how to quickly make the debt vanish

Paying for a college education very likely requires acquiring student loan debt (borrowing money). Reading this volume will enable you to clearly understand all the seeming government student loan gibberish and rules found on the applicable federal web site. You will be able to determine ongoing and total loan costs. You will become aware of the potentially very high debt possible and accompanying high cost. You will learn how to strategically assess and make the critical decisions about repayment, including the option of consolidating multiple student loans into a single loan.

I share vital behind the scenes information on how conditions set in a consolidated loan are determined by the lender. There are hidden pitfalls and you will see how to handle them allowing you to try to better negotiate if you don't like the terms you are offered. Then I show you how you can consolidate your student loans and repay them faster, saving buckets of money on interest.

Using my approaches to guide you and working together, parents and students will be confident credit and debit card worries will be vanquished. They will be well prepared to have all their student loans made and paid off in a wise manner! Students will walk down the Commencement aisle feeling much less financially overwhelmed than typically happens. Parents will watch with bigger smiles, feeling much more secure about having managed the finances involved in the college experience.

How to read this volume

THE COLLEGE EXPERIENCE is comprised of twenty (20) chapters, termed LESSONS. Collectively, the LESSONS teach the reader to be strategic in borrowing money and paying it back so as to minimize the costs. Sequentially, they are chronologically aligned to debt-based events encountered in a typical young person's life. In real-life, those events become increasingly more challenging. So it is in this book as well.

While text content carefully guides you along, the bulwark is the SITUATIONS presented within each LESSON. They are used to illustrate example debt circumstances and the math calculations associated with addressing them. As you progress through the LESSONS, the text and SITUATIONS each cover increasingly more involved debt needs and circumstances. The facts involved in each SITUATION constitute a monetary setting which the author uses to teach the reader either a good or a bad aspect of entering into and/or handling debt. In each, closing observations are made about the main points to be learned from the example. In some cases, tabulated information is then presented to provide useful, handy means to apply the concepts and methods without need of the lengthy calculations.

Each SITUATION involves re-use of high school level mathematics. Equations and methods involved are first covered in the text preceding the SITUATION(S). Typically, it's a prose description of a sequence of calculations with embedded illustrative math (numerical work). Then the SITUATIONS either extend those to a longer loan time frame or re-do them for different numerical values for the circumstance, such as a change in the rate of interest involved.

The suggested approach to each SITUATION is to carefully read the precedent text description and illustration, Then read through the SITUATION at a comfortable pace, but as quickly as manageable. Do that without delving into the weeds of the particular numbers being processed. The purpose of doing that is to see the flow of the calculations involved and the gist of what observations they lead to. Then go back and trace the actual numbers so as to learn how to do the calculations involved. If you can take time to confirm each calculated number, all the better. If you prefer to trust the author's math that is perfectly fine. Either way,

Periodic short Exercises (sort of optional homework) offer the reader check points to confirm his/her understanding of the subject matter. They provide a chance to see if you have learned the specifics of the calculation steps involved. I encourage you to try them and confirm the answers which I've given you. If you try hard and cannot get those results, don't hesitate to contact me about it. Whether you do them or not the answers (or partial answers) themselves provide additional learning and insight into the subject matter of the particular LESSON.

For pertinent external information and any thoughts that arise late in the publication process of a volume, I place them in an APPENDIX IV entitled Afterthoughts.

Meet my characters

In **THE COLLEGE EXPERIENCE**, you will meet my fictionalized Nicole and her advisor Dad. They serve three purposes. You will follow along as they jointly weave their way through their version of the college experience. Via that ongoing thread, I provide a continuing story of how a more or less typical young person encounters debt as she moves from high school into college and through the college years to graduation. Observing how she and her Dad verbally and relationally conduct each stage is the first target for learning. Observing the concepts, methods and calculations the Dad teaches to his daughter is the second aim. Observing how the Dad gradually and steadily helps his daughter ween away to increased self-reliance is the third aim.

The story begins with the seemingly simple SITUATION of teen-aged Nicole anxiously wanting a credit card. After asking parental approval, it proves to be not so simple to get one. Eventually she does. You will see how that happens.

As Nicole's life proceeds toward college, she confronts other SITUATIONS involving either the desire or the need to take on debt. The further she moves along the more serious the debt Situations she encounters. Simultaneously, when asked, her Dad intervenes to help. In a caring, knowledgeable, wise way her Dad teaches Nicole how to manage each SITUATION. Together they identify each and every issue and work together to resolve them. Each SITUATION enables you to learn from their personal interaction as well as the numerical work involved.

More and more Nicole learns to smartly take on debt and prepares to eventually handle it herself. At one point she even promises to outsmart her Dad, one day down the road. Watch as Nicole moves through her college experience and see if she reaches that point. In the end Nicole and her Dad have managed the college experience successfully. My hope and belief is then you will do so as well; in your own version of **THE COLLEGE EXPERIENCE**.

Contiguous with but subsequent to that central thread, many additional realistic SITUATIONS are described involving other fictional individuals living **THE COLLEGE EXPERIENCE**. Each SITUATION either emphasizes by hyperbole how debt can grow quickly or presents a fiscal circumstance and challenge experienced in ordinary life when money is borrowed. Each SITUATION details how the debt involved is handled either poorly or effectively.

The interaction of Nicole and her Dad and their dialogue offer valuable observations of how those two particular people approach it. For me it is an ideal I tried to reach with my own daughter, not always reaching it. But my intent for it always existed and often was achieved. In the youngest period it took patience and effort. Eventually it began to happen. In the case of Nicole's Dad, he was experienced in the debt matters she faced. He caringly but craftily weaned her into his comfort arena and himself into her comfort zone. As a result she learned to learn as much as how to handle the debt needs. Once she did she learned an awful lot.

Hopefully, for parent readers wanting to work closely with their child (young person) to develop similar skills to what Nicole learned, their example helps. Hopefully, this book is a vehicle in the path you take to get there. For the child (young person) of that parent, hopefully both of you are reading this book. Then it's very likely to come about more quickly than you think. If it's only one of you reading it, please encourage the other one to do so, for your sake, not mine.

Now let's begin to peek in on Nicole and her Dad. Then slowly but surely we'll push ourselves closer and closer to the action.

LESSON 1 Credit Cards: So Easy to Get – So Hard to Control!

It's an exciting time for 16-year old Nicole. Her junior year in high school has just begun. Like many teens reaching that age, she feels she has bridged the divide between being a kid and being an adult. Adulthood still awaits but she's unaware of and almost oblivious to that reality. She's feeling pretty grown up already.

Nicole has survived her driving lessons. Her parents have, too. She has yet to own a car, but that's unimportant to her. That's well down the road in her priorities. For now she does have "wheels" to go about her way for personal needs. Mom and Dad purchased a low cost, used VW NEW BEETLE for her. Of course they put "conditions on it". Though months have passed, the conversations with her Dad still reprise in her mind now and then. Sometimes that encore even seems to ring in her ears like a daily preset alarm clock doing its thing once again. Sometimes it just pieces of them. Sometimes they are complimentary. Sometimes they are otherwise.

"Nicole, you've turned sixteen and are well behaved and superb in the class room.

"You're probably itching to not have your parents driving you everywhere

"You earned a driving license in a commendable way.

"You drove carefully and safely when you trained in my car.

"So I've bought you a car. It's a used VW but I think you'll like it.

 "You are not to be a taxi service for your friends.

"If you are in an unavoidable accident, don't worry, the main concern is are you Ok.

"If you foolishly damage the car you pay to fix it. Until you do we drive you or you walk."

So Nicole drives alertly and mostly as a sole occupant.

But cars are not on her mind as she returns home from her first day of classes. Credit cards have entered her mindset. She wants to have one. She wonders how her request to her Dad will pan out. The car scenario flashes in her mind. But she is anxious to find out and feeling energetic.

Entering the house she calls out, "Hey Dad! Dad, are you home?"

Sofa back to her, her Dad slowly turns his seated body and acknowledges. "Yes I am! I right here Sweetie. What do you want?"

Nicole chimes out, "Some of my older friends in the senior class came back this year with a credit card. They were pretty proud, almost bragging about it.

"I never thought about it but now I'm sort of envious of them. We've never talked about credit cards, so I don't know anything about them. I guess I'll eventually need one, so can you explain them to me?

Then maybe I can get one too?"

"Well, Nicole. I'm just relaxing so we can talk about that right now."

Being very anxious to "get one", Nicole excitedly concurs. "That's terrific, Dad! Right now is what I was hoping for."

"Ok, come and sit down. Where do you want to start?"

"Well, how does someone get a credit card? How can I get one?"

Cautiously, Dad replies. "Let's cover your first question and hold off on the second one for a while.

"Nowadays, credit cards are offered in a lot of ways. Many, maybe most, adults are receiving mailed credit card offers as often as weekly from banks, insurance companies, colleges they attended, social groups etc. These are predominantly avenues that major credit card companies and banks use to reach the potential customers – persons who they are enticing to accept and use their particular credit card. College age kids get numerous offers almost from the moment they arrive on campus. Likely, your high school friends went with their parents to their bank to arrange one.

"I'm pretty sure their parents were filled with concerns about their high school kid's understanding of how a credit card works and his or her ability to manage one. Hopefully, they did their best to assure themselves about those concerns being alleviated. Before even considering your second question, I would do that with you. Do you understand that need?"

"Yeah, Dad, I do. Some of my friends who got one told me that when they learned more about credit cards they were actually a little afraid to get one. Some were very scared and decided against having one. But some did end up getting one so it must not be awful. And their parents must have been Ok with it. That's why I am asking how I can get one. So tell me more about them and why parents worry."

"Ok, let's start with how a credit card works.

"In effect, making purchases by use of a credit card is borrowing money. The purchases are a series of instantaneous loans. Each purchase occurs immediately and is electronically recorded by the credit card issuer as a debt the credit cardholder has incurred. In usual words, each purchase is charged to the credit card. By the vendor accepting a credit card charge, the credit card issuer has given the purchaser a loan of the funds needed to make the purchase. The debt is then owed to the credit card issuer, not to the vendor who sold the item. Of course, the credit card issuer charges interest for lending those funds to the credit cardholder."

"Dad, how would I pay the credit card issuer?"

"On a monthly basis, a credit card statement arrives in the mail or some offer a paperless (electronic) means to access your monthly billing. The credit card **MONTHLY STATEMENT** lists all the purchases you made up to a certain date over the preceding month. Those charges are compiled as part of the **BALANCE DUE** for that month.

"When you first begin to use a new credit card an **ANNUAL FEE** is typically charged at the outset and added to the debt incurred by making purchases. It is included in the **BALANCE DUE**. The **ANNUAL FEE** amount varies depending upon the interest rate structure of the particular credit card and how the card issuer applies its interest rates to charges left unpaid that month."

"That seems pretty straightforward, Dad. What's the worry?"

"In everyday life credit card purchases are made continuously. Each time an item is purchased using the credit card it is recorded as additional debt to the cardholder. Numerous instantaneous loans are incurred, indeed almost daily, over the course of each monthly billing period. Typical credit card balances are significant amounts. That's why most parents, including myself, worry about their child having access to a credit card. In one month of time you can make a lot of purchases and not see the total outcome until the end of that month.

"I am also very wary of passing credit card information and billing data electronically. Putting a card with access to incurring substantial debt in the line of fire of hackers and electronic thievery just does not sit well with me.

"Does that clarify the worries issue?"

"That helps and I see the scariness for you and me.

"It also seems to be almost free to use a credit card. Or did I miss something?"

"Well Peanut, I sure wish that was the case. But it isn't.

"A credit card issuer earns income in three ways. I already mentioned two of them.

"First, there is the **ANNUAL FEE** which the credit cardholder is charged for the use of the credit card, typically \$0.00-\$100.00. Generally, the lower is the **ANNUAL FEE** the higher will be the **ANNUAL RATE OF INTEREST** for purchases made using the credit card.

"Second, there is the interest charged. Although the **MONTHLY STATEMENT** indicates the accumulated **NEW BALANCE** due by a given date, the cardholder is not required to pay the entire amount. That person can pay any amount he or she wishes to pay either at or above a stated **MINIMUM PAYMENT** due. The remaining amount due is then carried forward into the next monthly billing period, that is it revolves over as a continuing debt. If the **NEW BALANCE** due on the credit card statement is not paid in full, then an **INTEREST CHARGE** is added on the next **MONTHLY STATEMENT**.

"Third, the credit card issuer charges the vendor who sells the item a fee for each purchase. Typically it's 2-4% of the cost of the item. Essentially, this fee is to compensate for the costs related to handling the implied loan of money. The vendor is the party who is charging the cardholder for the purchase. That might be a department store, an auto dealership, a charitable organization, etc. Once billed by the vendor, the card issuer pays the cost of the purchase to the vendor and awaits repayment by the purchaser. The fee paid by the vendor to the credit card issuer covers the cost of the card issuer's staff time and effort for doing that and includes a profit as well."

"Wow! That sure seems like highway robbery now."

"Well Nicole, it is close to that if you have a credit card with a high **ANNUAL RATE OF INTEREST**. And young people with their first credit card experience seem to be especially prey to that possibility."

"Dad, you mentioned a **NEW BALANCE** due. Seems it's critical to pay that in full. How is that amount determined?"

"Yes, I did. It's kind of involved. It can differ a bit for different card issuers. Let me try to explain it in detail for what generally happens. If you need to interrupt me as I go along, please do so.

"A **MONTHLY STATEMENT** covers a one month period of time, but not necessarily from the first day of the month to the last day of the month. It depends on what time period the card issuer assigns to your particular card. For example, your card may cover purchases made over a period time from the 5th day of a month through the 4th day of the next month.

"A **MONTHLY STATEMENT** lists a **PREVIOUS BALANCE** from the previous one; each item purchased during the prior month; the date each purchase was charged to the credit card; the identification of the vendor; and the cost of the item. Then the **NEW BALANCE** due is indicated. If it is the first month for using the credit card, the **PREVIOUS BALANCE** will be $0.00 and the **ANNUAL FEE** will be also listed as a **PURCHASE**.

"The **NEW BALANCE** is obtained from the **PREVIOUS BALANCE** of the prior month by subtracting any **PAYMENT** received during the month and adding the total cost of the **PURCHASES** made during the one month period covered by the **MONTHLY STATEMENT** plus the **INTEREST CHARGE** if applicable."

"Whoa! Dad, that's spinning my head a bit."

"I noticed that in your facial expression. Let me write it in a math way."

Nicole's Dad writes something down on a sheet of paper and gives it to her, saying "Does this help?"

He's written,

NEW BALANCE = PREVIOUS BALANCE – PAYMENT RECEIVED + PURCHASES + INTEREST CHARGE

Nicole studies it for a few moments and asks her Dad to repeat himself, which he does.

"Ok, now it's clear to me. Thank you."

Dad continues.

"The cardholder must make a payment to the credit card issuer by a date specified on the **MONTHLY STATEMENT**. The **MINIMUM PAYMENT** due is also shown, which is commonly about 2.00% of the **NEW BALANCE** due."

"How is the **INTEREST CHARGE** handled, Dad?"

"Not all cards work the same way but what typically happens is the following.

"At the outset of a new card, **MONTHLY STATEMENT 1** is received. If the payment made and received is the full amount of the **NEW BALANCE** then no interest charged. If any portion of the **NEW BALANCE** is not paid on time then it is carried over to the next month.

"The carried over amount is charged interest on **MONTHLY STATEMENT 2**. Because of the partial payment, additional purchases made since **MONTHLY STATEMENT 1** will also incur an **INTEREST CHARGE**. If the **NEW BALANCE** for **MONTHLY STATEMENT 2** is not paid in full then the further **INTEREST CHARGES** appear on **MONTHLY STATEMENT 3**.

"If partial payments continue to keep happening then this sequences keeps recurring. Once a subsequent month's **NEW BALANCE** is paid in full, the charging of an **INTEREST** will end.

"Still with me, Peanut?"

"It's kind of confusing. I sort of get it but I'm not sure."

"I'll be showing you a numerical example later. That should help,"

 Ok, Dad. You've told me when I must make a payment each, but not how?"

"You're right. One can make a payment by either mailing in a personal check or arranging to pay via a phone call. In the latter case, one arranges that via secure phone call the payment amount is to be withdrawn from a designated personal checking account. If your credit card is issued by a bank, you might be able to make the payment electronically as well but you must consider security as well."

 "Dad, how much is the **INTEREST CHARGE**?"

"The card issuer calculates that in a very detailed way. It's a bit involved. I'll explain the details later. For now, let me give it a try on generally how it works.

"Although monthly payments are involved in credit cards the interest rates for credit cards are marketed on the basis of an **ANNUAL PERCENTAGE RATE (APR)**. That indicates the percentage of interest one would be charged on a debt left unpaid for a full year. Essentially, it is an **ANNUAL RATE OF INTEREST**. APR levels of 15.00%-20.00% are not uncommon rates credit card issuers impose on cardholders. Indeed that rate can be even higher if you are careless in picking a credit card company."

"Wait Dad, I thought interest on a credit card debt was paid monthly?"

"You're correct. The **INTEREST CHARGE** occurs on a monthly billing basis. Remember credit card purchases occur from day to day. The **INTEREST CHARGE** has to reflect the ongoing daily change in debt owed on the card. Again I'll explain it in more detail later. For now, just accept that interest is charged for each day of the month that purchases remain unpaid. The **APR** is not used directly, but does dictate the amount of interest charged each day. That's the complicated part. Aside from that, the **INTEREST CHARGE** is the total of those daily amounts. Does that clear it up a bit?"

"I sort of get that my credit card purchases get charged interest each day they are left unpaid? Is that correct?"

"Yes, that's it in simple terms and enough for this moment. Let's continue. I want to show you another reason why parental worry comes about."

"Ok, I can wait for the detailed explanation."

"Let's look at a bigger problem that can occur if each month you only pay the **MINIMUM PAYMENT** amount.

"For the first month of a new credit card, even if you do not pay its **NEW BALANCE** in full, there is no **INTEREST CHARGE** shown. In the next **MONTHLY STATEMENT** an **INTEREST CHARGE** is made on its **PREVIOUS BALANCE** and added to the **NEW BALANCE** for the that month. Since you paid only the **MINIMUM PAYMENT** for the prior month, then it's highly likely the **INTEREST CHARGE** exceeds that paid amount. If so, even if you don't make more purchases, then the **NEW BALANCE** at the end of that next month will be higher than its **PREVIOUS BALANCE**. So your credit card debt will not have declined but rather it will have increased. Actual purchases made on any days during that next month are also added to its **NEW BALANCE**. That will only worsen things. Almost certainly the **NEW BALANCE** will be significantly higher than the **PREVIOUS BALANCE**.

"Do you follow that? Does it make sense?"

Scratching her head, Nicole replies, "I'm following it OK. You're saying that only making the **MINUMUM PAYMENT** is bad news."

"Yes, in simple words, that's it. That's one of the pitfalls of credit card debt: Paying only the minimum amount due each month and continuing to regularly use your credit card easily causes the debt to grow each month and potentially substantially so. Keep doing that and your credit card debt grows fast and faster and faster. It will be getting out of control.

"Are you still following this logic?"

"Yes, I think I am Dad. Just because I would only need to make a **MINIMUM PAYMENT** does not mean I should do that. If I keep doing it then I'll owe more and more money. You didn't say it but I realize I would also be paying whole lot of interest each month. I suppose that would be more and more each month too."

"Bingo! Exactly right. I'm getting even less worried about you possibly having a credit card. Smarty Pants!

"The possible uncontrolled debt is the biggest worry of a parent when their teenager or college kid wants a credit card. Often a need for a teenager to have a credit card arises at the outset of college studies. If the child is living away from home, then it's unavoidable. The logistics of making ongoing purchases such as books, supplies and groceries is in play. Hence the credit card option. Mostly, the parents will be paying for those charges. When responsible and attentive parents are paying the child's credit card bill, the uncontrolled debt should not happen. In your case, it certainly would not happen. We would plan to pay much more than the **MINIMUM PAYMENT** each month, ideally the entire **NEW BALANCE**. If your charges were excessive and out of line, we would cut up the card. Then we'd work out how you would help pay the excessive charges."

"Dad, that makes sense to me. And I know you would be stern about misuse and be ready to take out the scissors. And you just said you were getting even less worried about my possibly having a credit card. So can I get one?"

"On that request I need to point out something. Unfortunate for you but fortunate for Mom and me, you cannot get a credit card at your age. You have to be at least 18 years old. You would also need to have satisfactory creditworthiness. Under the age of 18 young people can become an authorized user of a parent's card. But it will not be their card. The parents would be responsible for paying your charges. This is a complication and risk many parents won't take. In our case despite my growing confidence in you, we will wait until you are older."

"Darn, that's a bummer! But I guess I understand why you want me to wait."

"You mentioned creditworthiness. What's that all about?"

"That's a lengthy sermon and really a topic for another time. At sixteen years old it is not urgent. Let's talk about it down the road. For now, it means the credit card issuer will check that you can dependably afford to or have resources to pay at least the anticipated maximum **MINIMUM PAYMENT**. That would be a percentage of the credit limit on the card. If you are working it helps justify that.

"When you are older and independent, the risks of excessive credit card debt will be your problem entirely. That's why I am very happy you brought this subject up. Eventually, I would have brought it up anyway. Either way I want you to fully understand credit card debt before ever getting a credit card. Even though getting one now is out of the picture, would you like to spend more time learning the monetary details about credit cards?"

"Yes, I would, if that makes you happy. Maybe it will help me tell all my friends why I cannot get one now. Maybe I will even know a lot more about credit cards then my friends who got one. That would be a winner, for sure."

"Ok, that's great. To do that I need to prepare some detailed stuff. Let's continue in a day or two."

"Ok."

After two days of Dad preparing his material, he and Nicole meet in his home office where he can access his computer.

SITUATION 1

"Nicole, to begin I will illustrate the flow of **MONTHLY STATEMENTS** for a hypothetical credit card situation. For ease of math let's look at that for a very simplified set of circumstances. Let's assume the following.

"You have a new credit card. You purchase a $1000.00 laptop computer on the first day of the first monthly period and no other purchases are ever made.

"The **ANNUAL FEE** is $0.00, and the monthly **MINIMUM PAYMENT** due is 2.00% of the **NEW BALANCE**. The **MINIMUM PAYMENT** is due on the second day of the month following receipt of the **MONTHLY STATEMENT**.

"The **APR** is 20.00%. Using the actual daily interest process is complicated and distracting at this point. Instead I simplified calculating the **INTEREST CHARGE** by applying a **MONTHLY RATE OF INTEREST** to the **PREVIOUS BALANCE**. You'll see how as we move along.

"Right now we'll take a look at what happens if only the **MINIMUM PAYMENT** due on that credit card debt is paid for each **MONTHLY STATEMENT**. But first, is the given information clear to you?"

"I get that one purchase was made at the outset. The amounts of the given information are clear too. But the matters of timing of payment and calculating interest have me scratching my head."

"That's good enough for now. I was anticipating some head scratching, too. So I prepared a summary flow of the monthly monetary events to use a reference. Here's a print out for the first three months of activity.

Monthly Statement	Previous Balance	Payment Received	Purchases Made	Interest Charge	New Balance	Minimum Payment	Cumulative Interest
1	0	0	1000.00	0	1000.00	20.00	0
2	1000.00	20.00	0	16.70	996.70	19.93	16.70
3	996.70	19.93	0	16.64	993.41	19.87	33.34

SITUATION 1 – CONTINUED

"This table shows the outcome of the first three **MONTHLY STATEMENTS**. It's only a summary of results, not actual **MONTHLY STATEMENTS**. Let's walk through it.

"Line 1 is for the first **MONTHLY STATEMENT**. It indicates a **PREVIOUS BALANCE** of $0.00, the single **PURCHASE** of $1000.00, and a **NEW BALANCE** of $1000.00. Because the **PREVIOUS BALANCE** is $0.00, the **INTEREST CHARGE** is $0.00. The **MINIMUM PAYMENT** due is 2.00% of $1000.00 = 0.02 x $1000.00 = $20.00. The last column shows the amount of **CUMULATIVE INTEREST** paid up to that time. None has been paid so far. You mail in the $20.00 by check.

"For the second **MONTHLY STATEMENT** the **PREVIOUS BALANCE** is $1000.00. Your $20.00 payment was received on time. The credit card issuer has applied a **MONTHLY RATE OF INTEREST** = 20.00%/12 months = 1.67% on the **PREVIOUS BALANCE**. An **INTEREST CHARGE** = (1.67/100) x $1000.00 = 0.0167 x $1000.00 = $16.70 is added to the **PREVIOUS BALANCE**.

"Your **NEW BALANCE** = **PREVIOUS BALANCE** – **PAYMENT RECEIVED** + **PURCHASES** + **INTEREST CHARGE** = $1000.00 - $20.00 + $0.00 + $16.70 = $996.70. The **MINIMUM PAYMENT** due = 0.02 x $996.70 = $19.93. The **CUMULATIVE INTEREST** is $16.70. You mail in a check for $19.93.

"Are you following this flow?"

"Yes I am Dad. It's very clear when I see it organized in the table."

"Good. Now notice that for Month 2, you have reduced your **PREVIOUS BALANCE** by only $3.30, not $20.00. Only $3.30/$20.00 x 100 = 16.5% of your $20.00 payment applied to the **PREVIOUS BALANCE**. The other 83.5% was used to pay the **INTEREST CHARGE**."

"Wow! That's very interesting."

"Now, continuing the flow, for the third **MONTHLY STATEMENT** the **PREVIOUS BALANCE** is $996.70. Your $19.93 payment is received on time. An **INTEREST CHARGE** = 0.0167 x $996.70 = $16.64 is added to the **PREVIOUS BALANCE**.

"Your **NEW BALANCE** is $996.70 - $19.93 + $0.00 + $16.64 = $993.41. The **MINIMUM PAYMENT** due = 0.02 x $993.41 = $19.87. The **CUMULATIVE INTEREST** increases by $16.64 to $33.34. You mail in a payment for $19.87.

"Note that you have reduced your **PREVIOUS BALANCE** by only $19.93 - $16.64 = $3.29, not $19.93. Only $3.29/$19.93 x 100 = 16.5% of your $20.00 payment applied to the **PREVIOUS BALANCE**. The other 83.5% was used to pay the monthly interest."

"WOW! Looks like I am throwing 83.5% of my $20.00 down the drain each month. Does it always stay that way?"

"Well, it's great that you sense that might be the case. This flow actually continues for many additional months. Let's look further."

Dad gives Nicole the following table which continues the summary results. For brevity he only shows selected **MONTHLY STATEMENTS**.

Monthly Statement	Previous Balance	Payment Received	Purchases Made	Interest Charge	New Balance	Minimum Payment	Cumulative Interest
1	0	0	1000.00	0	1000.00	20.00	0
2	1000.00	20.00	0	16.70	996.70	19.93	16.70
3	996.70	19.93	0	16.64	993.41	19.87	33.34
.	.	.	.	.	.	.	.
6	986.87	19.74	0	16.48	983.61	19.67	82.95
.	.	.	.	.	.	.	.
12	967.49	19.35	0	16.16	964.30	19.29	180.70
.	.	.	.	.	.	.	.
24	929.86	18.60	0	15.53	926.79	18.54	370.47
36	893.70	17.87	0	14.92	890.75	17.82	552.84
.	.	.	.	.	.	.	.
48	858.94	17.18	0	14.34	856.10	17.12	728.15
.	.	.	.	.	.	.	.
50	853.28	17.07	0	14.25	850.46	17.01	756.70

SITUATION 1 – CONTINUED

"Well Sweetie, what strikes you about the flow?"

"Hmmm? It's a lot of numbers and kind of overwhelming. Mainly I see it continues for a long time. To fifty months?"

"That's correct. My table lists results up to **MONTHLY STATEMENT 50**. That's truly a long time.

"It's important to observe several specific trends in the results.

"The **NEW BALANCE** is declining, but very slowly. After Month 6 it is $983.61. After month 12 it is $964.30. Even after Month 50 it is $850.46.

"Because the **NEW BALANCE** is lower each month the **MINIMUM PAYMENT** due is lower each month. But it is only slowly changing. In Month 6 the **MINIMUM PAYMENT** is $19.74. In Month 12 it is $19.35. In Month 50 it is $17.07."

"I see that Dad"

Dad asks, "And what is happening to the **INTEREST CHARGE**?"

"It's going down but very slowly too. By Month 50 it has only dropped from $16.70 to $14.25."

"That's right, Nicole. And because the monthly **INTEREST CHARGE** is decreasing slowly, the **CUMULATIVE INTEREST** is increasing quickly.

"After Month 12 (1 year) the **CUMULATIVE INTEREST** is $180.70. That's about 18% of the $1000.00 purchase.

"After Month 24 (2 years) $370.47 has been paid which is about 37% of the purchase.

"After Month 50 (4+ years), $756.70 has been paid, which is about 76% of the purchase."

"Whew! That's a huge amount, Dad."

"Indeed it is and the debt is far from being paid off.

"There's also a subtle point to make. At the end of each month the **INTEREST CHARGE** became part of the **NEW BALANCE** and thus became part of the **PREVIOUS BALANCE** for the following month. Then the **MONTHLY RATE OF INTEREST** was applied to it. Consequently, interest was being paid on interest.

"A more vital observation is not yet evident. To observe it, let's examine further in time."

Dad shows Nicole additional tabulated results.

Monthly Statement	Previous Balance	Payment Received	Purchases Made	Interest Charge	New Balance	Minimum Payment	Cumulative Interest
60	825.52	16.51	0	13.79	822.8	16.46	896.64
.	.	.	.	.	.	.	.
72	793.43	15.87	0	13.25	790.81	15.82	1058.58
.	.	.	.	.	.	.	.
84	762.58	15.25	0	12.74	760.07	15.20	1214.22
.	.	.	.	.	.	.	.
96	732.93	14.66	0	12.24	730.51	14.61	1363.8
.	.	.	.	.	.	.	.
108	704.42	14.09	0	11.76	702.09	14.04	1507.56
.	.	.	.	.	.	.	.
120	677.00	13.54	0	11.31	674.77	13.50	1645.73
.	.	.	.	.	.	.	.
240	455.27	9.11	0	7.60	453.76	9.08	2763.75
.	.	.	.	.	.	.	.
360	306.13	6.12	0	5.11	305.12	6.10	3515.49

.	.	.	.	.	.	.	.
600	**138.41**	**2.77**	**0**	**2.31**	**137.95**	**2.76**	**4361.06**

SITUATION 1 – CONTINUED

"What catches your eye this time, Nicole?'

"If I believe my eyes, this debt continues for a very, very long time. I'm seeing the bottom line is that for **MONTHLY STATEMENT** 600 a **NEW BALANCE** still exists. If that's the case then I say "Holy Cow!"""

"Yes indeed. The cow is praying this debt ends. Let's look closer."

"After Month 360 (thirty years) the **NEW BALANCE** is $305.12 and **CUMULATIVE INTEREST** is $3515.49. That's about 352% of the $1000.00 purchase.

"After Month 600 (fifty years) the **NEW BALANCE** = $137.95. The **NEW BALANCE** continues to be significant. And although the monthly **INTEREST CHARGE** is declining, the **CUMULATIVE INTEREST** has become an enormous $4361.06. That's 436% of the purchase. Why do you think this is so?"

"Yikes! I have no idea. But I sure do want to know."

"The reason is that each time the **MINIMUM PAYMENT** is made, only a portion is applied to the **PREVIOUS BALANCE**. Thus, a non-zero **NEW BALANCE** will <u>always</u> result. And each month a non-zero **PREVIOUS BALANCE** will exist, and additional interest will be incurred.

"I haven't listed it, but if carried out the payments to **MONTHLY STATEMENT** 2400 (200 years), an **INTEREST CHARGE** of $0.05 is incurred and the **CUMULATIVE INTEREST** reaches $5076.91, and the clock is still moving.

"As a result, the original loan of $1000.00 is **<u>NEVER GOING TO BE PAID OFF!</u>**

'What's your reaction to that outcome?'

"Well Dad, it's almost unbelievable. Maybe you are correct. I don't think I need a credit card at this time."

"Well Peanut, I do agree with that."

"But now you are informed of the danger and can avoid it. If you don't, then catch the trend ASAP. Pay off the entire **NEW BALANCE** and consider cutting up this credit card!"

Exercise 1: *For the trail of* ***MONTHLY STATEMENTS*** *in SITUATION 1 calculate the results for* ***MONTHLY STATEMENTS*** *13, 61, 121, 241, 361 and 601. Calculate the* ***PERCENT CUMULATIVE INTEREST*** *and* ***AVERAGE ANNUAL INTEREST*** *for each of those statements, and the corresponding average yearly values.*

Your __partial__ results should be:

Monthly Statement	Previous Balance	Payment Received	Purchases Made	Interest Charge	New Balance	Minimum Payment	Cumulative Interest
13	964.30	19.29	0	16.10	961.11	19.22	196.80
61	822.80	?	0	13.74	?	16.40	910.38
121	674.77	13.50	0	?	672.54	?	1657.00
241	453.76	?	0	7.58	452.26	?	?
361	305.12	6.10	0	5.1	?	6.08	3520.59
601	137.95	?	0	?	137.49	2.75	4363.36

"I've probably already frightened you enough about a credit card. But one day you will need one and will be able to act independently. Some credit card companies are ready, willing and able to allow you to get into this bind. If you do, then you are their best customer! And they are your worst enemy!

"I don't want to leave you scared and without knowing how to properly handle credit card debt. You've probably got homework from school or want to see your friend later. Why don't we talk some more tomorrow?"

"Ok, Dad. Let's do that after my classes"

Entering her Dad's office Nicole calls out, "Hi Dad! I don't have much homework for tonight. So I have time to talk more about those credit cards? Are you free?"

"That's good. Yes I am so let's start."

"Yesterday, I showed you how a credit card debt can go crazy. In reality, for SITUATION 1, other than the high **APR** I used, the card itself is not the problem. The problem is the inadequate rate of payment. You need to make monthly payments substantially larger than the **MINIMUM PAYMENT** requested by the credit card issuer. Let's look at the effect of doing that."

SITUATION 2

"Nicole, let's assume you make one change. You elect to pay the initial **MINIMUM PAYMENT** of $20.00 and then continue paying that amount as a fixed amount each month.

"I have done the calculations in my computer. Let's examine the outcome."

Monthly Statement	Previous Balance	Payment Received	Purchases Made	Interest Charge	New Balance	Minimum Payment	Cumulative Interest
1	0	0	1000.00	0	1000.00	20.00	0
2	1000.00	20.00	0	16.70	996.70	19.93	16.70
3	996.70	20.00	0	16.64	993.34	19.87	33.34
4	993.34	20.00	0	16.59	989.93	19.80	49.93
5	989.93	20.00	0	16.53	986.46	19.73	66.46
6	986.46	20.00	0	16.47	982.93	19.66	82.93
.	.	.	.	.	.	.	.
12	964.38	20.00	0	16.11	960.49	19.21	180.49
.	.	.	.	.	.	.	.
24	913.11	20.00	0	15.25	908.36	18.17	368.36
.	.	.	.	.	.	.	.
36	850.56	20.00	0	14.20	844.76	16.90	544.76
.	.	.	.	.	.	.	.
48	774.25	20.00	0	12.93	767.18	15.34	707.18
.	.	.	.	.	.	.	.
60	681.17	20.00	0	11.38	672.55	13.45	852.55
.	.	.	.	.	.	.	.
72	567.63	20.00	0	9.48	557.11	11.14	977.11
.	.	.	.	.	.	.	.
84	429.12	20.00	0	7.17	416.29	8.33	1076.29

.	.	.	.	.	.	.	.
96	260.15	20.00	0	4.34	244.49	4.89	1144.49
.	.	.	.	.	.	.	.
108	54.03	20.00	0	0.90	34.93	0.70	1174.93
109	34.93	20.00	0	0.58	15.51	0.31	1175.51
110	15.51	15.51	0	0.00	0.00	0.00	1175.51

SITUATION 2 – CONTINUED

"Nicole, what's different from before?"

"It's still a lot of numbers. But I do see the debt actually ends in Month 110?"

"That's right. But what's different in each month?"

"I'm not seeing it Dad."

"The main thing is that in the **PAYMENT RECEIVED** column the amount is always $20.00. Before, it was a smaller and smaller amount each month and the debt never got paid off. Now it is always higher than the **MINIMUM PAYMENT**. That's why the debt eventually does get paid off.

"Look. In Month 109 the **NEW BALANCE** = $15.51. For Month 110 only a final payment of $15.51 is necessary to complete paying off the debt. It takes just over nine years to do that. Compared to **NEVER PAID OFF**, this is a big improvement. Do you agree?"

"Yes, I do. That's really good."

"Yes it is. But it's still a long time. Do you see any other problem in the results?"

Nicole winces and rubs her chin. "Not seeing anything obvious, Dad."

"How much **CUMULATIVE INTEREST** have you paid?"

"Oh! I see. It's $1175.51. That's sort of a lot."

"Yes it is." That's about 118% of the purchase.

"After Month 108, it was $1174.93. That's a lot less than the $1507.56 for Month 108 in our first situation. And after the 9+ year period of time the debt ends. Even so, clearly this amount of **CUMULATIVE INTEREST** is excessive.

"Let's now look at significantly increasing the amount paid each month."

---

*Exercise 2: For the trail of **MONTHLY STATEMENTS** in SITUATION 2 calculate the results for **MONTHLY STATEMENTS** 13, 25, 49, and 97. Calculate the **PERCENT CUMULATIVE INTEREST** and **AVERAGE ANNUAL INTEREST** for each of those statements, and the corresponding average* *yearly values.*

Your *partial* results should be:

Monthly Statement	Previous Balance	Payment Received	Purchases Made	Interest Charge	New Balance	Minimum Payment	Cumulative Interest
13	960.49	20.00	0	16.04	?	19.13	196.53
25	908.36	?	0	15.17	903.53	18.07	?
49	?	20.00	0	?	759.99	15.20	719.99
97	244.49	20.00	0	4.08	?	?	1148.57

For **MONTHLY STATEMENTS** *25 and 49 the* **PERCENT CUMULATIVE INTEREST** *= 38.35% and 72.00. The* **AVERAGE ANNUAL INTEREST** *values are 18.41% and 17.63%. For* **MONTHLY STATEMENTS** *13 and 97* **AVERAGE ANNUAL INTEREST** *values are 18.14% and 14.21%.*

SITUATION 3

"Nicole, now let's assume you decide to pay $100.00 each month on time until the **NEW BALANCE** is at or below $100.00. At that time, you pay **NEW BALANCE** in full. I calculated the outcome of doing that. Here are my results.

Monthly Statement	Previous Balance	Payment Received	Purchases Made	Interest Charge	New Balance	Minimum Payment	Cumulative Interest
1	0	0	1000.00	0.00	1000.00	20.00	0.00
2	1000.00	100.00	0	16.70	916.70	18.33	16.70
3	916.70	100.00	0	15.31	832.01	16.64	32.01
4	832.01	100.00	0	13.89	745.90	14.92	45.90
5	745.90	100.00	0	12.46	658.36	13.17	58.36
6	658.36	100.00	0	10.99	569.35	11.39	69.35
7	569.35	100.00	0	9.51	478.86	9.58	78.86
8	478.86	100.00	0	8.00	386.86	7.74	86.86
9	386.86	100.00	0	6.46	293.32	5.87	93.32
10	293.32	100.00	0	4.90	198.22	3.96	98.22
11	198.22	100.00	0	3.31	101.53	2.03	101.53
12	101.53	100.00	0	1.70	3.23	0.06	103.23
13	3.23	3.23	0	0.00	0.00	0.00	103.23

SITUATION 3 - CONTINUED

"Sweetie-pie, having seen and discussed the previous situations, can you tell me what you see in these results?"

"Ok, let me try, Dad."

"Right away I see that in Month 13 the **NEW BALANCE** is $3.23 and is paid to end the debt. Compared to 9+ years before, that's something!"

"Yes, and compared to **NEVER PAID OFF**?"

"That's fantastic!"

"What do you see regarding the interest paid?"

"The **CUMULATIVE INTEREST** is $103.23. Wasn't it thousands of dollars before?"

"Yes, it was."

"I'm not clear why it became so much lower, though."

"The much higher **MONTHLY PAYMENTS** are the base reason. But let's look in detail.

"In SITUATION 1, when you paid only the **MINIMUM PAYMENT** the **NEW BALANCE** and **INTEREST CHARGE** declined slowly. That's because in each month only small amount of the payment was applied to reduce the **PREVIOUS BALANCE**. Let's look back at that table.

"Recall, in each month only 16.5% of the **MONTHLY PAYMENT** applied to the **PREVIOUS BALANCE**. In Month 50, the **MONTHLY PAYMENT** was still $17.07 and only $2.82 was applied to the **PREVIOUS BALANCE**.

"In SITUATION 2 where each payment was $20.00, it improves. I calculated and found that in Month 2, 16.5% goes to the **PREVIOUS BALANCE**. In Month 6 it is 17.6%. In Month 12 it is 19.45%. In Month 109, it is 97.1%. The reason for improvement is the increasing overpayment being made each month.

"For SITUATION 3, in Month 2 $16.70 of the $100.00 payment was the **INTEREST CHARGE**. $83.30 was applied to the **PREVIOUS BALANCE**. That's 83.3% of the $100.00. In Month 6, $10.99 of the $100.00 payment was the **INTEREST CHARGE**. $89.01 was applied to the **PREVIOUS BALANCE**. That's 89.0%. In Month 12, $1.70 of the $100.00 payment was the **INTEREST CHARGE**. $98.30 was applied to the **PREVIOUS BALANCE**. That's 98.3%.

"I've said a lot. Did you follow it, Nicole?"

"Maybe I regret asking. But actually, you are showing me that increasing the amount I pay above the **MINIMUM PAYMENT** helps reduce my **NEW BALANCES** fast**er**. And the larger the extra amount is the faster I pay off my credit card debt. Am I right?"

"Indeed you are! I'm proud you are so smart and attentive. Let me expand on that.

"As the debt steadily gets paid down the **INTEREST CHARGE** gets smaller and smaller each month. The amount by which you overpay the **INTEREST CHARGE** goes to reduce the **PREVIOUS BALANCE**; For example for **MONTHLY STATEMENT 2** the **PREVIOUS BALANCE** is $1000.00 and the **INTEREST CHARGE** is $16.30. So $100.00 - $16.70 = $83.30 goes to reduce the **PREVIOUS BALANCE** to a **NEW BALANCE** = $1000.00 - $83.30 = $967.70. Do you see that?"

"Yes, I do."

"Good, Peanut. For **MONTHLY STATEMENT 3**, the **PREVIOUS BALANCE** is $967.70 and the **INTEREST CHARGE** is $15.31. So $100.00 - $15.31 = $84.69 goes to reduce the **PREVIOUS BALANCE** to a **NEW BALANCE** = $967.30 - $84.69 = $832.01. And so on it goes for succeeding months.

"Now I really understand your table much better."

Now about that **CUMULATIVE INTEREST** piece. I'll continue.

"As you stated, for the present situation when the loan ended the **CUMULATIVE INTEREST** paid is $103.23. Let's compare that to SITUATION 1.

"Looking back at that table, after 1 year, the **NEW BALANCE** was $964.30 and the **CUMULATIVE INTEREST** paid was $180.70. After 2, 3, and 4 years; the **NEW BALANCE** amounts were $926.79, $890.75 and $856.10, respectively. The corresponding **CUMULATIVE INTEREST** amounts were $370.47, $552.84 and $738.15, respectively.

"After 10 years the **NEW BALANCE** was $674.77 and **CUMULATIVE INTEREST** was $1645.73. After thirty years the **NEW BALANCE** was $305.12 and the **CUMULATIVE INTEREST** was $3515.49. After fifty years the **CUMULATIVE INTEREST** was $4361.06 and the **NEW BALANCE** was still $137.95! And the loan would go on forever!

"Still following everything, Nicole?'

"Yup! I see the picture clearly. It's a horror show and Voldemort is my credit card issuer."

"Who is Val Damore?

"Now Dad, everyone knows who he is. And it's "Vol" not "Val".

"I guess I am nobody."

"Not to me, Dad. To me you're special."

"It's nice to hear that. But let's finish."

"Again, for SITUATION 2 it improved. The **NEW BALANCE** decreased noticeably faster and was paid off in Month 110. The **CUMULATIVE INTEREST** increased less and less, ending at the$1175.51. Looking back at the table you would see that but my point has been made.

"My last point is that by paying $100.00 per month the stated **APR** of 20.00% never materialized. The debt ended in Month 13 and the last **INTEREST CHARGE** was in Month 12. The resulting **CUMULATIVE INTEREST** was $103.23. That's only 10.32% of the purchase."

Exercise 3: Repeat SITUATION 3 but use a **MONTHLY PAYMENT** of $50.00 instead of $100.00. Do it for six months only.

Your *partial* results should be:

Monthly Statement	Previous Balance	Payment Received	Purchases Made	Interest Charge	New Balance	Minimum Payment	Cumulative Interest
1	0	0	1000.00	0	1000.00	20.00	0.00
2	1000.00	50.00	0	16.70	966.70	19.33	16.70
3	966.70	?	0	?	932.84	18.66	32.84
4	932.84	50.00	0	15.58	?	?	?
5	898.42	?	0	?	863.42	17.27	63.42
6	863.42	50.00	0	14.42	?	16.56	77.84
.	.	.	.	.	.	.	.
12	640.82	50.00	0	?	601.52	12.03	?
24	123.42	50.00	0	2.06	?	?	225.48
25	75.48	50.00	0	1.26	26.74	0.53	226.74

*For readers with computer capabilities and who do the entire table, additional partial results have been given for Months 12, 24 and 25. For **MONTHLY STATEMENT** 25 the **NEW BALANCE** is $26.74 is less than $50.00, so that amount is paid to end the debt.*

"Well Nicole, that's quite a bit of territory we covered. There's still a bit more I would like to cover. But maybe you've heard enough about credit cards for now?"

"It certainly was a lot of information. It took a lot of concentration, so I think a break would be good.

A couple hours later, Nicole and her Dad continue the conversation.

"Are you ready to start, Nicole?"

"I'm as ready as I can be, Dad."

"Ok. In our example situations the **APR** was 20.00%. That's darn high, but not unusual for new card holders with little credit background. One way to reduce credit card debt is to not accept a card that has a high **APR**. To avoid a high **APR** one should have a good to excellent creditworthiness. I thought it over and decided it would be good to cover that topic and how a teenager would establish creditworthiness. Once we do that I plan to talk about ways you can get a credit card once you turn 18. But before we do that, let's take a look at the difference in outcome if you had a credit card with a much lower **APR** than 20.00%."

"That's wonderful Dad! I'm really glad you thought it over. You really have me anxious to hear all that. Now I'm perked up and ready to give you my full attention and keep my brain in gear."

SITUATION 4

"Let's revisit the situation of paying $100.00 per month on that $1000.00 credit card purchase with one change. Your new credit card has an **ANNUAL RATE OF INTEREST** of 6.00%. Here are my results.

Monthly Statement	Previous Balance	Payment Received	Purchases Made	Interest Charge	New Balance	Minimum Payment	Cumulative Interest
1	0	0	1000.00	0	1000.00	20.00	0.00
2	1000.00	100.00	0	5.00	905.00	18.10	5.00
3	905.00	100.00	0	4.53	809.53	16.19	9.53
4	809.53	100.00	0	4.05	713.58	14.27	13.58
5	713.58	100.00	0	3.57	617.15	12.34	17.15
6	617.15	100.00	0	3.09	520.24	10.40	20.24
7	520.24	100.00	0	2.60	422.84	8.46	22.84
8	422.84	100.00	0	2.11	324.95	6.50	24.95
9	324.95	100.00	0	1.62	226.57	4.53	26.57
10	226.57	100.00	0	1.13	127.70	2.55	27.70
11	127.70	100.00	0	0.64	28.34	0.57	28.34
12	28.34	28.34	0	0	0.00	0.00	28.34

SITUATION 4 - CONTINUED

"Nicole, what do you see about how this situation ends?"

"The credit card debt is paid off in Month 12. Before, wasn't it in Month 13?"

"That's right. It's not much sooner, but how much is the **CUMULATIVE INTEREST**?"

"The **CUMULATIVE INTEREST** is $28.34."

"That's right. Oh, the $28.34 amount happens to be the same as the last payment amount, but that's just coincidental. The important thing is that despite being paid off just one month sooner, there's a lot less **CUMULATIVE INTEREST** than the $103.23 for the **APR** of 20.00%. And because the debt was paid off rapidly, the **APR** of 6.00% for the credit card never materialized. The $28.34 is 2.83% of the $1000.00 purchase. What's that teach you?"

"It's telling me to get that job right away so when I get my first credit card it will have a low **APR**."

Exercise 4: *Repeat SITUATION 4 but use an* ***APR*** *= 12.00% instead of 6.00%.*

Your <u>partial</u> results should be:

Monthly Statement	Previous Balance	Payment Received	Purchases Made	Interest Charge	New Balance	Minimum Payment	Cumulative Interest
1	0	0	1000.00	0	1000	20.00	0.00
2	1000.00	100.00	0	10.00	910.00	18.20	10.00
3	910.00	100.00	0	9.1	?	16.38	?
4	819.10	100.00	0	?	727.29	?	27.29
5	?	100.00	0	7.27	?	12.69	?
6	634.56	100.00	0	?	?	10.82	40.91
7	540.91	100.00	0	5.41	446.32	8.93	46.32
8	?	100.00	0	4.46	?	7.02	50.78
9	350.78	100.00	0	?	254.29	?	?
10	?	100.00	0	2.54	?	3.14	56.83
11	156.83	100.00	0	1.57	?	1.17	58.40

For **MONTHLY STATEMENT** *11 the* **NEW BALANCE** *of ? is less than $1000.00 and is paid to end the debt.*

"Dad, maybe it's nerdy, but I am still wondering exactly how that **INTEREST CHARGE** is calculated. Maybe you can cover that as well?"

"I haven't forgotten your surprising curiosity about that aspect. I plan to cover it after I close out where we are now. Oh, and I think of you as a smarty pants, not a nerd.

"Our SITUATION 1 had the debt going on forever. I did that for purposeful emphasis. For an actual credit card, a creditable card issuer normally prevents the debt from continuing endlessly. This is done by stating some <u>absolute</u> monthly **MINIMUM PAYMENT** due in addition to the automatically computed 2.00% (or other applicable % value). For instance the terms of the card might state that a minimum payment of say $50.00 is required in lieu of the amount based on a percentage of the outstanding debt.

"A responsible credit card issuer desires to avoid an endless debt and alerts the card user of the consequence of only paying the **MINIMUM PAYMENT** due versus some other larger monthly amount. But an unscrupulous card issuer can deliberately encourage a cardholder by simply stating the **MINIMUM PAYMENT** due and leave an unwise cardholder open to paying just that amount. That first situation emphasizes the cost of making a poor choice. The cardholder should always pay as much of the monthly **NEW BALANCE** as possible. The best choice is to pay that balance in full each month to avoid having any interest charges at all."

"I certainly get that message, loud and clear. It is eye opening."

"Also, the Situations showed the costliness of paying just the **MIMIMUM PAYMENT** versus making higher monthly payments but on just a single purchase. When many purchases are made over the month the debt grows rapidly. Fortunately, there is a limit to how much debt a cardholder can accumulate. A maximum amount that the cardholder can borrow is stated as a **UPPER LIMIT** and is based on the cardholder's credit standing established when the card is issued. The **UPPER LIMIT** can also be increased periodically when a track record of timely payments unfolds as well as when positive changes in an individual's credit rating occur. More secure individuals will be allowed a higher **UPPER LIMIT**.

"The **APR** charged is also based on one's credit rating. More secure individuals also will be offered a lower **APR** than those offered to individuals with low creditworthiness. For example the **UPPER LIMIT** and **APR** for a secure individual might be $10000.00 to $15000.00 and 6.00%-12.00%. For a less secure individual they might be $2000.00 to $5000.00 and 12.00%-20.00%, respectively. For a high risk individual they might be $500.00 to $1000.00 and 20.00%-24.00%, respectively. When you are eighteen years old and get your first credit card, it will be $300 to $500 and a high **APR**. I guess they see young people as being riskier, too."

"I cannot imagine me needing those large **UPPER LIMIT** amounts. But maybe as I get older they start to come into play."

"That's right, Nicole. When you graduate college bigger life needs arise. Buying a car is one example. The more important matter is you need to build creditworthiness for other purposes. For example, renting an apartment involves the landlord checking your creditworthiness. One day you will want to buy an apartment or condominium. When those needs enter your world, I'll be around for advice if you need it."

"I'm glad you will be even as I try to stand on my own two feet."

"Want to move on to those details about the **INTEREST CHARGE** now?"

"Actually, it's enough for today and I have my homework to do later. Why don't we do that tomorrow?"

"That's fine. I can also prepare some more information we can look at as a basis for talking."

The next afternoon after school Nicole meets with her Dad in his office. He is ready with some information.

"Ok Peanut, let's tackle those details you clamor about the **INTEREST CHARGE**!"

"I wouldn't say I am clamoring for them, but my math side is pinching me about them. I'm ready."

"The situations we used so far were simplified to a single purchase. I did that to separately focus on the consequences of paying only the **MINIMUM PAYMENT** due compared to paying a much larger amount each month. Typical adults make charges to their card on many days. To cover the details about interest we need to consider multiple purchases occurring in each month. But it can be done even if I limit it to just a few purchases each month. Then we won't get lost in the minutia of a sea of purchases."

"That sounds reasonable, Dad. I know you will do it as simply as possible."

"I've brought a copy from my own actual credit card statement to show you the back side of a page, where you will find the fine print. The stuff many people don't take the time to read."

"Sounds like it's going to be some involved but important stuff?"

"Well, yes. It does cause some head scratching when you see it for the first time. That's the case for you. But it's short and I hope to clear it up.

"Squint your eyes and notice the words, 'To figure your periodic interest charges for each billing cycle when a daily periodic rate(s) applies, we use the daily balance method (including new transactions). To figure your periodic interest charges for each billing cycle when a monthly periodic rate(s) applies, we use the average daily balance method (including new transactions).' If that's clear to you, then I guess we can just go out for ice cream?"

After struggling a bit to focus on the fine print, Nicole opines "Wow, that's Greek to me, so I don't think were headed out for ice cream."

"It is complicated. But let's give it a try.

"To start let's just say credit card issuers charge interest by using either of two methods.

"Let's call the first one the "**AVERAGE DAILY BALANCE METHOD** with a **MONTHLY PERIODIC RATE**.

"And let's call the second one the "**DAILY BALANCE METHOD** with a **DAILY PERIODIC RATE**".

"Those sure are tongue twisters."

"Yes they are a confusingly alike. I have a hard time with them, too.

"In each case the intent is to charge interest essentially on a "day to day basis". They are charging interest to you each and every day you owe them money, unless you pay your monthly bill in full all the time. Let's take them one at a time.

"For the first method, the **AVERAGE DAILY BALANCE** means the amount of money owed each day (including transactions that day) is summed for all the days of the monthly billing period and divided by the number of days in that period of time. The result is charged interest at the **MONTHLY PERIODIC RATE** which is the **APR/12 months**.

"Let's look at that on my monitor, Sweetie."

AVERAGE DAILY BALANCE METHOD with a MONTHLY PERIODIC RATE

MONTHLY PERIODIC RATE = APR/12

AVERAGE DAILY BALANCE = (SUM OF DAILY BALANCES)/DAYS

INTEREST CHARGE = (APR/12)% of AVERAGE DAILY BALANCE

"I see the equations and they look simple, Dad. The last one looks a little odd, though. And I'm not ready and able to apply them."

"Ok, let me illustrate that with a situation.

SITUATION 5

"You've just gotten your new card and there is no **ANNUAL FEE**. The **APR** is 12.00%. Assume the first monthly period is 30 days. On each of the first three days you spend $100.00 each day. Then there are no other purchases. The **MINIMUM PAYMENT** is 2.00%, so $6.00, but you pay $100.00 on time. The **INTEREST CHARGE** is based on the **AVERAGE DAILY BALANCE METHOD** with a **MONTHLY PERIODIC RATE**.

"Let's see what happens.

MONTHLY STATEMENT 1

PREVIOUS BALANCE = $0.00

Day 1: DAILY BALANCE = $100.00

Day 2: DAILY BALANCE = $100.00 + $100.00 = $200.00

Day 3: DAILY BALANCE = $200.00 + $100.00 = $300.00

Days 4-30 DAILY BALANCE = $300.00

NEW BALANCE = $0.00 + $300.00 = $300.00

You pay $100.00

SITUATION 5 - CONTINUED

"Do you follow that?"

"I do, Dad. What's next?"

"In the second monthly billing period, of 30 days you spend $100.00 on the each of the first two days. You also spend $100.00 on the tenth day. There are no other purchases. Your $100.00 previous payment is received and posted on the fifth day. You pay the entire **NEW BALANCE** on time.

"Let's see what happens.

MONTHLY STATEMENT 2

PREVIOUS BALANCE = $300.00

Day 1: DAILY BALANCE = $300.00 +100.00 = $400.00

Day 2: DAILY BALANCE = $400.00 + $100.00 = $500.00

Days 3 and 4: DAILY BALANCE =$500.00

Day 5: INTEREST CHARGE = $2.90, DAILY BALANCE = $500.00 + $2.90 = $502.90

Days 6-9: DAILY BALANCE = $502.90

Day 10: DAILY BALANCE = $502.90 + $100.00 = $602.90

Days 11- 30: DAILY BALANCE = $602.90

NEW BALANCE = $602.90

You pay $602.90.

SITUATION 5 - CONTINUED

"Do you still follow, Nicole?"

"I understand everything except where the **INTEREST CHARGE** of $2.90 came from. But I guess that's what you want to show me."

"Good! I do aim to show it. Here's that calculation.

MONTHLY PERIODIC RATE = APR/12 = 12.00%/12 = 1.00%

SUM OF DAILY BALANCES = $100.00 +200.00 +$300.00 + 27 x $300.00 = $8700.00

AVERAGE DAILY BALANCE = (SUM OF DAILY BALANCES)/DAYS

= $8700.00/30 = $290.00

INTEREST CHARGE = (APR/12)% of AVERAGE DAILY BALANCE

= 1.00% of $290.00 = 1.00/100 x $290.00

= 0.01 x $290.00 = $2.90

SITUATION 5 - CONTINUED

"Do you follow the **SUM OF DAILY BALANCES**, Sweetie?"

"If I'm correct, the **DAILY BALANCES** come from **MONTHLY STATEMENT 1**?"

"You're correct."

"I see the first three amounts are for days 1, 2 and 3. Then after day 3 there are 27 days of the $300.00 amount spent in the first three days. The average of all of them is $290.00."

"Exactly!

"Do you understand the **INTEREST CHARGE** better now?"

"Yes, Dad. Way back in in school I learned about percentages. So the **INTEREST CHARGE** is the **FRACTION** of 1.00/100 times the $290.00. You also used it the last time we talked."

"Super! Let's continue.

"Let's say in the third monthly period you make a $100.00 purchase on the first day. Your $602.90 payment for **MONTHLY STATEMENT 2** is received on the fifth day. Here are those results.

MONTHLY STATEMENT 3

PREVIOUS BALANCE = $602.90

Day 1: DAILY BALANCE = $602.90 +100.00 = $702.90

Days 2-4: DAILY BALANCE = $702.90

Day 5: PAYMENT $602.90, INTEREST CHARGE = $0.80

DAILY BALANCE = $702.90 -$602.90 + $0.80 = $100.80

Days 6-30: DAILY BALANCE = $100.80

NEW BALANCE = $100.80

SITUATION 5 - CONTINUED

"I suppose you do follow the day to day flow but want to see the calculation of the **INTEREST CHARGE**?"

"Yes I do follow the flow of **DAILY BALANCES**. But I paid the entire **NEW BALANCE** last month. So, why is there and **INTEREST CHARGE** at all? Yes, where does the $0.80 come from?"

"Great questions! There is an **INTEREST CHARGE** because until the payment is received any additional purchases you make in the next monthly period (Month 2 in this case) are charged interest. More specifically and important the **DAILY BALANCES** until that time are charged interest. Those charges are applied on the succeeding **MONTHLY STATEMENT** (Month 3 in this case). Let's me show you the calculations. Then you can take a moment to think them out."

SUM OF DAILY BALANCES = $400.00 +500.00 + 2 x $500.00 + $502.90 = $2402.90

AVERAGE DAILY BALANCE = (SUM OF DAILY BALANCES)/DAYS

= $2402.90/30 = $80.10

INTEREST CHARGE = 1.00% of $80.10 = $0.80

SITUATION 5 - CONTINUED

"Ok Nicole, what are you thinking?"

"Well, now the **DAILY BALANCE** amounts come from **MONTHLY STATEMENT 2**. I see that the **SUM OF DAILY BALANCES** is only for the first 5 days. The days until my payment is received and posted. But why is that sum divided by 30 days, not 5 days?"

"That's because you paid the prior **NEW BALANCE** in full. Once that $602.90 payment is received the subsequent **DAILY BALANCES** are not included. They are treated as $0.00.

"At this point you have a choice. If you pay the entire **NEW BALANCE** of $100.80 there is no **INTEREST CHARGE** on the next statement. If you do not pay the entire amount, then those subsequent **DAILY BALANCES** will be charged interest and it will be taken into account on **MONTHLY STATEMENT 4**. Do you understand that now?"

"I sort of do, Dad, but will think about it some more."

"A subtle aspect is that like a purchase from a vendor, the **INTEREST CHARGE** is an instantaneous loan and if left unpaid it will subsequently incur interest itself. In other words interest will be charged on unpaid interest. That occurs in the following **MONTHLY STATEMENT**.

"Do you understand my point?'

"I sort of interpret that if I don't pay the entire **NEW BALANCE**, I will be charged interest on the amount of charges I leave unpaid. And I will also be charged interest each day after that payment is accepted by the credit card company. As to 'interest charged on interest", you mentioned it last time too. It's fuzzy to me. I think it means the **INTEREST CHARGE** is just like a purchase and if unpaid later it would be charged interest itself for each day it is left unpaid. Have I got it right?"

"You sure do Smarty Pants! I am getting less and less worried about you possibly having a credit card.

"Now I'll explain the second method, the "**DAILY BALANCE METHOD** with a **DAILY PERIODIC RATE**". Let me pull that up."

DAILY BALANCE METHOD with a DAILY PERIODIC RATE

DAILY PERIODIC RATE = APR/365 days

DAILY INTEREST AMOUNT = (APR/365)% of DAILY BALANCE

INTEREST CHARGE = SUM OF DAILY INTEREST AMOUNTS

"To get the **DAILY PERIODIC RATE** they divide the **APR** by the number of days in a year. Then that **DAILY PERIODIC RATE** is applied each day to the **DAILY BALANCE** owed on that day. Then to get the **INTEREST CHARGE** the **DAILY INTEREST AMOUNTS** are summed for the entire month of that billing period. Do you see follow that?"

"Yeah, Dad, I do. It's easier to understand now that you explained the first method. I see the difference. Does it give the same result?"

"Let's try it and see."

SITUATION 6

"Let's use the same situation as we just examined, except the **INTEREST CHARGE** is based on the **DAILY BALANCE METHOD** with a **DAILY PERIODIC RATE**.

"The first **MONTHLY STATEMENT** is the same as before, so let's start with the second one."

MONTHLY STATEMENT 2

PREVIOUS BALANCE = $300.00

Day 1: DAILY BALANCE = $300.00 +100.00 = $400.00

Day 2: DAILY BALANCE = $400.00 + $100.00 = $500.00

Days 3 and 4: DAILY BALANCE =$500.00

Day 5: INTEREST CHARGE = $2.86, DAILY BALANCE = $500.00 + $2.86 = $502.86

Days 6-9: DAILY BALANCE = $502.86

Day 10: DAILY BALANCE = $502.86 + $100.00 = $602.86

Days 11- 30: DAILY BALANCE = $602.86

NEW BALANCE = $602.86

You pay $602.86.

SITUATION 6

"What difference do you notice, if anything?"

"Well, the amount of the **INTEREST CHARGE** is different. For this method it is $2.86 instead of $2.90. I guess that answers my question on that point. Can you show me the calculations?"

"I was going to do that next. Here they are."

DAILY PERIODIC RATE = APR/365 = 12.00%/365 = 0.0329% (rounded)

DAY 1: DAILY INTEREST AMOUNT = 0.0329% of $100.00

$$= 0.0329/100 \times \$100.00$$

$$= \$0.03 \text{ (rounded)}$$

DAY 2: DAILY INTEREST AMOUNT = 0.0329/100 x $200.00 = $0.07 (rounded)

DAY 3: DAILY INTEREST AMOUNT = 0.0329/100 x $300.00 = $0.10 (rounded)

DAYS 4-30: DAILY INTEREST AMOUNT = 0.0329/100 x $300.00 = $0.10 (rounded)

INTEREST CHARGE = SUM OF DAILY INTEREST AMOUNTS

$$= \$0.03 + \$0.07 + \$0.10 + 27 \times \$0.10 = \$2.90$$

SITUATION 6 – CONTINUED

"Well, well. Before you can even say it yourself, it seems we get $2.90, NOT $2.86. If that $2.90 I just got is correct, then the result for each method would be the same. So what's going? Before looking at that though, do you follow the procedure?"

"Yes, I do. I already said it was clearer than the first method. I see that the **DAILY PERIODIC RATE** is 0.0329, rounded. I guess it's rounded to that value to make the math easier. Then each day you just multiply its **DAILY BALANCE** by that 0.0329 to get the **DAILY INTEREST AMOUNT**. Each of those results is rounded to the nearest cent. Then you add them up for all the days. That gives you the $2.90"

"Good. And why is the $2.86 result on the **MONTHLY STATEMENT**?"

"If no rounding was done, then the result would the $2.86."

"That's terrific, Nicole! Your understanding is spot on. I recalculated the values with more precise numbers. Let's look at it."

DAILY PERIODIC RATE = APR/365 = 12.00%/365 = 0.0328767%

DAY 1: DAILY INTEREST AMOUNT = 0.0328767/100 x $100.00 = $0.0329 (rounded)

DAY 2: DAILY INTEREST AMOUNT = 0.0328767/100 x $200.00 = $0.0657 (rounded)

DAY 3: = DAILY INTEREST AMOUNT = 0.0328767/100 x $300.00 = $0.0986 (rounded)

DAYS 4-30: DAILY INTEREST AMOUNT = 0.0328767/100 x $300.00 = $0.0986 (rounded)

INTEREST CHARGE = SUM OF DAILY INTEREST AMOUNTS

= $0.0329 +$0.0657 + $0.0986 + 27 x $0.0986

= $2.8594 = $2.86 rounded

SITUATION 6 – CONTINUED

"So, Nicole, the more precise numbers do lead to the $2.86 amount. And indeed the result is different for each method."

"Maybe you are wondering why the two methods of determining the **INTEREST CHARGE** give different results?"

"Actually, I was too mesmerized by the decimal places in your precise calculations to have that enter my mind. But now that you mention it, why does that happen? I'm sure you were going to explain it anyway."

"It's kind of subtle, Nicole. When the **DAILY PERIODIC RATE** is used it is based on a year of 365 days. When calculating the **MONTHLY PERIODIC RATE,** the **APR** was divided by 12 months, which presumes the months all have same number of days. That's not correct. For the examples I used 30 days, which is only correct for 4 months in the year. Others have 31 days, expect February. February has 28 days (29 days in a Leap Year). It's kind of like assuming each year has 360 days. Or more technically, you have a different number of **DAILY BALANCES** based on the month at hand. As a result, the daily effect varies. For the **DAILY PERIODIC RATE** that does not matter, as each day has the same interest rate in play.

"There is an additional subtle consideration. In the above, when calculating the **DAILY PERIODIC RATE** the **APR** was divided by 365 days. In a Leap Year there are 366 days.

"Lenders actually take these differences into account in determining any monthly **INTEREST CHARGE**. They will usually show both an **ANNUAL RATE OF INTEREST** and an **APR**, and they will differ slightly. Credit card issuers do the same."

"That makes sense and seems pretty obvious once you describe it, Dad. It seems like it's just a small difference in the result, too."

"That small difference is insignificant when the credit card charges are hundreds of dollars. But for charges approaching high **UPPER LIMITS** of tens of thousands dollars, it's a little more significant. It's not enough to worry which method is used. The larger need is to know if the **INTEREST CHARGE** is correct, that no error was made.

"Whichever way it is done, the calculation of the **INTEREST CHARGE** is not shown in the **MONTHLY STATEMENT**. The credit card issuer has programmed the calculation into its computerized processing. If you did not pay your previous month's **NEW BALANCE** in full, then the **INTEREST CHARGE** for that amount is calculated. And they do that with precise numbers. The amount is indicated on your next **MONTHLY STATEMENT** as a charge you owe."

"How would I know if an error was made?"

"In normal use, credit card purchases are made on many days within a month. It would be very time consuming for the cardholder to actually check the amount of interest charged on a credit card each month. With a large number of transactions spread over many days, it quickly becomes unwieldy. That's because the **MONTHLY STATEMENT** does not show the **DAILY BALANCES**, only the amount of the charges. You have to calculate them yourself. Who has the time to do that? The point of the above explanation is for reader awareness of the complexity that is hidden behind the single line that indicates the **INTEREST CHARGE**. In essence the transparency of the calculation is minimal.

"There is no easy way to confirm the **INTEREST CHARGE** precisely. However, there's a simpler step one can take.

"For the **DAILY BALANCE METHOD** with a **DAILY PERIODIC RATE** there's an alternative way the **INTEREST CHARGE** can be calculated. To do the calculation, you don't have to do it day by day. You can sum the **DAILY BALANCES** and then apply the **DAILY PERIODIC RATE** to it. Let me show that.

INTEREST CHARGE = (APR/365)% of SUM OF DAILY BALANCES

"Can you deduce that this is correct and the result will be the same as doing it day by day?"

"Not really, Dad."

"If you think about your algebra, then you might see it is simple logic. But it's not worth explaining it that way. Just know it is the case."

"I agree Dad. I am taking algebra this year, so I'll think about another time."

"Ok. Here's confirmation it works for the situation we a have at hand.

INTEREST CHARGE = 0.0328767/100 x $8700.00 = $2.86 (rounded)

"But even this way one has to get the **SUM OF DAILY BALANCES**. Again, for a **MONTHLY STATEMENT** with a lot of charges, that's extremely tedious. A very approximate but quick alternative is helpful for months in which you do not pay the entire **NEW BALANCE**. Just apply the **MONTHLY PERIODIC RATE** to that **NEW BALANCE** amount.

"For our example, for **MONTHLY STATEMENT 1**, the **NEW BALANCE** is $300.00. 1.00% of that amount is $3.00 compared to $2.90 or $2.86.

"For **MONTHLY STATEMENT** 2, the **NEW BALANCE** is $602.90. If you do not pay that then the approximate **INTEREST CHARGE** on the next statement would be 1.00% of that, $6.03. If you calculate the actual result you will find it is $5.76. But I'm sure you get the point. If you want, you can consider confirming that value as your homework.

Exercise 5: *Calculate the above* ***INTEREST CHARGE*** *of $5.76.*

Your homework result should be: *$5.76*

"The result can be very approximate. However, it does give you "ball park" confidence that the actual amount is "about right." If you correctly calculate the approximate value and get $4.50 vs. say $15.00 charged, you should wonder "What's going on here?" and call your credit card issuer to explain their number.

"Of course all this fuss about the **INTEREST CHARGE** is only necessary if you are not going to pay the **NEW BALANCE** in full and on time. But you did ask for the details, Peanut."

"Yes, I did and maybe I should not have been so curious. At least I can use your quick check. Once I get a credit card I'll strive to always pay the entire **NEW BALANCE** every month."

"That's the bottom line lesson. Given the high **APR** values involved for credit card usage it comes at very high cost if the cardholder is careless about making payments. By paying the entire **NEW BALANCE** each month you create an effective interest rate of 0.00%. That does not mean the credit card issuer makes no money and will want to dump you. They still make the **ANNUAL FEE** and the typical 4.00% vendor fee on your purchases."

"I do see how complicated the **INTEREST CHARGE** is and why most people don't read the fine print. And if they do, maybe they don't dig into it like you do Dad. I guess I believe you when you call me a "smarty pants" because I seem to be just as curious as you about money matter details. Thank you so much."

"You're very welcome! Yeah, I tried to avoid the nuts and bolts of it. But you got what you asked for.

"Don't forget, Nicole. I said I had decided it would be good to cover how a teenager would establish creditworthiness?

"How could I forget, Dad. You also said you'd talk about ways you can get a credit card once I am eighteen.

"If you want to, we can talk about it now. Or if you're tired, we can cover that another day."

"I don't want to take any chance to let you forget that one. Let's get right to it."

"Ok, but let's take 15 minute time out. Then we'll go at it."

LESSON 4 *How Do I Love Creditworthiness? Let's Count the Ways*

Exactly 15 minutes later on the dot, Nicole and her Dad continue the conversation.

"Hi Dad! I'm raring to go."

"I'm ready, too, Nicole. Let me be more specific about the meaning of creditworthiness."

"Ok, that would be helpful."

"In general terms, creditworthiness means being financially reliable enough to be approved for a loan at a reasonable interest rate for a reasonably high amount of money. That is determined by your credit standing as measured by a credit rating bureau which scores you according to past history of many things, among them having paid debts (car loans, student loans, other credit cards, etc.) in a timely manner.

"Making all monthly payments on time for the full amount due is one key factor. A record of making less than the full amount due each month, especially if one only pays the minimum amount frequently suggests an inability to afford the purchase in the first place. Skipping even one payment a loan can prove detrimental to a credit rating score. The higher the amounts of various debts that you have successfully repaid on time the better is your creditworthiness."

"I'm not aware of having a credit standing? How do I get a credit card if I have no record of credit? And what's a credit rating bureau and credit rating score?"

"Let's not focus on the technical meanings quite yet. Let's first look at your burning question. How can you get a credit card? As a 16-year old all that is a tall order. Even as an 18-year old. Most kids don't have a credit rating score. In fact getting a credit card is one of the few ways you can start to establish one. My generation calls that a "Catch-22". It's from an old movie. Means you need to have something in order to first get the same thing."

"It must be a real old movie. I've never heard of it or that phrase."

"I mentioned that to get a credit card as a 16-year old you need to have your parents involved. As you become 18-years old and approach going to college, there will be other ways to get a credit card. Let's look at them.

"One way is to apply for a **student credit card**. You can do that at a bank. Using the one Mom and me use is maybe easiest, since they know us. You would have to qualify for the card. Each bank is different in that regard. For our bank you need to have a checking account at that bank. Then use it without ever having overdraft problems. That means not ever having written a check that exceeds the money you have in the account at that time. It is also necessary that you are working at least part time at a job with some regular earnings. That could be at a burger joint. It could be part-time work at the college. There are many jobs at colleges, such as an aide at the bookstore or a vendor at sports events."

"I guess I need to start preparing for that. Looks like I need a part-time job and a checking account?"

"Exactly, Peanut. But some banks accept the situation of a parent giving the student a regular monthly amount of money. When the time approaches we can look into that. For now it would be great if you could work part-time if it does not interfere with school. But there's more to consider.

"A student credit card is always for a very low credit limit. As I mentioned it's usually its $300 to $500. But that should be plenty of money, especially if we pay for your books. Student loans would cover that too and other academic expenses. You mainly need money for daily living. There's a drawback too. Until you establish enough credit it comes at a high **APR**, likely in that 18% to 20% range. You would have to be sure to pay the charges off in full each month.

"Another way is a **secured credit card**. That type of card requires being able to deposit enough funds to back up the card limit, that $300-$500. That's what "secured" means. At our bank you do that by having a separate bank account set up with that amount of funds deposited in it. If a credit card **MONTHLY PAYMENT** is not made, then the bank can withdraw that amount from that account. If that happens you would have to replace the funds or possibly have your card terminated. You avoid that by always paying the **MONTHLY PAYMENT** on time yourself from your checking account. But it too would come with a high **APR** until you build up more credit and qualify for a normal card with a lower **APR.** You do have to apply and qualify on the same basis as a student card but it is nearly automatic because of the secured aspect."

"So if I had a job, I could save up that $300- $500. Then I could open the bank account apply for the card myself?"

"That's the intent."

"Great! I was thinking about getting a job at Comic Cones."

"What's Comic Cones?"

"It's near the school. You buy ice cream and can hang around reading their comic books. A lot of my friends go there. One of them works there and said they always need help."

"Then I agree that would be great. So if you want to, go apply for a job at Comedy Cones for a few hours a week, maybe on weekends."

"Ok Dad, I will apply. And its Comic Cones not Comedy Cones. I don't want to be a comedian."

Smiling widely, "My mistake, I don't think I want you to be one either. There is one more way for you to get a credit card.

"If a parent is willing to do it, a **joint credit card account** can be established. Basically the parent and the child are co-applicants. A key advantage is the parent would demonstrate the needed creditworthiness. If applied for and approved each applicant would have separate credit cards. Yours would be in your name. The **MONTHLY STATEMENT** would identify your purchases and payments. You would have to make sure that the account is being reported on your credit report. That allows you to build up your creditworthiness. But both persons are responsible for the **MONTHLY PAYMENT** and are liable if it is not made. That's the rub I mentioned before. Misuse by the child would affect the parent's credit rating, too."

"Dad, how do I make sure the credit card activity I have is being reported on my credit report?"

"You would need to ask the card issuer if that is the case.

"By the way, if you do have your job at Comic Cones you might find you don't need a co-applicant. So even if you apply with one they might tell you it's not necessary."

"Wow! That would be great."

"For evaluating your creditworthiness, banks and credit union lenders commonly depend on your credit rating from one or more of the three major credit reporting agencies. They are referred to as credit bureaus. Those credit bureaus are Equifax, Experian and Transunion. So that answers that question.

"The information about you is detailed and when requested is provided in a credit report. The credit reports for the three agencies are not replicates. Each credit bureau does that differently and might have different information at hand. That's because they collect and update data on different timings, have different inquiry occurrences etc. The lender will request your credit report from one of them. If your credit is satisfactory, it is unlikely the lender will check more than that one."

"What's in a credit report?"

"A credit report shows your debt and repayment history in detail over a long period of time. Your history includes very detailed information on the types of credit (debt) you have and/or have had; how long you have and/or have had the credit (each debt); how much of each debt you still owe; your repayment history (were payments made on time, missed, gone into collection, etc.?); any new credit applications; inquiries from lenders regarding your loan and credit card applications; inquiries from promotional marketers; inquiries from potential employers etc."

"Can I get a credit report for myself?"

"Yes you can, Sweetie. You are entitled to a free credit report annually from each of the agencies. You can request them any time either via the Internet at www.annualcreditreport.com or calling 1-877-322-8228. It is a good idea to request one every four months and rotate the requests to each agency. That will give you a periodic general sense of your situation."

"If I get one, what should I look for in it?"

"You want to check the correctness of the information it reports about you and your credit history. If you find questionable and/or erroneous information you can act to try to get it corrected. Should that happen, you should investigate at the credit reporting agency from which the report at hand came. Once clarified and acted on, you should check your reports at the other two agencies, even if you have to pay for them."

"Does it have that credit rating score you mentioned?"

"No it does not. That's one of the oddities. You have to get that separately and pay for it."

"How would I do that and what does it cost and how do I do that?"

"For an overall "credit rating" these credit reporting agencies use a so-called **FICO SCORE**. Presently, it costs $15.95 to obtain a **FICO SCORE** via www.myfico.com, and you can include a request for either your Equifax or Transunion credit report. Fortunately, the situation appears to be changing. Some avenues to get a free **FICO SCORE** are slowly arising. But they appear to be mostly from someone trying to sell you something or their services or offer you a loan. More important there are fraudulent or imposter websites out there, often using the word free to entice one. It is worth the $15.95 to be sure you avoid accidentally using any of them. Likely, when a lender decides on a loan you can ask if your **FICO SCORE** was a factor. That lender might tell you your score and its effect on your outcome. My bank offers free **FICO SCORES** unconditionally."

"What is a **fyko score** and why is it called that? And how do you spell fyko, Dad?"

"It's **F-I-C-O**, Sweetie-pie. A **FICO SCORE** is a number and it is based on the information in your credit report. It's called that because the scoring system was developed by Fair, Isaac Corporation."

"How do they do that scoring?"

"The methodology and algorithm behind it are secret. That's for two main reasons. One is protection against competition seeing it. The other is that individuals would be able to see the details and argue about their **FICO SCORE** and the calculation details. Indeed, a person might take legal action to dispute their data used, importance of different components and the result."

"Then how does anyone know what led to their **FICO SCORE**?"

"If your score is high, then you likely don't care. If it is low, about the only thing you can do is look for negative information and the preponderance of it. You can see the trail of your activity and surmise which pieces contributed to it your score being low."

"What's a high score or a low score?"

"The highest **FICO SCORE** one can be given is 850. The lowest **FICO SCORE** is 300."

"How important is the **FICO SCORE**?

"Your **FICO SCORE** is a critical aspect of your creditworthiness. It's a significant factor in a lender's decision on loan applications, particularly car loans. The lower your **FICO SCORE** is the higher will be the **ANNUAL RATE OF INTEREST** a lender will charge you for a loan. Each lender will have its own criteria for matching an **ANNUAL RATE OF INTEREST** to your **FICO SCORE**.

"A **FICO SCORE** in the range of 750-850 is considered excellent. As you drop toward 700 you are nearing an average credit rating. **FICO SCORES** below 600 might prevent you from obtaining the loan. If you do get one it will be at a very high rate of interest.

"There are also other "credit scores" out there that some lenders use instead of or in addition to a **FICO SCORE**. The range of scores and their meaning will be entirely different. If so, you will need to research that particular scoring. One example is a Vantage Score which ranges from 501 to 990. Scores above 900 are excellent.""

"Golly Dad, I didn't realize these guys were out there collecting information about me. How do they get that stuff?"

"Well Nicole, that's why the government requires that anyone dealing with your financial information has to provide you a statement of their privacy policy.

"I mentioned that whichever way you get your first credit card at eighteen years old it will very likely have a high **APR**. Again, that's because most 18-year olds have yet to establish creditworthiness. You might be able to find a student or secured credit card with a low **APR** introductory offer. That means it would apply for a short time, maybe for 6 months. Then you have to solve the puzzle again. But introductory offers can present some other worries."

"Tell, me more about that Dad?"

"One caution about credit cards concerns a so-called "teaser rate." Credit card issuing entities often offer a teaser rate to entice one to accept their offer of a credit card. You have to be careful of that whenever you are offered a low **APR**, but especially so if your credit rating does not seem to justify it.

"A common approach is to offer a very low **APR** for transferring the outstanding balance of your present credit card (issued by another entity) to the new one they offer. While that is unlikely to come into play with your first credit card as an 18-years old student, it provides insight to what I mean about teaser rates."

"Yeah, that event sounds way ahead of me. But I am curious about it."

"Yes, it seems you are always curious about details. That's a very good thing. Always check things out carefully with credit cards or any other money matter.

"In essence, they offer a path by which your new credit card purchases the debt of your present credit card. That results in the outstanding balance (of your present credit card) being paid in full by charging it to your new credit card. For example, a credit card issuer offers to transact that for you and indicates the "introductory rate" is going to be "as low as" 2.99% **APR**.

"One pitfall is that by stating a 2.99% **APR** they are using an old trick of trying to make it look like a 2.00% **APR** rather than a 3.00% **APR** to the casual observer. Another pitfall is the meaning of the term "introductory rate." In the fine print, there will be several qualifiers. First, it will be indicated that the meaning of "as low as" is that the introductory rate is, for example, "2.99%-18.00% based on your creditworthiness". Second, it will indicated that the introductory rate only applies for an initial period of time, typically six to twelve monthly statement periods following the transfer of your outstanding balance. After that initial introductory period of time, the initial **APR** is to be increased to a much higher **APR**.

"For example, it might be stated that "after the introductory period, the interest rate will be 6.99% to 21.00% **APR** based on your creditworthiness". If you act carelessly you may inadvertently accept the above card thinking you have a 2.99% **APR** outright. It may turn out to be as high as 18.00% **APR** and become 21.00% **APR** in just six months. It may be that the initial introductory **APR** and/or subsequent delayed **APR** are/is higher than that of your existing credit card. Also, if your outstanding balance transfers in from your old card in the last few days of a month, you in effect have essentially one less month of the introductory period in play."

"That's kind of involved Dad but I get it."

"All this worry-wart stuff does not matter if you pay your monthly outstanding balances in full and on time. But you did ask about it all and got me to relent and spend time explaining how you can get a first credit card at a young age."

"Dad, when that time comes I will be careful about that and probably check with you first. It also adds to my feeling that maybe I should not be so anxious to get a credit card now, or even when I am eighteen years old."

"Sweetie, I have to admit it. That's nice music to my ears. But when you are eighteen years old I will be very anxious to help you walk through the hoops of getting your first credit card. Now that we spent all this time together on the topic, I actually look forward to that day.

"Unless you have other curiosities, I'm done with everything I wanted to share. How about heading for Comic Cones and some ice cream and light reading? It's my treat."

"Super! Let's go. I'll drive. What's your favorite flavor?"

"Pistachio! It's the color of money."

"Maybe I'll make that mine too. Thank you for everything Dad."

"You're awesome and very welcome!"

Nicole's junior year is moving along fast. Her school life is flashing by like scenes in an action packed video game. On the academic side she is doing great. Between working at Comic Cones on weekends, playing on the school volleyball team and taking private dance lessons, atop classes she is ready for the pause. Thanksgiving break is just a few days away.

Nicole alerts her Dad. "Dad, next week I am on break for Thanksgiving. In school they've been telling us about college entrance exams. I plan to take them next term. It's around $50.00 to take each exam. There are other fees if you register late, want to later get answers to the test questions, send scores to extra colleges and other things."

"Well Nicole, that's exciting. It's not a concern at all. Just go ahead and register whenever you need to do so. I'll do the payment whatever way is needed."

"Great Dad! I also wanted to meet with you some time to find out about the affordability of going to college. Once I take the entrance exams I'll have a better idea of my chances of admission at different colleges. So I can wait."

"Nicole, don't worry on that yet. When you have definite colleges in mind, we can discuss that aspect in some detail. Depending on the choices and costs, it might be that student loans would be involved. I'm not knowledgeable about the government student loan programs. But, we can look into the details of that together."

"I understand and appreciate that. If student loans are different than credit cards, I'm in the dark."

"Before looking into student loans I can teach you about other types of loans in general? We could begin that right away."

"How about Saturday morning, Dad? I don't have to work Saturday until 3."

"OK. Let's start around 10 in the morning in my office. I'll prepare some material like the time we discussed credit cards."

"Ok Dad, that way I can sleep a little later, too."

It's 10 AM that Saturday. Hearing Nicole come in, Dad turns from his computer. "There you are Peanut! I started a few minutes early to pull up some computer files."

"Good morning Dad, I'm ready to start."

"Ok. When we talked about credit cards you learned about the concept of revolving charges. If your end of month balance was not paid in full, then interest was charged on the unpaid portion. Because purchases occur on a daily basis, the interest charged was calculated on a daily basis. Do you remember that?"

"I do, Dad.. It was very complicated."

"It is. Revolving charges also occur if you purchase items on an account at a department store. Fortunately regular loans do not work that way. It's a lot easier."

"Sounds good to me."

"When a regular loan, such as a loan to purchase a car, occurs you are borrowing a fixed amount of money from a lender. For a car the lender would either be the car dealer or a bank. The lender intends to give you money because you intend to repay it back plus pay interest the lender will charge. That's called an agreement. The agreement is made with certain conditions in play. Those conditions are referred to as the **terms** of the loan.

"The **terms** of the loan refer to the details of the signed loan agreement made between the lender and borrower. The primary terms of the loan include the **LOAN AMOUNT**, **ANNUAL RATE OF INTEREST**, the **TERM** of the loan, details about the repayment process and any penalties involved should any scheduled payment be late, missed or skipped."

"Wait a moment Dad. You said the terms of the loan include the term. Sounds strange to me. Is that what you meant to say?"

"I did. It is confusing the first time you hear it. When I say **terms** it's written in lower case letters to distinguish it from the **TERM** which has no "s" and is written in capital letters. It's just happens to be the common business terminology. Let me define **TERM**. Oops, now there's an awkward wording."

"Sure is."

"The **LOAN AMOUNT** is amount of money borrowed at the outset. The **TERM** is amount of time that will pass until the loaned amount plus accumulating interest will be paid off. For repayment, typically incremental portions of the loaned amount plus accrued interest are due on a monthly basis.

"Although an **ANNUAL RATE OF INTEREST** is always specified, most actual loans are made on the basis of the borrower incurring interest on a monthly basis. Interest is incurred at the end of each month on the amount of unpaid debt that existed during that month. Unlike a credit card, no purchasing activity occurs in a loan after the initial **LOAN AMOUNT** is accepted by the borrower. The **MONTHLY RATE OF INTEREST** is the agreed to **ANNUAL RATE OF INTEREST** divided by twelve months."

"How much money and interest is owed each month? How is the amount of interest calculated?"

"You sure do like to know how interest is calculated. I'll get to that."

"The borrowed funds are paid back incrementally, with payment "in part" due each month. Payment "in total" is due after an agreed amount of time. The agreed amount of time what I called the "**TERM** of the loan". The **TERM** may extend to several months, a few years or many years, but the debt owed is visited every month by the lender. That is because the incremental payments due each month follow a payment schedule dictated by the **terms** of the loan.

"The **MONTHLY PAYMENTS** are based on agreeing to how much money must be paid each month so that the full amount borrowed plus the accumulating interest will be gradually paid by the end of the **TERM** of the loan. In many loans a process called **amortization** is used to determine the amounts. That has a bit of complex math involved and it's premature to get into it. Later we can talk about it. Right now I'll use a different process. That way the basic points are easier to see. It's not an imaginary process. It could actually occur if the **terms** of the loan specify it."

"How do you even spell "ammutization"? Sounds like I'd be getting my flu shot."

"Well that's not going to happen, Nicole. When we cover the topic I'll write it down. Let me describe the other approach.

"To begin, let's assume a certain amount of money is borrowed. What's that called?"

"The **LOAN AMOUNT**."

"Right. Then assume each month a specified portion of borrowed money is paid back at the end of the month. It could be a different amount each month. Call it the **SCHEDULED MONTHLY PAYMENT**. The **MONTHLY INTEREST** is an additional charge and is also owed at the end of each month. Each month the entire scheduled **MONTHLY PAYMENT** amount is to be applied to reduce the amount of money owed each month. A **MONTHLY STATEMENT** is received showing those amounts."

"So you get a statement similar to a credit card **MONTHLY STATEMENT**?"

"Yes, it is similar. But since there are no ongoing purchases it's a lot shorter.

"Once a loan is initiated, after the Month 1 a **MONTHLY STATEMENT** is received. The initial **OUTSTANDING BALANCE** is the **LOAN AMOUNT**.

"Then the **OUTSTANDING BALANCE** is reduced by the **PAYMENT RECEIVED**. **MONTHLY INTEREST** is obtained by applying the **MONTHLY RATE OF INTEREST** to that amount. Then the **MONTHLY INTEREST** is added to the **REDUCED BALANCE** to get the **NEW OUTSTANDING BALANCE**. It's also added to the **SCHEDULED MONTHLY PAYMENT** to get the **AMOUNT DUE**.

"Let me show all that as math equations.

MONTHLY STATEMENT 1

OUTSTANDING BALANCE = LOAN AMOUNT

REDUCED BALANCE = OUTSTANDING BALANCE – PAYMENT RECEIVED

RATIO = MONTHLY RATE OF INTEREST/100

MONTHLY INTEREST = RATIO x REDUCED BALANCE

NEW OUTSTANDING BALANCE = REDUCED BALANCE + MONTHLY INTEREST

AMOUNT DUE = SCHEDULED MONTHLY PAYMENT + MONTHLY INTEREST

"If the **AMOUNT DUE** is paid on time, then in the next month it is the **PAYMENT RECEIVED** amount.

"Are you following this OK?"

"That **RATIO** term is new to me. Since it's divided by 100, the **MONTHLY RATE OF INTEREST** must be a percentage?"

"That's correct. **RATIO** is just a math term used when the percentage is written in decimal form."

"Then I sort of understand the equations. But all the different names of balances is starting to spin my head a bit"

"Yes, as I describe it my mind spins a little bit too. Later I'll make that clearer by using a numerical example."

"Dad, I understand the meaning of the **NEW OUTSTANDING BALANCE**. But I tend to be confused about why the **AMOUNT DUE** is not equal to it."

"Recall that the **LOAN AMOUNT** is being repaid by incremental amounts each month. The **AMOUNT DUE** is that increment of money plus any interest charged for the amount of money that was left unpaid that month. You'll also see that more clearly in my numerical example."

"Ok. I'll wait for that."

"After the end of Month 2 the second **MONTHLY STATEMENT** arrives. The **NEW OUTSTANDING BALANCE** is carried forward as the **PREVIOUS OUTSTANDING BALANCE**.

"The **PREVIOUS OUTSTANDING BALANCE** is reduced by the **PAYMENT RECEVED**. **MONTHLY INTEREST** is obtained by applying the **MONTHLY RATE OF INTEREST** to that amount. Then the rest is like Month 1.

"Let's look at that in equation form.

MONTHLY STATEMENT 2

REDUCED BALANCE = PREVIOUS OUTSTANDING BALANCE – PAYMENT RECEIVED

MONTHLY INTEREST = RATIO x REDUCED BALANCE

NEW OUTSTANDING BALANCE = REDUCED BALANCE + MONTHLY INTEREST

AMOUNT DUE = SCHEDULED MONTHLY PAYMENT + MONTHLY INTEREST

"Do you follow it. Nicole?"

"I think so. It does seem a little similar to the credit card statements."

"This pattern continues each month until the loan is fully paid off, that is until all **SCHEDULED MONTHLY PAYMENTS** and calculated **MONTHLY INTEREST** amounts have been paid. Are you still with me?"

"Kind of."

"Let's look at an example with actual numbers. As you're too young to legally make such a loan, I'll use a hypothetical individual named Bradley."

SITUATION 7

"Bradley takes out a bank loan for $1000.00 to buy a guitar. By signed agreement the debt is due in one year. **MONTHLY PAYMENTS** of $85.00 are to be made at the end of each month for eleven months. A **MONTHLY PAYMENT** of $65.00 is to be made at the end of month twelve. The twelve payments total $1000.00. An **ANNUAL RATE OF INTEREST** of 5.00% is to be applied on a **MONTHLY INTEREST** basis each month in the manner I just described."

"Nicole, what's all that information called?

"I suppose those are the **terms** of the loan?" =

"That's right. Assume Bradley makes all payments including interest on time. Let's follow the repayment. First we need the **MONTHLY RATE OF INTEREST**. Let's get that and then look at the outcome after the first month.

MONTHLY RATE OF INTEREST = ANNUAL RATE OF INTEREST/12 months

= 5.00%/12 months = 0.417% per month

RATIO = 0.417%/100 = 0.00417

MONTHLY STATEMENT 1

OUTSTANDING BALANCE = LOAN AMOUNT = $1000.00

REDUCED BALANCE = OUTSTANDING BALANCE – PAYMENT RECEIVED

= $1000.00 - $0.00 = $1000.00

MONTHLY INTEREST = RATIO x REDUCED BALANCE = 0.00417 x $1000.00 = $4.17

NEW OUTSTANDING BALANCE = REDUCED BALANCE + MONTHLY INTEREST

= $1000.00 + $4.17 = $1004.17

SCHEDULED MONTHLY PAYMENT = $85.00

The AMOUNT DUE = $85.00 + $4.17 = $89.17 and is paid on time.

SITUATION 7 - CONTINUED

"Do you understand those calculations, Peanut?"

"Like you mentioned, it's sort of like a credit card repayment but a lot different. But I do mostly understand it. But why is the **PAYMENT RECEIVED** zero dollars?"

"Because it's the first **MONTHLY STATEMENT** no payment has been made. None is due until after that first statement is received."

"Ok, I realize that now. When are the **MONTHLY INTEREST** charged and the **AMOUNT DUE** paid?"

"I see I left that part out of the **term**s. You see on my monitor flow they are charged and due right at the end of the month. Let's assume that's stated in the **terms** of the loan. Assume Bradley pays by bank checks sent in the mail. Usually a so-called **grace period** of a few days, perhaps five to ten days is stated in the loan terms. That means Bradley would have that many days into the following month to have his check received by the lender. Is it all clear now?"

"Yes it's clear."

"Ok. Let's look at the next month's outcome.

MONTHLY STATEMENT 2

PREVIOUS OUTSTANDING BALANCE = $1004.17

PAYMENT RECEIVED = $89.17

REDUCED BALANCE = PREVIOUS OUTSTANDING BALANCE

– PAYMENT RECEIVED

= \$1004.17 - \$89.17 = \$915.00

MONTHLY INTEREST = 0.00417 x \$915.00 = \$3.82

NEW OUTSTANDING BALANCE = REDUCED BALANCE + MONTHLY INTEREST

= \$915.00 +\$3.82 = \$918.82

SCHEDULED MONTHLY PAYMENT = \$85.00

The AMOUNT DUE = \$85.00 + \$3.82 = \$88.82 and is paid on time.

SITUATION 7 - CONTINUED

"Are you still following it, Sweetie?"

"I sure am."

"That's great!"

"The monthly progression with a **MONTHLY PAYMENT** of \$85.00 repeats nine more times. I've condensed those results."

MONTHLY STATEMENTS 3 through 11

The sequence of results for REDUCED BALANCE, MONTHLY INTEREST is:

Month 3: \$830.00, \$3.46; *Month 4: \$745.00, \$3.11;* **Month 5: \$660.00, \$2.75***: Month 6: \$575.00, \$2.40;* **Month 7: \$490.00, \$2.04;** *Month 8: \$405.00, \$1.69;* **Month 9: \$320.00, \$1.33;** *Month 10: \$235.00, \$0.98;* **Month 11: \$150.00, \$0.63.**

Adding the two values will give the NEW OUTSTANDING BALANCE for each month.

SITUATION 7 - CONTINUED

"Still following me?"

"It takes a bit of eye attention, but yes, Dad. I see you skip the calculations and give the values of those two items for each of the next nine months. That's through Month 11. So what happens next?"

"I understand the eye strain. I wrote it in text to save space. Also if you want to see it as voluntary homework, you can fill in the details all the way through. But whoa on what happens next. First tell me what's happening to those values as the months pass?"

"Well they both keep getting lower."

"Why?"

"I guess it's because the **MONTHLY PAYMENTS** are reducing what is owed each month. So the amount of **MONTHLY INTEREST** is less each month."

"Very good! And it's not really a guess is it?"

"I suppose it's not. I kind of thought it out."

"Indeed you did, Smarty Pants."

"Notice that at the end of Month 11 the **REDUCED OUTSTANDING BALANCE** is $65.00. What's interesting about that?"

"If I remember correctly, the last **MONTHLY PAYMENT** is $65.00. And the loan will be paid off that month? That sort of makes sense."

"That's right. But there will also be **MONTHLY INTEREST** charged on that $65.00. Let's look at the last month."

"Ok. And maybe I will try that voluntary homework when I have the time to do it. At least I have the correct answers to check my work."

"Great and let me know if you encounter any trouble. Oh, I'll E-mail you those results, too."

MONTHLY STATEMENT 12

PREVIOUS OUTSTANDING BALANCE = $150.00 +$0.63 = $150.63

PAYMENT RECEIVED = $85.63

REDUCED BALANCE = $150.63 - $85.63 = $65.00

MONTHLY INTEREST = 0.00417 x $65.00 = $0.27

NEW OUTSTANDING BALANCE= $65.00 - $0.27 = $65.27

SCHEDULED MONTHLY PAYMENT = $65.00

The AMOUNT DUE = $65.00 + $0.27 = $65.27 and is paid on time and the loan ends.

SITUATION 7 - CONTINUED

"Indeed the loan has now been fully repaid. The **TOTAL INTEREST** paid is the sum of the twelve **MONTHLY INTEREST** amounts. So, the **TOTAL INTEREST** equals $4.17 + $3.82 + ... + $0.27. I calculated that and its $26.65. What's that as a percentage of the loan?"

"Hmm? I think I should know how to get that? But it escapes me right now."

"Look at my monitor, please."

FRACTION = TOTAL INTEREST/LOAN AMOUNT = $26.65/$1000.00 = 0.02665

PERCENT TOTAL INTEREST = 0.02665 x 100 = 2.67% (rounded)

SITUATION 7 – CONTINUED

"Yeah, I sort of remember now. To get the percentage something is of something else you divide the something by the something else and multiply by 100. It's sort of the reverse of calculating the something when you know the percentage and the something else. Seems like sort of the reverse of the **RATIO** term you used before."

"Well, Nicole, that's a mouthful and earful and sort of vague. But I do see you do kind of know it. To be specific, what are the something and something else?"

"Let me think. The something is the **TOTAL INTEREST**. The something else is the **LOAN AMOUNT**."

"Now you've got it. Notice the **PERCENT TOTAL INTEREST** is significantly less than the stated **ANNUAL RATE OF INTEREST** of 5.00%. That's due to the **OUTSTANDING BALANCE** declining each month. Similar to credit cards, the lesson here is to pay off your entire **AMOUNT DUE** each month and on time. Now I want to discuss what happens if you do not do that. That's an even more important lesson."

"I bet it is."

---

*Exercise 6: Repeat the first three months of SITUATION 7 for an **ANNUAL RATE OF INTEREST** of 10.00%*

*Your **partial** result should be: At the end of Month 2, **MONTHLY INTEREST** = $7.62, **OUTSTANDING BALANCE** = $830.00.*

"Our Bradley paid all of the scheduled **MONTHLY PAYMENT** and **MONTHLY INTEREST** amounts on time. Because of that the **OUTSTANDING BALANCE** and **MONTHLY INTEREST** amounts due declined each month. The loan was paid off on time in one year. But what would happen if he skips paying all the scheduled **MONTHLY PAYMENT** and **MONTHLY INTEREST** amounts?"

"Well his **OUTSTANDING BALANCE** would just get bigger and bigger each month. And the debt would not get paid."

"That's right, Nicole. And it's hard to imagine a lender letting Bradley get off "Scot-free". Typically, a **MONTHLY PENALTY** would be incurred when any **MONTHLY PAYMENTS** are skipped.

"For Bradley, let's say the **MONTHLY PENALTY** is a small percentage of the accumulated **OVERDUE MONTHLY PAYMENTS**. I'll call that the **MONTHLY PENALTY RATE** The skipped **MONTHY INTEREST** is of minor consequence to it so won't be included in calculating the **MONTHLY PENALTY**.

"Since nothing is being paid each month, there is no reduction in the **OUTSTANDING BALANCE**. But at the end of each month, the **MONTHLY INTEREST** and **MONTHLY PENALTY** amounts are added to the **PREVIOUS OUTSTANDING BALANCE**."

"Whoa, Dad! I'm starting to lose you."

"Righto! I was just about to show it in math equation form. Let's look at that now for a typical **MONTHLY STATEMENT**.

REDUCED BALANCE = OUTSTANDING BALANCE – PAYMENT RECEIVED

RATIO1 = MONTHLY INTEREST RATE/100

MONTHLY INTEREST = RATIO x REDUCED BALANCE

RATIO2 = MONTHLY PENALTY RATE/100

MONTHLY PENALTY = RATIO2 x OVERDUE MONTHLY PAYMENTS

NEW OUTSTANDING BALANCE = REDUCED BALANCE + MONTHLY INTEREST + MONTHLY PENALTY

AMOUNT DUE = SCHEDULED MONTHLY PAYMENT + MONTHLY INTEREST + MONTHLY PENALTY

"Does that make sense now, Sweetie?"

"It sort of helps me out. I see it's like before except now the **MONTHLY PENALTY** has been added to the **NEW OUTSTANDING BALANCE** and the **AMOUNT DUE**. But I'm not seeing the details. Like since Bradley does not make payments, why is there a subtraction of the **PAYMENT RECEIVED** from the **OUTSTANDING BALANCE**?"

"I added that because before we had Bradley making payments. Now I made it general in form. When he skips payments, the **PAYMENT RECEIVED** will be $0.00."

"I got it."

"Do you understand **RATIO1** and **RATIO2**?"

"I guess **RATIO1** is like the **RATIO** used before, so **RATIO2** is similar? Each changes its corresponding rate in percent to a decimal. They could be different values so we need the "1" and "2"?"

"There you go again smarty pants, not really guessing?"

"I guess you're right again. Oops, I mean your sort of right about that. My brain told me so."

"OK, now for that let me numerically illustrate the repayment flow for our Bradley's situation."

SITUATION 7A

"Bradley skips the **MONTHLY PAYMENT** and the **MONTHLY INTEREST** at the end of each month. Assume a **MONTHLY PENALTY RATE** of 2.00% of the cumulative overdue **MONTHLY PAYMENTS** is applied. Let's look at the first **MONTHLY STATEMENT**."

MONTHLY STATEMENT 1

OUTSTANDING BALANCE = LOAN AMOUNT = $1000.00

REDUCED BALANCE = OUTSTANDING BALANCE – PAYMENT RECEIVED

= $1000.00 - $0.00 = $1000.00

MONTHLY INTEREST = 0.417% of $1000.00 = 0.00417 x $1000.00 = $4.17

NEW OUTSTANDING BALANCE = REDUCED BALANCE + MONTHLY INTEREST + MONTHLY PENALTY

= $1000.00 + $4.17 + $0.00 = $1004.17

SCHEDULED MONTHLY PAYMENT = $85.00

The AMOUNT DUE = $85.00 + $4.17 = $89.17 and is not paid.

SITUATION 7A – CONTINUED

"If you examine it, Nicole, you will see **MONTHLY STATEMENT 1** is the same results as before. Why is that?"

"I don't know, Dad?"

"Like before the **OUTSTANDING BALANCE** is the **LOAN AMOUNT**. And as I said before, the **PAYMENT RECEIVED** is $0.00. That's because no payment activity occurs until the second month. Until then the lender does not know Bradley will not make any payment. Also, there also is no **MONTHLY PENALTY** yet, which makes that amount $0.00. So the results turn out the same as before. And the **NEW OUTSTANDING BALANCE** carries over to the next month as its **PREVIOUS OUTSTANDING BALANCE**.

"In **MONTHLY STATEMENT 2**, things change. In math equation form three things are different. And they apply to all subsequent months."

**REDUCED BALANCE = PREVIOUS OUTSTANDING BALANCE
– PAYMENT RECEIVED**

**NEW OUTSTANDING BALANCE = REDUCED BALANCE
+ MONTHLY INTEREST
+ MONTHLY PENALTY**

**AMOUNT DUE = PREVIOUS AMOUNT DUE + SCHEDULED MONTHLY PAYMENT
+ MONTHLY INTEREST + MONTHLY PENALTY**

SITUATION 7A – CONTINUED

"I think those differences are straightforward, right?"

"They seem so to me, Dad."

"Ok, let's look at the calculations for Month 2."

MONTHLY STATEMENT 2

PREVIOUS OUTSTANDING BALANCE = $1004.17

REDUCED BALANCE = PREVIOUS OUTSTANDING BALANCE – PAYMENT RECEIVED

= $1004.17 - $0.00 = $1004.17

MONTHLY INTEREST = 0.00417 x $1004.17 = $4.19

OVERDUE MONTHLY PAYMENTS = $85.00

MONTHLY PENALTY = 2.00% of $85.00 = 0.02 x $85.00 = $1.70

NEW OUTSTANDING BALANCE = REDUCED BALANCE + MONTHLY INTEREST + MONTHLY PENALTY

= $1004.17 + $4.19 + $1.70 = $1010.06

SCHEDULED MONTHLY PAYMENT = $85.00

AMOUNT DUE = $89.17 + $85.00 + $4.19 + $1.70 = $180.06 and is not paid.

SITUATION 7A – CONTINUED

"Check point again! Do you follow these calculations, Peanut?"

"Mostly, I do. But why is the **PAYMENT RECEIVED** amount $0.00 again?"

"In Month 1 it was because no payment was due yet. Here it's because Bradley skipped the **SCHEDULED MONTHLY PAYMENT**. That's also why the **OVERDUE MONTHLY PAYMENTS** amount is $85.00."

"I see. I sort of thought about the reason for the $85.00 but was going to ask to be sure. Thank you. I do understand that the **MONTHLY PENALTY** amount is 2.00% of that."

"What about the **NEW OUTSTANDING BALANCE** and the **AMOUNT DUE**?"

"Yes, I see how the amounts from Month 1were increased by the additional **MONTHLY INTEREST** and the **MONTHLY PENALTY** also came into play. The additional overdue **SCHEDULED MONTHLY PAYMENT** was also added to the **AMOUNT DUE**."

"That's perfect. Let's look at one more month."

MONTHLY STATEMENT 3

PREVIOUS OUTSTANDING BALANCE = \$1010.06

**REDUCED BALANCE = PREVIOUS OUTSTANDING BALANCE
– PAYMENT RECEIVED**

= \$1010.06 - \$0.00 = \$1017.67

MONTHLY INTEREST = 0.00417 x \$1010.06 = \$4.21

OVERDUE MONTHLY PAYMENTS = \$85.00 + \$85.00 = \$170.00

MONTHLY PENALTY = 2.00% of \$170.00 = 0.02 x \$170.00 = \$3.40

**NEW OUTSTANDING BALANCE = REDUCED BALANCE + MONTHLY INTEREST
+ MONTHLY PENALTY**

= \$1010.06 + \$4.21 + \$3.40 = \$1017.67

SCHEDULED MONTHLY PAYMENT = \$85.00

AMOUNT DUE = \$180.06 + \$85.00 + \$4.21 + \$3.40 = \$272.67 and is not paid.

SITUATION 7A – CONTINUED

"What's different here, Nicole, if anything?"

"Basically, I see that the **OVERDUE MONTHLY PAYMENTS** increased again by the amount of the second skipped payment. So the **MONTHLY PENALTY** also increased. Otherwise it's the same routine."

"Exactly.

"Let's give you some more voluntary homework. Here's a summary for rest of the months. Maybe you can try to confirm them, at least some of them."

The ensuing trail of MONTHLY INTEREST, OVERDUE MONTHLY PAYMENTS, MONTHLY PENALTY and NEW OUTSTANDING BALANCE is:

Month 4: \$4.24, \$255.00, \$5.10, \$1027.01; *Month 5: \$4.28, \$340.00, \$6.80, \$1038.09;* **Month 6:\$4.33, \$425.00, \$8.50, \$1050.92;** *Month 7: \$4.38, \$510.00, \$10.20, \$1065.50;* **Month 8: \$4.44, \$595.00, \$11.90, \$1081.64;** *Month 9: \$4.51, \$680.00, \$13.60, \$1095.95*; **Month 10: \$4.59, \$765.00, \$15.30, \$1119.84:** *Month 11: \$4.67, \$850.00, \$17.00, \$1141.5;* **and Month 12: \$4.76, \$935.00, \$18.70, \$1164.97.**

SITUATION 7A – CONTINUED

"It's bleary eyed again, but if you do the **MONTHLY STATEMENT** calculations, these are the primary answers."

"Once I get time for the previous homework, I'll think about that additional voluntary homework."

"It really is all voluntary. Doing it will reinforce everything. If you do try it, I'm around if you find you need my help"

"Let's look at the final outcome a bit more."

At the end of Month 12

TOTAL DEBT = NEW OUTSTANDING BALANCE = $1164.97

TOTAL INTEREST = $4.17 +$4.19 + $4.23 + … $4.76 = $52.77

TOTAL PENALTY = sum of the MONTHLY PENALTY amounts

= $1.70 + $3.40 + $5.10 + … + $18.70 = $112.20.

NOTE: As confirmation,

TOTAL DEBT – TOTAL INTEREST – TOTAL PENALTY = $1164.97 - $52.77 - $112.20

= $1000.00

= LOAN AMOUNT

For TOTAL INTEREST as a percentage of the LOAN AMOUNT:

FRACTION = $52.77/$1000.00 = 0.05277.

PERCENT TOTAL INTEREST = 0.05277 x 100 = 5.27% (rounded)

SITUATION 7A – CONTINUED

"The **PERCENT TOTAL INTEREST** slightly exceeds the stated **ANNUAL RATE OF INTEREST** of 5.00%.

"Since Bradley pays off the **TOTAL DEBT**, the **MONTHLY PENALTY** for Month 12 would not come into play. He has to pay only $1164.97 - $18.70 = $1148.27. The **TOTAL PENALTY** actually paid = $93.50. It is almost double the **TOTAL INTEREST**."

"Yeah, that's right Dad."

"Now let's consider the **TOTAL PENALTY** as a sort of additional interest."

EQUIVALENT INTEREST = \$52.27 + \$93.50 = \$145.77

FRACTION = \$145.77/\$1000.00 = 0.14578

PERCENT EQUIVALENT INTEREST = 0.14578 x 100 = 14.58%

SITUATION 7A – CONTINUED

"The **PERCENT EQUIVALENT INTEREST** is about triple the stated **ANNUAL RATE OF INTEREST** of 5.00%! So the **TOTAL PENALTY** of \$93.50 is the significant aspect."

"Wow! That's eye popping, Dad."

"Yes it is. Skipping scheduled **MONTHLY PAYMENTS** when a **MONTHLY PENALTY** is applied is very costly! Imagine if the **MONTHLY RATE OF INTEREST** and **MONTHLY PENALTY RATE** were even higher."

"I don't even want to think about it."

---

*Exercise 7: Repeat the first two months of SITUATION 7A for an **ANNUAL RATE OF INTEREST** of 10.00% and **MONTHLY PENALTY** of 3.00%.*

Your partial results should be: *At the end of Month 1, **AMOUNT DUE** = \$93.33, **OUTSTANDING BALANCE** = \$1010.88. At the end of Month 3, **MONTHLY INTEREST** = \$8.42, **MONTHLY PENALTY** = \$5.10 and **OUTSTANDING BALANCE** = \$1024.40.*

"You wanted to learn about loans in general loans. Hopefully all this helps you accomplish that."

"It sure does, Dad. Thank you so much."

"You're very welcome, Peanut! Is there anything else on your mind?"

"I haven't forgotten about that process you called "ammutization" or however you say it. You were going to explain that to me and how the darn word is spelled."

"It's actually **amortization** and it's spelled **a-m-o-r-t-i-z-a-t-i-o-n**. I haven't forgotten about that either. With our relatives coming here for Thanksgiving Day, it's going to be hectic. And you have that voluntary homework in sight. Maybe after your school term ends we can cover that process?"

"Ok let's do that. And I didn't promise to do that voluntary homework, but if I can fit it in I will at least try some of it."

"I'll be waiting to meet, but won't hold my breath on waiting for that voluntary homework."

LESSON 6 Amortized Loans = Getting Out of Debt Faster and Faster!

It's a blizzard-like December day and school is out. Snow is piled high so there's nowhere to go. Nicole asks her Dad, "Maybe this is a good time to talk about that amortization loan process? I don't know where the word comes from but at least I know how to say it now."

"That's a great idea. I've already been preparing to do that since we last talked. Let's go to my office.

"When we met before Thanksgiving I described two hypothetical loan situations. **MONTHLY PAYMENT** amounts of $85.00 and $65.00 were used. In the first situation all the **MONTHLY PAYMENTS** were paid on time. And the entire amount of each payment was applied to reduce **OUTSTANDING BALANCE** each month. In the second situation all the **MONTHLY PAYMENTS** were skipped and the loan was repaid after the 1-year **TERM** ended. The different outcomes illustrated the big benefit making all the payments on time."

"Dad, I recall that vividly. It was so eye opening."

"I used those situations as a simplification. That was because the amortization process has a bit of scary math involved in calculating the **MONTHLY PAYMENT** amount used in it.

"For a loan payment sequence developed by **amortization** the **MONTHLY PAYMENT** amount is the same each month. However, the portion of the payment that is used to reduce the debt <u>increases</u> each month and the portion that is used to pay interest <u>decreases</u> each month. Consequently, the borrower is getting out of debt faster and faster!

"You wondered about the source of the word itself. It actually comes from the Latin words for "to" and "death', which are "ad" and "mortem". In common terminology when the amortization process is to be used, one says they are going "to amortize" the loan. Albeit a morbid translation the phrase "to amortize" means "to die". I suppose the terminology came about because the amount of interest being paid each month from the fixed amortized **MONTHLY PAYMENT** amount gets less and less. And when the loan ends, it goes away."

"That's interesting. It makes sense."

"In practice, the **amortized MONTHLY PAYMENT** amount is determined by the lender using a specific mathematical equation. The lender only gives the borrower the resulting amount. But it is very useful and important for the borrower to be able to use that equation too. Let's call the amortized **MONTHLY PAYMENT** amount **MPAYMENT**. Here's the mathematical equation for it."

$$\textbf{MPAYMENT} = \textbf{PRINCIPAL} \times \textbf{MRATIO} \times (\textbf{MRATIO} + 1)^{\textbf{TERM}}/((\textbf{MRATIO} + 1)^{\textbf{TERM}} - 1)$$

"Holy cow! I can see why a lender does not show it to anyone and only gives the result."

"It does look a bit intimidating. Nonetheless I'll show you how to use it. I'll make it more palatable by applying it step-by-step."

"Hopefully you can use baby steps."

"That's my intention Peanut.

"Let's refer to the equation as the **AMORTIZATION EQUATION**. Looking at the right side of the equal sign, you see three words: **PRINCIPAL, MRATIO** and **TERM.** They are called the "variables" in the equation. To use the **AMORTIZATION EQUATION** one needs to specify their numerical values.

"Dad, I'm familiar with what is meant by the variables in the equation. I just had that in my math class."

"Ok, I figured you probably did.

"In this case, **PRINCIPAL** is the financial terminology for the amount of money to be borrowed. It's what I called **LOAN AMOUNT** before. **MRATIO** is the **MONTHLY RATE OF INTEREST** in ratio form. **TERM** is the desired number of months to pay off the loan. In other words, the variables are the numerical terms of the loan."

"Ok, I understand that part."

"The equation for **MPAYMENT** is more readily used if written in another way."

$$\textbf{MPAYMENT = NUMERATOR/DENOMINATOR}$$

where

$$\textbf{NUMERATOR = PRINCIPAL x MRATIO x (MRATIO + 1)}^{\textbf{TERM}}$$

and

$$\textbf{DENOMINATOR = (MRATIO + 1)}^{\textbf{TERM}} \textbf{– 1}$$

"Dad, it does look a little less intimidating, but not by much."

"That's true. This only breaks it into two main calculations. The actual sequence of calculations is best illustrated by numerical examples. Let me do that using imaginary actors to keep it interesting. To start we'll make the loan terms the same as for our prior Bradley."

SITUATION 8

"Consider a young woman named Vanessa. She needs to take out a loan from a bank for $1000.00 and wants to repay it over a period of one year.

"Based on her very good credit rating and current loan rates, her bank agrees to amortize the loan and offers her the loan at an **ANNUAL RATE OF INTEREST** of 5.00%. The loan officer indicates that the

---

amortized **MONTHLY PAYMENT** amount will be $85.61. That amount was obtained by the loan officer using computer software. Let's confirm that ourselves by using a calculator.

"Since a calculator is to be used, a decision about precision must be made. Let's assume the precision to be used is to round off all calculated values to "three significant figures". Do you know what that means?"

"When I first learned to use a calculator that topic was covered by my teacher. I think it means to round off numbers to three digits including decimal places."

"You're right. I've already done the actual calculations and have the step by step results. In my example, you will see that 0.416667 becomes 0.417 and 4.3785 becomes 4.38."

"Let's look at my calculations step by step."

$$\text{MONTHLY RATE OF INTEREST} = 5.00\%/12 \text{ months}$$
$$= 0.416667\%/\text{month}$$
$$= 0.417\%/\text{month (rounded)}$$

$$\text{MRATIO} = 0.417/100 = 0.00417 \text{ (rounded)}$$

$$\text{TERM} = 1 \text{ year} \times 12 \text{ months/year} = 12 \text{ months (therefore the exponent} = 12)$$

$$(\text{MRATIO} + 1)^{\text{TERM}} = (1 + 0.00417)^{12} = (1.00417)^{12}$$
$$= (1.00417)(1.00417)(1.00417)\dots \text{ twelve times!}$$
$$= 1.05120 = 1.05 \text{ (rounded)}$$

$$\text{NUMERATOR} = \text{PRINCIPAL} \times \text{MRATIO} \times (\text{MRATIO} + 1)^{\text{TERM}}$$
$$= 1000.00 \times .00417 \times 1.05 = 4.17 \times 1.05$$
$$= 4.37850 = 4.38 \text{ (rounded)}$$

$$\text{DENOMINATOR} = (\text{MRATIO}+1)^{\text{TERM}} - 1 = 1.05 - 1 = 0.05$$

$$\text{MPAYMENT} = \text{NUMERATOR/DENOMINATOR} = 4.38/0.05 = \$87.60$$

SITUATION 8 - CONTINUED

"Do you follow my calculations?"

"Everything except the calculation using the **TERM** is easy. I know from my school math that the number 12 is an exponent. And that 1.00417 is being raised to a power of 12. And that means multiplying 1.00417 times itself twelve times. At least those are the type of words my teacher used. We often used our calculator to raise a number to a power of 2 or to a power of 3. We just multiplied the number two or three times but never twelve times. That's takes a while and I probably would make mistakes."

"Calculations involving exponents require the use of a scientific calculator of the type used by high school students or via smart phones with such a calculator capability. You probably were taught to use functions on a calculator. Maybe you just don't do it often or forgot?"

"Yeah, you're right Dad. I have my smart phone. Can you remind me how to do it?"

"Can you find the function y^x?"

"I have it"

"Ok on your keypad, enter1.00417, then select y^x, then enter 12 to get 1.05120."

"Got it!"

"Ok, now what about the final result of $87.60? It's not the $85.61 that the bank officer stated to Vanessa is it?"

"I noticed that. What's wrong?"

"Actually, nothing's wrong. I rounded off all numbers to three significant figures. A bank officer's software would not round off numbers so roughly. I recalculated the results using nine significant figures."

$$(MRATIO + 1)^{TERM} = (1+.00416667)^{12}$$
$$= (1.00416667)(1.0041667)(1.0041667)...\text{twelve times!}$$
$$= 1.05116190$$

$$NUMERATOR = 1000.00 \times .00416667 \times 1.05116190 = 4.37984124$$

$$DENOMINATOR = (MRATIO+1)^{TERM} - 1 = 1.0511619 - 1 = 0.05116190$$

$$MPAYMENT = NUMERATOR/DENOMINATOR = 4.37984124/0.0511619$$
$$= \$85.607482 = \$85.61$$

SITUATION 8 - CONTINUED

"Bingo! Now we have the loan officer's result exactly.

"The approximate value based on rounded numbers is $1.99 higher than the precise value."

"But Dad, it's sort of tedious and anal to use nine significant figures. Isn't it?"

"Sure is! Nobody would keypunch numbers to that many places. It would drive them bananas. I used my computer and got them.

"Let's see what we get if all calculated values to are rounded to <u>four</u> significant figures. That might be palatable for some people."

MONTHLY RATE OF INTEREST = 5.00%/12 months
$$= 0.416667\%/\text{month} = 0.4167\%/\text{month (rounded)}$$

MRATIO = 0.4167/100 = 0.004167 (rounded)

TERM = 1 year x 12 months/year = 12 months

$(\text{MRATIO} + 1)^{\text{TERM}} = (1+.004167)^{12} = (1.004167)^{12}$
$$= (1.004167)(1.004167)(1.004167)..... \text{ twelve times!}$$
$$= 1.05120 = 1.051 \text{ (rounded)}$$

NUMERATOR = PRINCIPAL x MRATIO x $(\text{MRATIO} + 1)^{\text{TERM}}$
$$= 1000.00 \text{ x } .004167 \text{ x } 1.051 = 4.167 \text{ x} 1.051$$
$$= 4.383$$

DENOMINATOR = $(\text{MRATIO} + 1)^{\text{TERM}} - 1 = 1.051 - 1 = 0.051$

MPAYMENT = NUMERATOR/DENOMINATOR = 4.383/0.051
$$= \$85.941176$$
$$= \$85.94 \text{ (rounded)}$$

SITUATION 8 - CONTINUED

"The improved approximate value is $85.94. That's only $0.33 per month higher than the precise value of $85.61."

"I see that. But I cannot see myself keypunching even four decimal places."

"That's not my intent. The main reason to calculate it yourself is to roughly know the **MONTHLY PAYMENT** before you go to the lender. That way you know if you can afford it or not. In this case the $87.60 is close enough to know that. If you grin and bear it through four significant figures you get closer but it's a waste of time. And you can always use a computer to do it.

"These days you can even find an **app** to get the precise result. But without my lesson you would be getting it blindly. I want you to know how it actually is calculated and get into the habit of always wanting to know how money related calculations are actually done.

"And can you trust the result of an **app**? Chances are you confirm it too, at least the first few times."

"Dad, I didn't think you even knew about **apps**?"

"Surprise, Surprise! I do but having a whole bunch of those to access just drives me bananas. So I leave those to you young people. As time goes on you can teach dear old Dad more about them."

"When we talked about general loans a **LOAN AMOUNT** or **PRINCIPAL** of $1000.00 and an **ANNUAL RATE OF INTEREST** of 5.00% were also used. The **SCHEDULED MONTHLY PAYMENTS** used were $85.00 for eleven months and $65.00 for the twelfth month.

"For our Vanessa's amortized loan the **MONTHLY PAYMENT** value is $85.61 which is similar to the $85.00. But how it is applied differs. A portion of it is applied to pay the interest owed. The rest of it is applied to reduce the amount of money owed. Let me illustrate the contrasting computations of the sequence of payments involved in the amortization process."

SITUATION 8 - CONTINUED

"Let's say that the entire funds for Vanessa's loan are disbursed on the first day of a month. The first **MONTHLY PAYMENT** is due on the first day of the next month and subsequent payments are due on the first day of each month thereafter. If any scheduled **MONTHLY PAYMENT** is late by more than five days, a **PENALTY FEE** of $17.00 (about 20.00% of the **MONTHLY PAYMENT** amount) will be charged. If the **MONTHLY PAYMENT** is received before then, it is credited to the previous month.

"The loan papers are signed. The money is disbursed and the payments ensue. To avoid the penalty, Vanessa makes every payment on time. Let's trace the first two monthly outcomes."

MONTHLY RATE OF INTEREST is 5.00%/12 months = 0.417% per month

For Month 1:

PRINCIPAL = $1000.00.

MONTHLY INTEREST owed = 0.417% of $1000 = 0.00417 x $1000.00 = $4.17

SCHEDULED MONTHLY PAYMENT = $85.61 is paid on time.

Portion APPLIED TO INTEREST = $4.17

Portion APPLIED TO PRINCIPAL = $85.61-$4.17 = $81.44

OUTSTANDING PRINCIPAL = $1000.00 - $81.44 = $918.56

For Month 2:

MONTHLY INTEREST owed = 0.417% of $918.56 = 0.00417 x $918.56 = $3.83

SCHEDULED MONTHLY PAYMENT = $85.61 is paid on time.

Portion APPLIED TO INTEREST = $3.83

Portion APPLIED TO PRINCIPAL = $85.61- $3.83 = $81.78

OUTSTANDING PRINCIPAL = $918.56 - $81.78 = $836.78

SITUATION 8 - CONTINUED

"Peanut, do you follow this sequence of calculations?"

"The terminology is different, but I see what's happening. The **OUTSTANDING PRINCIPAL** is like what you called the **OUTSTANDING BALANCE** before. Like it, the **OUTSTANDING PRINCIPAL** got lower each month. But why is there a different terminology used?"

"That's because in amortized loans from a lender like a bank, they call the **LOAN AMOUNT** the **PRINCIPAL** and then say the amount of **PRINCIPAL** owed is declining. The amount currently owed is the **OUTSTANDING PRINCIPAL**. It's sort of standard wording.

"Did you notice the amount of interest was lower in Month 2 compared to Month 1? Why is that?"

"I did notice that, Dad. It's because the money owed in Month 2 is less than the amount owed in Month 1."

"Yes, that's correct. What happened to the portions of the **SCHEDULED MONTHLY PAYMENT**?"

"I see the portion **APPLIED TO INTEREST** got lower and the portion **APPLIED TO PRINCIPAL** got higher."

"Exactly, that's the key feature of the amortization process. It happens each month. Let's look at next month."

For Month 3:

MONTHLY INTEREST owed = 0.417% of $836.78 = 0.00417 x $836.78 = $3.49

SCHEDULED MONTHLY PAYMENT = $85.61 is paid on time.

Portion APPLIED TO INTEREST = $3.49

Portion APPLIED TO PRINCIPAL = $85.61-$3.49 = $82.12

OUTSTANDING PRINCIPAL = $836.78 - $82.12 = $754.66

SITUATION 8 - CONTINUED

"I see the trend now Dad."

"That's good. This continues for nine more months. Here are the rest of the results."

The scheduled MONTHLY PAYMENT remains $85.61."

The sequence of portion APPLIED TO INTEREST, portion APPLIED TO PRINCIPAL, and OUTSTANDING PRINCIPAL amounts will be:

Month 4: $3.15, 82.46 and $672.20; *Month 5: $2.80, $82.81 and $589.39;* **Month 6: $2.46, $83.15, and $506.24;** *Month 7: $2.11, $83.50 and $422.74;* **Month 8: $1.76, $83.85 and $338.89;** *Month 9: $1.41, $84.20 and $254.69;* **Month 10: $1.06, $84.55 and 170.15;***Month 11: $0.71, $84.90 and $85.25;* **and Month 12: $0.36, $85.25 and $0.00.**

SITUATION 8 - CONTINUED

"For homework, you can confirm these results. But I'm sure you would do it correctly. It's voluntary, too."

"I'm pretty sure I would, Dad. But if I find the time I might do it anyway."

"At the end of Month 12 the loan has been "paid off". The **CUMULATIVE INTEREST** paid = $4.17 + $3.83 + $3.49 … + $0.36 = $27.31. The original signed loan agreement would be returned to Vanessa by the bank and she could "tear it up". She is excited to be done with her payments, almost jumping with joy. It is best that Vanessa not "tear it up" until the document is no longer needed for either legal reasons or possible tax considerations."

"I'm sure I would enjoy "tearing it up", too, Dad."

"These results confirm my earlier general statement about an amortized loan payment process getting you out of debt faster and faster! As you observed the portion of the fixed **MONTHLY PAYMENT** that was **APPLIED TO PRINCIPAL** got larger and larger each month; starting at $81.44 in month 1 and gradually increasing each month to being $85.25 at the end of month 12.

"To reiterate, for Bradley's loan the **SCHEDULED MONTHLY PAYMENT** was $85.00 for each of the first eleven months and the portion applied to reduce the **OUTSTANDING BALANCE** was the <u>entire</u> amount! Each of those eleven payments was actually greater than each of the first eleven portions of the $85.61 payments involved in the amortization process. For example, for month 1 $85.00 is greater than $81.44. However, the **MONTHLY INTEREST** charged on the **OUTSTANDING BALANCE** was <u>additional</u> to those $85.00 payments. Of course, in the last month the $65.00 **SCHEDULED MONTHLY PAYMENT** was entirely different than the $85.61 in the amortized loan."

"Well, Nicole, I hope I eased you through the edgy math gently. Once the amortized **MONTHLY PAYMENT** amount, **MPAYMENT**, is known, the computations of monthly changes to **PRINCIPAL** are repetitious and comprised of ordinary multiplication and subtraction operations."

"Actually it was painless, unless I decide to try that voluntary homework."

"Again, it is not necessary for the borrower to do that math as the <u>lender</u> does it all. The detailed results are provided in the loan documents to be signed the bank. They are organized into what is called the **AMORTIZATION SCHEDULE** for the loan. But an ability to do that math is vital to being knowledgeable enough to confirm or to check the entries in the **AMORTIZATION SCHEDULE** . It also allows you to independently calculate different loan option scenarios before actually beginning to seek a loan. Then you can compare options, assess affordability and choose the best option."

"Ok, Dad. Now you've got me curious about what an **AMORTIZATION SCHEDULE** looks like."

"I'm glad your curiosity is peaked once again. My next part was to do exactly that. With those merits in mind, let's look at the process again but as it would be provided by a lender in the **AMORTIZATION SCHEDULE** format.

Loan Terms: PRINCIPAL: $1000.00, 5.00% ANNUAL RATE OF INTEREST (0.417% monthly), TERM: 12 months.

AMORTIZATION SCHEDULE :

Term in Years	Annual Rate of Interest	Month	Monthly Payment	Applied to Interest	Applied to Principal		Principal = $1000.00	
							Outstanding Principal	Cumulative Interest
1	5.00	1	85.61	4.17	81.44		918.56	4.17
		2	85.61	3.83	81.78		836.78	8.00
		3	85.61	3.49	82.12		754.66	11.49
		4	85.61	3.15	82.46		672.20	14.64
		5	85.61	2.80	82.81		589.39	17.44
		6	85.61	2.46	83.15		506.24	19.90
		7	85.61	2.11	83.50		422.74	22.01
		8	85.61	1.76	83.85		338.89	23.77
		9	85.61	1.41	84.20		254.69	25.18
		10	85.61	1.06	84.55		170.14	26.24
		11	85.61	0.71	84.90		85.24	26.95
		12	85.61	0.30	85.24		0.00	27.31

SITUATION 8 - CONTINUED

"For each month the **MONTHLY PAYMENT** is $85.61. It's called that because it is assumed the full scheduled payment will be made. For Month 1, the listed portion **APPLIED TO INTEREST** is $4.17 and the remaining $81.44 is the listed portion **APPLIED TO PRINCIPAL** by the bank to reduce the **OUTSTANDING PRINCIPAL** to $918.56. These are the values I showed before. The narrow seventh column will be needed later, but for now it is void.

"For Month 2 the listed **OUTSTANDING PRINCIPAL** of $918.56 for Month 1 is used to compute the $3.83 listed as the portion **APPLIED TO INTEREST**. The remaining $81.78 is the listed portion **APPLIED TO PRINCIPAL**. It reduces the **OUTSTANDING PRINCIPAL** to $836.78. The **CUMULATIVE INTEREST** listed in the rightmost column is a running total of the interest paid as it accumulates each month. After twelve months it is the $27.31. Those are the values I calculated before.

"The next ten lines of the **AMORTIZATION SCHEDULE** follow by repetition. Do you follow them?"

"I sure do Dad. But if I had not talked with you and got this table I would have been scratching my head."

"Let's look at the results if the improved approximate amortized **MONTHLY PAYMENT** value of $85.94 is used.

AMORTIZATION SCHEDULE :

Term in Years	Annual Rate of Interest	Month	Monthly Payment	Applied to Interest	Applied to Principal		Principal = $1000.00 Outstanding Principal	Cumulative Interest
1	5.00	1	85.94	4.17	81.77		918.23	4.17
		2	85.94	3.83	82.11		836.12	8.00
		3	85.94	3.49	82.45		753.67	11.49
		4	85.94	3.14	82.80		670.87	14.63
		5	85.94	2.80	83.14		587.73	17.43
		6	85.94	2.45	83.49		504.24	19.88
		7	85.94	2.10	83.84		420.40	21.98
		8	85.94	1.75	84.19		336.21	23.73
		9	85.94	1.40	84.54		251.67	25.13
		10	85.94	1.05	84.89		166.78	26.18
		11	85.94	0.70	85.24		81.54	26.88
		12	85.94	0.34	85.60		-4.06	27.22
		12	*81.88*	*0.34*	*81.54*		*0.00*	*27.22*

SITUATION 8 - CONTINUED

"As the payment is $0.33 per month higher than the precise bank value two things occurred.

"First, the last month results in a $4.06 overpayment. This is because $0.33 per month more was being than required; i.e. $0.33/month x 12 months = $4.00 in total. The $4.06 results because the all monthly values in the table were rounded to two decimal places. The bank would adjust the last amortized **MONTHLY PAYMENT** to equal the preceding **OUTSTANDING PRINCIPAL** plus the **MONTHLY INTEREST** on that amount, that is to $81.54 + 0.00417($81.54) =$81.54 + $0.34 = $81.88. I added the adjusted line to the **AMORTIZATION SCHEDULE** in italics.

"Second, the **CUMULATIVE INTEREST** paid is $26.88 +$0.34 = $27.22 which is $0.09 less than the precise result.

"Is this all clear, the flow of the numbers and the adjustment for Month 12?"

"Yes, it's just different numbers. And the adjustment makes sense to me."

Exercise 8: *Produce the* **AMORTIZATION SCHEDULE** *for SITUATION 8 using the approximate* **MONTHLY PAYMENT** *amount of $87.60.*

*Your **partial** results should be:*

AMORTIZATION SCHEDULE :

Term in Years	Annual Rate of Interest	Month	Monthly Payment	Applied to Interest	Principal		Principal = $1000.00	
							Outstanding Principal	Cumulative Interest
1	5.00	1	87.60	4.17	83.43		916.57	4.17
		2	87.60	3.82	83.78		832.79	7.99
		3						11.46
		4						14.58
		5						17.34
		6	85.61	2.46	83.15		506.24	19.76
		7	85.61	2.11	83.50		422.74	21.82
		8	85.61	1.76	83.85		338.89	23.52
		9						24.86
		10						25.85
		11	87.60	0.62	86.98		62.89	26.47
		12	87.60	0.26	87.34		-24.45	26.73
		12	63.13	0.26	62.87		0.00	26.73

"Ok, Nicole. Let's do one more step. Then I think we're done."

SITUATION 8A

"Assume Vanessa's **ANNUAL RATE OF INTEREST** is changed to 10.00%. The amortized **SCHEDULED MONTHLY PAYMENT** will change."

MONTHLY RATE OF INTEREST = 10.00%/12 months
$$= 0.833\%/\text{month (rounded)}$$
MRATIO = 0.833/100 = 0.00833 (rounded)
TERM = 1 year x 12 months/year = 12 months
$$(\text{MRATIO} + 1)^{\text{TERM}} = (1+.00833)^{12} = (1.00833)^{12}$$
$$= (1.00833)(1.00833)(1.00833)..... \text{ twelve times!}$$
$$= 1.105 \text{ (rounded)}$$
NUMERATOR = PRINCIPAL x MRATIO x (MRATIO + 1)^{TERM}
$$= 1000 \times .00833 \times 1.105$$
$$= 8.33 \times 1.105$$
$$= 9.205 \text{ (rounded)}$$

DENOMINATOR = $(MRATIO+1)^{TERM} - 1 = 1.105 - 1 = 0.105$ (rounded)

MPAYMENT = NUMERATOR/DENOMINATOR = 9.205/0.105 = $87.66

Using the more precise numbers:

$(MRATIO + 1)^{TERM} = (1+.00833333)^{12} = (1.00833333)^{12}$

$= (1.00833333)(1.00833333)(1.00833333)\ldots$twelve times!
$= 1.10471307$

NUMERATOR = 1000.00 x 0.00833333 x 1.10471307 = 9.20594223
DENOMINATOR = $(MRATIO + 1)^{TERM} - 1 = 1.10471307 - 1 = 0.10471307$
MPAYMENT = NUMERATOR/DENOMINATOR = 9.20594223/0.10471307
$= \$87.92$/month

SITUATION 8A – CONTINUED

"The new value of **MPAYMENT** is $87.92. What was it for the **ANNUAL RATE** OF **INTEREST** of 5%?"

"It was $85.61, Dad."

"That's not a huge difference. But let's look at the **AMORTIZATION SCHEDULE** .

AMORTIZATION SCHEDULE :

Term in Years	Annual Rate of Interest	Month	Monthly Payment	Applied to Interest	Applied to Principal		Outstanding Principal	Cumulative Interest
							Principal = $1000.00	
1	10.00	1	87.92	8.33	79.59		920.41	8.33
		2	87.92	7.67	80.25		840.16	16.00
		3	87.92	7.00	80.92		759.24	23.00
		4	87.92	6.32	81.60		677.64	29.32
		5	87.92	5.64	82.28		595.36	34.96
		6	87.92	4.96	82.96		512.40	39.92
		7	87.92	4.27	83.65		428.75	44.19
		8	87.92	3.57	84.35		344.40	47.76
		9	87.92	2.87	85.05		259.35	50.63
		10	87.92	2.16	85.76		173.59	52.79
		11	87.92	1.45	86.47		87.12	54.24
		12	87.92	0.73	87.19		-0.07	54.97
		12	*87.85*	*0.73*	*87.19*		*0.00*	*54.97*

SITUATION 8A – CONTINUED

"Due to round-off, an **OUTSTANDING PRINCIPAL** of $-0.07 remains at the end. The bank would subtract the $0.07 overcharge from the payment due that last month, making it $87.85. The **CUMULATIVE INTEREST** would be $54.24 + .008333($87.85) = $54.97. It's unchanged because the interest drop on $0.07 reduces it less than $0.01. Sweetie, how does the $54.97 compare to before?"

"Before the **CUMULATIVE INTEREST** was $27.31."

"It has doubled, right?"

"Yes it has."

"That's to be expected since the **ANNUAL RATE OF INTEREST** was doubled. The other point is that happened even though the **MPAYMENT** only went up a small amount."

---

*Exercise 9: Repeat SITUATION 8A using an **ANNUAL RATE OF INTEREST** of 20.00%. The bank calculated the amortized **SCHEDULED MONTHLY PAYMENT** as $92.64 per month.*

Your partial result should be:

Term in Years	Annual Rate of Interest	Month	Monthly Payment	Applied to Interest	Applied to Principal		Outstanding Principal	Total Interest
							Principal = $1000.00	
1	20.00	1	92.64	16.67	75.97		924.03	16.67
		2	92.64	15.40	77.24		846.79	32.07
								46.19
								59.00
								70.48
								80.60
								89.35
								96.70
								102.63
								107.11
		11	92.64	3.01	89.63		91.08	110.12
		12	92.64	1.52	91.12		-0.04	111.64

"Well Peanut, do you have any other curiosities?"

"Nothing I can think of right now. Maybe later something will hit me."

"Ok then. But let me leave you with one to think about. What would happen if you each month you paid more than the **SCHEDULED MONTHLY PAYMENT**? I do not want a reply from you right now. But it is called **acceleration** of the loan repayment. It's a very important topic, so we should discuss it at another time."

"That's interesting. That's a topic in my Physics class next term. Maybe I can get a head start on it. Since we're snowed in and I am on school break, how about in a day or two?

"That's fine with me. If we do it the day after tomorrow, I can get some things ready. And your mention of physics gives me an idea on how to prepare."

His mind perked by Nicole's mention of physics, Dad created an analogy to help illustrate the concept of **acceleration of loan repayment**. Since Nicole drives a car, he thought she might enjoy an illustration related to the phenomenon of an accelerating car. While a different from money matters, the effect is similar to that of loan repayment. He's prepared some material to compare the two.

"Hi Nicole! I'm ready to go and looking forward to explaining the process and effects of accelerating loan repayment. In fact I want to compare them to something you will study in physics."

"Hi Dad! That's sound neat."

"Ok. Before doing that let me ask you something.

"Have you heard the expression of "money burning a hole in your pocket"?"

"Sure Dad. And I suppose some of my spending is careless."

"Wouldn't it be nice if the money one owes on a loan could diminish with the rapidity of expending one's cash on hand?"

"If you're asking if I could repay one as easily as spending my money, how would I feel? Then I'm sure that would feel very good."

"The ability to reasonably increase the rapidity with which a loan is repaid is in everyone's reach. It can be done by the acceleration of loan repayment. To understand how that works, you need to know what the word acceleration means. Let's first look at its meaning in physics."

" Ok, Peanut. It will be new to me but I'll do my best to follow."

What's Acceleration?

"Since you drive a car now, Nicole, you know that when you press the peddle it begins to pick speed. That is the car accelerates?"

"Yeah, I do know that use of the word. But I only know it in general terms."

"When you're pressing the peddle of the car you are actually pressing on an accelerator. The end result is the gas gets into the engine faster and faster. So it picks up speed. But I don't want to discuss the details of auto parts. I want to explain the resulting movement of the car."

"I'm not ready for a lesson on car parts either. I just began driving one a few months ago."

"Don't worry. I am talking simple mechanics of motion, not auto mechanics work. We have all felt the thrill and/or fright of pressing the gas pedal of our car to the floor. The driver feels an exhilarating sensation as the accelerator is pressed down and the car surges forward faster and faster. If you press it all the way too quickly you pick up speed really fast. For my generation, "going from 0 to 60 in 10 seconds" is familiar driver's benchmark for that experience. Hopefully, you're not doing that."

"I've heard that phrase but I doubt I ever done it. Dad, I drive very carefully."

"It's good that you do drive safely. Let me explain the actual technical meaning of that expression?

"In basic terms the car is gaining speed over time. Initially the car is moving at 0 miles per hour and 10 seconds later it is moving at 60 miles per hour. In my younger days, that was called "scrubbing out" and it is the screeching sound of the tires that made it so. You are literally scrubbing rubber off your tires. But why is "going from 0 to 60 in 10 seconds" called acceleration? Well, a physicist might explain it like this.

"The speed (formally, she would call it "velocity") of the car increased (formally she would say "steadily increased") from a speed of 0 miles per hour to a speed of 60 miles per hour. It took 10 seconds to do that. So the speed of the car was increasing at an average rate of 60 miles per hour divided by 10 seconds, or 6 miles per hour per second. That physical phenomenon is called acceleration. The "6 miles per hour per second" is what a physicist would say is its acceleration. In simple terms, the speed is getting <u>faster</u> each second. Following me?"

"The "miles per hour per second" is fuzzy."

"Ok, Sweetie. Let me say it another way. If for each second the speed increases by the same amount than it did in the previous second the acceleration is constant. For every second it is accelerating the car gains 6 miles per hour in the speed at which it is moving. So in 1 second the car is moving 6 miles per hour; in 2 seconds the car is moving at 12 miles per hour; in 3 seconds it is moving at 18 miles per hour, and so on."

"That's clearer, Dad."

"Because in each second the speed of the car is getting faster by the same amount, its speed is said to be increasing "linearly". If instead the speed of the above car increases from 0 mph to 0.5 mph after 1 second, then to 2 miles per hour after 2 seconds, then to 5-mph after 3 seconds, and so on, then its speed is increasing <u>nonlinearly</u>. As time passes the speed is getting faster but is also doing it faster each second! For this circumstance the acceleration is not constant. Compared to constant acceleration which the speed is getting <u>faster</u> each second, in this case the speed of the car is getting <u>faster and faster</u> each second."

"Whew! That linear and nonlinear stuff goes over my head."

"I'm not surprised it does. Let's look at it visually. I made a plot that shows it.

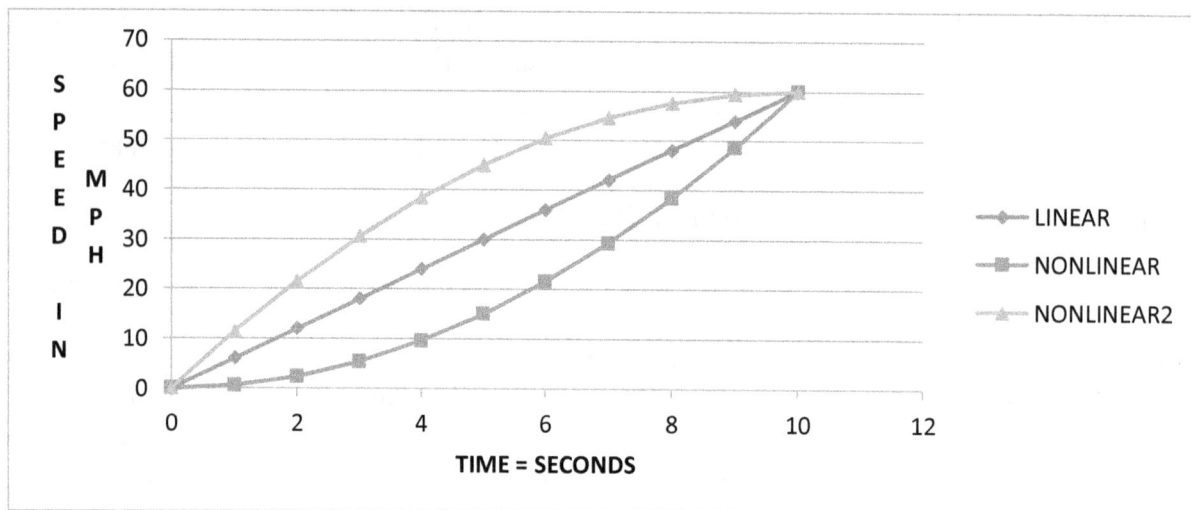

"Two of the plots are of the example of "going from 0 to 60 in 10 seconds". They're based on the numbers I described. The straight line is for the linear changes in velocity. The lower curved line is for the nonlinear changes in velocity. The third (upper) plot is for another possible nonlinear velocity pattern leading to the same end result. How's this all look to you."

"It helps a lot to see it graphically, Dad. I guess there are different ways to get the car up to 60 miles per hour?"

"I would say there are different ways to accelerate the car up to that speed. The ones I have shown are not the only ones. Which one happens depends on how you press the pedal. It's not important to go into that. The three I have shown make my point.

"But there's another effect involved that is not felt, it just happens unnoticed until the end. The distance the car travels increases even faster than its speed. During each second it will travel a greater distance than the one before. Consider the circumstance of going from 0 to 60 in 10 seconds (accelerating at a constant 6 miles per hour per second). I've done a plot of the distance (in feet) the car travels in 10 seconds. I won't go into the physics and math of how I calculated it. I'll leave that as a subject for your Physics teacher next term."

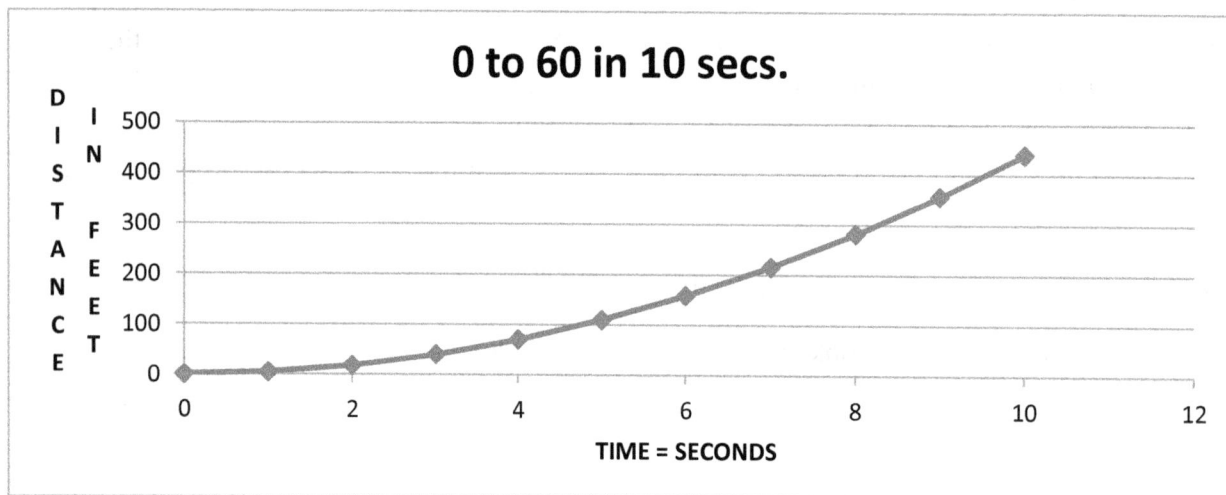

"Nicole, what's pertinent is what the plot shows. During the first second the car will travel 4 feet, during the next second it will travel another 13 feet, during the third second it will travel another 22 feet, during the fourth second it will travel another 31 feet and, and so on. After 4 seconds it will travel a total of 70 feet. In 10 seconds it will travel 440 feet! But in each second, it has moved by a different (and higher) amount. Do you understand the plot?"

"I do. It's also nonlinear."

"Yes it is. When the car is accelerating we can see it is getting to its destination "faster and faster and faster". Of course, if the car is you getting into debt the feeling of rapidity is there but not the exhilaration. But if you are accelerating the repayment of your loan, then you are paying it off and reducing your debt faster and faster and faster! As a result the debt ends sooner than the **TERM** of the loan. It will save you money and the more you accelerate the more you will save. That's a much more exhilarating sensation than speeding up a car's movement!"

"I get the general sense of it. But I don't get a feel for the effects on loan repayment."

"I'll get to numerical considerations soon. Let me add a little more, speaking generally.

"Another way of saying something is increasing over time is to say it is growing over time. "Rate of growth" means the speed at which something is growing as time passes. If the "something" is your savings, then that is good. If the "something" is your debt, then that is bad. In path 2 above the speed is getting faster and faster and not leveling off. In path 3 the speed is getting faster but the rate of increase is leveling off. It is slowing down. The latter is the first step in controlling debt. Once you get the debt to level off, then you can start to reduce the debt."

Acceleration of Credit Card Debt Repayment

"Now let's examine how to accomplish acceleration of loan repayment and the benefits of doing so. I'll go back to the example of credit cards, as that is likely the first kind of debt you will experience."

"When we discussed that topic, I used the illustration of a credit card holder making a single $1000.00 purchase. I showed that if he or she pays only the minimum **MONTHLY PAYMENT** due each month, then the loan would never be paid off. The reason was that the interest added each month exceeded the amount of the **MONTHLY PAYMENT**. So the debt grew bigger each month. Do you recall that happening?"

"Yes I do. It was so scary I couldn't forget."

"Then I altered the situation to where the cardholder increased the **MONTHLY PAYMENT** to a consistent $20.00 per month, an amount slightly above the **MONTHLY INTEREST** imposed by the credit card company. As a result, the debt was paid off in a little over 9 years with the **CUMULATIVE INTEREST** amounting to $1175.51. Next, I altered it again to where that individual made **MONTHLY PAYMENTS** of $100.00. As a result, the debt was paid off in 1 year with the **CUMULATIVE**

INTEREST amounting to $103.23. Do you remember that?"

"Not the numbers, Dad. But I do remember the **CUMULATIVE INTEREST** going down quite a bit."

"The particular numbers aren't so important. I had to look up them up before we met. That the reduction in **CUMULATIVE INTEREST** was significant is the general point of interest. By paying more than the minimum payment the loan was paid off sooner and at less cost. So it is a form of acceleration of loan repayment.

"The key to paying off a loan faster and faster is to **accelerate its repayment**. You do that by making as high a payment each month as possible and consistently do it. One way to do that is to take any cash that is burning a hole in one's wallet and pocket and use some of it to pay an extra amount toward the credit card debt. Have I explained the analogy well enough for you?"

"Yes, you have Dad. I see the part about paying off the credit card debt very clearly. I generally get the physics of the car aspects but will wait to learn more about it from my teacher. At least I have a leg up on it."

"Good for you.

"The acceleration approach is valid for any loan, not just a credit card loan. In particular, it is readily done for amortized loans. Let's take a look at that."

Acceleration of Amortized Debt Repayment

"With an amortized loan, a <u>fixed</u> amortized **MONTHLY PAYMENT** amount is established. Indeed, for such loans the loan is already being paid off faster and faster. That's because the amount of the **MONTHLY PAYMENT** that is **APPLIED TO INTEREST** gets lower and lower each month, resulting in the amount that is **AMOUNT APPLIED TO PRINCIPAL** getting higher and higher each month. Do you recall all of that Peanut?"

"It was only a couple days ago so it is still in my mind."

"In the context of acceleration of loan repayment, the amortized **MONTHLY PAYMENT** is "fixed" only in the sense that the amount is the same each month. It does not mean one cannot pay more than that, Peanut.

"The amortized **MONTHLY PAYMENT** is the counterpart to "minimum" amount due each month for credit card debt. Failure to pay the minimum amount results in a penalty being applied, which can range from nominal to severe. On the other hand, if the terms of the amortized loan permit it, the borrower can pay any amount above the "minimum" payment each month. Indeed, if the terms of the loan permit it, the entire **OUTSTANDING PRINCIPAL** can be paid off in full at any time."

"So if they let me then I can accelerate the repayment of an amortized loan. Why wouldn't they let me if I wanted to do it?"

"It's not very common, but the main reason is they want to have the loan in place for a satisfactory length of time to collect the interest on it. They want it to be enough to justify the time and effort and cost of making the loan in the first place. An extreme is someone borrows money for several years but pays it back in one month.

"The qualifier "if" is important as one should assure oneself that such terms of the loan exist before accepting the loan. It is important to have a clause present that allows one to "prepay the loan in full, without any prepayment penalty". If the loan is for buying a home then it is critical and crucial. Otherwise selling the property in order to move to another home has a financial constraint to overcome. The severity of the constraint depends upon the specific prepayment penalty clause in the terms of the loan. But home buying is well down the road for you. When that day comes, we can get together and discuss home mortgages.

"I'm sure I'll need to, Dad"

"Let me further illustrate the concept of accelerating the paying off of an amortized loan by reexamining a SITUATION we looked at previously."

SITUATION 9

"Let's return to that situation of Bradley taking out a loan from a bank for $1000.00 for a **TERM** of 1 year at an **ANNUAL RATE OF INTEREST** of 10.00%. The amortized **SCHEDULED MONTHLY PAYMENT** amount was $87.92. The resulting **CUMULATIVE INTEREST** was $54.97. It took one year to pay off the loan.

"Assume that Bradley receives a pay increase at his job and can afford to pay $120.00 per month. Here's the resulting **AMORTIZATION SCHEDULE** ."

| | | | | | | | PRINCIPAL = 1000.00 | |
Term in Years	Annual Rate of Interest	Month	Monthly Payment	Applied to Interest	Applied to Outstanding Principal	Additional Amount Applied To Outstanding Principal	Outstanding Principal	Cumulative Interest
1	10.00	1	87.92	8.33	79.59	32.08	888.33	8.33
		2	87.92	7.40	80.52	32.08	775.73	15.73
		3	87.92	6.46	81.46	32.08	662.19	22.19
		4	87.92	5.52	82.40	32.08	547.71	27.71
		5	87.92	4.56	83.36	32.08	432.27	32.27
		6	87.92	3.60	84.32	32.08	315.87	35.87
		7	87.92	2.63	85.29	32.08	198.50	38.50
		8	87.92	1.65	86.27	32.08	80.16	40.16
		9	87.92	0.67	87.25	32.08	-39.18	40.83
		9	32.75	0.67	32.08	0.00	0.00	40.83

SITUATION 9 - CONTINUED

"Notice that the **AMORTIZATION SCHEDULE** has an additional column labeled **ADDITIONAL AMOUNT APPLIED TO PRINCIPAL**. That column was present before but was narrow and void of contents. I said it would have a purpose."

"Here that column serves to indicate the difference between the actual monthly amount paid and the **SCHEDULED MONTHLY PAYMENT**. In this case that difference is $120.00 – $87.92 = $32.08. As the **MONTHLY INTEREST** amount has been met by a portion of the $87.92, this $32.08 is entirely used to further reduce the **PRINCIPAL** due the next month."

"I do see that, Dad. How does that come into the calculations?"

"Let's walk through that for the first two months of the table entries."

For Month 1

PRINCIPAL = $1000.00.

MONTHLY INTEREST owed = 0.833% of $1000 = 0.00833 x $1000.00 = $8.33

SCHEDULED MONTHLY PAYMENT = $87.92 is paid on time.

Portion APPLIED TO INTEREST = $8.33

Portion APPLIED TO PRINCIPAL = $87.92 - $8.33 = $79.59

ADDITIONAL AMOUNT APPLIED TO PRINCIPAL = $32.08

OUTSTANDING PRINCIPAL = $1000.00 - $79.59 - $32.08 = $888.83

For Month 2

MONTHLY INTEREST owed = 0.833% of $888.33 = 0.00833 x $888.33 = $7.40.

SCHEDULED MONTHLY PAYMENT = $87.92

Portion APPLIED TO INTEREST = $7.40

Portion APPLIED TO PRINCIPAL = $87.92 - $7.40 = $80.52

ADDITIONAL AMOUNT APPLIED TO PRINCIPAL = $32.08

OUTSTANDING PRINCIPAL = $1000.00 - $80.52 - $32.08 = $775.73

SITUATION 9 – CONTINUED

"Nicole, what is happening in the flow that is different from before?"

"The only difference I notice is that the **OUTSTANDING BALANCE** is being reduced by that $32.08 in addition to the amount from the **SCHEDULED MONTHLY PAYMENT**."

"Yes. So compared to before, will the sequence of **OUTSTANDING BALANCES** be lower or higher amounts?"

"Well, they would all be lower than before?"

"That's right, Sweetie. What about the amount of **MONTHLY INTEREST** being charged?"

"Because it is charged on the **OUTSTANDING BALANCE**, they would all be lower too."

"That's right. This sequence continues for seven more months, producing the rest of the **AMORTIZATION SCHEDULE** . The **CUMULATIVE INTEREST** paid should be noticeably lower than before. Let's look at the outcome.

"How long did it take to pay off the loan as compared to before?"

"I can see the loan has been paid off after nine months, instead of a full year. It looks like in Month 9 an adjustment is made in the final payment? I see that because there is an adjusted Month 9 line shown in italics."

"Indeed, in the original results for Month 9 an overpayment of $39.18 occurs. So, the last **ADDITIONAL AMOUNT APPLIED TO PRINCIPAL** of $32.08 is not needed. Even with that the debt is still overpaid by $39.18 - $32.08 = $7.10. The bank would adjust the last payment to be the **OUTSTANDING PRINCIPAL** after Month 8 plus the **MONTHLY INTEREST** due on that amount. That's $32.75, of which only $0.67 is **MONTHLY INTERREST**. The rest of it is $32.08 which pays off the debt.

"What's the amount of **CUMULATIVE INTEREST**?"

"It's $40.83."

"That's right. It compares to the **CUMULATIVE INTEREST** of $54.97 when only the **SCHEDULED MONTHLY PAYMENT** of $87.92 was paid.

"Although the dollar amounts involved are small, the relative benefit is clearly evident. By paying an extra $32.08 each month, Bradley reduced the time to pay off the loan by three months and the **CUMULATIVE INTEREST** by $54.97 - $40.83 = $14.14. The latter is a reduction of $14.14/$54.97 x 100 = 25.72%. I trust it's truly exhilarating reduce the cost of a loan debt by nearly 26%."

"It sure is Dad."

"I'll make one last point and then we're done.

"For the base amounts being **APPLIED TO PRINCIPAL** the amortized loan was already being paid off "faster and faster." That's because those amounts were getting larger and larger each month. The consistent **ADDITIONAL AMOUNT APPLIED TO PRINCIPAL** hastens the repayment even more. For that reason *Acceleration = Getting There Faster and Faster and Faster!*"

"It sure looks that way."

"Unless you have even more curiosities, we're done!"

"Sounds good! I can't think of anything else. Thank you Dad!""

"It's been my pleasure. So let's relax and enjoy being snowed in."

Exercise 10: *Bradley of SITUATION 9 is able to pay $50.00 as an* ***ADDITIONAL AMOUNT APPLIED TO PRINCIPAL***. *Calculate the first three lines and the last line of the* ***AMORTIZATION SCHEDULE*** .

Your *partial* results should be:

Term in Years	Annual Rate of Interest	Month	Monthly Payment	Applied to Interest	Applied to Principal	Additional Amount Applied to Principal	OUTSTANDING PRINCIPAL	Cumulative Interest
1	10.00	1	87.92	8.33	79.58	?	?	8.33
		2	87.92	?	?	?	739.76	?
		3	87.92	?	?	?	608.00	?
		-	-	-	-	-	-	-
		8	87.92	0.58	87.33	50.00	-67.41	35.92
		8	?	?	69.93	0.00	0.00	35.92

Exercise 10A: *Repeat SITUATION 9 using an* ***ANNUAL RATE OF INTEREST*** *of 20.00%. The bank calculated the amortized* ***MONTHLY PAYMENT*** *as $92.64 per month. Bradley pays an extra $25.00 per month.*

Your *partial* result should be:

Term in Years	Annual Rate of Interest	Month	Monthly Payment	Applied to Interest	Applied to Principal	Additional Amount Applied to Principal	OUTSTANDING PRINCIPAL	Cumulative Interest
1	20.00	1	92.64	16.67	?	25.00	899.03	?
		2	92.64	?	?	?	?	31.65
		3	92.64	?	79.37	?	?	44.92
		-	-	-	-	-	-	-
		10	92.64	0.47	92.17	25.00	-88.93	87.47
		10	?	0.47	?	0.00	0.00	87.47

Nowadays, most high school graduates continue on to some avenue of higher education. My fictionalized Nicole is about to become one of them. Her parents will accompany her along the path she will take to get there; her Dad primarily handling the financial costs aspects with her. That path will begin in the next Lesson. Before tagging along, they and we need a general roadmap in place. This Lesson provides one. It covers the setting and key elements of the academic decision making that parents and a child must work out. It also provides a look at what they need to accomplish as they begin to engage in financing a college education.

As a professor, I interfaced with thousands of college students. Most of them were majoring in my area of specialization, civil engineering. How each arrived at that choice of major and my institution's program is as varied as they were. But one thing is certain. It involved a lot of decision making. For traditional students entering directly from high school that decision making was a parent-child interface. Whether well-defined yet or not, the child's career aspirations versus the affordability of potential colleges to attend was at the forefront. The path from being a high school student to being enrolled in a specific college is a daunting one. That's just a given and a huge challenge in the parent-child interface involved. In succeeding Lessons we will watch as Nicole's Dad interacts with her to comfortably take on the challenge and help reach her goal. For now, let's look at that decision making process from my dual perspectives; as a parent and as a professor.

General Decision-Making Process

During my daughter's childhood and adolescent years many aspirations "came and went"; among them were architect, FBI agent, lawyer, and forensic chemistry. All children meander through such wanderlust as they grow up and eventually make a choice about their future career path. Eventually the widespread big dreams settle down and a choice is made. Like a growing number of individuals, to start her chosen dream vocation my daughter sought to and did attend college. Once that choice is made, the doorway into likely significant debt is entered. And the career choice significantly affects the level of awaiting costs. For example, it costs much more to become a doctor or engineer than to become a teacher.

I recall my daughter's path to "going to college" vividly. It was emotional, painstaking and filled with decisions by her and her parents. The obvious primary decision influencing future debt was where she would attend college. Of course, that choice was highly dependent on her educational interests, location, chances for admission etc. The financial commitment and level of debt potentially incurred are vital. The following are some of the significant financial aspects and decisions involved.

One vital consideration is the general affordability of the tuition and fees for colleges of interest. Over the recent decade college tuitions have soared. One reason for that is the increasing demand for a college education has led to a need for greater and greater capacity on college campuses. More laboratories, more technology infrastructure, more dormitories, more parking facilities, more buildings etc. cost a lot of money. Demand also requires paying for more faculty and staff. Looking at recent and projected trends in affordability as an important step.

There are a variety of higher education settings: small college, major college, university, community college, institute, two-year school, etc. Cost of attendance varies between and among them and for public vs. private colleges. The choice between private colleges vs. public colleges is a major issue. As tuition costs are dramatically higher for most private colleges, choosing a public college significantly decreases anticipated costs.

Annual tuition and fees at public college education can reach and exceed $15000 to $20000. However tuition rates at public colleges have been increasing dramatically, at a rate of 5-10% or more per year. In recent years the struggling economy has been a factor has been. With fewer people employed, less tax revenue exists for State government to finance salaries, benefits, and physical complex needs of public colleges. Other budget demands, such as K-12 costs, prisons, healthcare, also have cut the share of it going to higher education. That converts into increases in tuition rates.

Private colleges are not subsidized by government resources. They carry much more of the full burden of costs than public colleges, partially contributing to their much higher tuitions. With lessened donations from endowments and fundraising, they too have raised their tuition and fees. Private universities can reach and exceed $40000.00-$70000.00 annual cost of tuition plus fees. How to pay for such costs is a monumental consideration in weighing the decision to apply to private colleges. While many private institutions offer significant scholarships and other financial aid, few students receive full support.

Another primary factor in decision-making is the choice between in-state and out-of-state colleges. With the option of an in-state college, the student is availed of in-state tuition rates paid by a student whose home residence is in the state in which the public college is located. In-state tuition rates are dramatically less than out-of-state tuition rates. In-state tuition rates are commonly about one third to one-half of out-of-state rates. The general reason for the difference in rates is that formal residents pay state income and other state taxes. Part of that revenue is used to offset actual tuition costs, via the college setting in-state tuition rates at levels approved by the State government. Those rates reflect consideration of needed tax payer revenue and a desire to keep them affordable for the voting constituency. Out-of-state tuition rates reflect the actual full costs of providing the education. They also reflect some additional amounts needed to partially offset any subsidy given to residents beyond the tax revenue pot of money. Choosing and in-state college will predominately result in much lower costs of attendance.

In-state locations also offer the possibility of proximity to home, which can make commuting to campus a choice for family dependents still living at home. Choosing a more distant in-state college and any out of state college normally means incurring the cost of living in a dormitory or off-campus housing. Another financial factor in that choice is the type of location: small town vs. medium size town vs. urban area. Each of those settings infers a different cost of living. A smaller, but important, factor is costs for moving goods to that new location, albeit in the case of in-state colleges many families do that by a small caravan of family vehicles. Some do it that way even for more distant locations. Regardless, over four years that means as many as eight automobile trips. For out of state locations there are additional costs for traveling (often flying) home for holidays and for summers. So estimate those costs rationally and realistically.

The actual choice of a college is the outcome of balancing the academic and financial aspects. Parents want to have their child attend the best college possible that proves affordable. The meaning of "best" differs for each situation. Academic reputation of the college might be most vital, no matter the cost. Taking the best academic program available for their child's interests, regardless of cost, might be important. In some cases, carrying on a tradition of a trail of family members attending the local college might control. For many parents and students it is predominantly affordability. Proximity to home for either financial reasons or emotional reasons or both is sometimes a critical factor. In most cases the choice reflects a balance of academic fit and affordability. In the end, most parents want to manage the costs for the most affordable college that fits the child's academic area of interest and is at a location the child and they feels is the best fit for cost, location and success upon graduation.

For typical families, the cost of a college education is high even for the most cost-effective circumstance – commuting from home to the local public college. When the circumstance is otherwise costs dramatically increase. Rarely does the total cost get borne using only "out-of-pocket" resources, i.e. savings and ongoing income of the parents and the student. Financial aid in the form of scholarships for need and/or academic prowess and other forms of granted money assist many students. In limited cases such support might cover the full costs of the education, but not very often. Of most importance, many families have to plan for addressing the costs of college for more than one child.

Federal Student Aid Program

For most undergraduate students financing part of the cost involves seeking federal government aid. That means applying for assistance through the **Federal Student Aid (FSA)** program. The **FSA** program is operated as an Office of the **U.S. Department of Education (U.S.D.E.)**. Financial aid can be sought to help you pay for education expenses at an eligible college or career school. Grants, loans and work-study jobs are types of federal student aid. Amidst all the academic decisions to be made a complex maze of procedures and rules for seeking federal student aid have to be navigated. Some readers may be familiar with or see references to its extensive web site at http://www.direct.ed.gov/. As of March 15, 2016, that site was changed https://studentaid.ed.gov/sa/. The web site also includes nominal guidance regarding pursuit of non-federal aid including: from the state in which one live, the college one seeks to attend, non-profit and private organizations.

While some applicants are awarded **FSA** grants of funds, few get complete funding. Seldom does a student attend college without borrowing money. The **FSA** program offers subsidized and unsubsidized loans through its **Direct Loan** program. Indeed, they seem to have become an unavoidable fixture of paying for higher education pursuits. Parents can seek unsubsidized loans via its unsubsidized **Direct PLUS** program. Unsubsidized **Direct Loans** are also available for students continuing on to advanced degrees (graduate school).

Be rational and realistic about the debt level that lies ahead. Today's reality is that the need to borrow money for college costs is a norm, and significantly so. Many sources exist for accessing statistics about the past and recent trends in federal student loan debt. For more information on these, visit:

http://www.asa.org/policy/resources/stats/default.aspx

and

http://www.forbes.com/sites/halahtouryalai/2013/01/29/more-evidence-on-the-student-debt-crisis-average-grads-loan-jumps-to-27000.

By some accounts, in the recent half decade the average level of undergraduate student **FSA** loan debt has risen to more than $27000.00. About 10.00% of students owe more than $50000.00. Many parents also carry **FSA** debt as well, likely to similar levels. The cost of college educations for multiple children can be staggering, almost assuredly leading to significant borrowing. After home mortgage loans, student loan debt is likely the next most imposing debt to be incurred by parents and their children.

The nuts and bolts of the **FSA** website are complex to explore, especially for loans. Accomplishing the task of effectively utilizing the information, eligibility and other criteria, rules regarding potential loan amounts, annual rates of interest involved and paths to repayment is exhausting. But as Nicole and her Dad are about to tackle and navigate the financial aspects of her college education, they will have examined it closely. For purposes of subsequent Lessons the author prepared **APPENDIX I**. In it he has sorted out and summarized the main content of the federal web site. It's meant to constitute what Nicole and her Dad would have discovered. So do examine it before we start following them along their path in the succeeding Lessons.

Prior to beginning the actual process of applying to specific colleges the parents and student will want to estimate the affordability of potentially needed **LOAN AMOUNTS**. That's an understandable need. Unfortunately, addressing it is not straightforward. Dilemmas arise.

One dilemma is that future **FSA ORIGINATION FEES** and **ANNUAL RATES OF INTEREST** are unknown. Their values change each year and are dependent on the Congressional processes and politics for setting them. The government agency simply has not yet had them determined for future years. Only the present and past values in place when an application is made are known. For a student beginning college after June 30, 2018 the actual rates likely will different from those for the prior academic year.

A second dilemma is one does not know how much **FSA** money he or she will be allowed to borrow. Only upon acceptance into a college will the student be offered a financial aid package of grants and loans. For **FSA** funds the available amounts are based on the college receiving the outcome of the student's financial status information submitted to the **FSA**. The financial aid package also includes **FSA** loan amounts available to the parents. Offers will differ for each college of interest. The range of awarded amounts is not known until the student receives a financial aid package from each college of interest.

Those are significant dilemmas. Essentially the parents and student are empty handed when it comes to the specific monetary information needed for assessing affordability and doing associated financial planning. They're in a bit of pickle. They might feel they need a magic crystal ball to predict the future. Let's watch how Nicole and her Dad approached that dilemma.

Having completed her junior year in high school, Nicole is looking forward to summer. It was an interesting past year. As usual, she had excellent grades despite playing on the volleyball team, working at Comic Cones on weekends and having weekly private dance lessons. Preparation for attending college has begun.

Now she has a certain major in mind. She is looking forward to pursuing a degree in Journalism. She loves reading and writing and following news events and athletics. English teacher Mr. Carmichael, her favorite teacher, encourages her in that direction. She has high grades in English and Composition classes and enjoys meeting and talking with people. She occasionally submitted opinion articles to her high school's weekly newspaper *The Beacon - The Ears and Eyes of Mountain High*. Next term she plans to work on the staff of the paper.

Nicole has three specific colleges in mind: Sure Thing University One; Hoped For University; and Dream University.

Sure Thing University is a local public institution and she could commute. While ranked lower than her other choices, its Journalism program is very reputable. The tuition and fees of about $10000.00 per year are the most affordable of her three choices. Many students in her high school get accepted at that university, and always a few are admitted into the Journalism program. Those factors make Nicole feel certain about her acceptance and the affordability.

Mr. Carmichael suggested the Journalism program at Hoped For University as one Nicole should consider. It is a very reputable program. Hoped For University also has a superb English Department where she would likely take some courses as well. Nicole feels much more comfortable about being accepted into that program. It is out-of-state institution and has significantly higher tuition and fees of about $26000.00 per year.

Dream University is an out-of-state, top-tier private institution. Admission into its prestigious Journalism program is extremely competitive. Nicole feels uncertain of admission. She also is concerned about its very high cost being affordable to her parents. Its tuition and fees are about $35000.00 per year. So, Hoped For University is where she has set her more realistic sights.

Now that summer is at hand and she has specific degree aspirations and potential colleges in mind, Nicole asks her Dad when they could talk about her college goals, the costs and if loans will be needed.

"Hi, Dad! Over the last school term I've been thinking about college quite a bit. I've gotten some advice from a great teacher and have a direction I want to take. I'm interested in a career in Journalism. I've researched it and have three universities in mind that have great degree programs. You told me when I reached that point we could discuss the affordability and whether loans would be needed. Now that summer is here I plan to increase my hours at Comic Cones. But I'll still have a lot of free time. So when would you be available to do start doing that?"

"That's wonderful, Nicole. Why don't you tell me about those university programs right now? Then we can pick a time to talk about them at more length."

After listening to Nicole's description of the programs he opines. "Mom and I would want you to be able to attend the college that best fits your needs and comfort level. We also need to be able to pay the costs involved. Of course that's not just tuition and fees. For the medium to higher end it surely would require borrowing some of the funds needed. So let's investigate them all in a relative sense."

"I'm doing excellent in school, especially in courses related to journalism. I've had an article of mine published in the school paper and will get on the staff next year. Mr. Carmichael feels I could qualify for scholarships to cover some for the costs. The academic guidance counselor and he will help me with applying for them. He also feels all the colleges would compete to admit me, so I should get some partial grants of money. I guess that with luck I might get a lot, maybe all of it."

"That's super and part of the thinking out of options and calculating costs. But for once I'm agreeing with your "guessing" at it. So let's not quite go that far in our assumptions. We'll prepare for reaching realistic targets and options. If it works out you get full-ride scholarships or close to it, we celebrate big time. For now let's prepare to examine a range of hypothetical financial needs and possible financial pathways on a tentative basis. If we do that, then you can work on evaluating your choices on basis of academics. As you move closer we try for the best academic fit we can afford knowing we will do the best we possibly can. For me it begins with learning everything we can about the federal government grant and loan programs."

"That's sounds wonderful, Dad, and makes a lot of sense. Mr. Carmichael and the academic guidance counselor mentioned that federal grants and loans usually enter the picture. They said I would need to complete an application for the **Federal Student Aid** programs. Since I'm a dependent student it would include a lot of financial information about me and you and Mom. Based on that I might receive offers of grants and loans or both from the colleges I apply to. I guess how much depends on what is determined as my financial need. In any case, next fall the school will make presentations about those programs and parents can attend, too."

"Ok, that's to be expected. We'll get through it all. Those school presentations are a ways off. Let's start by learning on our own for a while. We can go to the website for the **FSA** programs and start there. I'll look around for other resources as well. Whenever we're ready we can meet to begin sorting it out."

During the next few weeks, Nicole and her Dad initially access and explore the **FSA** web site (https://studentaid.ed.gov/sa/). Expectedly, they encounter voluminous information (summarized in **APPENDIX I**). Realizing the complexity of it they agree that Dad will focus on deciphering it.

As grants of money involve no debt, he concentrates on the loan programs. Knowing the family financial means, he doubts that subsidized loans are in the picture. If they happen to be, then the government pays the ongoing interest, so in a way that money has no loan costs. The main issue is the calculation of costs for unsubsidized loans. So he absorbs the detailed information about them.

He's spoken to the **FSA** program personnel. He's also inquired to the student financial aid office of the local college about their process. More important for right now, he's aware of the above dilemmas involved in having to project future loan costs. He shares that information with his daughter indicating he has some ideas how to handle it. It will take a while but he will work on it. Here's what he does.

Undergraduate FSA loan rates

Dad realizes that the loan rates for the present and past loans are the only information he has available. He must utilize it in some way and he will. It takes time and effort but he locates that information via the Internet. For ease of reference he assembles the following table. It lists the current and recent past **FSA** loan rates for undergraduate students.

Undergraduate Direct Subsidized/Unsubsidized Loans				
Period of Disbursement				
July 1, 2014 – June 30, 2015	July 1, 2015 – June 30, 2016	July 1, 2016 – June 30, 2017	July 1, 2017 – June 30, 2018	
Annual Rate of Interest				
4.66%	4.29%	3.76%	4.45%	
Period of (First) Disbursement				
Dec. 1, 2013 - Sept. 30, 2014	Oct. 1, 2014 - Sept. 30, 2015	Oct. 1, 2015 - Sept. 30, 2016	Oct. 1, 2016 - Sept. 30, 2017	Oct. 1, 2017 – Sept. 30, 2018
Date of First Disbursement				
August 1, 2014	August 1, 2015	August 1, 2016	August 1, 2017	August 1, 2018
Origination Fee Rate				
1.072%	1.073%	1.068%	1.069%	1.066%

Dad arranges a time to share this information with Nicole. He begins their meeting by showing her the above table of present and past loan costs. He mentions what he had researched to develop it.

"I know it's a lot of information in one table. I'll walk through the details. Here's a print out of it. You saw the federal web site, too. Even though it's daunting at least your looking through it is helpful. Whenever you're losing me just slow me down with your questions."

"Ok Dad. There's some terminology in it that I remember being described in the government web site. It was pretty foggy and convoluted."

"Wow, convoluted? That's a fancy word you know. I agree it is pretty entangled when you read the web site content. I will explain the terminology as I go along."

"Loan funds are awarded in advance of the applicable academic year but not received until the student is actually enrolled in classes. Student loan rates are set annually by Congress to fit the typical academic yearly period. That's the period of July 1 of the applicable academic year through June 30 of the following year. That time period is called a **PERIOD OF DISBURSEMENT**. My table includes the present **PERIOD OF DISBURSEMENT** `of July 1, 2017 – June 30, 2018 and the three that preceded it. That's because I assumed it will take four years to complete studies and loans are needed and awarded each year. The **ANNUAL RATE OF INTEREST** is different for each **PERIOD OF DISBURSEMENT** and I've listed the applicable values. For example, for the present **PERIOD OF DISBURSEMEN** of July 1, 2017 – June 30, 2018 the **ANNUAL RATE OF INTEREST** is 4.45%. Do you follow me so far?"

"Um, I think so. If I graduate in four years, I might have loans during each of those years. The government charges a different interest rate for each of those years."

"That's correct."

"Dad, from skimming through the website, it seems to me I apply each year? And I submit a form to the government each year? I don't remember what it's called. It's looked pretty awful."

"That's right! In advance of each year, you'll have to complete and submit the **Free Application for Federal Student Aid** form. For short, it's called the **FAFSA** form. By your doing so, the government agency determines the amounts of grants, work-study funds, and loans for which you qualify; if any. The amount awarded likely changes each year. In reality, when the time comes, we'll have to prepare it together. The form involves a lot of financial status information about you and us, mostly about us."

"I figured that, too. And I peeked at the rest of your table. I don't get it at all. There's a bunch of words I that are new to me. What are subsidized and unsubsidized loans? And what do all those dates mean?"

"Basically for an unsubsidized loan, the borrower pays the interest. For a subsidized loan the government pays the interest. The subsidized loans are based on having financial need, low income etc. Most applicants including us won't qualify for them. I assumed the loans are unsubsidized."

ASIDE: Calculations are predominantly the same for subsidized loans. For subsidized loans the only difference is the **U.S.D.E.** pays the interest from the time of disbursement. The student incurs none.

"As to all those dates, you use them to determine **ORIGINATION FEE RATE**. For example…"

"Wait, Dad. I can't help frowning right away. What's that mean?"

"That's quite OK. Interrupt me any time you feel a need."

"For any student loan there is an **ORIGINATION FEE**. It's a loan processing fee that covers the cost associated with considering the application and handling the details of determining the awarded funds. Later the lender has to disburse the funds, receive and process payments, and track repayment. The **ORIGINATION FEE** is based on an **ORIGINATION FEE RATE**, which is a percentage of the loaned funds. Let's cover how all those dates come into play.

"The **ORIGINATION FEE RATE** is based on a **PERIOD OF (FIRST) DISBURSEMENT**, again that's the period of time in which the loan funds are disbursed. In this case, it's the period of time between Oct.1 of the applicable calendar year and September 30 of the following calendar year. Because that's a different period than for the **ANNUAL RATE OF INTEREST**, I added the word **FIRST** in parentheses. And I've tabulated five needed **PERIODS OF (FIRST) DISBURSEMENT**. The **ORIGINATION FEE RATE** differs for each them.

A **DATE OF (FIRST) DISBURSEMENT** is also in play. That's the first day that any part of or all money from a given annual award is disbursed to you. The funds are actually put into an account at the college. For a given loan award the applicable **ORIGINATION FEE RATE** is the one listed for the applicable **DATE OF (FIRST) DISBURSEMENT**. For example, for August 1, 2017 the **ORIGINATION FEE RATE** is 1.069%. Are you following me OK?'

"I think so. The **DATE OF (FIRST) DISBURSEMENT** is the first day I get some of the money for that academic year. And looking at your table, I guess that's August 1? I'm not sure why. And you also show five Augusts, not four?"

"Nice observation, Sweetie! Loan funds are not released until the student is actually on campus and enrolled in classes. I assumed that two semesters are in play and half the awarded funds are disbursed on August 1 of the first semester and the other half are disbursed in February 1 of the following semester. That implies that August 1 is the **DATE OF (FIRST) DISBURSEMENT**. That's why I used that date for each of the five **PERIODS OF (FIRST) DISBURSEMENT**.

"Unfortunately the timing of the **PERIOD OF (FIRST) DISBURSEMENT** for the **ORIGINATION FEE RATE** is for the out of synch with that of the **ANNUAL RATE OF INTEREST**. That disconnect necessitates being careful to select the proper and consistent values for both."

"Why would they do that, Dad?"

"Yes, it is an odd thing isn't it? It appears the federal government doesn't set the **ORIGINATION FEE RATE** until Oct. 1 of each year. That happens to coincide with the start of the annual budget year for the federal government, which runs from Oct 1 of a given year to Sept. 30 of the following year. As I mentioned, setting the **ANNUAL RATE OF INTEREST** on a different timing for seems to be an exception to make it compatible to the outset of the college academic year. It helps students and parents better anticipate the cost of loan needs for the coming academic year."

"It still seems silly that they would have different periods of time, and confusing."

"I agree, but we'll have to love with it as we look ahead to your student loan need."

Repayment of Student Loans

"I spoke with a financial aid staff person of the local college about student loan repayment timing. There isn't a fixed federal date for disbursing student loan funds. They can be disbursed at any time and differently for each student. Also, a borrower can pay any partial repayment amount at any time, including the entire **OUTSTANDING BALANCE**. The borrower might skip payments or pay them erratically. For those reasons, **FSA** loan interest is calculated on a daily basis."

"Sounds like it's just like how a credit card account works?"

"Good recall, Sweetie. It is indeed similar to how interest is charged on a credit card statement.

"To calculate the interest on a daily basis for a student loan, the daily **OUTSTANDING BALANCE** is multiplied by **DAILY INTEREST RATE** times. Then the daily amounts are added up. The **DAILY INTEREST RATE** is the **ANNUAL RATE OF INTEREST** divided by the number of days in the year. Back when you learned about credit cards, you saw the awkwardness and complexity that creates. I needed a simpler way to do it. As you saw, I used the **AMORTIZATION PROCESS** in my approach. Here's why.

"The financial aid staff person told me that, typically, the borrower sets up automatic monthly repayments to be taken from a bank account. Many borrowers make timely **MONTHLY PAYMENTS** on a consistent, scheduled monthly timing. In that case, the repayment is essentially the same as for an amortized loan. I checked it out numerically for some trial circumstances and it gives essentially same results as using the **FSA** daily basis calculation. I don't think it's necessary to show you that."

"That's Ok with me, Dad. I'm sure you convinced yourself and I trust you completely."

"OK. In reality, annually only one awarded loan amount is in play. Then split disbursements, daily interest and monthly payments are tracked. To examine the isolated cost effects of each disbursement I will consider each to be a separate loan. If you're still with me, I'll show how it works numerically?"

"I'm right there, Dad."

ASIDE: Disbursements could be other than once per semester, such as in a "quarter system" where funds are disbursed partially each quarter. But for timely monthly payments, amortization would still give correct results. For readers in that circumstance, the illustrated loan calculations would have to be expanded to more than two loans per academic year. The process is the same but more calculation work is involved.

ASIDE: Here-in, for applying **FSA** loan criteria it is assumed that the undergraduate student is dependent on her or his parents and the parents are eligible for **Direct PLUS loans**. Such is the case for Nicole and her parents.

Undergraduate Base Loans

Dad recognizes he will have to examine various scenarios for possible loan terms. His mental light bulb comes on and the idea of an approach of using "base loans" comes to his mind. In each base loan the **LOAN AMOUNT** is $1000.00. The monetary results for a base loan could then be multiplied by ("scaled" by) a **SCALING FACTOR** to obtain the corresponding results for any other **LOAN AMOUNT**.

He develops the idea and does the calculations needed to develop the results needed base loans for undergraduate student loan.

"Good. Now I want to show you a concept I came up with to facilitate calculating student loans. I call it **base loans**. Since you're not in college yet, I used a hypothetical person to illustrate how to calculate loans costs for a base loan."

SITUATION 10

"Baxter is in his final year pursuing a 4-year undergraduate degree. He will graduate in May, 2018. He had obtained an **FSA loan** for a **LOAN AMOUNT** of $1000.00. It was awarded in April, 2017. Half the funds were disbursed on August 1, 2017 and the remainder will be on February 1, 2018. He is on the **Standard** repayment plan with a 5-year **TERM**."

"What's a standard repayment plan?"

"That's the usual option for a borrower. Typically the repayment is over a 5-year or 10-year timing. There is also an **Extended** repayment plan for people who have borrowed enough to qualify for longer timing, up to twenty five years. There are other plans during periods of differing conditions of financial constraint.

"In my table you should see the applicable **ANNUAL RATE OF INTEREST** is for the period of July 1, 2017 – June 30, 2018, so 4.45%. The applicable **ORIGINATION FEE RATE** is for August 1, 2017, so 1.069%."

"I do see that."

"Assume Baxter is deferring repayment until he graduates and will use the 6-month grace period. Do you know what that is?"

"I remember seeing something about that on the website. He can delay payment while he is school and until 6-months after he completes his studies. Right?"

"Yes, and he can choose to either pay or skip the **MONTHLY INTEREST**. Assume he is paying the ongoing **MONTHLY INTEREST** during that deferred/grace period. Consequently his **PRINCIPAL** will be unchanged each month. As a refresher, here is my calculation of his subsequent **MONTHLY PAYMENT**.

ORIGINATION FEE = (1.069%/100)($1000.00) = $10.69
PRINCIPAL = **LOAN AMOUNT** - **ORIGINATION FEE** = $1000.00 - $10.69
= $989.31
MONTHLY RATE OF INTEREST = 4.45%/12 months
= 0.371%/month (rounded)
MRATIO = 0.371/100 = 0.00371
TERM = 5 years x 12 months/year = 60 months
$(MRATIO + 1)^{TERM} = (1 + 0.00371)^{60} = (1.00371)^{60}$
= (1.00371)(1.00371)(1.00371)….. 60 times! = 1.25 (rounded
NUMERATOR = **PRINCIPAL** x **MRATIO** x $(MRATIO + 1)^{TERM}$
= 989.31 x 0.00371 x 1.25 = 4.59 (rounded)
DENOMINATOR = $(MRATIO + 1)^{TERM} - 1$ = 1.25 - 1 = 0.25
MPAYMENT = **NUMERATOR/DENOMINATOR** = 4.59/0.25 = $18.36 (rounded)

SITUATION 10 - CONTINUED

"Notice that the **LOAN AMOUNT** is reduced by the **ORIGINATION FEE** resulting in a **PRINCIPAL** of $989.31. That's because it is taken out automatically at the time of the first disbursement."

"I see that. I suppose it has to be taken into account when we figure out how much to borrow?"

"That's right. If we need $5000.00 and are awarded exactly that, we are short a little bit."

"Using more precise calculations, **MPAYMENT** is actually $18.42. Using that value and continuing with precise numbers, I produced the partial **AMORTIZATION SCHEDULE**."

Loan Amount	1000.00							Principal = 989.31	
Origination Fee Rate	1.069%								
Origination Fee	10.69								
Term in Years	Annual Rate of Interest	Month	Monthly Payment	Applied to Interest	Applied to Principal		Outstanding Principal	Cumulative Interest
5	4.45	1	18.42	3.67	14.75	0.00	974.67	3.67
		2	18.42	3.61	14.81	0.00	959.86	7.28
		12	18.42	3.06	15.37	0.00	808.71	40.37
		24	18.42	2.36	16.07	0.00	619.80	72.54
		36	18.42	1.63	16.79	0.00	422.31	96.12
		48	18.42	0.87	17.56	0.00	215.84	110.74
		60	18.42	0.07	18.35	0.00	0.00	115.96

SITUATION 10 - CONTINUED

"When the loan ends **CUMULATIVE INTEREST** paid totals $115.96. Combined with the **ORIGINATION FEE**, Baxter will have paid a **TOTAL COST** = $115.96 + $10.69 = $126.65.

"Baxter also paid the **MONTHLY INTEREST** during the differed/grace period. Later, I'll show you a quick way to calculate it. How that amount is determined is covered subsequently. For subsidized loans it is not an issue as the above repayment begins at the time of loan disbursement and **U.S.D.E.** pays the interest."

"In Baxter's situation the **LOAN AMOUNT** is the base loan amount of $1000.00. That's why I call it a base loan. In reality, it would be different and various amounts. I'll show how to handle that later.

"Baxter's loan is for the academic year of July 1, 2017 - June 30, 2018. It could have been otherwise."

SITUATION 10A

"Let's say Baxter <u>also</u> had obtained a prior **FSA** loan for a **LOAN AMOUNT** of $1000.00. The **ORIGINATION FEE RATE** was timed to the disbursements. Half the funds were disbursed on August 1, 2016 and the remainder of the funds was disbursed on February 1, 2017. He is on the **Standard** repayment plan with a 5-year **TERM**.

"What are the **ANNUAL RATE OF INTEREST** and **ORIGINATION FEE RATE**?"

"From your table I see the **ANNUAL RATE OF INTEREST** for the period of July 1, 2016 – June 30, 2017, so 3.76%. The applicable **ORIGINATION FEE RATE** is 1.068%."

"Good. Like before, Baxter deferred repayment until he graduates and uses the 6-month grace period. Until then he pays the **MONTHLY INTEREST** due. Here are his subsequent repayment results."

ORIGINATION FEE = (1.068%/100)($1000.00) = $10.68
PRINCIPAL = LOAN AMOUNT - ORIGINATION FEE = $1000.00 - $10.68
$$= \$989.32$$
MONTHLY RATE OF INTEREST = 3.76%/12 months
$$= 0.313\%/\text{month (rounded)}$$
MRATIO = 0.313/100 = 0.00313
TERM = 5 years x 12 months/year = 60 months
$$(\text{MRATIO} + 1)^{\text{TERM}} = (1 + 0.00313)^{60} = (1.00313)^{60}$$
$$= (1.00313)(1.00313)(1.00313)..... \text{ 60 times!}$$
$$= 1.21 \text{ (rounded)}$$
NUMERATOR = PRINCIPAL x MRATIO x (MRATIO + 1)^{TERM}
$$= 989.32 \times 0.00313 \times 1.21 = 3.75 \text{ (rounded)}$$
DENOMINATOR = (MRATIO + 1)^{TERM} – 1 = 1.21 – 1 = 0.21

MPAYMENT = NUMERATOR/DENOMINATOR = 3.75/0.21

= **$17.86(rounded)**

= **$18.11 (with precise numbers)**

Partial AMORTIZATION SCHEDULE :

Loan Amount	1000.00						Principal 989.32	
Origination Rate	1.068%							
Origination Fee Rate	10.68							
Term in Years	Annual Rate of Interest	Month	Monthly Payment	Applied to Interest	Applied to Principal		Outstanding Principal	Cumulative Interest
5.00	3.76	1.00	18.11	3.10	15.01		974.31	3.10
		2.00	18.11	3.05	15.06		959.25	6.15
		12.00	18.11	2.57	15.54		806.03	34.06
		24.00	18.11	1.98	16.13		615.72	61.11
		36.00	18.11	1.36	16.75		418.14	80.88
		48.00	18.11	0.72	17.39		212.99	93.09
		60.00	18.11	0.06	18.06		0.00	97.45

SITUATION 10A - CONTINUED

"When the loan ends how much **CUMULATIVE INTEREST** has Baxter paid?"

"It's $97.45."

"Right! And if we add in the **ORIGINATION FEE** then the **TOTAL COST** = $97.45 + $10.68 = $108.23."

"Baxter would also be repaying the loan of SITUATION 10. Baxter also paid the interest for both loans during their deferred/grace periods. When he begins repaying the loans, he still owes their entire initial **PRINCIPAL**. As the **TERM** is the same for both loans, they would end simultaneously. He would be repaying them together when he graduates."

Combined ORIGINATION FEES = $10.68 + $10.69 = $21.37

Combined MONTHLY PAYMENTS = $18.11 + $18.42 = $36.53

Combined CUMULATIVE INTEREST = $97.45 + $115.96 = $213.41

Combined TOTAL COST = $231.41 + $21.37= $252.78

SITUATION 10A - CONTINUED

"Dad, I see the routine of it. There's a lot of effort involved to get these results. If the student has 4 years of loans, it has to be done two more times"

"Technically that's correct for any particular student. Recall that my table of loan rates lists them for the present and three past loan disbursements. For current graduating college students at-large they could have loans for all of those years. There also could be a different **TERM** for each loan. For general purposes having base loan results for all of them would be useful. That's a lot more than two times that the base loan calculations have to be redone. For you that is not the case right now. Later I will show you how to use those base loan rates to approximately project future loan costs."

Undergraduate Base Loan Table

"Since I had my computer routines available, I calculated base loan costs for all the possibilities. I've listed the summary results in a table. I'll call it the **UNDERGRADUATE - BASE LOAN TABLE** or **UG-BASE LOAN TABLE** for short.

UNDERGRADUATE-BASE LOAN TABLE								
				STANDARD REPAYMENT		EXTENDED REPAYMENT		
LOAN AMOUNT = 1000.00			**TERM**	**5 Years**	**10 Years**	**15 Years**	**20 Years**	**25 Years**
PERIOD DISBURSED	**ANNUAL RATE OF INTEREST**	**ORIG. FEE**	**PRINCIPAL**	MONTHLY PAYMENT				
7/1/14-6/30/15	4.66%	10.72	989.28	18.52	10.33	7.65	6.34	5.59
7/1/15-6/30/16	4.29%	10.73	989.27	18.35	10.15	7.46	6.15	5.38
7/1/16-6/30/17	3.76%	10.68	989.32	18.11	9.90	7.20	5.87	5.09
7/1/17-6/30/18	4.45%	10.69	989.31	18.42	10.23	7.54	6.23	5.47
PERIOD DISBURSED	**ANNUAL RATE OF INTEREST**	**ORIG. FEE**	**PRINCIPAL**	CUMULATIVE INTEREST				
7/1/14-6/30/15	4.66%	10.72	989.28	121.63	250.23	387.55	533.38	687.41
7/1/15-6/30/16	4.29%	10.73	989.27	111.65	229.06	353.91	486.02	625.16
7/1/16-6/30/17	3.76%	10.68	989.32	97.45	199.15	306.58	419.65	538.22
7/1/17-6/30/18	4.45%	10.69	989.31	115.96	238.20	368.41	506.42	651.95

"Whew! That's a lot of stuff for my eye to absorb. Let me study it a bit."

Moments later, Nicole observes "Ok, I see that in the upper part you give the **ORIGINATION FEE** and **MONTHLY PAYMENT** for each of the four **PERIODS OF DISBURSEMENT**. In the lower part you give the **CUMULATIVE INTEREST**."

"Exactly. And what about the **TERMS**?"

"You give results for repayment plans for different **TERMS**. Where did those come from?"

"That's right. When I spoke to the **FSA** staff, they indicated those are the possible **TERMS** the lenders assign for each.

"Now let's take a break and after it I will show you how use the **UG-BASE LOAN TABLE**."

"Hi Nicole! Are you ready to continue?'

"Yes I am. What's next?"

"I want to show you how base loan results can be "scaled" to give us loan costs for any other **LOAN AMOUNT**."

"Will I have to climb a mountain to do that?"

"Figuratively, the FSA loan process is sort of like climbing one. But the scaling I mean is pretty easy to do. But it does help us climbing that mountain a lot faster."

Using the Undergraduate Base Loan Table

"In Baxter's situation the **LOAN AMOUNT** is the base loan amount of $1000.00. In reality, it would be various amounts. So let's look at how to scale the base results accordingly.

"The results for the actual **LOAN AMOUNT** are obtained by multiplying the base loan results by the applicable **SCALING FACTOR**. The **SCALING FACTOR** is equal to the **LOAN AMOUNT** divided by $1000.00. Mathematically that's given by this equation.

SCALING FACTOR = LOAN AMOUNT/$1000.00

"Let's use Baxter to illustrate the necessary computations. Assume Baxter in our Situation 10 actually borrowed a **LOAN AMOUNT** of $4000.00 for his. Here are the calculations."

SCALING FACTOR = $4000.00/$1000.00 = 4.00

ORIGINATION FEE = 4.00 x $10.69 = $42.76

LOAN AMOUNT = 4.00 x $989.31 = $3957.12

MONTHLY PAYMENT = 4.00 x $18.42 = $73.68

CUMULATIVE INTEREST = 4.00 x $115.96 = $463.84

"Do you understand them?"

"Yes, I understand. To obtain the monetary outcomes, the base results you got before are multiplied by 4.00. That's easy."

"The base loan results for other loan disbursement periods can be calculated similarly. For example, consider if Baxter's prior loan in SITUATION 10A was also $4000.00. Although it has a different disbursement period, we can multiply the combined base loan results by the common **SCALING FACTOR**.

$$\text{Combined ORIGINATION FEES} = 4.00 \times (\$10.68 + \$10.69)$$
$$= 4.00 \times \$21.37 = \$85.48$$

$$\text{Combined MONTHLY PAYMENTS} = 4.00 \times (\$18.11 + \$18.42)$$
$$= 4.00 \times \$36.53 = \$146.12$$

$$\text{Combined CUMULATIVE INTEREST} = 4.00 \times (\$97.45 + \$115.96)$$
$$= 4.00 \times \$213.41 = \$853.64$$

$$\text{Combined TOTAL COST} = \$853.64 + \$85.48 = \$939.12$$

If instead his second **LOAN AMOUNT** was say $2000.00, its **SCALING FACTOR** = $2000.00/$1000.00. The scaled results would be,

$$\text{Combined ORIGINATION FEES} = 4 \times \$10.68 + 2.00 \times \$10.69 = \$64.10$$

$$\text{Combined MONTHLY PAYMENTS} = 4.00 \times \$18.11 + 2.00 \times \$18.42 = \$109.28$$

$$\text{Combined CUMULATIVE INTEREST} = 4.00 \times \$97.45 + 2.00 \times \$115.96 = \$621.72$$

$$\text{Combined TOTAL COST} = \$621.72 + \$64.10 = \$685.82$$

"Do you follow that, too?"

"Yes. Having those base loan values really simplifies things."

Average and Maximum Loan Costs

"Results in the **UG-BASE LOAN TABLE** can be scaled any **LOAN AMOUNT**. I did that in a table for two **LOAN AMOUNTS** of interest. I used the **PERIOD OF DISBURSEMENT** of 7/1/17-6/30/18, so for current loans."

UNDER-GRADUATE			STANDARD REPAYMENT		EXTENDED REPAYMANT		
DISBURSED 7/1/17-6/30/18	ANNUAL RATE OF INTEREST = 4.45%	TERM	5 Years	10 Years	15 Years	20 Years	25 Years
LOAN AMOUNT	ORIGINATION FEE RATE = 1.069%)	PRINCIPAL	MONTHLY PAYMENT				
1000.00	10.69	989.31	18.42	10.23	7.54	6.23	5.47
30000.00	320.70	29679.30	552.60	306.90	226.20	186.90	164.10
57500.00	614.68	56885.33	1059.15	588.23	433.55	358.23	314.53
LOAN AMOUNT	ORIGINATION FEE (RATE = 1.069%)	PRINCIPAL	CUMULATIVE INTEREST				
1000.00	10.69	989.31	115.96	238.2	368.41	506.42	651.95
30000.00	320.70	29679.30	3478.80	7146.00	11052.30	15192.60	19558.50
57500.00	614.68	56885.33	6667.70	13696.50	21183.58	29119.15	37487.13

"It's less busy on my eyes than the **UG-BASE LOAN TABLE**. I'm not quite figuring it out, though."

"I'll walk you through it. Here's a print out for reference."

"Entries in the $1000.00 lines are the base loan results taken from the **UG-BASE LOAN TABLE** for that period of disbursement. For the base **LOAN AMOUNT** of $1000.00 the **ORIGINATION FEE** = $10.69. The **PRINCIPAL** = **LOAN AMOUNT** – **ORIGINATION FEE** = $1000.00 - $10.69 = $989.31.

"The base **MONTHLY PAYMENT** amounts for the various **TERMS** are $18.42, $10.23, $7.54, $6.23 and $5.47, respectively. The base **CUMULATIVE INTEREST** amounts for the various **TERMS** are $115.96, $238.20, $368.41, $506.42, and $651.95, respectively.

"Do you see where the base loan values came from in my print out my other table?"

"Yes I do. So the **ORIGINATION FEE** is the same for all **TERMS**?"

"That's very observant! It's because the **ORIGINATION FEE** is taken from the awarded **LOAN AMOUNT** at the outset. It's the same amount regardless of which **TERM** is chosen. You choose that **TERM** when the loan is first disbursed. That's also why there is only one **PRINCIPAL** amount listed.

"Let's confirm some results.

For the average LOAN AMOUNT = $30000.00

SCALING FACTOR = $30000.00/$1000.00 = 30.00

ORIGINATION FEE = 30.00 x $10.69 = $320.70

For example, for a 5-year TERM:

MONTHLY PAYMENT = 30.00 x $18.42 = $552.60

CUMULATIVE INTEREST = 30.00 x $115.96 = $3478.80

(**ASIDE**: The **SCALING FACTOR** can also be calculated using the values of the **PRINCIPAL**. For the **PRINCIPAL** of $29679.30 the **SCALING FACTOR** = **$29679.30**/$989.31 = 30.00)

"Do you follow these calculations and are they what's listed in my table?"

"Yes I do and they are the same. But why did you use $30000.00 and $57500.00?"

"In my research, I found the average cumulative amount borrowed for all undergraduates is about $30000.00.In the **FSA** web site, it indicates the maximum amount of money the student can borrow over the time they qualify for loans. It's called the **AGGREGATE LOAN LIMIT**. For an undergraduate student it's $57500.00.

"In a bit, I'll show you results for $57500.00. I want to see the outcome if we had to borrow that **LOAN AMOUNT**, even though I doubt very much we will. Having the two results will provide a glimpse at the range of loan costs possible for between an average debt and the maximum debt that can occur."

"That makes sense to me. But is sure seems like a whole lot of money involved."

"It sure can be but that's why we're examining them. Later we can try other more likely amounts.

"Now that you see where the values come from let's look at the tabulated results some more.

For the average LOAN AMOUNT = $30000.00

ORIGINATION FEE = $320.70

For the <u>Standard</u> 5-year TERM the MONTHLY PAYMENT is $552.60. For the 10-year TERM of 10 years it is $306.90, much lower.

For the <u>Extended</u> 15-year TERM, it decreases to $226.20. For 20-year and 25-year TERMS it decreases to $186.90 and $184.10, respectively.

For the Standard 5-year TERM, the CUMULATIVE INTEREST is $3478.80. For the 10-year TERM, it increases significantly to $7446.00.

For the Extended 15-year TERM, it increases to $11052.30. For 20-year and 25-year TERMs, it increases to $15192.60 and $19558.50, respectively.

"Wow! That's a whole bunch of money, Dad."

"Yes, at your age it must seem incredible. Even at my age, the larger amounts are pretty steep.

"Notice two trends. As the repayment TERM increases, the MONTHLY PAYMENT decreases and the CUMULATIVE INTEREST increases. For a student with an average FSA loan debt, as the repayment TERM incrementally increases from five years to twenty five years, the MONTHLY PAYMENT incrementally decreases from $552.60 to $164.10. Correspondingly, the CUMULATIVE INTEREST incrementally increases from $6667.70 to $19558.80.

"What's that tell you?"

"It's like we saw back when you first talked with me about amortization. The lower is my MONTHLY PAYMENT the longer it takes to pay off my loan, and the more is the CUMULATIVE INTEREST I pay."

"You've got it, basically. However there's a subtle difference. For an FSA loan, you choose the TERM which then dictates the results. The longer is the TERM you choose, the lower is your MONTHLY PAYMENT and the more is the CUMULATIVE INTEREST you pay. The borrower should select the shortest TERM for which he or she can afford the MONTHLY PAYMENT."

"Ok, I understand that difference."

"Notice that the CUMULATIVE INTEREST can reach $19980.80. That's more than half the LOAN AMOUNT, actually about 67% of it.

"Yikes!"

"I agree. Let's look some more.

For the maximum LOAN AMOUNT of $57500.00

ORIGINATION FEE = $614.68

For the Standard 5-year TERM the MONTHLY PAYMENT is $1059.15. For the 10-year TERM, it decreases substantially to $588.23.

For the <u>Extended</u> 15-year TERM it decreases to $433.55. For the 20-year and 25-year TERMs, it decreases to $358.23 and $314.53, respectively.

For the 5-year TERM the CUMULATIVE INTEREST amount is $6667.70. For the 10 year TERM it increases to $13696.50.

For the 15-year TERM, it increases to $21183.58. For the 20-year and 25-year TERMs, it increases to $29119.15 and $37487.13, respectively. Again, the latter is more than half the LOAN AMOUNT.

"The main point is for the worst possible case borrowing up to the limit for a 25-year **TERM**, the **CUMULATIVE INTEREST** is $37487.13. That amount of money might pay the tuition and fees for some public universities for an entire four years."

"Holy moly! That's amazing and scary."

"Again, I agree with you. That's the big observation to this point. Now I'll move on to another topic."

Estimating Future Student Loan Costs

"When it's early in the process of planning for paying college costs, we don't have much factual information. Until you apply and are accepted we don't know your financial aid situation. So we don't know specifically how much **FSA** borrowing will be involved. Even if we did, there's another problem. The loan rates for the present and past loans are the only information we have now. In forthcoming years they will be different. We have no magic crystal ball to find them out. But what we do have at hand is still useful information."

"I'm all ears, Dad. You must have something up your sleeve. You always do."

"I do try my best to figure a way out any puzzle. So here's what I have considered for this one. A first step is simply to use the **UG-BASE LOAN TABLE** values for the current year of July 1, 2017 – June 30, 2018 and scale them to give a ball park estimate for future years. They're based on **ANNUAL RATE OF INTEREST** = 4.45%.

"A second step is to look at the trend in bank loan rates. While it's an assumption to correlate them we can look at the trend in bank interest rates. If they are rising, then we might scale the tabulated base loan results for an **ANNUAL RATE OF INTEREST** of 4.66%. That's the rate for the period of July 1, 2014 - June 30, 2015. If they are falling, then we might scale them for an **ANNUAL RATE OF INTEREST** of 3.76%. That's the rate for the period of July 1, 2016 - June 30, 2017. Doing both would provide a fairly dependable range of results

"Does that seem like a reasonable approach to you?"

"I understand your logic and it makes sense, Dad."

"Ok, so let's look at using it."

SITUATION 11

"Assume undergraduate student Emily is considering admission to a private college in August, 2018. Loan rates for that timing are not known. She does not anticipate any "full-ride" scholarships but expects she will get some partial ones. Each year of study, she expects to apply for **FSA** loans for between $5500.00 and $7500.00.

"Using the **UG-BASE LOAN TABLE** she develops a table of possible loan costs for each **LOAN AMOUNT**. She includes the results for each of three loan **TERMS**. They are for the current known rates, the highest recent and the lowest recent rates. The listed loan costs were calculated by multiplying the base loan values for each case by the applicable **SCALING FACTOR**."

For a LOAN AMOUNT = $5500.00

SCALING FACTOR = 5500.00/$1000.00 = 5.50

UNDER - GRADUATE				TERM	5 Years	10 Years	15 Years
DISBURSED	ANNUAL RATE OF INTEREST	LOAN AMOUNT	ORIGINATION FEE	PRINCIPAL	MONTHLY PAYMENT	MONTHLY PAYMENT	MONTHLY PAYMENT
7/1/14-6/30/15	4.66%	5500	58.96	5441.04	101.86	56.82	42.08
7/1/16-6/30/17	3.76%	5500	58.74	5441.26	99.61	54.45	39.60
7/1/17-6/30/18	4.45%	5500	58.80	5441.21	101.31	56.27	41.47
PERIOD DISBURSED	ANNUAL RATE OF INTEREST	LOAN AMOUNT	ORIGINATION FEE	PRINCIPAL	CUMULATIVE INTEREST	CUMULATIVE INTEREST	CUMULATIVE INTEREST
7/1/14-6/30/15	4.66%	5500	58.96	5441.04	668.97	1376.27	2131.53
7/1/16-6/30/17	3.76%	5500	58.74	5441.26	535.98	1095.33	1686.19
7/1/17-6/30/18	4.45%	5500	58.80	5441.21	637.78	1310.10	2026.26

For a LOAN AMOUNT = $7500.00

SCALING FACTOR = $7500.00/$1000.00 = 7.50

UNDER-GRADUATE				TERM	5 Years	10 Years	15 Years
DISBURSED	ANNUAL RATE OF INTEREST	LOAN AMOUNT	ORIGINATION FEE	PRINCIPAL	MONTHLY PAYMENT	MONTHLY PAYMENT	MONTHLY PAYMENT
7/1/14-6/30/15	4.66%	7500	80.40	7419.60	138.90	77.48	57.38
7/1/16-6/30/17	3.76%	7500	80.10	7419.90	135.83	74.25	54.00
7/1/17-6/30/18	4.45%	7500	80.18	7419.83	138.15	76.73	56.55
PERIOD DISBURSED	ANNUAL RATE OF INTEREST	LOAN AMOUNT	ORIGINATION FEE	PRINCIPAL	CUMULATIVE INTEREST	CUMULATIVE INTEREST	CUMULATIVE INTEREST
7/1/14-6/30/15	4.66%	7500	80.40	989.28	121.63	250.23	387.55
7/1/16-6/30/17	3.76%	7500	80.10	7419.90	730.88	1493.63	2299.35
7/1/17-6/30/18	4.45%	7500	80.18	989.31	115.96	238.20	368.41

"Do you follow what's in the tables?"

"I see that they're like those you did for the average and maximum **LOAN AMOUNTS**. And I understand that each line is gotten by multiplying the base loan values by the **SCALING FACTOR**. But how are they used?"

"Let me explain. In each table, the bottom line listing of **MONTHLY PAYMENTS** and **CUMULATIVE INTEREST** are projected results for the current loan rates for one year. The two lines above them provide a range for a possible lower or higher loan rates for one year. Emily can use any or all of them to consider different scenarios.

"One simple one is for Emily to assume that for each of the four years she borrows $5500.00 for a 5-year **TERM** and that the current loan rate of 4.45% applies. She then multiplies those listed results by 4 to get her projected loan costs for the 4-year period."

ORIGINATION FEE = 4 x $58.80 = $235.18

MONTHLY PAYMENT = 4 x $101.31 = $405.24

CUMULATIVE INTEREST = 4 x $637.70 = $2551.12

"Another easy one is to assume she borrows the funds and the highest loan rate of 4.66% applies. She then multiplies the listed results by 4."

ORIGINATION FEE = 4 x $58.96 = $235.84

MONTHLY PAYMENT = 4 x $101.86 = $407.44

CUMULATIVE INTEREST = 4 x $668.97 = $2675.88

"But more useful way is to also do it for the lowest loan rate of 3.76%. Here are those results."

ORIGINATION FEE = 4 x $58.74 = $234.96

MONTHLY PAYMENT = 4 x $99.61 = $398.42

CUMULATIVE INTEREST = 4 x $535.98 = $2143.90

"Doing that gives her projected ranges for the **LOAN AMOUNT** of $5500.00."

RANGES FOR LOAN AMOUNT = $5500.00

ORIGINATION FEE is between $234.96 and $235.84

MONTHLY PAYMENT is between $398.42 and $407.44

CUMULATIVE INTEREST is between $2143.90 and $2675.88

"The **ORIGINATION FEE** for the current **ANNUAL RATE OF INTEREST** of 4.45% is $235.18."

"That's awesome Dad. I see she can also do it for the **LOAN AMOUNT** of $7500.00."

"Well, thank you for the praise. I actually did that, too. Here are the overall results."

RANGES FOR LOAN AMOUNT = $7500.00

ORIGINATION FEE is between $315.32 and $321.60

MONTHLY PAYMENT is between $544.80 and $555.60

CUMULATIVE INTEREST is between $6008.40 and $7297.80

"Maybe for homework you can confirm my answers?"

"Who knows Dad, maybe I'll try that. For now I understand it and trust your results."

Exercise 11: *Verify the above results Nicole's Dad got for the **LOAN AMOUNT** of $7500.00.*

Your results should be: *Same as Dad's.*

"Combining both results gives Emily the following results.

RANGES FOR LOAN AMOUNT from $5500.00 to $7500.00

ORIGINATION FEE is between $234.96 and $321.60

MONTHLY PAYMENT is between $398.422 and $555.60

CUMULATIVE INTEREST is between $2143.90 and $3648.90

"These results apply to the 5-year **TERM** only. Emily has the 10-year and 15-year **TERMS** to consider as well. So she can work on those to her heart's content. It also gives you plenty more optional HW."

"Ha! Ha!"

"Let's investigate another scenario that's more involved but maybe more rational. Emily considers the possibility that for the first two years, she would take out loans of $5500.00 at the 4.45% interest rate and the next two she would take out loans of $7500.00 at the 4.66% interest rate. How would she calculate that possibility?"

"Let me think, Dad. Hmm? Hmm? I believe she just takes 2 times the results for the $5500.00 and 4.45% and adds it to 2 times the results for the $7500.00 and 4.66%."

Intentionally delaying, Dad mutters "Hmm? Hmm?" Then, "Yeah, you've got it Peanut. Now I am certain you can skip all the optional homework.

"Here are the numerical answers."

ORIGINATION FEE = 2 x $58.80 + 2 x $80.40 = $278.40

MONTHLY PAYMENT = 2 x $101.31 + 2 x $138.90 = $480.42

CUMULATIVE INTEREST = 2 x $637.78 + 2 x $912.23 = $3100.01

Exercise 12: *Calculate the loan repayment results for Emily of SITUATION 11 for a 10-year* **TERM** *for: a) four consecutive loans of $5500.00 and b) four consecutive loans of $7500.00 Use an* **ANNUAL RATE OF INTEREST** *of 3.76%.*

Your *partial* results should be:

For a):

ORIGINATION FEE = $234.96

MONTHLY PAYMENT = $398.42

CUMULATIVE INTEREST =?

For b):

ORIGINATION FEE =?

MONTHLY PAYMENT =?

CUMULATIVE INTEREST = $2923.50

Exercise 13: *Repeat Exercise 12 for an* **ANNUAL RATE OF INTEREST** *of 4.66%*

Your *partial* results should be:

For a):

ORIGINATION FEE =?

MONTHLY PAYMENT =?

CUMULATIVE INTEREST = $5505.06

For b):

ORIGINATION FEE = $309.90

MONTHLY PAYMENT = $555.60

CUMULATIVE INTEREST =?

Exercise 14: Jonathan anticipates borrowing two consecutive **FSA** loans. Loan 1 is for a **LOAN AMOUNT** of $6500.00 for 5 years at an **ANNUAL RATE OF INTEREST** of 4.45%. Loan 2 is for a **LOAN AMOUNT** of $3500 for 10 years at an **ANNUAL RATE OF INTEREST** of 4.66%. Calculate his loan repayment results.

Your _partial_ results should be:

For Loan 1:

ORIGINATION FEE = $69.49

MONTHLY PAYMENT =?

CUMULATIVE INTEREST =$753.74

For Loan 2:

ORIGINATION FEE =?

MONTHLY PAYMENT = $36.16

CUMULATIVE INTEREST =?

"You're really amazing Dad. Maybe you should write a book about loans for parents and young people?"

"That would take ages. But I'll think about as my potential long-term homework. Before I even consider that there's still more to show you. My watch indicates we've been at this for almost an hour. So do you want to tackle that another day?"

"Thank you, Dad. Honestly, it just flew right by. I'm really enjoying it and learning a lot. So you can continue."

"Ok, you asked for it."

Comparing Multiple FSA Loan Offers

"When a student is accepted into more than one university, he or she will receive different financial aid offers from each. That student will have to compare them. That probably will be the situation for you. Let's look at that for a hypothetical situation for a student who applied for the academic year of July 1, 2015- June 30, 2016."

SITUATION 12

"Lisa applied to two nearby in-state universities for the fall semester of 2017. Their programs of study in her major are comparable and she can commute to either one. As part of her financial aid package, University A offered her an unsubsidized **FSA** loan of $5500.00. The repayment **TERM** would be 10 years. As part of theirs, University B offered an unsubsidized **FSA** loan of $4000.00. The repayment **TERM** would be **5** years. She compared the costs of the two loans."

For Loan A

SCALING FACTOR = 5.50

ORIGINATION FEE = 5.50 x $10.69 = $58.80

MONTHLY PAYMENT = 5.50 x $10.23 = $56.27

CUMULATIVE INTEREST = 5.50 x $238.20 = $1310.10

TOTAL COST OF LOAN A = $58.80 + $1310.10 = $1368.90

TOTAL PAYMENTS = 120 x 56.27 = $6752.40

For Loan B

SCALING FACTOR = 4.00

ORIGINATION FEE = 4.00 x $10.69 = $42.76

MONTHLY PAYMENT = 4.00 x $18.42 = $73.68

CUMULATIVE INTEREST = 4.00 x $115.96 = $463.84

TOTAL COST OF LOAN B = $42.76 + $463.84 = $506.60

TOTAL PAYMENTS = 60 x 73.68 = $4420.80

SITUATION 12 - CONTINUED

"By accepting the offer of University A, Lisa would receive $5500.00 in loan funds and pay $1368.90 in **TOTAL COST OF LOAN**. Her **TOTAL PAYMENTS** is $6752.40. By accepting the offer from University B, Lisa would receive $4000.00 in loan funds and pay $506.60 in **TOTAL COST OF LOAN B**. Her **TOTAL PAYMENTS** is $4420.80. To equate the offers, she would have to pay $1500.00 out of pocket. Combined with the **TOTAL PAYMENTS**, Lisa pays $5920.80. That's $831.60 less than for **LOAN A**. After considering the rest of her aid package; difference in tuition, fees and other costs; etc. of the two universities she can make her choice."

"I see now how your table simplifies things and will be really helpful when we consider my college options. When will we get to that?"

"Soon enough, Sweetie! I'm not done showing you the base loan approach. So let's move on."

Repaying Multiple FSA Loans

"Usually, upon completing studies, a borrower has multiple **FSA** loans. We saw that with the Baxter example, who had two. As you observed earlier, an undergraduate student might have as many as four consecutive annual loan awards.

"Usually, each loan is on the same repayment plan option and **TERM.** The **ANNUAL RATE OF INTEREST** differs for each loan. Each has a different starting date. If each loan is being repaid starting immediately then they must be tracked separately as overlapping (not coincident) loans. One can do that using the base loan results. It just takes time and effort.

"But often the borrower defers repayment during the years of study and takes advantage of a grace period. So at the outset of repayment, the loan repayments are coincident. Having base results for each allows for that circumstance to be handled readily. So let's examine different hypothetical situations for students who will graduate at the end of the academic year of July 1, 2015- June 30, 2016 with multiple deferred loans."

SITUATION 13

"David began his 4-year undergraduate degree in August, 2014. As a part of his aid package each year he obtained an unsubsidized **FSA** loan. The **LOAN AMOUNTS** were: Loan 1 = $3200.00, Loan 2 = $3400.00, Loan 3 = $4100.00 and Loan 4 = $3000.00, totaling $13700.00.

"Each loan is on the **Standard** repayment plan with a 5-year **TERM.** The **ORIGINATION FEE RATES** were timed to first disbursements. For each loan, half the funds were disbursed on August 1and the remainder was disbursed on February 1.

"David will graduate in May 2018 and will begin repayment after a 6-month grace period. He will have paid the **MONTHLY INTEREST** during the entire deferred/grace period, so his **PRINCIPAL** amounts will be unchanged.

"Using the **UG-BASE LOAN TABLE,** here are the scaled repayment results."

SCALING FACTORS are: Loan 1 = $3200.00/$1000.00 = 3.20; likewise Loan 2 = 3.40 Loan 3 = 4.10, and Loan 4 = 3.00.

ORIGINATION FEES = 3.20 x $10.72 + 3.40 x $10.73

$$+ 4.10 \times \$10.68 + 3.00 \times \$10.69$$
$$= \$34.30 + \$36.48 + \$43.79 + \$32.07 = \$140.64$$

$$\textbf{MONTHLY PAYMENTS} = 3.20 \times \$18.52 + 3.40 \times \$18.35$$
$$+ 4.10 \times \$18.11 + 3.00 \times \$18.42$$
$$= \$59.26 + \$62.39 + \$74.25 + \$55.26$$
$$= \$251.16$$

$$\textbf{CUMULATIVE INTERESTS} = 3.20 \times \$121.63 + 3.40 \times \$111.65$$
$$+ 4.10 \times \$97.45 + 3.00 \times \$115.96$$
$$= \$389.22 + \$379.61 + \$399.55 + \$347.88$$
$$= \$1516.25$$

$$\textbf{TOTAL COST OF LOAN} = \$143.87 + \$1516.25 = \$1767.62$$

$$\textbf{PERCENT TOTAL COST} = \textbf{FRACTION} \times 100 = \$1767.62/\$13700.00 \times 100 = 12.90\%.$$

"That's rapid fire, Nicole. But do you follow it and see how I got the base loan values?"

"Hmm? Let me look at my print out."

"No hurry, I'll wait."

After wincing and rubbing her forehead for a while, Nicole replies.

"I've got it now. In the **UG-BASE LOAN TABLE** you just took them for each of the four **PERIOD DISBURSED** listings. They come from the columns labeled **ORIGINATION FEE** and **STANDARD REPAYMENT** for 5 Years. All four numbers listed vertically in those columns apply."

"Terrific, Nicole! And you follow how I used them?"

"Yes, you multiplied the values for the first year by its **SCALING FACTOR**, the values for the second year by its **SCALING FACTOR** and so on. Then you added them up."

"Well Miss Smarty, that's excellent. Maybe you're already qualified for college."

"My senior year will probably fly by. So I can wait for that."

Exercise 15: *Redo SITUATION 13 for David having yearly **LOAN AMOUNTS** of $5500.00, $6500.00, $7500.00 and $7500.00 (a combined **LOAN AMOUNT** of $27000.00). Do it for a) a 5-year TERM and b) a 25-year TERM.*

Your partial result should be:

ORIGINATION FEE *= $288.98*

For a 5-year TERM: ***MONTHLY PAYMENT*** *= $495.11*

For a 25-Year TERM: ***CUMULATIVE INTEREST*** *= $16770.57*

"Let's look at a more involved modification of SITUATION 13.

SITUATION 13A

"Let's say the **TERMS** for David's four consecutive loans are 10 years, 10 years, 15 years and 15 years. Here are my results for his loan costs."

For the 10-year TERM

For **Loan 1** and the $1000.00 base loan, the ORIGINATION FEE = $10.72, MONTHLY PAYMENT = $10.33 and CUMULATIVE INTEREST = $250.23.

For **Loan 2** and the $1000.00 base loan, the ORIGINATION FEE = $10.73, MONTHLY PAYMENT = $10.15 and CUMULATIVE INTEREST = $229.06.

Taken together:

ORIGINATION FEES = 3.20 x $10.72+ 3.40 x $10.73= $70.79

MONTHLY PAYMENTS = 3.20 x $10.33 + 3.4 x $10.15 = $67.57

CUMULATIVE INTERESTS = 3.20 x $250.23+ 3.4 x $229.06 = $1579.54

For the 15-year TERM

For **Loan 3** and the $1000.00 base loan, the ORIGINATION FEE = $10.68, MONTHLY PAYMENT = $7.20 and CUMULATIVE INTEREST = $306.58.

For **Loan 4** and the $1000.00 base loan, the ORIGINATION FEE = $10.69, MONTHLY PAYMENT = $7.54 and CUMULATIVE INTEREST = $368.41.

Taken together:

ORIGINATION FEES = 4.10 x $10.68 + 3.00 x $10.69 = $75.86

MONTHLY PAYMENTS = 4.10 x $7.20 + 3.00 x $7.54 = $52.14

CUMULATIVE INTERESTS = 4.10 x $306.58 + 3.00 x $368.41= $2362.21

For the four loans combined:

ORIGINATION FEES = $70.79 + $75.86 = $146.65

For 10 years: combined MONTHLY PAYMENT = $67.57 + $52.14 = $119.71

For the next 5 years: combined MONTHLY PAYMENT = $52.14

After 15 years: combined CUMULATIVE INTEREST = $1579.54 + $2362.21= $3941.75

TOTAL COST = $146.65 + $3941.75 = $4088.40

PERCENT TOTAL COST = $4088.40/$13700.00 = 29.84%

Exercise 16: Repeat SITUATION 13A for **LOAN AMOUNTS** *of $5500.00, $6500.00, $7500.00 and $7500.00 (combined* **LOAN AMOUNT** *of $27000.00). The consecutive* **TERMS** *are 5 years, 5 years, 25 years, and 25 years.*

Your **<u>partial</u> results should be**: *For the combined 5-year* **TERM** *loans*: **CUMULATIVE INTEREST** = *$1394.69. For the combined 25-year* **TERM** *loans*: **MONTHLY PAYMENT** = *$79.20. For the combined four loans the* **ORIGINATION FEE** = *$288.99 and the* **TOTAL COST** = *$10310.97.*

"Whew! Dad. That's a lot to absorb. But it does show me the versatility available by having your **UG-BASE LOAN TABLE**. I really see its value. Is there any more to see?"

"Well, I think that's plenty of numbers for one day. But before we call it a night, let me mention the bottom line quandary with any amortized loan. Reducing one's payment by extending the loan **TERM** is costly. A while back when you were only a small child, there was a commercial about auto filters. It showed a man who ignored replacing his inexpensive auto filter for a long time. Then he developed engine problems and had to pay for major repair costs. The punch line was 'You can pay me now, or you can pay me later!' The counterpart in student loans herein is "How much can I afford to borrow and for what amount of time? The longer you wait to pay it off the more it costs and by a lot more."

"I've been getting that message loud and clear, Dad. When I do get to taking out loans I will always try to pay them back as quickly as I can afford to do."

"In other types of amortized loans, that added cost of a longer **TERM** can be partially offset by negotiating a lower **ANNUAL RATE OF INTEREST**. But for **FSA** loans negotiation is not an alternative. All **ANNUAL RATES OF INTEREST** are fixed by government legislation. Using those and the available options for **TERMS**, the borrower must navigate his or her way through various loan options. Using the **UG-BASE LOAN TABLE** eases that work. Then the borrower can consider the trade-offs involved between present affordability of the **MONTHLY PAYMENT + ORIGINATION FEE** (the "pay me now") and the long term **CUMULATIVE INTEREST** (the "pay me later") of each option. Based on that he or she can choose a loan option best suited to his or her personal income and financial resources.

"That's what we will need to do ourselves, for your student loans if you need them, Peanut."

"That's what I am waiting to find out, whether or not loans are needed for the colleges I am considering."

"We'll get to that down the road when you are actually considering specific colleges. For now there's more for me to show you. Can we do that tomorrow?"

"That should work as I'm not getting much take home school work yet. I'll see you tomorrow."

As arranged, the next day Nicole and her Dad meet to continue discussing student loans. He begins, "Nicole, before starting my next topic I need to point out something by asking you a question? Do you realize that for everything I said yesterday, the loans being described are loans that the student is eligible to take out, not the parents? That means you yourself."

"Gee actually I didn't. That's a surprise. So I have to pay them off, not Mom and you?"

"Technically, yes. Does it make sense that parent would take on their child's debt for up to twenty five years? Not really. So how do parents pitch in? It depends on the particular parents and the total costs involved compared to their financial means and parenting approach.

"One way is the parents choose to pay for the costs not covered by the student loan awards. Another is to help the student pay their loans for a few years. They face the same concerns, is it necessary for them to take out loans to do that? If they want to help pay their child's loans, they could ongoing budgeted money, savings and private loans.

"But the **FSA** program is also available for parents to take out loans. When **FSA** loans are awarded to the student, the college also indicates what amount of money the parents can borrow too. So you need to know about the parent **FSA** loans too. They are essentially the same as Undergraduate loans except for the interest rates. So let's take a look at the differences."

Parent loan FSA Loan Rates

"An undergraduate student can get **FSA** awarded assistance from his or her parents by their taking out what are called **Direct PLUS Loans**. For a **Direct PLUS Loan** the amount the parents are allowed to borrow is also determined by the college their child enters. The maximum combined amount the student and parents can borrow is the cost of attendance (tuition, fees, room and board, and other school charges) minus any other financial assistance. Repayment options are the same for parents as for students. As I mentioned, the loan rates differ. So I put together a table for those in my computer. Here's a print out as well."

Parent Direct PLUS Loans				
Period of Disbursement				
July 1, 2014 - June 30, 2015	July 1, 2015 - June 30, 2016	July 1, 2016 - June 30, 2017	July 1, 2017 - June 30, 2018	
Annual Rate of Interest				
7.210%	6.840%	6.310%	7.00%	
Date of First Disbursement				
August 1, 2014	August 1, 2015	August 1, 2016	August 1, 2017	August 1, 2018
Origination Fee Rate				
4.288%	4.292%	4.272%	4.276%	4.264%

"You can see it's just like the one I did for Undergraduate loans. But all the values for loan rates are different. So, are they lower or higher values? And what does it indicate about the parents' loan costs compared to the student for the same **LOAN AMOUNT**?"

After looking at both print outs, Nicole responds. "The loan rates are a lot higher. So the parents' loan costs will be higher."

"That's right. So let's look into that."

Parent Base Loans

"Similar to what I did for an Undergraduate loan, let's examine a Parent **Direct PLUS Loan** for a base **LOAN AMOUNT** of $1000.00."

SITUATION 14

"Assume Tina is pursuing a 4-year undergraduate degree. She had taken out an unsubsidized **FSA** loan for a **LOAN AMOUNT** of $1000.00 that was disbursed half on August 1, 2017 and half on February 1, 2018. To assist her, Tina's parents also took out a **Direct PLUS Loan** for a **LOAN AMOUNT** of $1000.00.

"For both loans the **ORIGINATION FEE RATE** was timed to the first disbursement. Both are on the **Standard** repayment plan with a 5-year **TERM**. Tina and her parents defer repayment on the loan until she graduates in May 2018 and will use the 6-month grace period. Since they will pay the **MONTHLY INTEREST** due during the differed/grace period, their **PRINCIPAL** amounts will be unchanged.

"Tina's repayment is exactly the same as for Baxter in SITUATION 10. Let's examine the repayment results for her parents' loan. Looking at my table, what are the loan rates?"

Looking it over, Nicole indicates, "The **ORIGINATION FEE RATE** is 4.276%. The **ANNUAL RATE OF INTEREST** is for the period of July 1, 2017 – June 30, 2018, so 7.00%."

"You're correct. I've done the loan costs calculations so let's look at them."

ORIGINATION FEE = (4.276%/100) ($1000.00) = $42.76
PRINCIPAL = LOAN AMOUNT – ORIGINATION FEE
$= \$1000.00 - \$42.76 = \$957.24$
MONTHLY RATE OF INTEREST = 7.00%/12 months = 0.583%/month (rounded)
MRATIO = 0.583/100 = 0.00583
TERM = 5 years x 12 months/year = 60 months
$(\textbf{MRATIO} + 1)^{\textbf{TERM}} = (1 + 0.00583)^{60} = (1.00583)^{60}$
$= (1.00583)(1.00583)(1.00583)..... \textbf{60 times!}$
$= 1.42 \textbf{ (rounded)}$

$$\text{NUMERATOR} = \text{PRINCIPAL x MRATIO x (MRATIO + 1)}^{\text{TERM}}$$
$$= 957.24 \times 0.0583 \times 1.42 = 7.92 \text{ (rounded)}$$
$$\text{DENOMINATOR} = \text{(MRATIO + 1)}^{\text{TERM}} - 1 = 1.42 - 1 = 0.42$$
$$\text{MPAYMENT} = \text{NUMERATOR/DENOMINATOR} = 7.92/0.42$$
$$= \$18.86 \text{ (rounded)}$$
$$= \$18.95 \text{ (more precise)}$$

AMORTIZATION SCHEDULE :

Loan Amount	1000.00						Principal 957.24	
Origination Fee Rate	4.276%							
Origination Fee	42.92							
Term in Years	Annual Rate of Interest	Month	Monthly Payment	Applied to Interest	Applied to Principal		Outstanding Principal	Cumulative Interest
5	7.00	1	18.95	5.58	13.37		697.10	5.58
		2	18.95	4.07	14.89		435.44	9.65
		12	18.95	4.70	14.25		791.54	61.76
		24	18.95	3.67	15.28		613.87	111.54
		36	18.95	2.57	16.39		423.35	148.47
		48	18.95	1.38	17.57		219.06	171.64
		60	18.95	0.11	18.84		0.00	180.03

SITUATION 14 – CONTINUED

Dad asks, "How much is the parents' **CUMULATIVE INTEREST** compared to Tina's loan?"

"Well it's $180.03. I see that it was $115.96 for Baxter, I mean Lisa. It's higher."

"Ok. What about the **TOTAL COST,** adding in the **ORIGINATION FEE**?"

"Tina's parents pay $180.03 + $42.76 = $222.79 in **TOTAL COST**. From SITUATION 10 Tina's base loan the **TOTAL COST** was $126.65. I don't have a calculator to get the difference, but her parents pay a lot more."

"That's right. Let me do it in mine. The parents pay $222.79 - $126.65 = $96.14 more than Tina. That's 78.90% more **TOTAL COST**. That occurred even though their **MONTHLY PAYMENT** was $18.95 compared to $18.36 for their daughter."

"Hmm? That's something, Dad. Why did that happen?"

"One reason is the much higher **ORIGINATION FEE RATE** they paid. Another reason is their **ANNUAL RATE OF INTEREST** of 7.00%, compared the 4.45% of their daughter, leads to a much higher portion of their **MONTHLY PAYMENT** being **APPLIED TO INTEREST**."

Parent Base-Loan Table

"Having the results for a Parent base loan of $1000.00, Tina and her parents could scale them for any **LOAN AMOUNT** each might take out. The amounts could be different for each of them, too. But it's a lot easier if they have a table like the **UG-BASE LOAN TABLE** I developed for the Undergraduate loans. I put one together.

"I repeated SITUATION 14 for the other disbursement periods and the possible **TERMs** of the loan. I've listed the summary results in a **PARENT-BASE LOAN TABLE** or **P-BASE LOAN TABLE** for short."

PARENT-BASE LOAN TABLE							
				STANDARD REPAYMENT		EXTENDED REPAYMENT		
LOAN AMOUNT = 1000.00			TERM	5 Years	10 Years	15 Years	20 Years	25 Years
DISBURSED	ANNUAL RATE OF INTEREST	ORIG. FEE	PRINCIPAL	MONTHLY PAYMENT				
7/1/14-6/30/15	7.21%	42.88	957.12	19.05	11.22	8.72	7.54	6.89
7/1/15-6/30/16	6.84%	42.92	957.08	18.88	11.03	8.52	7.33	6.67
7/1/16-6/30/17	6.310%	42.72	957.28	18.64	10.78	8.24	7.03	6.35
7/1/17-6/30/18	7.00%	42.76	957.24	18.95	11.11	8.60	7.42	6.77
DISBURSED	ANNUAL RATE OF INTEREST	ORIG. FEE	PRINCIPAL	CUMULATIVE INTEREST				
7/1/14-6/30/15	7.21%	42.88	957.12	185.71	388.90	611.69	852.88	1110.92
7/1/15-6/30/16	6.84%	42.92	957.08	175.67	366.97	576.00	801.78	1043.04
7/1/16-6/30/18	6.310%	42.72	957.28	161.43	335.99	525.77	730.02	047.81
7/1/17-6/30/18	7.00%	42.76	957.24	180.03	376.46	591.47	822.91	1072.43

"Do you see the similarity, Nicole?"

"Yes, I do. It looks like the same table but of course all the listed values are different."

"That's right. The next thing I did was to scale the base results for the **LOAN AMOUNTS** of $30000.00 and $57500.00. That way we can compare the results with those for an Undergraduate loan. Here are those scaled results."

PARENT							
DISBURSED 7/1/15-6/30/16	ANNUAL RATE OF INTEREST = 7.00%%	TERM =	5 Years	10 Years	15 Years	20 Years	25 Years
LOAN AMOUNT	ORIGINATION FEE (RATE: 4.276%)	PRINCIPAL	MONTHLY PAYMENT				
1000.00	42.92	957.08	18.88	11.03	8.52	7.33	6.67
30000.00	1282.80	28717.20	568.50	333.30	258.00	222.60	203.10
57500.00	2458.70	55041.30	1089.63	638.83	494.50	426.65	389.28
LOAN AMOUNT	ORIGINATION FEE (RATE: 4.292%)	PRINCIPAL	CUMULATIVE INTEREST				
1000.00	42.92	957.08	175.67	366.97	576.00	801.78	1043.04
30000.00	1282.80	28717.20	5400.90	11293.80	17744.10	24687.30	32172.90
57500.00	2458.70	55041.30	10351.73	21646.45	34009.53	47317.33	61664.73

"Other than the resulting values being different, you can see the replication again. How do the results generally compare with what I got for the Undergraduate loans?"

Looking over both results, Nicole observes "All the **MONTHLY PAYMENT** and **CUMULATIVE INTEREST** values are higher for the parents than for the student."

"Yes, that's as expected. I calculated how much difference there is.

"For the **LOAN AMOUNT** of $30000.00, the **MONTHLY PAYMENT** is noticeably higher for each **TERM**. It ranges from $568.50 for 5 years down to $203.10 for 25 years. These compare to $552.60 and $164.10, respectively, for the undergraduate student. The amount for the parents is about 3% higher for the former and 24% higher for the latter.

"The **CUMULATIVE INTEREST** is dramatically higher, ranging from $5400.90 for 5 years up to $32172.90 for 25 years. These compare to $3478.80 and $19558.50, respectively, for the undergraduate student. The amount for the parents is about 55% higher for the former and 65% higher for the latter."

"Gosh, Dad, when you do it that way it really shows how much more parents have to pay in loan costs."

"There's more to observe. For the 25-year **TER** the **CUMULATIVE INTEREST** of $32172.90 is more than the **LOAN AMOUNT** of $30000.00. To be specific it's 107% of it. If you look back, you'll see that for the Undergraduate loan it was only 65%."

Astonished, Nicole gasps, "I kind of remember that and thinking 65% was Yikes! It's beyond incredible to see the 107%. It's interesting that it happens even though the **MONTHLY PAYMENT** doesn't change nearly as much."

Dad points out, "These results illustrate that if the child and parents each borrow the same total **LOAN AMOUNT**, it is not actually a 50-50 deal. Indeed, it's far from it. But parents being parents, they probably would be pleased that their son or daughter chose to incur loans for half of the needed **LOAN AMOUNT** as opposed to expecting them to incur 100.00% while the child incurs 0.00%. The child would benefit by not being required to pay the entire amount, either.

"Nicole, what do you think happens with the **LOAN AMOUNT** of $57500.00?"

"Wouldn't the all the loan cost results be almost twice as much?"

"That's right. However, the two values for percent increases are only a little lower. The actual values are 64% and 105%."

"Notice that for a 25-year **TERM**, the **CUMULATIVE INTEREST** is $61664.73!"

"I saw that. I cannot even imagine so much interest."

"And if you combine it with the student's interest it's about $100000.00!"

"Let's take a look at a more realistic example."

SITUATION 15

"Assume the parents of David in our SITUATION 13 assisted him by using **Direct PLUS Loans** over the same disbursement periods for the duration of his education. They were for the same **LOAN AMOUNTS** but had a 10-year **TERM**. They also began repaying after David's 6-month grace period. All **MONTHLY INTEREST** during the deferred/grace period was paid.

"How do we calculate the loan costs, Sweetie?"

"I guess it's the same way you did it for David, except you use the base results for the **P-BASE LOAN TABLE**."

"You guessed right again, if it was a guess. Here are my calculations."

The SCALING FACTORS are the same values as for David.

$$\text{ORIGINATION FEES} = 3.20 \times \$42.88 + 3.40 \times \$42.92$$
$$+ 4.10 \times \$42.72 + 3.00 \times \$42.76$$
$$= \$137.22 + \$145.93 + \$175.15 + \$128.28$$
$$= \$586.58$$

$$\text{MONTHLY PAYMENTS} = 3.20 \times \$11.22 + 3.40 \times \$11.03$$
$$+ 4.10 \times \$10.78 + 3.00 \times \$11.11$$
$$= \$35.90 + \$37.50 + \$44.20 + \$33.33$$
$$= \$150.93$$

$$\text{CUMULATIVE INTEREST} = 3.20 \text{ x } \$388.90 + 3.40 \text{ x } \$366.97$$
$$+ 4.10 \text{ x } \$335.99 + 3.00 \text{ x } \$376.46$$
$$= \$1244.48 + \$1247.70 + \$11377.56 + \$1129.38$$
$$= \$4999.12$$

$$\text{TOTAL COST} = \$586.58 + \$4999.12 = \$5585.70$$

$$\text{PERCENT TOTAL COST} = \text{FRACTION x } 100 = \$5585.70/\$13700.00 \text{ x } 100 = 40.77\%$$

SITUATION 15 - CONTINUED

"Nicole, what's the parents' **TOTAL COST** compared to David's?"

"Let me check that. Oh, I see for David it was $1767.62. His is a whole lot lower."

"Indeed it is. Adding the two, their combined **TOTAL COST** is $5585.70 + $1767.62, which is $7353.32. Of that the parents paid about 76% of it."

"The parents' **PERCENT TOTAL COST** is 40.77%. How's that compared to David's?"

"For David it was 12.90%. His is a whole lot lower, too."

"Yes it is. That's because David had a much lower **ORIGINATION FEE RATE** and **ANNUAL RATE OF INTEREST**.

"Let me make another observation. David incurs $13700.00 plus $1767.62 toward his college costs. That's $15467.62. For his parents the amount is $13700.00 + **$5585.70** = $19285.70. Combined that's $34753.32. Of that David incurs about 45%. His parents incur about 55%. David's **MONTHLY PAYMENT** is $251.16. His parents' is $150.93. But his parents pay twice as long.

"If David's parents used a 5-year **TERM** like he did, then their **TOTAL COST** would be considerably lessened. I calculated it. It would be $2980.08. As to the shared cost overall, it would become $16680.08 for the parents. That changes the proportions to 48% for David and 52% for his parents. It's closer to a 50-50 arrangement. However, the parents' **MONTHLY PAYMENT** would be $258.43, considerably higher"

"Based on my hypothetical SITUATION, what's your reaction, Nicole?"

"It's interesting how that comes out. It's strange the parents are charged more to borrow the same amount of money. It doesn't seem fair."

"Maybe it isn't. In the end it's a matter of the student and parents working together to figure out the puzzle involved in evaluating the costs of different colleges, the necessity and/or desirability of borrowing the some or all of funds and the ability to afford their repayment. In order to do that it is necessary to estimate future costs of any **Direct PLUS Loans**. That can be done in the same way as I did for Undergraduate loans, just using their corresponding loan rates.

"As the simplest approach, the base results for the current **ANNUAL RATE OF INTEREST** of 7.00%

would be scaled for the **LOAN AMOUNTS** of interest. Otherwise, the base results for the **ANNUAL RATE OF INTEREST** of either the lowest rate 6.31% or highest rate of 7.21% could be used based on the trend of bank interest rates. Doing both would provide a rational range of projected costs.

"I think you know the drill?"

"I can see it's the same as you showed me for Emily, just using the different numbers from your **PARENT-BASE LOAN TABLE**. I think I can do it."

"I think so too. In case you want to try it here are some voluntary homework exercises and some of the answers."

Exercise 17: *For the parents of Emily in SITUATION 11, develop a corresponding table for their estimated loan costs for the same LOAN AMOUNTS and TERMS..*

Your __partial__ results should be:

PARENT				TERM	5 Years	10 Years	15 Years
DISBURSED	ANNUAL RATE OF INTEREST	LOAN AMOUNT	ORIGINATION FEE	PRINCIPAL	MONTHLY PAYMENT	MONTHLY PAYMENT	MONTHLY PAYMENT
7/1/14-6/30/15	7.21%	5500.00	235.84	?	104.78	61.71	?
7/1/16-6/30/17	6.31%	5500.00	?	5265.14	102.52	?	45.32
7/1/17-6/30/18	7.00%	5500.00	235.18	5264.82	?	61.11	?
7/1/14-6/30/15	7.21%	7500.00	?	7178.40	142.88	?	65.40
7/1/16-6/30/17	6.31%	7500.00	320.40	7179.60	?	80.85	61.80
7/1/17-6/30/18	7.00%	7500.00	320.70	?	140.40	83.33	?
					CUMULATIVE INTEREST	CUMULATIVE INTEREST	CUMULATIVE INTEREST
7/1/14-6/30/15	7.21%	5500.00	235.84	?	?	2138.95	3364.30
7/1/16-6/30/17	6.31%	5500.00	234.96	5265.04	887.87	1847.95	?
7/1/17-6/30/18	7.00%	5500.00	?	5264.82	990.17	?	3253.09
7/1/14-6/30/15	7.21%	7500.00	?	7178.40	1392.83	?	?
7/1/16-6/30/17	6.31%	7500.00	320.40	7179.60	1210.73	2519.93	3943.28
7/1/17-6/30/18	7.00%	7500.00	320.70	?	?	2823.45	4436.03

Exercise 18: *Calculate the results for David's parents in SITUATION 15 for consecutive LOAN AMOUNTS of $5500.00, $6500.00, $7500.00 and 7500.00; a total of $27000.00. Do it for a) a 5-year TERM and b) a 25-year TERM.*

Your <u>partial</u> results should be:

ORIGINATION FEE *= $1155.92*
For 5-year TERM: ***CUMULATIVE INTEREST*** *= $4724.21*
For 25-year ***TERM: MONTHLY PAYMENT*** *= $229.64*

"Maybe I'll give them a try later."

"It's almost dinner time so let's stop for now. Tomorrow is Saturday. Can we continue then?"

"Dad, I work but will be free after one in the afternoon. How about three o'clock?"

"Ok, let's meet then."

Other Shared Loan Proportions

Typically a high school graduate would not have cash in an amount necessary for college educational costs. The author assumed that the child and parents each made a commitment to **FSA** loans. <u>Each</u> borrowed <u>half</u> the total loan funds amount needed. In the SITUATIONS and Exercises the **LOAN AMOUNTS** for Parent loans were equal to those of the accompanying Undergraduate student loans. Baxter and his parents borrowed the same amount. David and his parents borrowed the same amount. Other parents might do otherwise. As indicated in **APPENDIX I**, there are also **ANNUAL** and **AGGREGATE LIMTS** on the **LOAN AMOUNTS** a student can borrow; but not the parents. (Indeed those amounts were used in Exercises 16 and 18.) That circumstance can necessitate that the parents borrow more than the student. Whatever the arrangement chosen, the tabulated results in the **UG-** and **P-BASE LOAN TABLES** can be used to determine the respective loan costs. Of course, usually the parents would also incur the costs not covered by the loans and any financial aid grants the child might receive.

Apart from the dialogue between Nicole and her Dad, let's look at some other shared loan scenarios.

SITUATION 16

Phil needed **FSA** loans to complete his undergraduate degree. He graduated in May, 2018 and had needed to borrow $45000.00. His parents agreed to incur $18000.00 if Phil incurred $27000.00, which he did. Phil's **LOAN AMOUNTS** for each year were Loan 1 = $5500.00, Loan 2 = $6500.00, Loan 3 = $7500.00 and Loan 4 = $7500.00. Phil's parents' amounts were of his. For all loans Phil has a **TERM** of 15 years. His parents' loans have a **TERM** of 10 years.

Each yearly award was disbursed half on August 1and half on the following February 1. All repayments were deferred until his graduating and repayment begin after a 6-month grace period. All **MONTHLY INTEREST** was paid during the deferred/grace periods. Using the base results for the **UG-BASE LOAN TABLE** and the **P-BASE LOAN TABLE**, the repayment results are:

For Phil's Loan:

The SCALING FACTORS are: Loan 1 = 5.50, Loan 2 = 6.50, Loan 3 = 7.50, and Loan 4 = 7.50.

$$\text{ORIGINATION FEES} = 5.50 \times \$10.72 + 6.50 \times \$10.73$$
$$+ 7.50 \times \$10.68 + 7.50 \times \$10.69$$
$$= \$288.98$$

$$\text{MONTHLY PAYMENTS} = 5.50 \times \$7.65 + 6.50 \times \$7.46$$
$$+ 7.50 \times \$7.20 + 8.50 \times \$7.50$$
$$= \$201.12$$

$$\text{CUMULATIVE INTEREST} = 5.50 \times \$387.55 + 6.50 \times \$353.91$$
$$+ 7.50 \times \$306.58 + 7.50 \times \$368.41$$
$$= \$9494.37$$

The TOTAL COST = \$288.98 + \$9494.37 = \$9783.95. The PERCENT TOTAL COST = FRACTION x 100 = \$9783.95/\$27000.00 x 100 = 36.23%.

For his Parents' loans:

The SCALING FACTORS (rounded) are Loan 1 = 3.67, Loan 2 = 4.33, Loan 3 = 5.00 and Loan 4 = 5.00.

$$\text{ORIGINATION FEES} = 3.67 \times \$42.88 + 4.33 \times \$42.92$$
$$+ 5.00 \times \$42.72 + 5.00 \times \$42.76$$
$$= \$770.61$$

$$\text{MONTHLY PAYMENTS} = 3.67 \times \$11.22 + 4.33 \times \$11.03$$
$$+ 5.00 \times \$10.78 + 5.00 \times \$11.11$$
$$= \$198.39$$

$$\text{CUMULATIVE INTEREST} = 3.67 \times \$388.90 + 4.33 \times \$366.97$$
$$+ 5.00 \times \$335.99 + 5.00 \times \$376.46$$
$$= \$6578.49$$

The TOTAL COST = \$770.61+ \$6578.49 = \$7349.11. The PERCENT TOTAL COST = FRACTION x 100 = \$7349.11/\$18000.00 x 100 = 40.83%.

SITUATION 16 – CONTINUED

"For the shared loans, the combined **TOTAL COST** = \$9494.37 + \$7349.11 = \$16843.48. Of this amount, Phil incurs about 56% and his parents incur about 44%.

Exercise 19: *Repeat SITUATION 16 if Phil considers a* **TERM** *of 10 years and his parents consider a* **TERM** *of 15 years.*

Your partial results should be:

For Phil's loans: **MONTHLY PAYMENT** = $273.77, **CUMULATIVE INTEREST** = $6145.28.

For his parents' loans: **ORIGINATION FEE** = $770.61; **MONTHLY PAYMENT** = $153.09.

For Phil's and his parents' loans combined: **TOTAL COST** = $17530.06. *Phil pays about 36.7% of the* **TOTAL COST.**

SITUATION 17

Betsy, an undergraduate student, graduated in May 2018. She needed **FSA** loans to complete her degree. She only borrowed money in the last two years of her studies. The **LOAN AMOUNT** was $5500.00 each year. Her parents borrowed $2500.00 each year. Half was disbursed on August 1 and half on the following February 1. Betsy's loans each have a **TERM** of 10 years. Her parents have a **TERM** of 5 years. Repayment will begin after a 6-month grace period. During deferment and grace periods, the **MONTHLY INTEREST** was and will be paid.

Using the base results for the **UG**- and the **P-BASE LOAN TABLE**, the repayment results are:

For Betsy's loans:

The SCALING FACTORS are: Loan 1 = 5.50 and Loan 2 = 5.50.

ORIGINATION FEES = 5.50 x $10.68 + 5.50 x $10.69 = $117.54

MONTHLY PAYMENTS = 5.50 x $9.90 + 5.50 x $10.23 = $110.72

CUMULATIVE INTEREST = 5.50 x $199.15 + 5.50 x $238.20 = $2405.43

Betsy's TOTAL COST = $117.54 + $2405.43 = $2522.96. Her PERCENT TOTAL COST = FRACTION x 100 = $2522.96/$11000.00 x 100 = 22.94%.

For her parents' loans:

The SCALING FACTORS are Loan 1 = 2.50 and Loan 2 = 2.50.

ORIGINATION FEES = 2.50 x $42.72 + 2.50 x $42.76 = $213.70

MONTHLY PAYMENTS = 2.50 x $18.64 + 2.50 x $18.95 = $93.98

CUMULATIVE INTEREST = 2.50 x $161.43 + 2.50 x $180.03 = $853.65

Betsy's parents' TOTAL COST = $213.70 + $853.65 = $1067.35. Their PERCENT TOTAL COST = FRACTION x 100 = $1067.35/$5000.00 x 100 = 21.35%.

SITUATION 17 – CONTINUED

For the shared loans the combined **TOTAL COST = $2522.96 + $1067.35 = $3590.01**. Of this amount, Betsy incurs about 70% and her parents incur about 30%. Betsy's face sags. Her parents smile.

Exercise 20: *Reverse the circumstances in SITUATION-17. Betsy borrowed $2500.00 with a* **TERM** *of 5 years. Her parents borrowed $5500.00 with a* **TERM** *of 10 years.*

Your *partial* results should be*:

The outcome for Betsy is the **ORIGINATION FEE** *= $53.43 and* **TOTAL COST** *= $586.95.*

The outcome for the parents is the **MONTHLY PAYMENT** *= $120.40 and* **TOTAL COST** *= $4388.62.*

Of the combined **TOTAL COST***, Betsy incurs about 12% and her parents incur about 88%. Betsy smiles. Her parents' faces sag.*

It's Saturday afternoon. At 2:30, Nicole's cell phone sounds out its Walk in the Forest alarm tone. Being tired after work at Comic Cones, she had set it so she could rest before meeting with her Dad at 3:00. Knowing her future college costs are the topic, she springs up readily. A quick face wash and she's on her way to his office.

"Hi Dad! Are you ready to tell me which of my college choices we can afford?"

"Hi Nicole! Good afternoon.

"I haven't got that magic crystal ball yet and I don't see one in your arms. So that's not quite in the cards. But we can get a reasonable look at it. Nothing firm yet, but a sense of what we can estimate and what we cannot is what we'll try for. Then we'll crunch some trial numbers. Actually, we'll crunch a lot of numbers. So are you in a number crunching mood?"

"Sounds like a dance, but I know it isn't. I'm as ready as I'll ever be. So let's start crunching those digits."

"Ok, let's start with a bigger picture of the costs involved in going to college. I actually went to some college web sites to see what they say about costs. They all seem to have a lot of detailed cost data. There's more to it than just tuition and fees. I knew that but it was helpful to see how those colleges list them.

"Typically, costs are separated into Direct Costs and Indirect Costs. Direct Costs include tuition, fees and room and board. When enrolled they are fixed and billed by the university to the student's account. Room and board rates are given for a double room and a full meal plan. Indirect Costs include books, supplies, transportation, and miscellaneous expenses. They base them on average living costs. Of course the university does not bill them. For books and supplies, usually an account can be set up with the campus bookstore. Often an account system exists for students to also charge other things on campus such as food at vendors in the student center. I'm not sure but I suppose they can be like a debit card system. Otherwise, a normal credit card can be used as well. Transportation is pay as you go. As students may or may not have a car, may or may not live close enough for occasional trips home there's a lot of variation. So their estimate is stated as a rough number, what we call a "ball park" figure."

"What's a debit card system?"

"Basically, you would have an account set up and place a certain amount of money in it. Then you spend it down as you pay for things using your debit card. Periodically you replenish it. Since it does not involve paying interest it's not actually like a credit card where there interest charges are involved. So I won't go into the details. Besides, that's how a bank basically does it. I don't know how a college does it. At the time they'll tell you all about it.

"Of course, for a public college, tuition is much lower for residents of the state than for non-residents. And for some resident students, they could be commuting from home. For others and non-resident students they might be living off campus, paying rent and buying groceries. So on-campus room and board would not be applicable. But until it's a reality, let's just assume the estimate for room and board is good enough for off-campus living if you have a roommate. Of course you might have several roommates, so rent could be much lower. Those details we address when they become reality.

"Without looking into what some call top tier colleges, I got a general feel for yearly costs for public and private colleges. For private colleges, tuition and fees are between $30000 and $50000. They're essentially the same for residents and non-residents. For public colleges, they're between $10000 and $12000 for residents. For non-residents they're between $25000 and $30000. Room and board costs between $9000 and $12000. For finishing a degree in four years, multiply those by 4. Some students in fields like engineering and the sciences don't finish in four years; they take longer to complete their degrees.

"For yearly cost of indirect items, books seem to be about $1000 to $1200 per year, transportation around $1000. Miscellaneous other costs are about $1000 to $1500."

"That's an amazing amount of money Dad."

"Yes, it is.. But people manage to get through it. Most students get some amount of granted financial aid. Then they just add a lot of debt.

"For our purposes, let's settle on some costs to use for number crunching. The colleges you are considering have costs at the lower end, which is helpful. For the local Sure Thing University tuition and fees are $10000.00 and assume you would commute. For Hoped For University they are $26000.00. For Dream University the tuition and fees are $35000. Since the last two are both out–of–state add in $11000 for room and board. Let's add in $3500 for the indirect costs.

"For totals Sure Thing University is $13500, Dream University is $49500, and Hoped For University is $40500. Sure Thing University is by far the least cost. If you were to live on campus it would still only be $24500. Those costs will be going up each year, too."

Nicole sighs and the comments, "I'm seeing why Hoped For University and Dream University have fitting names. So am I headed to Sure Thing University?"

"That's not the point. We want to see if we can afford any one of them."

Estimating Loan Needs and Affordability

"Let's assume the costs go up 4% each year. So to get each succeeding year we multiply by 1.04 each time. We can then add them up to get the 4-year total. I did that and here are the results."

YEARLY COSTS

	Year 1	Year 2	Year 3	Year 4	TOTAL	AVERAGE
Sure Thing	13500	14040	14602	15040	57181	14295
Sure Thing-R&B	24500	25480	26499	27559	104038	26010
Hoped For	40500	42120	43805	45557	171982	42995
Dream	49500	51480	53539	55681	210200	52550

"Let's now assume the colleges give you financial aid. Based on your academics they give you gift aid of one third of the costs. From what I researched at other colleges, that's not unreasonable. Here are those amounts."

YEARLY GIFT AID

0.33333	Year 1	Year 2	Year 3	Year 4	TOTAL	AVERAGE
Sure Thing	4500	4680	4867	5013	19060	4765
Sure Thing-R&B	8167	8493	8833	9186	34679	8670
Hoped For	13500	14040	14601	15186	57327	14332
Dream	16500	17160	17846	18560	70066	17516

"Subtracting them reduces the costs to the following results."

YEARLY COSTS – YEARLY GIFT AID

0.666667	Year 1	Year 2	Year 3	Year 4	TOTAL	AVERAGE
Sure Thing	9000	9360	9734	10026	38121	9530
Sure Thing-R&B	16333	16987	17666	18373	69359	17340
Hoped For	27000	28080	29203	30371	114655	28664
Dream	33000	34320	35693	37121	140133	35033

"Mom and I have been saving money toward your college education. We've been doing that ever since we could afford to start doing so. Almost since the day you were born. So we saved $50000.00. That gives us $12500.00 per year. So let's now subtract that amount. That gives these results."

YEARLY COSTS – YEARLY GIFT AID – YEARLY SAVINGS

12500	Year 1	Year 2	Year 3	Year 4	TOTAL	AVERAGE
Sure Thing	-3500	-3140	-2766	-2474	-11879	-2970
Sure Thing-R&B	3833	4487	5166	5873	19359	4840
Hoped For	14500	15580	16703	17871	64655	16164
Dream	20500	21820	23193	24621	90133	22533

"What do these results tell you, Sweetie?"

"I see that if I commute then the cost of Sure Thing University is negative. So I guess they are going to pay us that amount? Just kidding, Dad! I understand it means you and Mom have saved enough money to pay for that option. That's wonderful that you did that."

"That's right. That's why we did it.

"But it also means we count on Sure Thing University giving you one third of the total cost. That's $19060. If they don't, we need to come up with $19060 – $11879 = $7181. That's only $1795 per year. So we can surely do that. So you can go to Sure Thing University but you don't necessarily have to do so."

"I don't intend to falter at school or get "senioritis" so my grades will still be great. I did very good on the college entrance exams and expect to do better the second time. So maybe I will get that gift aid."

"Ok, I'm confident you will. Mom and I can budget money during your college years. Right now it looks like about $1000 per month, which is $12000 annually. Let's say half that amount is for loan payments and half is for ongoing other college costs. If we subtract the $6000 for ongoing college cost we get this table."

YEARLY COSTS – YEARLY GIFT AID – YEARLY SAVINGS – YEARLY BUDGET

6000	Year 1	Year 2	Year 3	Year 4	TOTAL	AVERAGE
Sure Thing	-9500	-9140	-8766	-8474	-35879	-8970
Sure Thing-R&B	-2167	-1513	-834	-127	-4641	-1160
Hoped For	8500	9580	10703	11871	40655	10164
Dream	14500	15820	17193	18621	66134	16534

"I did a table for the costs assuming you get no gift aid. I think that's very unlikely but it gives us worst case costs. If we add gift aid amounts back in to the previous table the result is this one."

NO GIFT AID: YEARLY COSTS – YEARLY SAVINGS – YEARLY BUDGET

	Year 1	Year 2	Year 3	Year 4	TOTAL	AVERAGE
Sure Thing	-5000	-4460	-3898	-3460	-16819	-4205
Sure Thing-R&B	6000	6980	7999	9059	30038	7510
Hoped For	22000	23620	25305	27057	97982	24495
Dream	31000	32980	35039	37181	136200	34050

"For Sure Thing University, whether you live on campus or not, if you get the gift aid we can afford the costs without loans. If you did not get any gift aid then we would need **FSA** loans then we need loans for you to live on campus. It would be $7510 per year."

"So if I wanted to live on campus Sure Thing University is a not a sure thing for me unless I get gift aid?"

"We would just have to be able to borrow $7510 each year. That's probably easily workable. We'll look at it in a bit. What I'm doing now is seeing the **LOAN AMOUNTS** needed for different possibilities at each college. Now let's look at Hoped For University.

"Assuming you get the gift aid, we need $40655 in **FSA** loans. That's $10164 per year."

"That's an awful lot of money Dad. I only make about $350 a month working 12 hours each week at Comic Cones."

"At your age it is a lot of money. Once you finish college and work as a journalist it won't seem as bad. Now back to Hoped For University.

"If you don't get any gift aid, then we would need $97982 in **FSA** loans. That's $24495 per year."

"Now, that really is a lot of money even if I become a journalist."

"Indeed it is, even for Mom and Dad. But let's continue and look at Dream University.

"Assuming you get the gift aid, we would need $66134 in **FSA** loans. That's $16534 per year.

"If you don't get any gift aid, then we have $136200 in **FSA** loans. That's $34050 per year."

"Does a journalist even make that much money, Dad?"

"I don't know. It's something to consider though. What really counts is how much the **MONTHLY PAYMENT** and **CUMULATIVE INTEREST** amounts would be. We'll look at that too. Now you can see why students borrow so much money and can take up to twenty five years to repay their loans. And recall that a student can only borrow up to $57500 in total. That's why Parent loans come into the picture."

"Maybe I shouldn't become a journalist at all?"

"Peanut, I think you should pursue what your mind and heart gives you the passion to pursue. What we are doing now is examining how to finance that passionate pursuit. Examining the choices of college tells us the monetary targets in play. Then we see if we can reach them. No matter what, Sure Thing University really is a sure thing for you. It's our insurance policy. Now were working on the other choices."

Estimating Loan Costs and Affordability

"Here's a summary of the **FSA** loan needs. As you said, negative amount means we don't need any."

	With Gift Aid		Without Gift Aid	
LOAN AMOUNTS	**Total**	**Per Year**	**Total**	**Per Year**
Sure Thing	-35879	-8970	-16819	-4205
Sure Thing-R&B	-4641	-1160	30038	7510
Hoped For	40655	10164	97982	24495
Dream	66134	16534	136200	34050

"Wow! It's eye popping to see it all together, Dad."

"It is but it's also helpful. Now we can use these numbers to predict the **FSA** loan costs. I showed how we can do that in detail for a series of four annual loans. Once you are actually receiving acceptances and financial aid packages we would do that. But at this point in time and for our goal of a general assessment, we don't need to be that detailed.

"A dependent student can borrow up to $27000, if that amount is awarded. Right away we see some total **LOAN AMOUNTS** exceed that amount. Without gift aid they exceed them by a very large margin. That's when Parent loans come into play. You might say that's when the parents come to the rescue."

"I sure see that I need your help, indeed a rescue effort."

"From our parent perspective let's assume you borrow a total of $27000 for each case that the needed amount exceeds that amount. Your resulting loan needs are as follows."

	With Gift Aid		Without Gift Aid	
LOAN AMOUNTS	**Total**	**Per Year**	**Total**	**Per Year**
Sure Thing	-17939	-4485	-8409	-2102
Sure Thing-R&B	-2320	-580	15019	3755
Hoped For	20328	5082	27000	6750
Dream	27000	6750	27000	6750

"I've shown an average per year, but the individual **LOAN AMOUNTS** for the $27000 would be $5500, $6500, 7500 and $7500.

"How's that look to you Nicole?"

"That sure look less eye popping. But it's still lots of money."

"What we see is that if you do get the gift aid, then the resulting **LOAN AMOUNTS** are not so surprising. Recall that the average Undergraduate **FSA** loan debt is about that $28750. Most must be borrowing the full amount and even $31000 if they take more than four years to graduate. For Dream

University you need only $20328. That's encouraging."

"Let's turn to the Parent loans. That's an entirely different situation. Here are those needs."

	With Gift Aid		Without Gift Aid	
LOAN AMOUNTS	Total	Per Year	Total	Per Year
Sure Thing	-17939	-4485	-8409	-2102
Sure Thing-R&B	-2320	-580	15019	3755
Hoped For	20328	5082	70982	17746
Dream	39134	9784	109200	27300

"What do you see in these results, Sweetie?"

"I see how important the gift aid is to the affordability. Without it you have borrow an astounding amount of money. Without it, Hope For University and Dream University look like dead ends? If I don't get enough gift aid, I guess I'm headed to Sure Thing University?"

"I wouldn't say that yet. It's not encouraging but let's take a quick look at the projected loan costs. Later, we can look into it in more detail."

"Assume you get the gift aid and project the loan costs for the needed amounts. Also assume we pay only the interest during your school years and 6-month grace period. After that repayment will start on the four loans coincident and you will owe the full **LOAN AMOUNTS**. For simplicity, assume the four loans will be consolidated. I'll teach you about that as the time approaches. Basically you convert them to one loan for the combined amount owed. Let's use the highest listed **ANNUAL RATE OF INTEREST** of 4.66%. Scaling the base loan results for each university, here are the results."

UNDER-GRADUATE			STANDARD REPAYMENT		EXTENDED REPAYMANT		
DISBURSED 7/1/14-6/30/15	ANNUAL RATE OF INTEREST = 4.66%	TERM	5 Years	10 Years	15 Years	20 Years	25 Years
LOAN AMOUNT	ORIGINATION FEE (RATE = 1.072%)	PRINCIPAL	MONTHLY PAYMENT				
1000	10.72	989.28	18.52	10.33	7.65	6.34	5.59
HF 20328	218	20110	376	210	156	129	114
D 27000	289	26711	500	279	207	171	151
LOAN AMOUNT	ORIGINATION FEE (RATE = 1.072%)	PRINCIPAL	YEARLY AMOUNT				
1000	10.72	989.28	222	124	92	76	67
HF 20328	218	20110	4518	2520	1866	1547	1364
D 27000	289	26710	6000	3347	2479	2054	1811

LOAN AMOUNT	ORIGINATION FEE (RATE = 1.072%)	PRINCIPAL	CUMULATIVE INTEREST				
1000	10.72	989.27	122	250	388	535	687
HF 20328	218	28442	2472	5087	7878	10883	13974
D 27000	290	26710	3284	6756	10464	14401	18560
PERCENT CUMULATIVE INTEREST			12	25	39	54	69
PERCENT CUMULATIVE INTEREST/TERM			2.43	2.5	2.58	2.67	2.75

"To distinguish the two colleges I put an **HF** and **D** on the **LOAN AMOUNTS**. To avoid getting lost in decimal places I rounded the scaled results to whole numbers. I've also multiplied the **MONTHLY PAYMENT** amounts by 12 to get the **YEARLY AMOUNTS**. And I added a line showing the **PERCENT CUMULTIVE INTEREST** for each **TERM**.

"Let's consider the **YEARLY AMOUNT** values. How do they look to you, Nicole?"

"Compared to the huge numbers we were looking at before, they're a lot smaller. That's feels good, Dad. But what do they mean about affordability?"

"In the case of Hoped For University they range between $4518 for a 5-year **TERM** down to $1364 for a 25-year **TERM**. Having these you can consider how much a journalist makes yearly and get an idea of proportions.

"For example, if you earned $36000 per year, then after withholdings you might have $30000. Considering Hoped For University, $1364 is a very small proportion of that, so affordable. The $4518 amount is a lot more but probably affordable too. Actually, any repayment **TERM** is affordable. You should be able to afford any of the **MONTHLY PAYMENT** amounts."

"Oh, I see now. But what are "withholdings"?"

"For each monthly paycheck, an estimated amount is taken out for income taxes, social security and some other things. For your Comic Cones job you earn a very small amount so likely the withholding amounts for taxes are zero. For social security it would be pretty small amount. So you probably wouldn't notice."

"Well, you told me I did not have to file a tax return? And what's social security?"

"That's right. And you didn't. That's because what you earned was less the minimum amount for which you would have to pay taxes. One day you will have enough income and I will help you file tax returns. Social security is a government retirement program that you pay money into. When you are old enough to and do retire you will begin getting paid back out of this funds. At your age it's too early to think about."

"OK, I understand."

"For Hoped For University all the **TERMS** are affordable, but the 5-year **TERM** has **YEARLY**

AMOUNT of $4518, which is a **MONTHLY PAYMENT** of $376. Its **CUMULATIVE INTEREST** is only $2472.

"Perhaps the 10-year **TERM** with a **YEARLY AMOUNT** of $2520, which is a **MONTHLY PAYMENT** of $210, is a more manageable cost choice. But its **CUMULATIVE INTEREST** doubles to $5087. Possibly the 15-year **TERM** is necessary despite its even higher **CUMULATIVE INTEREST**. But we can decide that once we are considering actual financial aid packages.

"Nicole what about the affordability of the **MONTHLY PAYMENTS** and **YEARLY AMOUNTS** for Dream University?"

"Well, Dad. The **MONTHLY PAYMENTS** range from $500 down to $151. The **YEARLY AMOUNTS** range from $6000 down to $1811. So it seems it's not affordable for the 5-year **TERM**."

"You're correct for that **TERM**. But the **YEARLY AMOUNT** for a 10-year **TERM** is $3347, a **MONTHLY PAYMENT** of $279. The **CUMULATIVE INTEREST** is $6756. So, Dream University should be a manageable cost for that **TERM** and for longer ones."

"I can see that because you said the $4518 amount for Hoped For University was probably affordable. And $3347 is a lot less."

"Exactly! And, as expected, we see that as the **TERM** increases the **CUMULATIVE INTEREST** amount increases. For a 15-year **TERM** the **CUMULATIVE INTEREST** increases to $10464. We know that if a **MONTHLY PAYMENT** is manageable then so is the **CUMULATIVE INTEREST**. But is it a reasonable cost is the question.

"What are important now are the corresponding **PERCENT CUMULATIVE INTEREST** values. What do you see there and deduce?"

"Dad, I see that they increase from 12% to 69%. I know I want to keep that as low as possible. But I can't be and more specific."

"That's what I wanted you to see. If you divide them by the **TERM** you get an average yearly cost. . I did that and the results are in the bottom line of the tables. You see they increase from 2.43% per year to 2.75% per year. They're lower than the stated **ANNUAL RATE OF INTEREST** of 4.66%. That's due to the declining balance of amortization. They are reasonable. It's a choice of just how much is willing to pay in total as a percentage of the **LOAN AMOUNT**.

"Now let's look at the combined Parent loans using the highest listed **ANNUAL RATE OF INTEREST** of 7.21%. Here are my tabulated results."

PARENT							
DISBURSED 7/1/14-6/30/15	**ANNUAL RATE OF INTEREST = 7.21%%**	**TERM =**	**5 Years**	**10 Years**	**15 Years**	**20 Years**	**25 Years**
LOAN AMOUNT	**ORIGINATION FEE (RATE: 4.288%)**	**PRINCIPAL**	**MONTHLY PAYMENT**				
1000	42.88	957.12	19.05	11.22	8.72	7.54	6.89
HF 20328	872	19456	387	228	177	153	140
D 39134	1678	37456	746	439	341	295	270
LOAN AMOUNT	**ORIGINATION FEE (RATE: 4.288%)**	**PRINCIPAL**	**YEARLY AMOUNT**				
1000	42.88	957.08	229	135	105	90	83
HF 20328	872	19456	4647	2737	2127	1839	1681
D 39134	1678	37456	8946	5269	4095	3541	3236
LOAN AMOUNT	**ORIGINATION FEE (RATE: 4.288%)**	**PRINCIPAL**	**CUMULATIVE INTEREST**				
1000	42.88	957.08	186	389	612	853	1111
HF 20328	872	19456	3775	7906	12434	17337	22583
D 39134	1678	37456	7268	15219	23938	33377	43475
PERCENT CUMULATIVE INTEREST			19	39	61	85	111
PERCENT CUMULATIVE INTEREST/TERM			3.71	3.89	4.08	4.26	4.44

"For Hope For University our **LOAN AMOUNT** is the same as yours. We will pay somewhat more **CUMULATIVE INTEREST** than you, but the outcome is essentially the same as yours.

"As expected, for Dream University the **MONTHLY PAYMENT** amounts are noticeably higher. However, at face value the Undergraduate **MONTHLY PAYMENT** amounts that are affordable for you should be affordable for us, too. However, we have a much higher /interest rate than you.

"For a 20-year **TERM** our **MONTHLY PAYMENT** is $295, which is close to your $279. Our **YEARLY AMOUNT** is $3541, which close to your $3347. Both are just a wee bit higher. But our **CUMULATIVE INTEREST** is $33377 compared to your $6756.

"For a 15-year **TERM** our **MONTHLY PAYMENT** increases to $341 and the **YEARLY AMOUNT** is $4095, which is $423 less than that $4508 amount. And the **CUMULATIVE INTEREST** drops tp $23928. But we can afford those payments, as we budgeted $500 per month. We can even afford a 10-year **TERM**, the same as you. In that case, our **MONTHLY PAYMENT** increases to $439 but our **CUMULATIVE INTEREST** drops to $15219.

"It seems pretty clear that we cannot afford the **MONTHLY PAYMENT** of $746 for a 5-year **TERM** for Dream University.

"Are you with me on those observations, Peanut?"

"I follow what you said and it's clear you have more costs to cover than I do, by a lot."

133

"Nicole, what do you observe about the **PERCENT CUMULTIVE INTEREST** values?"

"They're a lot higher than mine. But I realize they should be."

"Right. For us it's much more costly and limiting the **TERM** is even more cost effective than for you. For our 10-year **TERM** it's 39% compared to your 25%. For our 15-year **TERM** it's 61% compared to your 39%. For our 20-year **TERM** it's 85% compared to your 54%."

"Dad, those percentages look very steep to me even at 25%?"

"I can understand But if you divide them by the **TERM** it look a lot better. Those values range from 3.71% to 4.44%. They are much less than the stated **ANNUAL RATE OF INTEREST** of 7.21%

"Now let's take on the possibility of no gift aid arising, albeit unlikely. Most likely you will receive some even if less than 1/3 of the costs. So we are looking a worst case situation. In your case, the **LOAN AMOUNT** is $27000 for both universities. Consequently, the results are the same for each and are equal to what they were for Dream University when gift aid was available. Nevertheless, it's useful to the tabulate the results."

UNDER - GRADUATE			STANDARD REPAYMENT		EXTENDED REPAYMANT		
DISBURSED 7/1/14-6/30/15	ANNUAL RATE OF INTEREST = 4.66%	TERM	5 Years	10 Years	15 Years	20 Years	25 Years
LOAN AMOUNT	ORIGINATION FEE (RATE = 1.072%)	PRINCIPAL	MONTHLY PAYMENT				
1000	10.72	989.28	18.52	10.33	7.65	6.34	5.59
HF 27000	289	26711	500	279	207	171	151
D 27000	289	26711	500	279	207	171	151
LOAN AMOUNT	ORIGINATION FEE (RATE = 1.072%)	PRINCIPAL	YEARLY AMOUNT				
1000	10.72	989.27	222	124	92	76	67
HF 27000	289	26710	6000	3347	2479	2054	1811
D 27000	289	26710	6000	3347	2479	2054	1811
LOAN AMOUNT	ORIGINATION FEE (RATE = 1.072%)	PRINCIPAL	CUMULATIVE INTEREST				
1000	10.72	989.27	122	250	388	535	687
HF 27000	290	26710	3284	6756	10464	14401	18560
D 27000	290	26710	3284	6756	10464	14401	18560
PERCENT CUMULATIVE INTEREST			12	25	39	54	69

"What does that mean regarding affordability, Nicole?"

"Hmm? I suppose if $27000 was affordable before, then it here too. That I can afford to pay my loans even if I don't get any gift aid."

"Precisely, Peanut. Let's look at the Parent loans if no gift aid materializes. I tabulated the results for our **LOAN AMOUNTS**."

PARENT							
DISBURSED 7/1/15-6/30/16	**ANNUAL RATE OF INTEREST = 7.21%%**	**TERM =**	**5 Years**	**10 Years**	**15 Years**	**20 Years**	**25 Years**
LOAN AMOUNT	**ORIGINATION FEE (RATE: 4.288%)**	**PRINCIPAL**	**MONTHLY PAYMENT**				
1000	42.88	957.12	19.05	11.22	8.72	7.54	6.89
HF 70982	3044	67938	1352	796	619	535	489
D 109204	4683	104521	2080	1225	952	823	752
LOAN AMOUNT	**ORIGINATION FEE (RATE: 4.288%)**	**PRINCIPAL**	**YEARLY AMOUNT**				
1000	42.88	957.08	229	135	105	90	83
HF 70982	3044	67938	16226	9557	7428	6422	5869
D 109204	4683	104521	24964	14703	11427	9881	9029
LOAN AMOUNT	**ORIGINATION FEE (RATE: 4.288%)**	**PRINCIPAL**	**CUMULATIVE INTEREST**				
1000	42.88	957.08	186	389	612	853	1111
HF 70982	3044	67938	13182	27605	43419	60539	78855
D 109204	4683	104521	20280	42469	66799	93138	121317
PERCENT CUMULATIVE INTEREST			19	39	61	85	111

"In regard to Hoped For University it appears that we would need to take out a loan for either a 20-year or a 25-year **TERM**. For the former it would stretch the **MONTHLY PAYMENT** to $535, a bit more than our planned budget of $500. But if we save a little more, we could manage that. On the other hand, the **CUMULATIVE INTEREST** is substantial, $60539 or $78855.."

"For Dream University, even with a 25-year **TERM** our **MONTHLY PAYMENT** is $752. That's 50% more than we budgeted."

"If I understand you Dad, the Parent loans Hoped For University are feasible even without gift aid but at a high loan cost. And, oh gosh, without gift aid **DREAM UNIVERISITY** is out is out of reach. So I better get that gift aid?"

"You're correct on the loan observations. As to feeling you "better get that gift aid?" That's an incorrect perspective. This exercise is not intended to put pressure on you about that. As I said before, it is to look at a worst case outcome. Above all, I have no doubt that you will get gift aid. Yes, the results are telling me that to afford Dream University, getting one-third of the cost covered by gift aid is needed. We'll just have to wait and see if you get that. It could be more or less than that. If it's more, then that's all the better. And you'll be learning Dream University's alma mater. If it's lower, as long as it's in the ball park, then your dream might be in reach even without gift aid. If turns out to be the best academic decision, we take a much closer look at it once you are admitted to these colleges and have actual financial aid packages to look at."

"That makes me feel so wonderful Dad, that you want me to h ave the chance so much. But I do plan to keep up my school work no matter what so I can get as much gift aid as possible, to keep costs as low as possible. In time, with my teachers and you helping me, I will figure out which of these universities is the correct academic choice for me."

"I just remembered one sort of secondary consideration. The **LOAN AMOUNTS** are our projected needs, but when the funds are disbursed the **ORIGINATION FEE** is taken out at the outset. So the net funds are less than the projected need. When gift aid is included, the **ORIGINATION FEE** is only a few hundred dollars for the Undergraduate loans, so relatively very small compared to the other loan costs. For Parent loans it can reach about $1400, so more noticeable. I don't see that as an obstacle, and it could turn out that the gift aid is a bit higher than we estimated. Without gift aid, it is still hundreds of dollars for the Undergraduate loans. But for the Parent loans it's a few thousand dollars. Relatively it's still very small, but in actual dollars it isn't. It's not worth the time to consider it now. But once we are doing this for real, if necessary we would tweak things to take into account."

Paying Interest While in Deferment

"Another consideration is the **CUMULATIVE INTEREST** amount that would be paid while you are in college and deferment. For the analysis we did, it was assumed that would be paid during that time. So let's estimate how much that would be."

"Yeah, and if I need to be paying that then I would need to work during college."

"Actually we would aim to pay that for you during that time. If you do work and it does not interfere with your studies, you can use it for some of the living costs to offset it a bit."

"That's great Dad and I appreciate it very much."

"The four annual loans occur in different years. And actually half of the **LOAN AMOUNT** is disbursed in each semester. So there are eight timings. Each succeeding disbursement is in place for a shorter time than the preceding one. The calculation could be done in a very detailed way by treating each of the disbursements separately. Then one calculates the **CUMULATIVE INTEREST** for the applicable period of time for each of them. Until we have actual situations at hand, that's too involved. Instead I did the following approximate calculations.

"I used the **ANNUAL RATE OF INTEREST** of 4.66%. I have the average annual **LOAN AMOUNT** for each scenario. Those amounts are for the split loans. I multiplied that amount by 4.66/100 to get the interest for 1 year and then by 4 to get **APPROXIMATE YEARLY INTEREST** for the four annual loans combined.

"Assuming each loan is disbursed in total on August 1 and including a 6-month grace period, the first loan has 51 months of payments. The fourth loan has only 15. The average number is 33 months, 2 years plus 9 months. That's 2.75 years. So I multiplied the **APPROXIMATE YEARLY INTEREST** by 2.75 to get the **APPROXIMATE CUMULATIVE INTEREST** for the four loans. Does that make sense to you?"

"Sort of, Dad. But to be sure I would have to think it out a little more as to why it works, especially for the number of months. But I trust you on it?"

"I understand you might be mentally scratching your head, Sweetie."

"To illustrate the calculations, I'll use Hoped For University and case of gift aid being awarded. For that case average yearly **LOAN AMOUNT** was $10164. Split in two that was $5082. Here is the calculation."

$$\textbf{APPROXIMATE YEARLY INTEREST = AVG. LOAN AMOUNT x 4.66/100 x 4}$$

$$\textbf{= \$5082 x 4.66/100 x 4 = \$947 (rounded)}$$

$$\textbf{APPROXIMATE CUMULATIVE INTEREST = \$947 x 2.75 = \$2604}$$

"Is it clearer now?"

"I do see how the calculations are done, but still will trust you on the nitty gritty of the logic. But, that's a lot of interest to be paid."

"Yes, it does look so. But that's paid over 51 months, so on average it is $2604/4.33 = $601 per year. That's $50 per month. So for this case and the Undergraduate loans it's not awful. And we are using averages. In reality, it starts with just one loan. Without explaining why, for that first loan it's about that amount divided by 2.5, or $20 per month. When the next loan kicks in it becomes $40 per month. When the third and fourth ones kick in it becomes $60 per month and then $80 per month.

"I also did the calculation for the Parent loan using an **ANNUAL RATE OF INTEREST** of 7.21%."

$$\textbf{APPROXIMATE YEARLY INTEREST = AVG. LOAN AMOUNT x 7.21/100 x 4}$$

$$\textbf{= \$5082 x 7.21/100 x 4 = \$1466}$$

$$\textbf{APPROXIMATE CUMULATIVE INTEREST = \$1466 x 2.75 = \$4032}$$

"Wow! Dad. That's a lot more than for my loans."

"Yes it is. On average that's $403/4.33 = $931 per year, $78 per month. For the first loan it's about $78/2.5 = $31 per month. When the next loans kick in it becomes $62 per month then $93, then $124 per month.

"Combining Undergraduate and Parent loans, the **APPROXIMATE CUMULATIVE INTEREST** = $2604 + $4032 = $6636. Adding the monthly amounts, for the first loan it is $51 per month. As the other loans occur it becomes $102 per month, then $153 per month and then $204 per month. With additional money we save next year and increasing earnings, those should be manageable."

"That's sounds great Dad. What about Dream University?"

"I also calculated that case. I put the results both cases into a table. Look it over for as long as you need and let me know if you see how the calculated results for both are organized."

With Gift Aid		Approx. YI	Approx. CI	CI Per Year	CI Per Month	M1	M2	M3	M4	TI
UG	Hoped For	947	2604	601	50	20	40	60	80	2640
P	Hoped For	1466	4032	931	78	31	62	93	124	4092
Combined	Hoped For	2413	6636	1532	128	51	102	153	204	6732
UG	Dream	1258	3460	799	67	27	54	81	108	3564
P	Dream	2835	7796	1800	150	60	120	180	240	7920
Combined	Dream	4093	11256	2599	217	87	174	261	348	11484

After several minutes Nicole indicates, "Looking at the Hoped For entries, I do see most of it. **YI** is **YEARLY INTEREST** and **CI** is **CUMULATIVE INTEREST**. Those columns have the **APPROXIMATE** amounts you calculated and I see those. The **APPROXIMATE CI** is the total for all four loans until the end of the grace period. Then you listed the average amount of **CUMULATIVE INTEREST** per year and per month. But what are **M1**, **M2**, **M3** and **M4**? And what's **TI**?"

"That's very good so far, Nicole. Now recall I used the average **CUMULATIVE INTEREST** per month to estimate how much would be paid each month for the first loan, then after the second loan kicked in and so on. Those amounts are what I listed in the **M1**, **M2**, **M3** and **M4** columns. Recall that for the Undergraduate loans, they were $20, $40, $60 and $80 and that's what's listed. Do you see it now?"

"I do remember you saying those numbers and what they are. I kind of remember you mentioning the numbers you have listed for the Parent loan, too. So, OK. Then I recognize that for Dream University that you are skipping showing me the calculations and just listed the results. That's fine as I follow how you calculated them for Hoped For University."

"That's great! So looking here's what I see. For Dream University, the combined amount of interest for each month is about 70% higher than for Hoped For University. So it's more of a challenge to handle that. Perhaps with you working during college the reduced amount of living expenses Mom and I have to pay may free up enough. We'll just have to wait and see what the future holds. Again we don't have that magic crystal ball but I did manage to simulate one."

"You sure did Dad. Thank you for imagining a way we could have one, as my generation would say, "virtually"."

"Oh, you asked me about **TI**. Remember I said the first loan lasts 51 months. If you check it out the succeeding ones last 39 months, 27 months and 15 months. But it's just 12 months less for each succeeding one. So I multiplied **M1** by 51 and **M2** by 39 etc. and added the results together. That gives me the **TOTAL INTEREST** based on those values. It's also approximate but I can compare with the **APPROXIMATE CI**. They should be about the same and they are. It gives me a check that my monthly values are about right."

"That's interesting Dad. I think I follow it. I'll think on it some more later."

"Well so far its good news if you get the gift aid. I also applied my virtual crystal ball to the case of no gift aid being awarded. Of course, that outcome is not so encouraging."

"I forgot all about that part. The spoil sport in the virtual crystal ball is in play, I suppose."

"Well that's a fun way of putting it. Let's just see if that's the case. Here are my results."

Without Gift Aid		Approx. YI	Approx. CI	CI Per Year	CI Per Month	M1	M2	M3	M4	TI
UG	Hoped For	1258	3460	799	67	27	54	81	108	3564
P	Hoped For	5118	14075	3251	271	108	216	324	432	14256
Combined	Hoped For	6376	17535	4050	338	135	270	405	540	17820
UG	Dream	1258	3460	799	67	27	54	81	108	3564
P	Dream	5118	14075	3251	271	108	216	324	432	14256
Combined	Dream	9131	25111	5799	484	194	388	582	776	25608

"What the spoil sport tells me about Hoped For University is that amount of interest each month starts out low enough, **M1** being $135 per month. **M2** is fine too. Maybe **M3** at $324 per month is OK but begins to stretch things. **M4** at $540 per month would be a challenge. So at that time we have to face the music, somehow. We'll just have to wait until you are accepted and know the gift aid award. Likely it's going to be enough to take that concern away."

"That's encouraging Dad. What about the results for Dream University?"

"As you can see **M1** at $194 is fine and **M2** at $388 is beginning to stretch things. Then **M3** and **M4** at $582 and $768 become a big problem. We would be counting on as high a gift aid amount as possible. Again we wait out the actual financial aid events, Sweetie."

"Dad, I can see that and understand the virtual crystal ball is just being used to estimate the worst case outcome. You already put me at ease about not pressuring me on gift aid. Regardless I fully intend to have academic performance in high school that makes these colleges intensely want to admit me. Then they would also maximize their gift aid. I'll also be trying for scholarships elsewhere as my teachers will help me find them and apply for them."

"That's a great attitude, Nicole. I'm sure you mean do to it. At this point I've covered all of what I feel is relevant at this time. Knowing you always have unending curiosity, is there anything else you are curious about?"

"Actually I do. You always have done a lot of calculations and creating all these tables you've shown me each time we meet. That has to take a lot time and effort. And you figure out numbers for a lot of different options and outcomes. So how do you get it all done using your computer?"

"That's an excellent question. For most of it I created what is called a **spreadsheet**. Do you know what a spreadsheet is?"

"Actually I have heard of them. I'll be learning about them in one of my courses next term. Some of my geek friends seem to know how to use them already. But I don't know what they do."

"Basically, a spreadsheet for say an **AMORTIZATION SCHEDULE** is a way of writing the table in invisible equation form behind the scenes of the spreadsheet. The tables I have shown you are the visible numerical results, not the equations. The visible table locations are called cells. Each visible cell either has words or numbers. Some of the visible cells have numerical values of what are called the variables. Other visible cells contain numerical values that have been calculated by the computer using the hidden equations. In the case of an **AMORTIZATION SCHEDULE** the variables are the **LOAN AMOUNT**, **ANNUAL RATE OF INTEREST** and the **TERM** of the loan. One of the calculated numbers is **MONTHLY PAYMENT**. One of the hidden cells contains the amortization equation. Let's look at one of my spreadsheets."

After opening his spreadsheet file for amortization calculations (not shown) Dad describes it.

"Each line of the visible contains hidden cells to calculate the amount **APPLIED TO INTEREST**, amount **APPLIED TO PRINCIPAL**, **OUTSTANDING PRINCIPAL** and **CUMULATIVE INTEREST**. By typing the desired values of all the variables, the visible spreadsheet results appear automatically. In this case the results are the full **AMORTIZATION SCHEDULE** for the loan – month by month. The spreadsheet software does the calculations invisibly. More importantly, if you want to examine different values of the variables, you just change the values in those variable cells of the spreadsheet. As you do that the calculated values change accordingly. Once done with all of them, voila! You have the new results to reflect the changes in values of the variables. Let me show you.

"I'm changing the values of the **LOAN AMOUNT**, **ANNUAL RATE OF INTEREST** and **TERM**. See how all the other values in the spreadsheet become new values."

"Wow Dad! That's awesome. How does the computer know how to do that?"

"That's why it called creating a spreadsheet. I had to figure out how to make it do all those things by forming the mathematical logic and flow of it. Then I had to put equations into the cells to make it happen."

"Sounds like you have to be really smart to create a spreadsheet?"

"When you learn the basics it's not as challenging as it seems. A smarty pants like you will have no trouble learning how to do that in your school class. And anytime you need some help from me, just ask me. For now, it's premature to start on that. It's more important that you see and comprehend the manual math processes within subjects I've been showing you. It would be a distraction to put spreadsheet learning atop that and defeat my purpose.

"Once you are learning about spreadsheets in school, you'll begin to see how my presentations of the information actually provide easy to follow roadmaps for you to create the spreadsheets that underlie them. Showing you the invisible workings of mine defeats my purpose too. You can readily look at the hidden cell math content but figuring out the flow of all them is the creative part."

"It's great to see the purpose of a spreadsheet and a glimpse at one. Now I can't wait to learn how to do them. Thank you so very much Dad."

"You're very welcome Nicole. For me it's fun and a labor of love. Let's call it a day, or few days and await the actual college application and acceptance process to unfold. We're well armed to tackle the decisions that await you, Mom and me."

Exercise 21: *Assume Nicole receives 40% in gift aid, her parent have saved $32000, and have budgeted $800 per month ($9600 annually) for her college costs. Half of the savings will be used for educational costs.*

Develop:

a) the table for **YEARLY COSTS – YEARLY GIFT AID – YEARLY SAVINGS – YEARLY BUDGET**,

b) **YEARLY COSTS – YEARLY SAVINGS – YEARLY BUDGET**,

c) needed Undergraduate **LOAN AMOUNTS** *(assuming Nicole borrows no more than a total of $27000),*

d) Undergraduate loan costs for Hoped For University and Dream University (Disbursed 7/1/14-6/30/15, assume gift aid is awarded),

e) **APPROXIMATE CUMULATIVE INTEREST** *paid (total amount) for Hoped For University and Dream University during deferment (assume 33 months, assume gift aid is awarded).Use 4.66% and 7.21% as the applicable* **ANNUAL RATE OF INTEREST** *values.*

Your results should be: *Detailed results are given in APPENDIX 3.*

LESSON 13 Decision Time: Where Oh Where Shall I Attend?

Summer ended. The school year is bringing more good things. Nicole's soap box articles for the school paper led to working on the staff. While not exactly her thing, in fall term she wrote the fashion articles as nobody else wanted to do it. Readers loved her sense of style. She helped proofread the sports articles and became editor for that section in spring term. She retook the college entrance exam and got WOW scores on composition and related parts. While not zooming on math she raised her score to a very good one. She had her results sent to her three target colleges. She and Dad had completed the tedious and exhaustive **FAFSA** application.

Armed with excellent grades and great entrance exam scores, she applied to her target colleges. By early March, all three had sent acceptance letters and charmed her with attractive financial aid packages. Happily all were more or less in line with what her Dad and she had projected more than a year ago. With actual information in hand, the period for assessment, personal and academic soul searching, and finalizing monetary matters had been activated.

For brevity and ease of following numbers, the amounts for the offers from the colleges are taken as exactly as estimated in Lesson 12. Of course that would not be the case in actuality. Carrying over those details, avoids the interjection of somewhat different numbers and redoing Dad's calculations. There is no need to repeat that entire process. The important next steps are the decision making and final decisions.

Nicole and her Dad arranged to meet to discuss the offers and begin the process of acting on them. So let's look in as they go about it.

"Hello Dad. I'm so excited to begin evaluating my college financial aid offers. At the same time it feels a little intense and possibly nerve wracking. But I am ready to get started. I've also got some interesting news and suggestions from Mr. Carmichael and the school guidance counselors."

"Interesting news you say? Tell me about that."

"Ms. Taylor spoke with Mr. Carmichael about my interests. She's the teacher who advises the school newspaper team. You won't believe what she told him and what happened."

"Now you've got me excited to hear all about it."

"Ms. Taylor told him I was a super student and would have a promising chance for a journalism career. Apparently she had an inquiry from the employment office of our local newspaper. The Sentinel is introducing a column to be done by a local high school student about identifying career interests, choosing a college, graduating and preparing for entering college. If it goes well they might continue it as that student works his or her way through the transition. She wanted to recommend me and was asking Mr. Carmichael if he agreed. When she told me about it Ms. Taylor said Mr. Carmichael gave me a great recommendation. Then she smiled and called it a "high five" opinion.

"Later that day Ms. Taylor stopped me in the hallway and said she wanted to ask me about something. Right away I got goosebumps. We met and she said she wanted to recommend me for that job if I was interested and had the time to do it. She said I could do it on my own time and from home, as long as I met a deadline. They would pay me for each column. If I was picked I would meet some columnists first at the publications building and get some guidance and advice. One of them would oversee my column, proofreading and approving each one. If I want to do it I will be interviewed, but she said I will pass with flying colors."

"That really is exciting information. I'm so proud of you, almost as much as Mom will be when you tell her. What did Mr. Carmichael suggest to you?"

"It was regarding my starting college. As this opportunity fits me like a glove, I should do it. It also gives me invaluable experience heading into college. It will be a nice professional item for my resume. Knowing the colleges I have in mind, he suggested I think about doing my first year here at Sure Thing University. That would make me available to do the column during my first year. Since I've already been accepted, that part is in place if I opt to go there."

"What about your ambitions for Hoped For University and Dream University?"

"That's the other great part Mr. Carmichael pointed out. By attending Sure Thing University, I can get my first year of general courses out of the way and at lower cost. Things like math, a basic science course etc. Almost all of them don't directly pertain to a degree in Journalism and Media Communication. That's the type of degree all three colleges offer. Even courses like Composition or Speech can be taken anywhere. They all would transfer to either of my other college choices."

"I can see his point on that. Are you telling me you would prefer to go to Sure Thing University for one year and then transfer to one of the others?"

"Yes, I think it's a good plan. That way I can be here and do my column. I feel fine about it. He also said if the column writing gig worked well, who knows they might continue me as an intern. If so, then a second year at Sure Thing University might be workable and not hinder me from transferring. That would also save more money. But he advised I check that out. He does think I should pursue either Hoped For University or Dream University for the eventual degree."

"Well that sure gives a lot of food for thought. No doubt it takes a lot of financial cost away. That gives us flexibility in that regard. To me the most important aspect is that you do eventually finish at either of the other colleges. At least get what you hope for and at best achieve your dream. Let's analyze it.

"Since I mentioned the basics of spreadsheets to you last time we talk, we can produce tables of costs for the revised options on the fly. How's that sound?"

"Wonderful, Dad, I can watch you do it."

"Knowing the gift aid is in place for all three colleges I'll remove the results for no gift aid. That assumes the other universities will offer similar when you transfer. I think that's a sure bet. And if experience blossoms at the local newspaper, they might even offer you more. My first question is will you commute?"

"Yes Dad. I see no point of living on campus. I can do my columns in more peace and quiet from home. And why pay room and board costs if I don't need to do so."

"All right, then. Let me pull up our data from last time and take that option out."

YEARLY COSTS – YEARLY GIFT AID

0.666667	Year 1	Year 2	Year 3	Year 4	TOTAL	AVERAGE
Sure Thing	9000	9360	9734	10026	38121	9530
Sure Thing-R&B	16333	16987	17666	18373	69359	17340
Hoped For	27000	28080	29203	30371	114655	28664
Dream	33000	34320	35693	37121	140133	35033

"The values reflect gift aid. If you attend Sure Thing University for one year and commute, we can delete the second row of costs. We can also change Year 1 costs for the other colleges to zero."

YEARLY COSTS – YEARLY GIFT AID

0.666667	Year 1	Year 2	Year 3	Year 4	TOTAL	AVERAGE
Sure Thing	9000	9360	9734	10026	38121	9530
Hoped For	0	28080	29203	30371	87655	29218
Dream	0	34320	35693	37121	107134	35711

"Mom and I have $50000 saved for college costs. For Year 1 we only need to spend $9000 of it. Sure Thing University is done so I can remove it. That leaves us with $41000 or $13667 per year for the next 3 years. So let me subtract those in my spreadsheet. Here are the results."

YEARLY COSTS – YEARLY GIFT AID –YEARLY SAVINGS

0.666667	Year 1	Year 2	Year 3	Year 4	TOTAL	AVERAGE
Hoped For	0	14413	15536	16704	46654	15551
Dream	0	20653	22026	23454	66133	22044

"Now we account for Mom and I having budgeted $12000 per year, $6000 going to loan repayment and $6000 to **YEARLY COSTS**. Because Sure Thing University is paid for in Year 1 we won't need to spend the $6000 on loan repayment. That $6000 can be used for ongoing costs in the next three years. As a result, we have $2000 per year to also apply atop the budgeted $6000 per year. We can now subtract $8000 from each cell. Do you recall the meaning of cell?"

"Yes I do Dad. It's a cubicle in the spreadsheet."

"Ok. Here are the results, Nicole. What are the total loan needs for each college choice?"

YEARLY COSTS – YEARLY GIFT AID – YEARLY SAVINGS – YEARLY BUDGET

8000	Year 1	Year 2	Year 3	Year 4	TOTAL	AVERAGE
Hoped For	0	6413	7536	8704	22654	7551
Dream	0	12653	14026	15454	42133	14044

"For Hoped For University it's $22654. For Dream University it's $42133."

"Ok and course they are noticeably lower than before. Now we divide those by two for the separate Undergraduate and Parent loans amounts. That's $11327 and $21067. Because you would take no loans in Year 1, your **Aggregate Loan Limit** is $27000 - $5500 = $21500 which is greater than $21067.

"Let me pull up the table for applicable base loans. I don't know the actual loan rates for the next academic year. So we'll use the values we used last time, 4.66% and 7.21%. Now I'll scale base results loan costs to get them for those numbers. Here are the Undergraduate results."

UNDER - GRADUATE			STANDARD REPAYMENT		EXTENDED REPAYMANT		
DISBURSED 7/1/14-6/30/15	ANNUAL RATE OF INTEREST = 4.66%	TERM	5 Years	10 Years	15 Years	20 Years	25 Years
LOAN AMOUNT	ORIGINATION FEE (RATE = 1.072%)	PRINCIPAL	MONTHLY PAYMENT				
1000	10.72	989.28	18.52	10.33	7.65	6.34	5.59
HF 11327	121	11206	210	117	87	72	63
D 21067	226	20841	390	218	161	134	118
LOAN AMOUNT	ORIGINATION FEE (RATE = 1.072%)	PRINCIPAL	YEARLY AMOUNT				
1000	10.72	989.28	222	124	92	76	67
HF 11327	121	11205	2517	1404	1040	862	760
D 21067	226	20841	4682	2611	1934	1603	1413
LOAN AMOUNT	ORIGINATION FEE (RATE = 1.072%)	PRINCIPAL	CUMULATIVE INTEREST				
1000	10.72	989.27	122	250	388	535	687
HF 11327	122	11205	1378	2834	4390	6042	7786
D 21067	226	20841	2562	5272	8165	11237	14482
PERCENT CUMULATIVE INTEREST			12	25	39	54	69

"For Hoped For University, what sticks out for you, Nicole?'

"The main thing is that for a 5-year **TERM** the **MONTHLY PAYMENT** is $210. Last time we were fine with amounts way higher, even considering some above $400. I see that as doable and so is any other **TERM**."

"That's what I primarily see, too. The **YEARLY AMOUNT** is $2517 so that's pretty good for your potential net annual pay of $30000. The **CUMULATIVE INTERES**T is only $1378 so really low. It's just 12% of the **LOAN AMOUNT**. What about Dream University, Nicole?'

"The **MONTHLY PAYMENT** is much higher. But for a 5-year **TERM** it's $390. So being below $400 it seems it might be manageable. But the **YEARLY AMOUNT** of $4682 is not so good. For a 10-year **TERM** the **MONTHLY PAYMENT** is $218 and the **YEARLY AMOUNT** is only $2611. That's very good. Yikes, I can't believe I am actually saying $2611 is very good. The **CUMULATIVE INTEREST** is $5272, which is a bit scary."

"I agree with your reactions. Remember you will be earning a journalist's salary, not Comic Cones pay."

"Yeah, I know that Dad."

"Yes the **CUMULATIVE INTEREST** seems high. But last time we were OK with amounts at least double that amount. And it's an average of $527 a year, so not scary."

"I can see that now, Dad."

"Let's look at the results for the Parent loans.

PARENT							
DISBURSED 7/1/14-6/30/15	**ANNUAL RATE OF INTEREST = 7.21%%**	**TERM =**	**5 Years**	**10 Years**	**15 Years**	**20 Years**	**25 Years**
LOAN AMOUNT	**ORIGINATION FEE (RATE: 4.288%)**	**PRINCIPAL**	**MONTHLY PAYMENT**				
1000	42.88	957.12	19.05	11.22	8.72	7.54	6.89
HF 11327	486	10841	216	127	99	85	78
D 21067	903	20164	401	236	184	159	145
LOAN AMOUNT	**ORIGINATION FEE (RATE: 4.288%)**	**PRINCIPAL**	**YEARLY AMOUNT**				
1000	42.88	957.08	229	135	105	90	83
HF 11327	486	10841	2589	1525	1185	1025	937
D 21067	903	20164	4816	2836	2204	1906	1742
LOAN AMOUNT	**ORIGINATION FEE (RATE: 4.288%)**	**PRINCIPAL**	**CUMULATIVE INTEREST**				
1000	42.88	957.08	186	389	612	853	1111
HF 11327	486	10841	2104	4405	6929	9661	12583
D 21067	903	20164	3912	8193	12886	17968	23404
PERCENT CUMULATIVE INTEREST			19	39	61	85	111

"As before whatever **TERM** is manageable for you would be so for us. So let's look at the combined amounts for the Undergraduate loans plus the Parent loans. I just have to add the two tables."

Dad works a few minutes as Nicole watches. "Here are the results."

COMBINED							
DISBURSED 7/1/14-6/30/15	**ANNUAL RATE OF INTEREST = 4.66%, 7.21%%**	**TERM =**	**5 Years**	**10 Years**	**15 Years**	**20 Years**	**25 Years**
LOAN AMOUNT	**ORIGINATION FEE (RATE: 1.072%, 4.288%)**	**PRINCIPAL**	**MONTHLY PAYMENT**				
2000	53.60	1946.40	37.57	21.55	16.37	13.88	12.48
HF 22654	607	22047	426	244	185	157	141
D 42134	1129	41005	791	454	345	292	263
LOAN AMOUNT	**ORIGINATION FEE (RATE: 1.072%, 4.288%)**	**PRINCIPAL**	**YEARLY AMOUNT**				
2000	53.60	1946.40	451	259	196	167	150
HF 22654	607	22047	5107	2929	2225	1887	1696
D 42134	1129	41005	9498	5448	4138	3509	3155
LOAN AMOUNT	**ORIGINATION FEE (RATE: 1.072%, 4.288%)**	**PRINCIPAL**	**CUMULATIVE INTEREST**				
2000	53.60	1946.40	307	639	999	1386	1798
22654	607	22047	3481	7239	11318	15702	20370
42134	1129	41005	6475	0	0	0	37885
PERCENT CUMULATIVE INTEREST			15	32	50	69	90

"Now that I've learned about spreadsheets in school, I followed what you did."

"That's great. Now let me examine these results."

After a few minutes, "Since you might attend Sure Thing University for two years, it prompted another aspect. I've been thinking about the possibility of starting to repay these loans at the time they are disbursed. Until you graduate, Mom and I would have to repay both loans. For Hoped For University, it appears possible with a 5-year **TERM**. The combined **MONTHLY PAYMENT** is $426. We have $500 per month in our budget. The three loans come in one at time, so we begin with a lower amount and it increases each year reaching $426 in the last year."

"Do you really mean that, Dad?"

"I do. As a result, by the time you graduate you would owe less money. We also save paying extra interest by not deferring the loans. We can look at those things, too.

"For Dream University it looks like that's possible with a 10-year **TERM**. The combined **MONTHLY PAYMENT** is $454. It too starts lower and reaches $454 in the third year. So it works for either college.

"Because there are three years, I'll divide the $454 by 3. That's $151. Because the first year has the lowest **LOAN AMOUNT** its combined **MONTHLY PAYMENT** is somewhat lower, perhaps $135. So this can be readily done.

"To know the result of the 10-year loan after 3 years, the **AMORTIZATION SCHEDULE** would have to be produced for all three loans, as they start at different times. That's a lot of time. It's not necessary, as we know it's a lot less owed once you graduate. Once you get there we will know, but when I get a chance I might do those calculations sometime. It's more interesting to me to look at what happens if you decide to stay a second year at Sure Thing University. So let's take break for 15 minutes and then do those calculations."

"It's terrific Dad to know my going to Sure Thing University allows me to reach Dream University without it costing a fortune. I'm really wondering what going there two years does for the situation. Just in case a good break occurs at the local newspaper. But a short break is good."

After the fifteen minutes, they continue. "All right, Nicole, I pulled up our cost data from last time again. If you attend Sure Thing University for two years, we can take delete the Year 1 and Year 2 results for the other colleges. So I've done that and got these results."

YEARLY COSTS – YEARLY GIFT AID

0.666667	Year 1	Year 2	Year 3	Year 4	TOTAL	AVERAGE
Sure Thing	9000	9360	9734	10026	38121	9530
Hoped For	0	0	29203	30371	59575	29787
Dream	0	0	35693	37121	72814	36407

"For Year 1 plus Year 2 we only need $18360. From the $50000 savings we have $31640 left over. That's $15820 per year left for the next 2 years. So let me subtract those in my spreadsheet. Sure Thing University is done so I can remove it. Here are the results."

YEARLY COSTS – YEARLY GIFT AID –YEARLY SAVINGS

0.666667	Year 1	Year 2	Year 3	Year 4	TOTAL	AVERAGE
Hoped For	0	0	13383	14551	27935	13967
Dream	0	0	19873	21301	41174	20587

"We do not need to spend $6000 in Year 1 and Year 2 for loan repayment. We can apply that $12000 for ongoing costs Year 3 and Year 4. That's $6000 per year added to the $6000 we planned. We can now subtract $12000 from each cell.

 "OK, here are the results."

YEARLY COSTS – YEARLY GIFT AID – YEARLY SAVINGS – YEARLY BUDGET

12000	Year 1	Year 2	Year 3	Year 4	TOTAL	AVERAGE
Hoped For	0	0	1383	2551	3935	1967
Dream	0	0	7873	9301	17174	8587

"Looking at them, Nicole, what are the total loan needs for each college choice?"

"Wow, For Hoped For University it's only $3935. For Dream University it's down to $17174."

"I see that too. And now we divide those by two for the separate Undergraduate and Parent loans amounts. That's $1978 and $8587. It looks like a no brainer. For your loan it's so low, we might not bother with a loan, and pull it from savings. Also because you would take no loans in Years 1 and 2 your Aggregate Loan Limit is $27000 - $5500 - $6500 = $15000, which is greater than $8567."

"That's sure incredible. It feels like college tooth fairy sprinkled star dust on me."

"Maybe so. Let's run the loan costs anyway."

UNDER-GRADUATE			STANDARD REPAYMENT		EXTENDED REPAYMANT		
DISBURSED 7/1/14-6/30/15	ANNUAL RATE OF INTEREST = 4.66%	TERM	5 Years	10 Years	15 Years	20 Years	25 Years
LOAN AMOUNT	ORIGINATION FEE (RATE = 1.072%)	PRINCIPAL	MONTHLY PAYMENT				
1000	10.72	989.28	18.52	10.33	7.65	6.34	5.59
HF 1798	19	1779	33	19	14	11	10
D 8587	92	8495	159	89	66	54	48
LOAN AMOUNT	ORIGINATION FEE (RATE = 1.072%)	PRINCIPAL	YEARLY AMOUNT				
1000	10.72	989.28	222	124	92	76	67
HF 1798	19	1779	400	223	165	137	121
D 8587	92	8495	1908	1064	788	653	576
LOAN AMOUNT	ORIGINATION FEE (RATE = 1.072%)	PRINCIPAL	CUMULATIVE INTEREST				
1000	10.72	989.27	122	250	388	535	687
HF 1798	19	1779	219	450	697	959	1236
D 8587	92	8495	1044	2149	3328	4580	5903
PERCENT CUMULATIVE INTEREST			12	25	39	54	69

"It's amazing Dad. For a 5-year **TERM** the **MONTHLY PAYMENT** for Hoped For University is just

$33. That's not even close to the allowance Mom and you give me. For Dream University it's $159 and I could pay for that just working at Comic Cones."

"And maybe we'll let you do that, Sweetie.

"I'm just kidding, Peanut. You'll actually be away from here in Years 3 and 4. And once there you'll find a much better part-time job. And while you here you likely will too. Plus you have that column at the local newspaper. And maybe bigger things will come.

"Let's look at the Parent side of it."

PARENT							
DISBURSED 7/1/14-6/30/15	ANNUAL RATE OF INTEREST = 7.21%%	TERM =	5 Years	10 Years	15 Years	20 Years	25 Years
LOAN AMOUNT	ORIGINATION FEE (RATE: 4.288%)	PRINCIPAL	MONTHLY PAYMENT				
1000	42.88	957.12	19.05	11.22	8.72	7.54	6.89
HF 1798	77	1721	34	20	16	14	12
D 8587	368	8219	164	96	75	65	59
LOAN AMOUNT	ORIGINATION FEE (RATE: 4.288%)	PRINCIPAL	YEARLY AMOUNT				
1000	42.88	957.08	229	135	105	90	83
HF 1798	77	1721	411	242	188	163	149
D 8587	368	8219	1963	1156	899	777	710
LOAN AMOUNT	ORIGINATION FEE (RATE: 4.288%)	PRINCIPAL	CUMULATIVE INTEREST				
1000	42.88	957.08	186	389	612	853	1111
HF 1798	77	1721	334	699	1100	1533	1997
D 8587	368	8219	1595	3339	5253	7324	9539
PERCENT CUMULATIVE INTEREST			19	39	61	85	111

"For a 5-year **TERM** Hoped For University has a **MONTHLY PAYMENT** of just $34. Maybe we switch things and you can pay for our loan too."

"Maybe I'll surprise you and do that, Dad."

"That would be a surprise, and a nice one. For Dream University the **MONTHLY PAYMENT** is $164. Maybe you can pay that as well?"

"If I can then maybe I will and surprise you even more."

"Keep on doing that one, Smarty Pants.

"Well let's get back to Earth and look at the combined costs."

"Beam me down Scotty! Isn't that what your generation liked to say, Dad?"

"Even though Star Trek is still around, I'm surprised you know that phrase from it."

"Actually when we want to get somewhere quickly would use Harry Potter and "disapparate". It has nothing to do with getting from space to earth, it's like disappearing. I know you don't want me to disapparate right now, and neither do I."

"Who's Harry Potter? Just kidding, I know he's some imagined geek behaving like an imagined non-geek in in an imagined world. And he has special powers. So maybe he can make our college costs disappear. Since he hasn't yet, let's continue. Let me add things together."

"Ok done. Here are the combined results."

COMBINED							
DISBURSED 7/1/14-6/30/15	**ANNUAL RATE OF INTEREST = 4.66%, 7.21%%**	**TERM =**	**5 Years**	**10 Years**	**15 Years**	**20 Years**	**25 Years**
LOAN AMOUNT	**ORIGINATION FEE (RATE: 1.072%, 4.288%)**	**PRINCIPAL**	**MONTHLY PAYMENT**				
2000	53.60	1946.40	37.57	21.55	16.37	13.88	12.48
HF 3596	96	3500	68	39	29	25	22
D 17174	460	16714	323	185	141	119	107
LOAN AMOUNT	**ORIGINATION FEE (RATE: 1.072%, 4.288%)**	**PRINCIPAL**	**YEARLY AMOUNT**				
2000	53.60	1946.40	451	259	196	167	150
HF 3596	96	3500	811	465	353	299	269
D 17174	460	16714	3871	2221	1687	1430	1286
LOAN AMOUNT	**ORIGINATION FEE (RATE: 1.072%, 4.288%)**	**PRINCIPAL**	**CUMULATIVE INTEREST**				
2000	53.60	1946.40	307	639	999	1386	1798
HF 3596	96	3500	553	1149	1797	2492	3233
D 17174	460	16714	2639	0	0	0	15442
PERCENT CUMULATIVE INTEREST			15	32	50	69	90

"Looking at Dream University, for a 5-year **TERM** the **MONTHLY PAYMENT** is $323 and well within our budget of $500. No need to look at the rest of it."

"I can't believe it. I must be dreaming. If I want to make my dream come true it looks like it will happen. Mom and you are my fairy godmother and fairy godfather atop being my Mom and Dad. You are the best parents in the world."

"I can remember when you were turning teenager, you sometimes said something entirely reverse to that. It's nice that phase faded away. Now, let's wrap this meeting up.

"I agree with your teachers recommending you go to Sure Thing University first. So go ahead and do it. It's not the money aspect, albeit that is a great development. It's that they think so highly of you to recommend the opportunity to be working on the local newspaper. I'm already waving your columns in front of our relatives and friends.

"I want you to get to either Hoped For University or Dream University as soon you can. Attending Sure Thing University for one year is a game changer. I have little doubt you will be awarded gift aid. If you get enough gift aid, then we see now we can afford either one for three years.

"With gift aid, if you go to Sure Thing University for two years then Dream University is certainly realistic for the following two years. It appears we could even readily start repayment of each of all the loans as they are disbursed, too. That would save us a fair amount of interest.

"If it turns out you attend Sure Thing University for only for one year, it looks like Dream University is still possibly in the cards, at least on a loan repayment basis. It's more of a stretch. It would a 10-year loan. We would have to look at it in more detail. As for starting repayment of each loan as it is disbursed, I did not look at that. So we don't know yet. I would want to look at that in detail as well. But as it is involved to do so let's wait, watch and see what plays out.

"I'd like very much to see you take on your dream, Dream University. You see, when I was your age and had my chance at mine, I never got there. My parents simply could not afford it so I let go of it. I've had a fantastic career anyway and great life, only with more effort I imagine. So let's make it a lot easier for you.

"Now run off and tell your Mom all the great news!"

Exercise 22: *For the conditions of Exercise 21 (of Lesson 12) repeat Dad's calculation of the cost benefit of Nicole attending Sure Thing University for* <u>*one year*</u>. *Develop: a) the table for* **YEARLY COSTS – YEARLY GIFT AID – YEARLY SAVINGS – YEARLY BUDGET,** *b) needed Undergraduate* **LOAN AMOUNTS** *(assuming half shares), and c) Undergraduate loan costs for Hoped For University and Dream University (Disbursed 7/1/14-6/30/15, assume gift aid is awarded*

Your results should be: *Detailed results are given in APPENDIX 3.*

Exercise 23: *For the conditions of Exercise 21 (of Lesson 12) repeat Dad's calculation of the cost benefit of Nicole attending Sure Thing University for <u>two years</u>. Develop: a) the table for* **YEARLY COSTS – YEARLY GIFT AID – YEARLY SAVINGS – YEARLY BUDGET***, and b)Undergraduate loan costs for Hoped For University and Dream University (Disbursed 7/1/14-6/30/15, assume gift aid is awarded*

Your results should be*: Detailed results are given in APPENDIX 3.*

LESSON 14 Why Pay All That Deferment Interest?

It's nearing the end of Nicole's last term at Mountain High School. In August she will begin studies at Sure Thing University and begin taking on student loans.

The experience of writing a regular column at the Sentinel is going very well. Frequent messages to her professional Email address and hits in her Twitter account are evidence of a high level of readership interest in them. She apparently has lots of young fans, an audience so to speak. She enjoys following up and providing further insight to them. She has learned to smoothly handle the occasional senders of less than positive messages.

As time moved along the columnist who oversaw her column had less and less need for edits and giving guidance. Nicole progressed to confidently standing on her own two feet. Now and then the Editor took time to give positive reactions, too. Half way along in the experience Nicole sensed she might be given some opportunity to continue for a second year and beyond in some capacity. Nothing actually has been said to her.

She had already taken Mr. Carmichael's advice to check out the viability of doing that vis-à-vis the breadth and timing of courses in the academic programs at Hoped For University and Dream University compared to Sure Thing University. As a result she was pretty sure she wanted to transfer to one of them after just one year at Sure Thing University. So she met with her Dad to express that and explain her reasons.

"Dad, I've been looking into the relative merits of the curricula at the three universities. Mr. Carmichael had said I should do that to help decide when to transfer. I reviewed their catalog contents. He was correct about the first year. In each case, practically all first year courses were not directly related to my program of study. The exception was two semesters of Introduction to Journalism. Those courses were very similar at all of them. After that things are different.

"I found there was more to majoring in Journalism than journalism. Each program contained courses regarding journalism but they were much broader. Areas such as Advertising, Broadcast News, Broadcast Production, and News-Editorial were included. It was not limited to newsprint. One could take courses related to radio, television, magazines, book publishing, marketing, international mass communication, public relations, digital and electronic news and others.

"I saw considerably more course offerings at Hoped For University and at Dream University than at Sure Thing University. It made me realize I should apply to get transferred in to one of them as a sophomore; next fall. Being hesitant to directly inquire about transfer credit possibilities, either with staff at Sure Thing University or the two others, I asked Mr. Carmichael about it. He kindly acted to inquire at the two other colleges himself, in a general way. Readily, he found there would be no problem.

"What about the Sentinel?"

"I haven't mentioned anything. The possibility of anything more than the present column job is simply conjecture. There's no reason to forewarn them that I will only be available for one year. Once I act to reapply for readmission and am accepted I would give my boss the good news. Of course, I'll indicate the column work was a very helpful piece in my applications for transfer."

"That's very mature thinking. What do you want to do?"

"Overall I felt that Dream University has the strongest program and reputation. And their web site information highlighted a very high percentage of post degree employment and with high quality employers. Based on that, I would like to transfer there. I also take to heart your wish that I fulfill my dream and enroll at Dream University. But I know there is higher cost involved overall by not staying at Sure Thing University for two years. And you said under that circumstance the numbers for Dream University would have to be looked at more carefully."

"Peanut, that's wonderful and very interesting. You sure did great homework on that. Maybe that's why you skipped a lot of my optional homework on the costs"

"Maybe so, Dad. Mostly I felt I knew how to do much of it."

"No matter, I knew you did, too. Remember it is my wish that you transfer to either Hoped For University or Dream University as soon you can, if you wanted it. Mom and I are on the same page in that regard.

"Now that I know you will only attend Sure Thing University for just one year, I will take the time to run some more loan numbers on Dream University. When we first looked at it, the main concern about Dream University was the uncertainty of beginning repayment at the outset of each loan. But if f we can do that we would avoid interest that would otherwise be paid during a deferment. It would be helpful to the decision itself. I'll do that and some other things. Then we can discuss them. How about doing that next Saturday morning, about 10 AM?"

"OK, that's great. I'll see you next Saturday "

Dad spends the next few days working on several things. Then he meets with Nicole to discuss the results.

"Hi Peanut! I've done a lot looking into the Dream University possibility. I have a bunch of stuff to share."

"Hi Dad! That's great. As always I greatly appreciate the time you take to examine things and share them with me and show me how you do it."

"You're very welcome. It's always very enjoyable for me."

"Here's the summary loan information we had gotten for Dream University last time we met."

YEARLY COSTS – YEARLY GIFT AID – YEARLY SAVINGS – YEARLY BUDGET

	Year 1	Year 2	Year 3	Year 4
Dream	0	12653	14026	15454

"These are the needed total **LOAN AMOUNTS** based on your decision to only attend Sure Thing University for one year. We each would borrow half the amounts. Also they are reduced a little by the **ORIGINATION FEES** paid at the outset. After subtracting them these are the results."

	LOAN AMOUNT	LA/2	ORIG. FEE	PRINCIPAL
UG-Loan 1	12653	6327	68	6259
P-Loan 1	12653	6327	271	6055
UG-Loan 2	14026	7013	75	6938
P-Loan 2	14026	7013	301	6712
UG-Loan 3	15454	7727	83	7644
P-Loan 3	15454	7727	331	7396

Beginning Repayment upon Disbursements - Interest Saved

"We'd like to know how much interest we saved by starting repayment immediately, instead of paying only the **MONTHLY INTEREST**. How do we determine that, Sweetie?"

"Hmm?" After thinking for a few minutes, Nicole replies, "That's a good question. I think you covered something about that but I don't remember."

"Yes, I did. Here's a hint. If we pay only the **MONTHLY INTEREST** then the **OUTSTANDING BALANCE** will remain the same for the entire time. So how much interest will we pay over that time? For example, what would the amount be up to end of the grace period for the first loans?"

"Ah! Now I remember it. We apply the **ANNUAL RATE OF INTEREST** for the number of years we do that. For my first loan that's 39/12 = 3.25 years. So for my first loan, the **CUMULATIVE INTEREST** paid equals 3.25 x 4.66/100 x $6259. I'll do it on my cell phone calculator. OK I get $948. For your loan it's 3.25 x 7.21/100 x $6055. OK I get $1419. Adding them together, it's $2367. That's a lot of money saved."

"Terrific! Smarty Pants. And that's just for the first loans. For the second and third loans the amounts saved will be lower because they involve less years. If you calculate the amounts for the second loans you'll get $727 +$1089 = $1816. For the third loans you'll get $445 + $667 = $1112. Adding them up, the combined **CUMULATIVE INTEREST** saved is $5295. That's a whole lot of money saved. You can check those results as optional homework."

"I doubt I'll have the time given my college homework. But I'm sure I could do it using your spreadsheet. But now I can develop one myself if I had to."

"I'm certain the college girl you could, too. Maybe you would find I made some mistakes."

"I really doubt that, Dad, so I'll still pass."

Amortization Schedules

"At the time you had decided to spend a year or two at Sure Thing University, we estimated the resulting **LOAN AMOUNTS** for each year at Dream University. What we need now are the **AMORTIZATION SCHEDULE S** for each of loan based on assuming repayment starts while you are in college. That will show how much would be paid off at the time you graduate, how much **CUMULATIVE INTEREST** we paid (did not save), and how much remains to be repaid. We each have three loans involved, too. That's six in total. It's tedious because they start at different times It took a little more work than I figured. But I've done it."

"You always go the extra mile for me, Dad."

"I do but there's benefit to both of us.

"As an example here's the partial one for the first Undergraduate loan."

UG-Loan 1							
Loan Amount	6327						
Origination Fee Rate	1.072						
Origination Fee	68					**Principal = 6259**	
Term in Years	**Annual Rate of Interest**	**Month**	**Monthly Payment**	**Applied to Interest**	**Applied to Principal**	**Outstanding Principal**	**Cumulative Interest**
10	4.66	1	65.35	24.31	41.05	6217.95	24.31
		2	65.35	24.15	41.20	6176.75	48.45
		12	65.35	22.52	42.83	5755.80	281.01
		24	65.35	20.48	44.87	5228.64	538.07
		33	65.35	18.89	46.47	4816.87	714.45
		39	65.35	17.79	47.56	4534.26	823.96
		120	65.35	0.25	65.10	0.00	1583.13

"It includes results for the length of time you are in college plus a 6-month grace period. Since repayment is already ongoing, it's actually a grace period we give ourselves in case you need it before getting and starting a job. During that time, Mom and I would keep making the payments on both loans. For this loan it's 33 months to graduation and 39 months to the end of a grace period, respectively. That assumes you graduate in May and our grace period includes that month.

"After Month 33 the **OUTSTANDING PRINCIPAL** is $4817, rounded. That's how much is still owed. The **CUMULATIVE INTEREST** paid is $714. After Month 39 the **OUTSTANDING PRINCIPAL** is $4534. The **CUMULATIVE INTEREST** paid is $824."

"Ok, I see that Dad."

"Here's the corresponding partial **AMORTIZATION SCHEDULE** for the first Parent loan.

P - 1								
Loan Amount	6327							
Origination Fee Rate	4.288							
Origination Fee	271						Principal = 6259	
Term in Years	Annual Rate of Interest	Month	Monthly Payment	Applied to Interest	Applied to Principal		Outstanding Principal	Cumulative Interest
10	7.21	1	70.96	36.38	34.58		6020.42	36.38
		2	70.96	36.17	34.79		5985.63	72.55
		12	70.96	34.03	36.94		5626.04	422.57
		24	70.96	31.27	39.69		5165.12	813.18
		33	70.96	29.07	41.89		4797.02	1083.72
		36	70.96	28.31	42.65		4669.84	1169.43
		39	70.96	27.54	43.42		4540.36	1252.83
		120	70.96	0.42	70.54		0.00	2460.29

"After Month 33 the **OUTSTANDING PRINCIPAL** is $4797. The **CUMULATIVE INTEREST** paid is $1084. After Month 39 the amounts are $4540 and $1253.

'Here's a summary of the results for all six loans."

	LA	LA/2	OR. FEE	PRINCIPAL	MONTHS	OUT. PRINC.	CUM. INT.	MONTHS	OUT. PRINC.	CUM. INT.
UG	12653	6327	68	6259	Grad 33	4817	714	Grace 39	4534	824
P	12653	6327	271	6055	Grad 33	4797	1084	Grace 39	4540	1253
UG	14026	7013	75	6938	Grad 21	5945	528	Grace 27	5645	663
P	14026	7013	301	6712	Grad 21	5857	797	Grace 27	5592	1004
UG	15454	7727	83	7644	Grad 9	7186	260	Grace 15	6871	425
P	15454	7727	331	7396	Grad 9	7007	391	Grace 15	6735	639
SUM UG	42133	21067	226	20841	Graduate	17948	1502	Grace	17050	1912
SUM P	42133	21067	903	20163	Graduate	17661	2272	Grace	16867	2896
TOTAL	84266	42134	1129	41104	Graduate	35609	3779	Grace	33917	4808

"I had to abbreviate the some headings; but I think they are obvious. Let's walk through the first line.

"**UG** indicates its results for an Undergraduate loan. This line is for the first one of three loans. The **LOAN AMOUNT** is $12653 and half that is $6327. We each have a loan for that amount. The **ORIGINATION FEE** is $68 leaving a **PRINCIPAL** of $6259.

"Graduation occurs in Month 33.At that time the **OUTSTANDING PRINCIPAL** is $4817 and the **CUMULATIVE INTEREST** paid is $714. At the end of the grace period the **OUTSTANDING PRINCIPAL** is $4534 and the **CUMULATIVE INTEREST** paid is $824. So you still owe $4534. Did you follow that?"

"Yes, Dad, I did and it helps a lot."

"The next line is the corresponding data for the first Parent loan.

"The next two lines are for the second loans. For those loans graduation occurs in Month 21 and the grace period ends in Month 27. The next two lines are for the third loans. For those loans graduation occurs in Month 9 and the grace period ends in Month 15.

"Now for all the loans we know how much we still owe and how much **CUMULATIVE INTEREST** we have paid when you graduate and at the end of the grace period.

"The bottom two lines sum up the amounts for all the Undergraduate loans and for all the Parent loans. What do you observe in those totals, Nicole?"

"The first thing I see is that the reduction from the initial **PRINCIPAL** to **OUTSTANDING PRINCIPAL** is less for each successive loan. I suppose that's because we're paying each one off for a shorter period time.

"The second thing I see is the combined effect for both sets of loans. For my Undergraduate loans, at the time of graduation the initial combined **PRINCIPAL** of $20841 is reduced to $17948, by about $2900. At the end of the grace period it has been reduced to $17050, by about $3800."

"That's right, as usual, Smarty Pants.

"Let's look back at the **AMORTIZATION SCHEDULE S** for our first loans in Month 120. That's when the loans end. They show the **CUMULATIVE INTEREST** amounts paid are $1583 and $2460, a total of $4043. For the second loans I got $1755 + $2819, a total of $4574. For the third loans I got $1933 + $3005, a total of $4938. The combined **CUMULATIVE INTEREST** paid for the six loans is $13555.That shows the relative significance of the $5295 we avoided."

"That sure looks great Dad. You aren't going to suggest I check those results as optional homework, are you?"

"Nope! I'm certain you can do that too if you had to. I want to move along to another very important step."

Accelerating the Loan Repayment

"Notice that the **MONTHLY PAYMENT** amounts in the **AMORTIZATION SCHEDULE S** are $65.35 and $70.96. For our second loans, the amounts are $72.44 and $78.66. For the third loans they are $79.82 and $86.67. Although pretty nominal, they are additive. As the loans kick in, the sum of the **MONTHLY PAYMENTS** increases.

"If you don't need a grace period, then during college the repayment track for your loans is:"

UG + P Loans 1	NO GRACE PERIOD							
Months of Repayment		**Loans Being Paid**	**TRACK OF OWED MONTHLY PAYMENTS**					
From	To		UG	P	Sum	Running Sum	Number of Monthly Payments	Total of Owed Monthly Payments
1	12	1	65.35	70.96	136.31	136.31	12	1635.72
13	24	1, 2	72.44	78.66	151.10	287.41	12	3448.92
25	33	1, 2, 3	79.81	86.68	166.49	453.90	9	4085.10
							SUM	9169.74

"If you do need a grace period, then the only difference is we pay $453.90 for another six months. That's $2723.40. The **SUM** increases to $11893.14.

"Mom and I had budgeted $500 per month for loan repayment. But the tracks indicate we don't need that much. For the first twelve months we only need $136.31. For the next twelve months we only need $287.41. For the next nine months or fifteen months we only need $453.90. That means we can comfortably manage the repayment. In fact, we can afford to pay an extra amount each month on each loan as an **ADDITIONAL AMOUNT APPLIED TO PRINCIPAL**. If we do that what's it called?"

"Acceleration! I'll never forget your analogy of a car "going from 0 to 60 in 10 seconds". We would be accelerating the loan repayment."

"Exactly!

"These track results show the amounts owed. We can actually use the $500 per month in any proportions we want. I redid the **AMORTIZATION SCHEDULE S** with acceleration included. Based on what came out of it, I did something different with the $500. Let's look at it dividing it equally between your loans and ours,

"For the first Undergraduate loan the **ADDITIONAL AMOUNT APPLIED TO PRINCIPAL** is $250.00 - $65.35 = $184.65. Here are the amortized results."

UG-Loan 1								Principal = 6259	
Loan Amount	**6327**								
Origination Fee Rate	**1.072**								
Origination Fee	**68**								
Term in Years	**Annual Rate of Interest**	**College Month**	**Month**	**Monthly Payment**	**Applied to Interest**	**Applied to Principal**	**Additional Amount Applied to Principal**	**Outstanding Principal**	**Cumulative Interest**
10	4.66	1	1	65.35	24.31	41.05	184.65	6033.31	24.31
		2	2	65.35	23.43	41.92	184.65	5806.74	47.74
		12	12	65.35	14.48	50.88	184.65	3492.07	233.07
		24	24	65.35	3.26	62.09	184.65	593.41	334.41
		26	26	65.35	1.34	64.01	184.65	97.06	338.06
		27	27	65.35	0.38	64.97	184.65	-152.57	338.43
		27	*27*	*65.35*	*0.38*	*64.97*	*32.09*	*0.00*	*338.43*

"Note that I added a column to track the College Month. In this case it parallels the loan months. In Loan 2, that will change. I will explain it when we get to that loan."

"OK, I'll wait to see that."

"What do you notice about the outcome, Nicole?"

"What stands out to me is that the loan is paid off in Month 27. That means it's paid off before I graduate. That's amazing!"

"That's the power of acceleration. Notice the **CUMULATIVE INTEREST** is only $338.43. That's a lot lower than without acceleration.

"Now let's look at the effect of accelerating repayment of the first Parent loan. The **ADDITIONAL AMOUNT APPLIED TO PRINCIPAL** is $250.00 - $70.96 = $179.04. Here's that result."

P-Loan 1								Principal = 6055	
Loan Amount	**6327**								
Origination Fee Rate	**4.288**								
Origination Fee	**271**								
Term in Years	**Annual Rate of Interest**	**College Month**	**Loan Month**	**Monthly Payment**	**Applied to Interest**	**Applied to Principal**	**Additional Amount Applied to Principal**	**Outstanding Principal**	**Cumulative Interest**
10	7.21	1	1	70.96	36.38	34.58	179.04	5841.38	36.38
		2	2	70.96	35.10	35.86	179.04	5626.48	71.48
		12	12	70.96	21.83	49.13	179.04	3405.13	350.13
		24	24	70.96	4.82	66.14	179.04	557.77	502.77
		26	26	70.96	1.87	69.09	179.04	62.99	507.99
		27	27	70.96	0.38	70.58	179.04	-186.63	508.37
		27	*27*	*63.37*	*0.38*	*62.99*	*0.00*	*0.00*	*508.37*

"This loan also ends in Month 27. The **CUMULATIVE INTEREST** is bit higher, $508. But it's still a lot lower than without acceleration."

"Will that happen for the other loans?"

"Actually, very different things occur. Let's look at the second loans."

For those loans we cannot accelerate until College Month 28."

"Why not?"

"We don't free up the $250 being paid on Loan 1 until then."

"Yeah! That makes sense, Dad."

"Great! And actually for that last month, College Month 27, the **ADDITIONAL AMOUNT APPLIED TO PRINCIPAL** needed on Undergraduate Loan 1 is only $32.09. For the Parent loan 1 it's zero. So let's assume we just start paying $250 on Loan 2 in College Month 27.

"Here are the results for Undergraduate Loan 2."

UG-Loan 2									
Loan Amount	7013								
Origination Fee Rate	1.072								
Origination Fee	75							**Principal = 6938**	
Term in Years	**Annual Rate of Interest**	**College Month**	**Loan Month**	**Monthly Payment**	**Applied to Interest**	**Applied to Principal**	**Additional Amount Applied to Principal**	**Outstanding Principal**	**Cumulative Interest**
10	4.66	13	1	72.44	26.94	45.50	0.00	6892.50	26.94
		14	2	72.44	26.77	45.67	0.00	6846.83	53.71
		24	12	72.44	24.96	47.48	0.00	6380.21	311.50
		26	14	72.44	24.59	47.85	0.00	6284.70	360.87
		27	15	72.44	24.41	48.04	177.56	6059.10	385.27
		33	21	72.44	19.10	53.34	177.56	4687.02	513.19
		39	27	72.44	13.67	58.78	177.56	3282.65	608.82
		-	28	72.44	12.75	59.69	0.00	3222.96	621.57
		-	76	72.44	0.54	71.90	0.00	67.74	943.50
		-	77	68.00	0.26	67.74	0.00	0.00	943.76

"Note the College Month and Loan Month are not the same. I said I would explain why. But can you deduce why that is so?"

Pausing a bit, Nicole then replies. "Aha! I think I've got it. Loan 2 starts 1 year later then Loan 1. It begins in College Month 13. That is Loan Month 1 corresponds to College Month 13, Loan Month 2 corresponds to College Month 14, and so on. But why is that needed?"

"Excellent! I had to do that to track when to start and end the **ADDITIONAL AMOUNT APPLIED TO PRINCIPAL**. The amount is $250.00 – $72.44 = $177.56.

"What strikes you about the results?"

"I see this loan ends in Loan Month 77, a whole lot sooner than its **TERM**. The **CUMULATIVE INTEREST** of $943.76 must be a lot lower than if we don't accelerate repayment?"

"You're right.

"Do you follow the switch at Loan Month 28?"

"Well, you sort of told me. I suppose that's because it's the end of the grace period? So you stop paying for me. At that time the extra $177.56 disappears."

"That's right. It might actually happen at Loan Month 21 (College Month 33) when you graduate so I included that month too. That gives us the status at that time."

"Oh I see that too."

"Here's the result for the Parent loan 2."

P-Loan 2										
Loan Amount	7013									
Origination Fee Rate	1.072									
Origination Fee	301								**Principal = 6712**	
Term in Years	**Annual Rate of Interest**	**College Month**	**Month**	**Monthly Payment**	**Applied to Interest**	**Applied to Principal**	**Additional Amount Applied to Principal**		**Outstanding Principal**	**Cumulative Interest**
10	7.21	13	1	78.66	40.33	38.33	0.00		6673.67	40.33
		14	2	78.66	40.10	38.56	0.00		6635.10	80.43
		24	12	78.66	37.72	40.94	0.00		6236.50	468.43
		26	14	78.66	37.22	41.44	0.00		6153.87	543.12
		27	15	78.66	36.97	41.69	171.34		5940.85	580.09
		33	21	78.66	29.18	49.48	171.34		4635.55	774.79
		39	27	78.66	21.10	57.56	171.34		3282.48	921.72
		-	28	78.66	19.72	58.94	0.00		3223.54	941.44
		-	75	78.66	0.56	78.10	0.00		14.57	1429.52
		-	76	14.66	0.09	14.57	0.00		0.00	1429.60

"I trust you see the similarity. This one actually ends one month sooner too.

"Yes, I do and I noticed that earlier end too, Dad."

"What can you deduce about the third loans? Think about it a bit."

A few moments later Nicole replies, "It seems that you've used up all the acceleration possibilities. So you cannot acceleration them."

"Why so?"

"It's because you already had to pay the **ADDITIONAL AMOUNT APPLIED TO PRINCIPAL** on Loans 2 all the way to the end of the grace period, College Month 39. After that month you no longer have to pay it, I do."

"Perfect! Here are the two amortized results for the third loans."

UG-Loan 3								Principal 7644	
Loan Amount	7013								
Origination Fee Rate	1.072								
Origination Fee	83								
Term in Years	Annual Rate of Interest	College Month	Loan Month	Monthly Payment	Applied to Interest	Applied to Principal	Additional Amount Applied to Principal	Outstanding Principal	Cumulative Interest
10	4.66	25	1	79.81	29.68	50.13	0.00	7593.87	29.68
		26	2	79.81	29.49	50.32	0.00	7543.55	59.17
		33	9	79.81	28.11	51.71	0.00	7185.78	260.09
		39	15	79.81	26.89	52.92	0.00	6871.29	424.48
		-	120	79.81	0.31	79.50	0.00	0.00	1933.45

P-Loan 3								Principal 7396	
Loan Amount	7727								
Origination Fee Rate	1.072								
Origination Fee	331								
Term in Years	Annual Rate of Interest	College Month	Month	Monthly Payment	Applied to Interest	Applied to Principal	Additional Amount Applied to Principal	Outstanding Principal	Cumulative Interest
10	7.21	25	1	86.68	44.44	42.24	0.00	7353.76	44.44
		26	2	86.68	44.18	42.49	0.00	7311.27	88.62
		33	9	86.68	42.36	44.31	0.00	7006.59	390.67
		39	15	86.68	40.74	45.93	0.00	6735.06	639.21
		-	120	86.68	0.52	86.16	0.00	0.00	3005.17

"Now as to what it all means. In the following table I've summarized the results after repayment is over. As I go along, let me know if you are following my explanation."

	OUTSTANDING PRINCIPAL			CUMULATIVE INTEREST		
	Graduation	Grace	Loan Ends	Graduation	Grace	Loan Ends
UG L1	0	0	0	338	338	338
UG L2	4687	3283	0	513	609	944
UG L3	7186	6871	0	260	425	1933
SUM UG	11873	10154	0	1111	1372	3215
P L1	0	0	0	508	508	508
P L2	4636	3282	0	775	922	1430
P L3	7007	6735	0	391	639	3005
SUM P	11643	10017	0	1674	2069	4943
COMBINED	23516	20171	0	2785	3441	8158

"If you do not use a grace period, then the Graduation amounts apply. The individual **OUTSTANDING PRINCIPAL** amounts for your Undergraduate Loans are as listed. They sum to $11873. The individual **CUMULATIVE INTEREST** amounts sum to $1111. For the Parent loans the listed the individual **OUTSTANDING PRICIPALS** sum to $11643. The individual **CUMULATIVE INTEREST** amounts sum to $1674. The **COMBINED** amounts for all six loans amounts are as listed in the bottom line."

"Are you following everything, Peanut?"

"Yes, I see all of it"

 "At the end of the grace period, the individual **OUTSTANDING PRINCIPAL** amounts for your Undergraduate Loans sum to $10154. The individual **CUMULATIVE INTEREST** amounts sum to $1372. We will have paid that for you. For the Parent loans the individual **OUTSTANDING BALANCE** amounts sum to $10017. The **CUMULATIVE INTEREST** amounts sums to $2069. The **COMBINED** amounts for all six loans are as listed in the bottom line."

"I'm OK on that too."

"When you are independent and working, you'll take over repayment of the Undergraduate loans. We will continue repayment on ours. Whether that's at graduation or the end of a grace period, the applicable listed **OUTSTANDING BALANCES** are what we each will owe at that time. When the time comes we each can decide if we can and want to pay anything as **ADDITIONAL APPLIED TO PRINCIPAL**. My results listed amounts for when the loans end are based on assuming we do not do that. In that case the combined **CUMULATIVE INTEREST** is $8158. That's $5397 less than the $13555 paid if the loans are not accelerated."

"If we elect to continue to accelerate the loans in some way, then the **AMORTIZATION SCHEDULE S** can be adjusted to reflect whatever amounts we each decide to use. That will further reduce the combined **CUMULATIVE INTEREST** accordingly. And the loans would end sooner."

"Dad, I do realize and understand that. I'll be looking forward to being a journalist and being paid well enough to take on the repayment of my loans and possibly use acceleration to some extent."

"OK. By that time, as a college graduate, you should be able to figure out a choice on your own.

"Another acceleration option is to do the following. In the first year we could split the $500 between the two loans, $250 shares. In the next year split it between the four loans, $125 shares. In the last nine or fifteen months split it among the six loans, $62.50 shares. The amount of the share that exceeds the **MONTHLY PAYMENT** due is the **ADDITIONAL AMOUNT APPLIED TO PRINCIPAL**. Here's a summary of results for the Undergraduate loans using that approach."

Loan	Principal	College Month	Month	Monthly Payment	Applied to Interest	Applied to Principal	Additional Amount Applied to Principal	Outstanding Principal	Cumulative Interest
UG-1	6259	1	1	65.35	24.31	41.05	184.65	6033.31	24.31
		13	13	65.35	13.56	51.79	59.65	3380.63	246.63
		25	25	65.35	8.26	57.10	0.00	2068.77	375.12
		33	33	65.35	6.46	58.89	0.00	1603.95	433.11
		39	39	65.35	5.07	60.28	0.00	1245.75	467.02
		-	58	65.35	0.47	64.89	0.00	54.91	517.85
		=	59	55.13	0.21	54.92	0.00	0.00	518.07
UG-2	6938	13	1	72.44	26.94	45.50	52.56	6839.94	26.94
		14	2	72.44	26.56	45.88	52.56	6741.50	53.50
		25	13	72.44	22.27	50.17	0.00	5685.68	320.12
		33	21	72.44	20.69	51.75	0.00	5277.28	491.24
		39	27	72.44	19.48	52.96	0.00	4962.55	611.16
		-	106	72.44	0.50	71.94	0.00	57.65	1429.07
		-	107	57.87	0.22	57.65	0.00	0.00	1429.29
UG-3	7644	25	1	79.81	29.68	50.13	0.00	7593.87	29.68
		26	2	79.81	29.49	50.32	0.00	7543.55	59.17
		33	9	79.81	28.11	51.71	0.00	7185.78	260.09
		39	15	79.81	26.89	52.92	0.00	6871.29	424.48
		-	119	79.81	0.62	79.20	0.00	79.50	1933.14
		-	120	79.81	0.31	79.50	0.00	0.00	1933.45

"It turns out that after College Month 24, the $62.50 share is less than the normal **MONTHLY PAYMENT** for each of the loans. So acceleration ends after that month. Indeed that means we then have to make up a shortage. For Loan 1 it's $65.35 - $62.50 = $1.83. For Loan 2 it's $72.44 - $62.50 = $9.94. Loan 3 has no acceleration at all. That loan begins in College Month 25. A shortage $79.81 – $62.50 = $17.31 exists at the outset. We probably just come up with those extra amounts. Or we could slightly reduce the acceleration shares in the other loans.

"As is, when the loans all end the <u>sum</u> of the **CUMULATIVE INTEREST** amounts for the Undergraduate loans is $518 + $1429 + $1933 = $3880. I did a corresponding table for the Parent loans. Without showing it a similar sequence occurs. The sum of their **CUMULATIVE INTEREST** amounts is $774 + $2226 + $3005 = $6005. The combined amount is $9885. That's $1727 more than the $8158 for the approach I took. It means this approach is more costly."

"That's all pretty involved, Dad. But it's very interesting. I can see by taking the time to play around with it we could minimize the interest paid."

"That's right! The most effective way would be to apply all $500 of acceleration to just the Parent loans,"

"Why?"

"Because of their higher **ANNUAL RATE OF INTEREST**, 7.21% compared to 4.66%. That's evident from the preceding results. In each acceleration option the **CUMULATIVE INTEREST** portion of the Parent loans was much higher than for the Undergraduate loans.

In fact I did calculate that third option. Without the details, the result is the consecutive Parent loans end at 14 months, 17 months and 20 months. The summed **CUMULATIVE INTEREST** = $252 + $314 + $392 = $958. The Undergraduate loans have no acceleration and run the full 10-year **TERM**. Their summed **CUMULATIVE INTEREST** = $1583 + 1755 + 1933 = $5271. Combined, that's $6229. But you take the brunt of the hit! So we wouldn't do that."

"But you pay a part of it while I am in college, Dad."

"Actually, you're correct. But I still wouldn't do it, Peanut.".

Consolidation

"There is another matter which will arise. If you recall, I did mention the action of combining all of one's individual loans can be done by consolidation."

"I remember you saying that, Dad."

"We could each do that. But we can only do that when you've completed your studies. There are advantages and disadvantages for doing it. When graduation is nearing I can dig into the details and we can look it over together. We will see if that is an even better path."

"Even if I am a lot smarter by then I am sure I will need and want your help. You'll always be smarter than me. At least until the one day arises where I can outsmart you on a money matter."

"One thing is for sure, Smarty Pants. You'll know a ton more about journalism and media than I ever will. More important, you'll be learning most of it at Dream University."

"I have you and Mom to thank so much for that. I'm about to cry."

It's midway through spring semester at Dream University. Nicole is a sophomore transfer student and well into her second semester in the Journalism and Media Communications program, Let's peek in on an interesting episode in Nicole's college life.

Nicole is enjoying college and making new friends at Dream University. Along the way she met a young woman named Timmy, also a sophomore. They are becoming close friends. Timmy takes Nicole into confidence about a money management plight. Maybe it's more a plea for help than sharing in confidence. Evidently, Timmy has not had the same experience as Nicole when it comes to managing a credit card. Timmy has been pretty careless and naïve with hers. She is falling further and further behind. She is aware that Nicole is a great manager of money and that she learned about handling a credit card properly before she got hers. She asks Nicole for HELP!

SITUATION 18

Timmy receives $600.00 each month from her parents for expenses such as groceries, laundry, etc. and activities. Being old enough to act independently, as an entering first year student, she acted on her own to get a credit card. She was cajoled into getting one by a bank vendor booth outside the campus bookstore. In due time it arrived in her mail and she signed the back side and phoned in to activate the card. Unwittingly, because her creditworthiness turned out to be low her credit card came with an **UPPER LIMIT** of $1000.00 and **APR** of 18.00%. The **MINIMUM PAYMENT** due each month was either 4.00% of the **OUTSTANDING BALANCE** or $25.00, whichever is higher. But if the **BALANCE DUE** in a **MONTHLY STATEMENT** is paid in full no interest is charged.

Timmy has been charging $400.00 in purchases each month, primarily for groceries. As she decided she wanted extra money, primarily "cosmetics money" plus "doing things" she decided to pay the higher amount of either the half of the **NEW BALANCE** each month or the minimum amount due each month. Each payment is received on time.

NOTE: As for Nicole in an earlier lesson the **INTEREST CHARGE** will be obtained by applying the **MONTHLY RATE OF INTEREST** to the **PREVIOUS BALANCE** shown on the **MONTHLY STATEMENT**. The following shows the track of the monthly activity for eighteen months.

The first **MONTHLY STATEMENT** was received and it indicated a **PREVIOUS BALANCE** of $0.00, the $400.00 of purchases, and a **NEW BALANCE** of $400.00. No interest was charged. The **MINIMUM PAYMENT** due = 0.04 x $400.00 = $16.00. Half the **NEW BALANCE** was 0.50 x $400.00 = $303.00. A payment of $200.00 was made and received on time.

The second **MONTHLY STATEMENT** was received. The **PREVIOUS BALANCE** is $400.00. The credit card issuer applied a **MONTHLY RATE OF INTEREST** = 18.00%/12 months = 1.50% to that amount. Thus, the **INTEREST CHARGE** = 0.015 x $400.00 = $6.00 and was added to the **PREVIOUS BALANCE**. Additional **PURCHASES** of $400.00 were charged. The **NEW BALANCE** = **PREVIOUS BALANCE** – **PAYMENT** + **PURCHASES** + **INTEREST CHARGE** = $400.00 - $200.00 + $400.00 +$6.00 = $606.00. The **MINIMUM PAYMENT** due = 0.04 x $616.00 = $24.24. Half the **NEW BALANCE** is 0.50 x $616.00 = $303.00. The $303.00 amount was paid and received on time.

The third **MONTHLY STATEMENT** was received. The **PREVIOUS BALANCE** is $606.00. Thus, the **INTEREST CHARGE** = 0.015 x $606.00 = $9.09 and is added to the **PREVIOUS BALANCE**. Additional **PURCHASES** of $400.00 were charged. The **NEW BALANCE** = $606.00 - $303.00 + $400.00 + $9.09 = $712.09. The **MINIMUM PAYMENT** due = 0.04 x $712.09 = $28.48. Half the **NEW BALANCE** was 0.50 x $712.09 = $356.05. That $356.05 amount was paid and received on time.

The extended trail of **MONTHLY STATEMENTS** is as follows.

Monthly Statement	Previous Balance	Payment Received	Purchases Made	Interest Charge	New Balance	Minimum Payment	Cumulative Interest
1	0	0	400.00	0	400.00	16.00	0.00
2	400.00	200.00	400.00	6.00	606.00	24.24	6.00
3	606.00	303.00	400.00	9.09	712.09	28.48	15.09
4	712.09	356.05	400.00	10.68	766.73	30.67	25.77
5	766.73	383.36	400.00	11.5	794.86	31.79	37.27
6	794.86	397.43	400.00	11.92	809.35	32.37	49.19
7	809.35	404.68	400.00	12.14	816.82	32.67	61.33
8	816.82	408.41	400.00	12.25	820.66	32.83	73.58
9	820.66	410.33	400.00	12.31	822.64	32.91	85.89
10	822.64	411.32	400.00	12.34	823.66	32.95	98.23
11	823.66	411.83	400.00	12.35	824.18	32.97	110.58
12	824.18	412.09	400.00	12.36	824.45	32.98	122.94
13	824.45	412.22	400.00	12.37	824.59	32.98	135.31
14	824.59	412.30	400.00	12.37	824.67	32.99	147.68
15	824.67	412.33	400.00	12.37	824.70	32.99	160.05
16	824.70	412.35	400.00	12.37	824.72	32.99	172.42
17	824.72	412.36	400.00	12.37	824.73	32.99	184.79
18	824.73	412.37	400.00	12.37	824.73	32.99	197.16
19	824.73	412.37	400.00	12.37	824.73	32.99	209.53

SITUATION 18 - CONTINUED

Not unexpectedly, Timmy does not have the above physical trail to look at. She just sees what her **NEW BALANCE** is on each **MONTHLY STATEMENT**. She knows something's wrong. But not knowing what is wrong, she immaturely had been ignoring the matter.

Clearly, Timmy's credit card debt (**NEW BALANCE**) is not declining. Instead it is <u>growing!</u> However, after the end of Month 6, it begins to level off. That's because at the end of Month 6, her **PAYMENT RECEIVED** was $404.68. For that month and thereafter her **PAYMENT RECEIVED** exceeds the $400.00 in monthly purchases. In Month 17, her **NEW BALANCE** became $824.73 and remained at that amount for each succeeding month. Starting in Month 13, the **INTEREST CHARGE** also leveled off at $12.37. She was not adding to her net debt but she was accumulating more and more **CUMULATIVE INTEREST**. At the end of Month 18, if she could pay the **NEW BALANCE** of $824.73 Timmy will have paid in full and in Month 19 as her **PREVIOUS BALANCE** would be $0.00. Then in the next month she would begin with a fresh round of $400.00 in purchases and might repeat the above monthly events.

If, instead, at the end of Month 18 Timmy continues her pattern of paying only half the **NEW BALANCE** she pays $412.37, and then her **NEW BALANCE** of $824.73 for Month 18 becomes the **PREVIOUS BALANCE** for Month 19. She then accrues another **INTEREST CHARGE** of $12.37.

For Month 19 the **NEW BALANCE** = $824.73 - $412.37 + $400.00 + $12.37 = $824.73, again. This will occur again for each succeeding month. That's because her **MONTHLY PAYMENT** has become a constant $412.37. So no progress is being made in reducing the **NEW BALANCE**, that is, her credit card debt will stay constant from then on and **NEVER GET PAID OFF** and the **CUMULATIVE INTEREST** will keep growing by the $12.37 each month.

Seeing this happening Timmy contacts her parents and asks if they will help in paying off $824.73 of her debt. Wisely, they point out that as she acted alone to get a credit card and did it carelessly. She acted to not pay $400.00 each month, so she is responsible for the debt. They advise her to drink water, eat peanut butter sandwiches and "Ramen" for a good while and do crossword puzzles and Sudoku for entertainment, so she can have more money available to increase her monthly credit card payment and eventually pay off her $824.73 debt.

That's Timmy's credit card debt situation when she has the desperation and courage to chat with Nicole.

Exercise 24: *For SITUATION 18 extend the results through MONTHLY STATEMENT 21.*

Your __partial__ results should be

Monthly Statement	Previous Balance	Payment Received	Purchases Made	Interest Charge	New Balance	Minimum Payment	Cumulative Interest
19	824.73	412.37	400.00	12.37	824.73	32.99	209.53
20	824.73	412.37	400.00	12.37	824.73	32.99	221.90
21	824.73	412.37	400.00	12.37	824.73	32.99	234.27

SITUATION 18 - CONTINUED

Nicole is feeling concerned about her friends predicament. Inside she gleams a bit about herself, knowing she is well prepared to help. It feels nice to be able mimic her Dad's role when he taught her. She also feels a bit special that she can put her relative prowess with spreadsheets in play. Atop her

Dad's help, she got an A+ on that topic in high school.

Being a caring friend, Nicole wants Timmy to learn a practical lesson. She wants to shows her how to calculate that if she had made a $400.00 payment each month, she would have kept her credit card **NEW BALANCE** at $400.00, just at the amount of her new purchases. And she indicates that if Timmy made those payments on time she would incur no **INTEREST CHARGES**. She asks Timmy for permission to take all her **MONTHLY STATEMENTS** for a while. She indicates she will dig into and try to help fix it. Timmy jumps at the chance.

Nicole spends some time during the next week to develop a spreadsheet for the flow of Timmy's credit card monthly outcomes. She produces what was shown earlier as the extended trail of her payment history

Meanwhile, Timmy's parents have told her that unless she gets her credit card **NEW BALANCE** to $0.00 in two months, they will stop sending her money. They also unconditionally give her a copy of a prior edition of this book (void of this Lesson) and indicate they used it to learn to do the calculations they have shown her, and much, much more! They simply "suggest" that she consider reading it and learn what they have learned.

Feeling even more pressured Timmy decides she has no time to read a book. Why should she? She has Nicole digging into her problem.

When Nicole next meets Timmy, she gives her the direct evidence by showing her results to Timmy and explaining them to her.

Nicole gives Timmy the following tabulation. It shows the trial of **MONTHLY STATEMENT** outcomes if Timmy had paid the full $400.00 monthly.

Monthly Statement	Previous Balance	Payment Received	Purchases Made	Interest Charge	New Balance	Minimum Payment	Cumulative Interest
1	0.00	0.00	400.00	0	400.00	16	0.00
2	400.00	400.00	400.00	0	400.00	16	0.00
3	400.00	400.00	400.00	0	400.00	16	0.00
4	400.00	400.00	400.00	0	400.00	16	0.00
5	400.00	400.00	400.00	0	400.00	16	0.00
6	400.00	400.00	400.00	0	400.00	16	0.00

SITUATION 18 - CONTINUED

Nicole explains the trail and points out that, as intended, the **NEW BALANCE** is $400.00 each month because the payment of $400.00 cancels the **PREVIOUS BALANCE**. She notes that since it was paid on time, the **INTEREST CHARGE** is $0.00. Then each time Timmy makes the next month **PURCHASES** of $400.00,

NEW BALANCE = PREVIOUS BALANCE – PAYMENT + INTEREST CHARGE + PURCHASES

$$= \$400.00 - \$400.00 + \$0.00 + \$400.00 = \$400.00$$

It seems to be sinking in. She asks Timmy if she follows it all and Timmy nods affirmatively.

Nicole does not to overly interfere with Timmy's parents' strong intention for Timmy to figure the way out of her present credit card debt herself. She asks Timmy if she can do spreadsheets. She does. So Timmy tells her to try taking the next step on her own, to figure out plan of action based on calculating different repayment paths.

Timmy is reluctant to do so. But she would really like to stop appearing to be incompetent. So she agrees to try.

Timmy lingers for a few days. As her food supply is running down, she opts to plan to drink water and eat peanut butter sandwiches and Ramen. She tries to think out how she can pay down her credit card debt in two months. She "gets nowhere." So Timmy "caves in" to her parents' admonition and advice. She begins to read this book. Not being a "math major" but knowing mathematics well, she is surprised how quickly she reads it. She finishes enough of it before her next credit card payment is due. So she takes action.

Timmy's first step is to avoid any more purchases on her credit card. Her second step is to estimate that she will spend only $50.00 per month on her new diet, and pay for it in cash. Her third step is to estimate that each month she needs have $50.00 for a book of Sudoku puzzles, a book of crossword puzzles, and "just in case she needs cash for something". Her fourth step is to compute what happens if she uses the remaining $500.00 per month to make payments on her credit card. The results of her calculations are as follows.

Monthly Statement	Previous Balance	Payment Received	Purchases Made	Interest Charge	New Balance	Minimum Payment	Cumulative Interest
18	824.73	412.37	400.00	12.37	824.73	32.99	197.16
19	824.73	500.00	0	12.37	337.10	13.48	209.53
20	337.10	500.00	0	5.06	-157.83	-6.31	214.59

SITUATION 18 - CONTINUED

Timmy's reaction is **WOW**! She sees that she can readily solve her problem. For Month 19, her **NEW BALANCE** is only $337.10. Paying $500.00 that month would result in overpayment of $157.83. She actually can end her debt by paying $337.10. That's because by paying the **PREVIOUS BALANCE** in full, she avoids the **INTEREST CHARGE** in Statement 20.

Despite initially falling prey to bad money and credit card management, Timmy actually loves math and is very capable at it. Indeed she is clever enough to deduce that she can take an alternative path. Instead of paying $500.00 at the end of Month 19, she can reduce that amount to free up more of her budget for other needs. She deduces she can do that by making equal payments of less than $500.00 for each month. Timmy tries $425.00. The results are:

Monthly Statement	Previous Balance	Payment Received	Purchases Made	Interest Charge	New Balance	Minimum Payment	Cumulative Interest
18	824.73	412.37	400.00	12.37	824.73	32.99	197.16
19	824.73	425.00	0	12.37	412.10	16.48	209.53
20	412.10	425.00	0	6.18	-6.71	-0.27	215.72

SITUATION 18 - CONTINUED

Almost **VOILA!** Her **NEW BALANCE** in Month 19 is only $412.10. Math whiz Timmy wants each payment to be exactly equal. So her current plan is **NOT QUITE VOILA!** Timmy experiments by slightly changing the payment a few times she gets the following result.

Monthly Statement	Previous Balance	Payment Received	Purchases Made	Interest Charge	New Balance	Minimum Payment	Cumulative Interest
18	824.73	412.37	400.00	12.37	824.73	32.99	197.16
19	824.73	418.55	0	12.37	418.55	16.74	209.53
20	418.55	418.55	0	6.28	6.28	0.25	215.81

SITUATION 18 - CONTINUED

VOILA! Timmy need only pay $418.55 for **MONTHLY STATEMENT 19** and **MONTHLY STATEMENT 20**.

Consequently, Timmy has regained money in her monthly budget. Specifically, she has an extra $600.00 - $418.55 = $181.45 per month available for two months. So she can spend that on better food and/or a movie or two or three each month etc. She can eat hot dogs and hamburger instead of bread, peanut butter and Ramen and perhaps buy some soda pop, and maybe still take in one movie per month. She also understands that thereafter she can charge $400.00 each month on food. If pays the **NEW BALANCE** of $400.00 each month as Timmy showed her above, she will have $200.00 each month for other expenses. What's the best part? Timmy "thinks" she has outsmarted her parents. In reality, they have outsmarted her. They had actually done the above calculations themselves and simply waited to see if their daughter would get to the answer. Along the way, she learned a great lesson about managing credit card debt. Priceless!

They don't know about Nicole's intervention. If they did, they would see it was in response to a call for help to a peer. That's OK. They would also see that Nicole simply got Timmy started in the right direction and she was whiz once on that path. That would be even better than OK. It would be another Priceless finding.

Timmy also has a Priceless moment. She happily shares her steps and results with Nicole. Nicely, Nicole tells Timmy that she knew she was a smarty pants and she just had to put them on and start walking, then running. And that now she was going full speed ahead.

That's what makes a good friend. And borrowing her Dad's favorite line just added a nice touch to it.

At a glance, credit card loans have characteristics and implications similar to loan SITUATIONS covered in Lesson 5 regarding debt on loans with a **MONTHLY RATE OF INTEREST**. However, there is a significant, mathematically involved difference. Each time a purchase is made it becomes an instantaneous additional debt added to the credit card **OUTSTANDING BALANCE**. The preceding SITUATIONS involved a consistent $400.00 each month, but without specifying when they occurred. In effect they were treated as if they each occurred on a single day and were subject to one month of interest if left unpaid. That was done as a simplification to facilitate the initial presentation of the concepts. In reality, the $400.00 would be spent sporadically in various amounts on different days. Theoretically, she could have made small purchases on each day of the month. If so, then the money is actually being loaned on a daily basis and debt is growing on a daily basis.

LESSON 16 *I'll Be Graduating Soon, Now What?*

While moving along in her studies to Nicole it seems like completing her degree was always far off in the distance. Dedicated but demanding work was an almost constant presence. Social life and occasionally attending sports and other events offered respites. Semester breaks offered pauses. But even those breaks included some work.

Now, realizing she is almost midway through her final semester, it feels like it has all flown by. In about two months she will be graduating. She's busy job searching. She had considered graduate school, but opted to wait on that if she did it at all. Recent graduates returning as speakers or for alumni events were mixed on that point. But most felt progressing in the journalism or media fields was best served by getting a running start and thus experience. Having that enables better insight as to what line of graduate studies would best fit one's career directions. In some cases it a Master's degree simply was not needed. So Nicole elected as she did, the job path.

Another matter is on her mind, the repayment of her **FSA** loan debt. Her parents had indeed opted to begin accelerated repayment on all loans during her time in college. At the time her Dad had projected the outcome of doing that. Nicole's reverie brings to mind her Dad's alert that as her graduation neared they would work together on the post-graduation loan repayment approach. She remembered his mention of consolidation of her loans. So she phones him to remind him and that she could come home over Spring break to do that.

"Yes Nicole, I can do that. Since its a couple weeks away I can research it and be prepared. So let's plan on it."

When the time arrives, Dad begins with some general information.

"Typically, just like with our situation, once college studies are about to be completed a student and parent each have several individual **FSA** loans in place. That's the consequence of awarded loans being disbursed separately during each school year. When graduation is nearing, the primary decision borrowers must make is whether to consolidate their multiple loans into a single loan debt or not. I've looked into that option and it's pretty straightforward as to how it works"

"That's nice to hear. So would we be consolidating all of six of our loans, mine and yours?"

"Consolidating the Undergraduate loans together with the Parent loans is not allowed. Each set must be treated separately.

"The first step in consolidation is to determine what the resulting **LOAN AMOUNT, ANNUAL RATE OF INTEREST** and **TERM** will be for the consolidated loan. Functionally, the information is obtained from a potential lender. As your graduation is approaching, the government agency and/or private agency issuer(s) of your individual **FSA** loans will alert you that the beginning of repayment is close at hand. So you should receive that alert soon. Details of the status your loans and terms of them will be provided. The lenders will also inquire as to our desire to consolidate them or not. Just as with getting numerous credit card offers, you likely will receive several to many inquiries from other lenders offering an opportunity to consolidate via them. That's because in addition to government based lenders, private entities have been contracted to service student loans. They will offer about the same terms for consolidation."

"How do we determine those things now, Dad?"

"I spoke to the **FSA** staff by phone. There is an array of lenders out there. So I also spoke to one of them, in general terms. But the procedure is essentially the same for all of them. There is no **ORIGINATION FEE** for a consolidated loan. The **LOAN AMOUNT** is the total owed on all the individual loans you would be consolidating. Typically, one considers consolidating them all, but that is not required. You can retain some of the individual loans and consolidate the others. It is our option to investigate any combination we wish to include, either all of them or some subset. The lenders will presume the former unless you inform them otherwise. We'll just assume we will consolidate all of them. To do otherwise is more involved and I doubt we would do it anyway.

"The lender I spoke with indicated for them the determination of the **TERM** is automatic. It's based on the **LOAN AMOUNT** and its fit within some brackets. I had already found them at the **FSA** website, too. I wrote them out."

LOAN AMOUNT	TERM
$0.00 to $7499.99	10 years
$7500.00 to $9999.99	12 years
$10000.00 to $19999.99	15 years
$20000.00 to $39999.99	20 years
$40000.00 to $59999.99	25 years
$60000.00 or more	30 years

"That looks easy, Dad. I noticed that if we owe $60000.00 or more then the **TERM** will be 30 years. I don't think that's a good thing for **CUMULATIVE INTEREST**."

"That's correct.

"The **ANNUAL RATE OF INTEREST** will be a new <u>fixed</u> rate. It will be the **weighted average** of the individual rates on the separate loans being consolidated, rounded up to the nearest 0.125%. When you inquire with a potential lender, they will provide you the values once you have specified which loans you are consolidating. We are considering consolidating all three loans for each of us.

"Let's look at the case of your loans and assume you use the grace period. At the time you were deciding to enroll at Sure Thing University for just one year, I had worked up what the **OUTSTANDING BALANCES** would be when you reached that point."

"That was more than four years ago. I remember you doing that but not the amounts of course."

"I wouldn't either. But I still have them in my computer. At the time of your Graduation the projected **OUTSTANDING BALANCES** for your loans were $0, $4687 and $7186, which total $11873."

ASIDE: At that time Dad used the **ANNUAL RATE OF INTEREST** of 4.66% for all the loans. He didn't have a magic crystal ball for seeing the future rates. As Nicole actually proceeded along in college, new rates would come into play each year. The resulting **OUTSTANDING BALANCES** at the time of graduation would also differ somewhat than the approximate amounts Dad calculated. Without a magic crystal ball, at the time of writing this book the author cannot calculate the actual **OUTSTANDING BALANCES** either.

The author could have assumed new values for the actual **ANNUAL RATES OF INTEREST**. To get the actual **OUTSTANDING BALANCES** one would redo all his previous calculations using those rates. That would create an inconsistency. That lengthy repetition of the process is also unnecessary in this book and avoided by using a simplification. The author will use the estimated results previously projected by Dad, based on the 4.66% interest rate. That allows results from Dad's past **AMORTIZATION SCHEDULE S** to be carried over.

"Well, Nicole, what is the **TERM** for the **LOAN AMOUNT** of $11873?"

"From the brackets, I see it would be 15 years."

"The **WEIGHTED AVERAGE INTEREST RATE** is the **WEIGHTED INTEREST RATE** divided by the **LOAN AMOUNT**. Here is the calculation.

WEIGHTED INTEREST RATE = $4687 x 4.66% + $7186 x 4.66% = 57022 $ x %.

(NOTE: "$ x %" are the "units" of the value, albeit odd looking.)

WEIGHTED AVERAGE INTEREST RATE = 57022 $ x %/$11873 = 4.66
= 4.75% (rounded upward)

"Do you understand it?"

"Yes, I do. I learned about calculating a weighted average in a business course I took."

"Oddly, although both loans had the same **ANNUAL RATE OF INTEREST** of 4.66%,the required rounding up results in a different (and higher) value for the consolidated loan. While sort of an anomaly, in reality it is possible the **ANNUAL RATE OF INTEREST** could be the same for two consecutive loan years."

Exercise 24: Repeat Dad's calculation of the **WEIGHTED AVERAGE INTEREST RATE** *using* **ANNUAL RATES OF INTEREST** *of 4.75% and 5.00% for the consecutive loans.*

Your results should be:

WEIGHTED INTEREST RATE = 37452 $ x %. WEIGHTED AVERAGE INTEREST RATE = 4.875% (rounded upward).

"With the terms of the consolidation loan established, I did the **AMORTIZATION SCHEDULE**."

Consolidated Undergraduate							Principal = 11873	
Loan Amount	11873							
Origination Fee Rate	0.00							
Origination Fee	0							
Term in Years	**Annual Rate of Interest**	**Month**	**Monthly Payment**	**Applied to Interest**	**Applied to Principal**	**Additional Amount Applied to Principal**	**Outstanding Principal**	**Cumulative Interest**
15	4.75	1	92.35	47.00	45.35	0.00	11827.65	47.00
		2	92.35	46.82	45.53	0.00	11782.11	93.82
		12	92.35	44.98	47.37	0.00	11316.74	551.96
		36	92.35	40.27	52.08	0.00	10121.88	1573.56
		60	92.35	35.09	57.26	0.00	8808.20	2476.32
		84	92.35	29.40	62.95	0.00	7363.87	3248.43
		108	92.35	23.14	69.22	0.00	5775.89	3876.90
		132	92.35	16.25	76.10	0.00	4029.98	4347.45
		156	92.35	8.69	83.67	0.00	2110.44	4644.35
		180	92.35	0.36	91.99	0.00	0.00	4750.36

"The **CUMULATIVE INTEREST** paid is $4760. That's additional to the amount paid during your studies."

"So should I consolidate my loans, Dad?"

"Well, that depends. Let's look further and see what happens if you don't."

"Remember I did the **AMORTIZATION SCHEDULE** for each of the separate loans if you continued paying on the 10 year **TERMS**. When all those loans have ended the **CUMULATIVE INTEREST** amounts for the Undergraduate loans are $3215. At Graduation you will have paid $1112 of it already. Thereafter you will pay the rest, $2103.

"That compares to the $4750 for the consolidated loan. So what do you conclude, Nicole?"

"It looks like consolidation is not a wise choice. The **CUMULATIVE INTEREST** is awhole bunch higher."

"That's how I see it, too. I actually played around with it trying different loan circumstances and apparently the consolidation always leads to significantly more **CUMULATIVE INTEREST**. The reason is the longer **TERM** for the consolidated loan. But I've got an extra card up my sleeve. So let's play it."

"You always have surprises Dad. And the older I get the bigger they seem to be. But college has been expanding my brain cells, so now when you spring one on me I catch on to it much more quickly. So play your card, please."

"I certainly see how much four years of college time has matured you. Our playing field is leveling off more and more as each year passes. For sure, one of these years you will outsmart your dear old Dad."

"I'll try to do it before too long."

"Let's continue "smarter pants". What I investigated is accelerating repayment of the consolidated loan in a specific way. The **MONTHLY PAYMENT** for the consolidated loan is $92.35. The combined **MONTHLY PAYMENTS** for the individual loans is $63.55 + $72.44 + $79.81 = $215.81. That's $123.46 more. If you have to pay that much more, why not see what that extra amount does if it is used as **ADDITIONAL AMOUNT APPLIED TO PRINCIPAL** on a consolidated loan?"

"I don't see any reason why not. It makes a lot of sense to try that."

"Here's the result of doing it"

Consolidated Undergraduate							Principal = 11873	
Loan Amount	11873							
Origination Fee Rate	0.00							
Origination Fee	0							
Term in Years	Annual Rate of Interest	Month	Monthly Payment	Applied to Interest	Applied to Principal	Additional Amount Applied to Principal	Outstanding Principal	Cumulative Interest
15	4.75	1	92.35	47.00	45.35	123.46	11704.19	47.00
		2	92.35	46.33	46.02	123.46	11534.70	93.33
		62	92.35	1.00	91.36	123.46	36.72	1544.06
		63	92.35	0.15	92.21	123.46	-178.95	1544.21
		63	36.87	0.15	36.72	0.00	0.00	1544.21

"Nicole, how much **CUMULATIVE INTEREST** is paid now compared to before?"

"It's $1544 compared to $3726 when the consolidated loan is not accelerated. That's less than half of it. And it's also a lot less than the combined **CUMULATIVE INTEREST** of $2103 that I'd pay for the individual loans. That sure is interesting. Now it looks like accelerating repayment of a consolidated loan is the best path."

"And, when does this loan get paid off?"

"Gee, Dad. It gets paid off in Month 63. That's just a little more than five years, instead of twelve."

"It works out that way for these circumstances. I did it for the Parent loans and got a similar outcome. It's not necessary to show that to you. Maybe it does for other loan circumstances, too. When I get a chance to play around with the concept a lot more, I will have a definitive finding on it.

"For now my conclusion and advice are to pursue the consolidated loan and accelerate it. There's another valuable incentive for doing that. If it becomes difficult to pay the **ADDITIONAL AMOUNT APPLIED TO PRINCIPAL**, you can reduce it or even stop it. You would have to be careful. If you do it too soon and too long, you're headed toward the **CUMULATIVE INTEREST** of $3726. But I'm certain you know enough about doing **AMORTIZATION SCHEDULE S** you would be able to check it out in advance and along the way. For the **MONTHLY PAYMENT** amounts involved here I doubt you will have difficulty maintaining a **MONTHLY PAYMENT** of $215.81. But you never know what comes along. If something serious happens we might bail you out, too.

"Oh by the way, I have some optional homework. You can rework all this for the circumstance of your using the grace period. Because the **OUTSTANDING BALANCES** are so much lower, I suspect the results are less dramatic in absolute dollars, so I passed on it. But you're welcome to try it."

"I sure would like to Dad, But you see, a place called Dream University is keeping me busy almost over my head until I graduate, so I'll concur with you and pass on it too."

"That's right, I sort of got lost in all this. Mom and I can hardly wait. We're already practicing our wide smiles and yelling, That's our daughter! That's our daughter! Yay Nicole!"

"I'll be all ears for that. Thank you for all your time and effort and working through all this for and with me."

"You're very welcome, smarter pants."

Although about 80% of high school graduates continue on to college, most stop upon completion of a Bachelor's degree. Some may be pursuing a career where advanced studies are not required. Others may prefer to explore their career first to assess its fit and the need for another degree. Some gradually earn an advanced degree while being employed. Their employer might help support such an interest. Others may simply not academically qualify for advanced studies.

Pursuing an advanced degree involves a continuation of the high costs involved in pursuing a college education. Completing a Master's degree will add one to two years of costs. Completing a Doctoral degree will add three years of costs. Completing Professional studies (e.g. medical school) will add even more time. Typically tuition rates are higher than for an undergraduate degree. If one elects to pursue graduate/professional studies then **FSA** loans are available to assist with costs. But the criteria and terms are much different than for undergraduate students.

Graduate/professional student borrowers are considered to be independent and solely responsible for their costs of living. So the amounts they are allowed to borrow are significantly more than those of an undergraduate student. In effect, the **U.S.D.E.** assumes an undergraduate has his/her cost of living primarily covered by the parents and a graduate/professional student does not. The student might actually still be a financial dependent of the parents. Regardless, the **U.S.D.E.** treats the situation like he or she is not dependent. There are important implications.

Herein, the focus is on graduate students. The loan cost rates are the same for professional students but the permissible borrowing amounts are higher and rules more involved than for graduate students. **APPENDIX I** includes a summary of the **FSA** web site for information.

Graduate FSA Loan Rates

Graduate students can apply for **Graduate Unsubsidized FSA Loans**. Details of those loans are addressed in this Lesson. Subsidized loans are not available. The **ORIGINATION FEE RATES** are the same as for Undergraduate loans. But the **ANNUAL RATES OF INTEREST** are higher. The applicable values are listed in following table.

Graduate Direct Unsubsidized Loans				
Period of Disbursement				
July 1, 2014 - June 30, 2015	**July 1, 2015 - June 30, 2016**	**July 1, 2016 - June 30, 2017**	**July 1, 2017 - June 30, 2018**	
Annual Rate of Interest				
6.21%	5.84%	5.31%	6.00%	
Date of First Disbursement				
August 1, 2014	**August 1, 2015**	**August 1, 2016**	**August 1, 2017**	**August 1, 2018**
Origination Fee Rate				
1.072%	1.073%	1.068%	1.069%	1.066%

A graduate student can also apply for **Direct PLUS Loans**. But his/her parents are not permitted to apply for **Direct PLUS Loans** of their own. The loan costs are the same as for parent **Direct PLUS Loans** as covered in Lesson 11. That content carries over to this Lesson. For convenience the loan rates are repeated below.

Graduate/Parent Direct PLUS Loans				
Period of Disbursement				
July 1, 2014 - June 30, 2015	July 1, 2015 - June 30, 2016	July 1, 2016 - June 30, 2017	July 1, 2017 - June 30, 2018	
Annual Rate of Interest				
7.210%	6.840%	6.310%	7.00%	
Date of First Disbursement				
August 1, 2014	August 1, 2015	August 1, 2016	August 1, 2017	August 1, 2018
Origination Fee Rate				
4.288%	4.292%	4.272%	4.276%	4.264%

The **Direct PLUS Loan** costs are higher than for a **Graduate Unsubsidized FSA Loan**. Usually a graduate student will be approved for a certain amount of **Graduate Unsubsidized FSA Loan** funds. Should the amount be less than needed, the student can elect to apply for additional funds via **Direct PLUS Loans**. But he/she will pay the higher loan costs.

Graduate Base Loans

Similar to Lesson 11, the approach herein is the use of base loans and a scaling of those results for other **LOAN AMOUNTS**. The following SITUATION exemplifies development of base loan results for a **Graduate Unsubsidized FSA Loan**.

SITUATION 19

Carmelo pursued a Master's degree which he will complete in May 2018. He obtained a **Graduate Unsubsidized FSA Loan** for the period July 1, 2017 – June 30, 2018. The loan has a 5-year **TERM**. He will begin repayment after using the 6-month grace period. All interest charged during the deferred/grace period will be paid.

The **LOAN AMOUNT** was $1000.00. Half was disbursed on August 1, 2017 and the other half was disbursed on February 1, 2018. The **ORIGINATION FEE** was paid when the disbursements were made. The following details the costs of repaying the loan.

The applicable **ORIGINATION FEE RATE** is 1.066%.

ORIGINATION FEE = (1.066%/100)($1000) = $10.66
LOAN AMOUNT = $1000.00 - $10.66 = $989.34
MONTHLY RATE OF INTEREST = 6.00%/12 months
= 0.50%/month (rounded)

MRATIO = 0.50/100 = 0.00500
TERM = 5 years x 12 months/year = 60 months
$(MRATIO + 1)^{term} = (1 + 0.00500)^{60} = (1.0500)^{60}$
= (1.00500)(1.00500)(1.00500)….. 60 times!
= 1.35 (rounded)
NUMERATOR = PRINCIPAL x MRATIO x $(MRATIO + 1)^{TERM}$
= 989.34 x 0.00500 x 1.35 = 6.68 (rounded)
DENOMINATOR = $(MRATIO + 1)^{TERM} - 1$ =1.35 – 1 = 0.35
MPAYMENT = NUMERATOR/DENOMINATOR = 6.68/0.35
= $19.09/per month (rounded)

Using more precise calculations, MPAYMENT = $19.13.

AMORTIZATION SCHEDULE :

Loan Amount	1000.00							
Origination Rate	1.066%							
Origination Fee	10.66						Principal 989.34	
Term in Years	Annual Rate of Interest	Month	Monthly Payment	Applied to Interest	Applied to Principal		Remaining Principal	Cumulative Interest
5	6.00	1	19.13	4.95	14.18		975.16	4.95
		2	19.13	4.88	14.25		960.91	9.82
		12	19.13	4.15	14.98		814.42	54.60
		24	19.13	3.22	15.90		628.71	98.42
		36	19.05	2.18	16.87		430.56	127.16
		48	19.13	1.20	17.93		222.23	150.97
		60	19.13	0.10	19.03		0.00	158.26

SITUATION 19 - CONTINUED

When the loan is paid off the **CUMULATIVE INTEREST** is $158.26. That does not include the interest Carmelo paid during the deferred/grace period. Together with the **ORIGINATION FEE**, the **TOTAL COST** = $158.26 + $10.66 = $168.92. Referring to SITUATION 10 of Lesson 9, for a comparable $1000.00 base loan for an undergraduate student the **TOTAL COST** was $122.38. So, Carmelo pays $46.64 more (about 35% more) **TOTAL COST** than if he were an undergraduate student. That occurs even though his **MONTHLY PAYMENT** is only $19.13 compared to $18.35 for the undergraduate student. Because of the higher **ANNUAL RATE OF INTEREST**, a much higher portion of his **MONTHLY PAYMENT** was **APPLIED TO INTEREST**.

Graduate-Base Loan Table

Similar to Lessons 9 and 11, a **GRADUATE– BASE LOAN TABLE (G - BASE LOAN TABLE)** can be developed by repeating SITUATION 19 for the other periods of disbursement and **TERMS** of the loan. The author did that and the results are:

GRADUATE-BASE LOAN TABLE								
LOAN AMOUNT = 1000.00			TERM	5 Years	10 Years	15 Years	20 Years	25 Years
DISBURSED	ANNUAL RATE OF INTEREST	ORIG. FEE	PRINCIPAL	MONTHLY PAYMENT				
7/1/14-6/30/15	6.21%	10.72	989.28	19.22	11.09	8.46	7.21	6.50
7/1/15-6/30/16	5.84%	10.73	989.27	19.05	10.90	8.26	7.00	6.28
7/1/16-6/30/17	5.31%	10.60	989.40	18.31	10.64	7.98	6.70	5.96
7/1/17-6/30/18	6.00%	10.66	989.34	19.13	10.98	8.35	7.08	6.37
DISBURSED	ANNUAL RATE OF INTEREST	ORIG. FEE	PRINCIPAL	CUMULATIVE INTEREST				
7/1/14-6/30/15	6.21%	10.72	989.28	164.06	341.24	533.66	740.61	961.18
7/1/15-6/30/16	5.84%	10.73	989.27	153.84	319.16	498.03	689.87	893.87
7/1/16-6/30/17	5.31%	10.60	989.40	139.31	287.94	447.84	618.62	799.76
7/1/17-6/30/18	6.00%	10.66	989.34	158.26	328.70	513.41	711.77	922.96

Using the Graduate-Base Loan Table

Let's consider two specific **LOAN AMOUNTS** of interest. If a graduate student has not taken out any Undergraduate loans, then maximum amount that he/she can be borrow is $138500.00. The **SCALING FACTOR** for that **LOAN AMOUNT** is 138.50. The maximum a dependent undergraduate student can borrow is $31000.00. The maximum amount an independent undergraduate student can borrow is $57500.00. As worst case, if a graduate student previously has taken out the latter amount, then only $81000.00 remains as the maximum amount that he/she can take out during graduate studies. The **SCALING FACTOR** for that **LOAN AMOUNT** is 81.00. For those **LOAN AMOUNTS**, the scaled results for loans disbursed in the current academic years are as follows:

GRADUATE							
DISBURSED 7/1/17-6/30/18	**ANNUAL RATE OF INTEREST = 6.00%**	**TERM**	**5 Years**	**10 Years**	**15 Years**	**20 Years**	**25 Years**
LOAN AMOUNT	**ORIGINATION FEE (RATE = 1.066%)**	**PRINCIPAL**	**MONTHLY PAYMENT**				
1000.00	10.66	989.34	19.13	10.98	8.35	7.08	6.37
81000.00	863.46	80136.54	1549.53	889.38	676.35	573.48	515.97
138500.00	1476.41	137023.59	2649.51	1520.73	1156.48	980.58	882.25
LOAN AMOUNT	**ORIGINATION FEE (RATE = 1.066%)**	**PRINCIPAL**	**CUMULATIVE INTEREST**				
1000.00	10.66	989.34	158.26	328.70	513.41	711.77	922.96
81000.00	863.46	80136.54	12819.06	26624.70	41586.21	57653.37	74759.76
138500.00	1476.41	137023.59	21919.01	45524.95	71107.29	98580.15	127829.96

The monetary implications of such high **LOAN AMOUNTS** for a graduate student are significant. Let's examine them.

SITUATION 20

In May 2018, Genevieve will earn a Bachelor's degree in Biological Engineering. She realizes that to excel in that field she needs to earn Masters and Doctoral degrees. She did not take out any **FSA** loans as an undergraduate student. She has not learned if she will be offered non-government financial aid. Over the course of her advanced studies she could borrow as much as $138500.00 in **FSA** loans. She examines that as a worst case possibility using the loan cost rates for the current academic year.

Referring to the above tabulated results, Genevieve would incur an **ORIGINATION FEE** of $1476.41. Yes, that's $1486.41 paid "up front" just to take out the loan. It is subtracted from the **LOAN AMOUNT**. Consequently, it's that much less funds being used for the academic need.

For a 5-year **TERM**, the **MONTHLY PAYMENT** would be $2649.51 per month. The **CUMULATIVE INTEREST** would be $21919.01 (about 16% of the borrowed amount). The maximum **TERM** allowed for **Standard** repayment is ten years. For that **TERM**, the **MONTHLY PAYMENT** decreases substantially to $1520.73 but the **CUMULATIVE INTEREST** more than doubles to $45524.95 (about 33% of the borrowed amount).

Longer **TERMS** apply to the **Extended** repayment plan. For the 15- and 20-year **TERMS** the **MONTHLY PAYMENT** amounts decrease further to $1156.48 and $980.58, respectively. The corresponding **CUMULATIVE INTEREST** amounts increase further to $71107.29 (about 52% of the borrowed amount) and $98580.15.00 (about 72% of the borrowed amount), respectively.

The maximum **TERM** for the **Extended** repayment plan is twenty five years. For that **TERM** the **MONTHLY PAYMENT** decreases further to $882.25 per month. The **CUMULATIVE INTEREST** increases further $127829.96 (about 93% of the borrowed amount).

The differences starkly reiterate the significance of Genevieve's choice of a repayment option. As the **TERM** increases, the **MONTHLY PAYMENT** decreases from $2649.51 to $882.25. Correspondingly, the **CUMULATIVE INTEREST** increases from $21919.01 to $127829.96. If she does not receive non-governmental financial aid she must make a choice that balances the affordability of the **MONTHLY PAYMENT** and the ultimate cost in **CUMULATIVE INTEREST**. Of course, as her graduate studies begin and continue the applicable loan rates will be changing. But that won't significantly affect the above big picture.

SITUATION 21

Leonard was a non-traditional, independent undergraduate student. He completed a Bachelor's degree in Chemistry in May 2018. He took out **FSA** loans to the maximum amount allowable at the undergraduate level, specifically $57500.00. $81000.00 is left as the maximum he can borrow for graduate studies. During the deferment/grace period, the interest due on his Undergraduate is being paid. The costs for repaying his undergraduate loans would be based on Lesson 9 and the details of the various disbursements. That is bypassed here.

After a 3-month hiatus (within the 6-month grace period) he will begin Master's degree studies in August 2016. As a worst case possibility, he investigates the consequences of borrowing the $81000.00 in **FSA** loans. He uses the July 1, 2017-June 30, 2018 loan cost rates. He plans to pay the interest due on his loans during the deferment/grace period. For the **LOAN AMOUNT** of $81000.00 his results are as follows.

The **ORIGINATION FEE** is $863.46. The **MONTHLY PAYMENT** varies between $1549.53 for a 5-year **TERM** to $515.97 per month for a 25-year **TERM**. Conversely, the **CUMULATIVE INTEREST** varies from $12819.06 or a 5-year **TERM** to $74759.76 for a 25-year **TERM**. He would face a decision about potential loan **TERMS** with results ranging between those limits. For those loans alone, he could pay **CUMULATIVE INTEREST** as low as 16% and as high as 93% of the $81000.00 he borrows.

NOTE: The % values are the same regardless of the **LOAN AMOUNT**.

The above loan costs are much less than for SITUATION 20, wherein Genevieve also borrowed $138500.00. However, she had no undergraduate loans. Leonard has $57500 in undergraduate loans to pay as well. However the interest rates would be much less than for the graduate loans. So overall he has less cost than Genevieve.

If Leonard actually needs to borrow $138500.00 during graduate studies, then he would be $57500.00 short. He cannot use **Direct PLUS Loans** as he has already reached his **Aggregate Limit** for **FSA** loan funds. That shortage (or any lesser amount) would have to come from savings, income or private loan sources. Any possible assistance from parents would have to come that way as well.

The preceding SITUATIONS dramatize the very significant debt that an individual can incur by pursuing graduate studies. If a student fails to achieve non-governmental financial support, it is preferable to work at a job before and/or during pursuit of the advanced degrees. That lessens the amount of financial aid one must take out in the form of **FSA** loans. The student can also consider private bank personal loans, but that is not advisable as they could involve substantially higher interest rates and less flexible repayment then **Direct PLUS Loans**. A parent can do that too.

Let's look at a Graduate loan for a more reasonable **LOAN AMOUNT**.

SITUATION 22

Vincent completed a graduate degree in History. He had **FSA** loans for those studies only. During that period he was in deferment and paid only the interest owed. He had received a significant fellowship from the Smithsonian Institute, greatly reducing his **FSA** borrowing needs. Upon graduating in May 2015 he immediately started repayment of a **Graduate Unsubsidized FSA Loan** disbursed in the July 1, 2014 – June 30, 2015 period. The **LOAN AMOUNT** was $10750.00 and the **TERM** was 10 years.

The **SCALING FACTOR** = $10750.00/$1000.00 = 10.75. Using the **G-BASE LOAN TABLE**, the **ORIGINATION FEE** = 10.75 x $10.72 = $115.24 and was taken out of the **LOAN AMOUNT** at the time the loans were disbursed. The **MONTHLY PAYMENT** = 10.75 x $11.09 = $119.22. Once paid in full, his **CUMLATIVE INTEREST** will be 10.75 x $341.24 = $3668.33.

Exercise 25: Repeat SITUATION 22 with the following changes. Vincent borrows $14100.00. The loan was disbursed in the July 1, 2015 – June 30, 2016 period. The **TERM** of his repayment loan is 15 years.

Your results should be: The **ORIGINATION FEE** = $115.35, **MONTHLY PAYMENT** = $88.80 and **CUMULATIVE INTEREST** = $5353.82.

Exercise 26: Repeat SITUATION 22 with the following changes. Vincent borrows $21000.00. The loan is disbursed in the July 1, 2016 – June 30, 2017 period. The **TERM** of his repayment loan is 20 years.

Your results should be: The **ORIGINATION FEE** = $222.60, **MONTHLY PAYMENT** = $140.70 and **CUMULATIVE INTEREST** = $12991.02.

For simplicity of illustration, SITUATION 22 involved a single past loan. For graduate studies multiple loans are a near certainty. The student need might also involve both **Graduate Unsubsidized FSA Loans** and **Direct PLUS Loans**. The following SITUATIONS illustrate how to address those matters.

SITUATION 23

Loretta earned an undergraduate degree in Biology. She completed those studies in May 2015. She had "full-ride" scholarships, so had no **FSA** loans. In August 2015, she undertook a Master's degree at a prestigious university, which she completed in May 2017. She had some other partial support for those years. For her first year she took out $3000.00 in **Graduate Unsubsidized FSA Loans** and plans to take out $3600.00 in her second year. Both loans will have a 5-year **TERM**.

Loretta plans to begin a Doctoral degree in August 2017, which she hopes to complete in three years. She will proceed only if she has significant non-government financial aid. If so, she estimates she will need about $6400.00 per year in **Graduate Unsubsidized FSA Loans**. She will defer all the loans but pay the interest during that period. She plans to have a professional job upon completing those studies, but assumes a 6-month grace period. For all loans, she will use a 10-year **TERM**.

Loretta projected her loan repayment costs for the M.S. loans are as follows.

For August 2015 – June 2016:

The **SCALING FACTOR** = 3.00.

The **ORIGINATION FEE** = 3.00 x $10.73 = $31.19 and was taken out of the **LOAN AMOUNT** at the time the loans were disbursed. Her **MONTHLY PAYMENT** = 3.00 x $19.05 = $57.15. Once paid in full, her **CUMLATIVE INTEREST** will be 3.00 x $153.84 = $461.52.

For August 2016 – June 2017:

The **SCALING FACTOR** = 3.60.

The **ORIGINATION FEE** = 3.60 x $10.60 = $38.16 and was taken out of the **LOAN AMOUNT** at the time the loans were disbursed. Her **MONTHLY PAYMENT** = 3.60 x $18.31 = $65.92. Once paid in full, her **CUMLATIVE INTEREST** will be 3.60 x $139.31 = $501.52.

....

Loretta projected her loan repayment costs for the Doctoral loans as follows.

For August 2017 – June 30, 2018:

The **SCALING FACTOR** = 6.40

Using the July 1, 2016 – June 30, 2017 loan costs, the **ORIGINATION FEE** = 6.40 x $10.66 = $68.22 and will be taken out of the **LOAN AMOUNT** at the time the loans are disbursed. Her **MONTHLY PAYMENT** = 6.40 x $10.98 = $70.27. Once paid in full, her **CUMLATIVE INTEREST** will be 6.40 x $328.70 = $2103.68.

In case loan rates rise, Loretta repeated her estimate using the higher loan cost parameters for August 2014 – June 30, 2015. The **ORIGINATION FEE** = 6.40 x $10.72 = $68.61. Her **MONTHLY PAYMENT** = 6.40 x $11.09 = $70.98. Once paid in full, her **CUMLATIVE INTEREST** will be 6.40 x $341.24 = $2183.94.

In case loan rates fall, she repeated her estimate using the lower the loan costs parameters for August 2016 – June 30, 2017. The **ORIGINATION FEE** =6.40 x $10.60 = $68.10. Her **MONTHLY PAYMENT** = 6.40 x $10.64 = $68.42. Once paid in full, her **CUMLATIVE INTEREST** will be 6.40 x $287.94 = $1880.64.

For August 2018 – June 30, 2020:

Because the loan rates for the succeeding years are unknown, Loretta applies the preceding results to the next two years. Her estimated combined loan costs for the Doctoral degree are three times those amounts.

SITUATION 24

Patrick is pursuing a Doctoral degree in Anthropology, which he began in August 2015. He completed a Bachelor's degree and a Master's degree in related pre-requisite studies with no **FSA** student loans.

On August 1, 2014 and August 1, 2015, he took out consecutive yearly **Graduate FSA Loans** of $7500.00.

On August 1, 2016 and August 1, 2017, he took out consecutive yearly **Graduate FSA Loans** of $7500.00. But he needed more funds so also took out **Direct PLUS Loans** for $2500.00 each year.

All amounts were disbursed half on August 1 and half on February 1 of the following year. Patrick deferred all payments until he completed his degree in May, but did not take a 6 month grace period. He has a 20-year **TERM** for each loan. 2018. Here are the loan costs.

For the Graduate FSA Loans:

Using a SCALING FACTOR = 7.50 and various amounts G-BASE LOAN TABLE Patrick's loan costs are as follows.

The combined LOAN ORIGINATION FEE = 7.50 x ($10.72 + $10.73 + $10.60 + $10.66) = $320.33.

The combined MONTHLY PAYMENTS = 7.50 x ($7.21 + $7.00 + $6.70 + $7.08) = $209.93.

The combined CUMULATIVE INTEREST = 7.50 x ($740.61 + $689.87 + $618.62 + $711.77) = $20706.53.

For the Direct PLUS Loans:

Using a SCALING FACTOR = 2.50 and various amounts in P-BASE LOAN TABLE of Lesson 11, Patrick's loan costs are as follows.

The combined LOAN ORIGINATION FEE = 2.50 x ($42.72 + $42.76) = $213.70.

The combined MONTHLY PAYMENTS = 2.50 x ($7.03+ $7.42) = $36.13.

The combined CUMULATIVE INTEREST = 2.50 x ($730.02 + $822.91) = $3882.33.

SITUATION 24 - CONTINUED

For all loans together: The **TOTAL LOAN AMOUNT** = $35000.00, **TOTAL ORIGINATION FEE** = $534.03, **TOTAL MONTHLY PAYMENT** = $246.06, and **TOTAL CUMULATIVE INTEREST** = $24588.86. The **TOTAL COST** = $534.03 + $24588.86 = $25122.89 (about 72% of the borrowed funds).

Exercise 27: *Ben started a Master's degree in Mathematics in August 2016 and completed it in May 2018. He had no undergraduate **FSA** loans. Each year he had a **Graduate FSA Loan** with a 15-year **TERM**. In his first and second year he borrowed $8450.00 and $9375.00, respectively. Each was first disbursed on August 1. He deferred repayment but paid the **MONTHLY INTEREST**. He and will begin repayment upon graduating.*

*What are the **TOTAL ORIGINATION FEE, TOTAL MONTHLY PAYMENT, TOTAL CUMULATIVE INTEREST** and **TOTAL COST** amounts?*

Your partial results should be: ***The TOTAL ORIGINATION FEE*** *= $189.51. For the first loan, the MONTHLY PAYMENT = $67.43. For the second loan, the **CUMULATIVE INTEREST** = $4813.22. The **TOTAL CUMULATIVE INTEREST** is 48.23% of the borrowed funds. The **TOTAL COST** = $8786.97.*

Exercise 28: *Mandy is pursuing a Master's degree in Business Administration which she began in 2014 and will it complete in May 2018. As an undergraduate student she used **Graduate FSA Loans** and borrowed $5000.00 each of her last two years (2014-2015 and 2015-2016).*

For her graduate studies, in 2016-2017 Mandy was awarded $9000.00.

*For the period July 1, 2017 – June 30, 2018 she projects that she will receive only $3000.00 in **Graduate FSA Loans**. She projects she will augment that by obtaining $6000.00 in a **Direct PLUS Loan**.*

*All loans were or will be disbursed half on August 1 and half on February 1 of the following year. Each has a **TERM** of 10 years. All have been deferred with the **MONTHLY INTEREST** being paid. Simultaneous repayment will begin immediately after her graduation.*

*What are the **TOTAL ORIGINATION FEE, TOTAL MONTHLY PAYMENT, TOTAL CUMULATIVE INTEREST and TOTAL COST** amounts?*

Your __partial__ results should be:

Period of Disbursement	Loan Type	Origination Fee	Monthly Payment	Cumulative Interest
2014-2015	UG	53.60	?	1251.16
2015-2016	UG	?	50.75	1145.30
	COMBINED	107.23	?	2396.45
2016-2017	G	95.40	?	2591.46
2017-2018	G	31.98	32.94	?
2017-2018	PLUS	?	?	2258.76
	COMBINED	?	99.60	?
2014-2018	TOTAL	491.17	309.31	8232.77

The overall **TOTAL COST = $8723.94.**

For all example loans used there is the additional cost of the **CUMULATIVE INTEREST** paid during the deferred/grace period. The amount can be calculated either approximately or in detail as shown by Nicole's Dad in Lessons 12-14. However, the **ANNUAL RATES OF INTETREST** for the graduate **Direct PLUS** loans are applicable. The interested reader can do the calculations.

If the loans are deferred and ongoing **MONTHLY INTEREST** is not paid, then the loan balances at graduation or the end of a grace period would rise. The consequence of that is more interest is subsequently incurred than otherwise. Calculation of the extra amount is a covered subsequently in Lesson 18.

If the repayment of the loans begins immediately upon disbursement, then these two additional interest costs do not occur.

Non-Government Financial Aid for Graduate Students

Undergraduate students can reduce the need for student loans via scholarships and other competitive or needs based avenues. But those avenues are highly competitive and the pool of applicants is enormous. Fortunately, graduate students can obtain other forms of financial aid more readily. So it is vital to be fully aware of them when assessing one's potential student land debt situation. Acceptance into graduate school requires a high academic performance as an undergraduate student as a key factor. With a very high academic performance, the student can apply for non-government based financial assistance in the form of **fellowships**, **graduate teaching assistantships (GTAs)**, **graduate research assistantships (GRAs)** or other forms of support. These awards can substantially reduce or possibly eliminate the need for **FSA** loans during that period of education.

Fellowships cover a substantial portion (in many cases, all) of the educational cost and sufficient cost of living funds. Most commonly, fellowships are available from foundations and other organizations and are open to nationwide application in any or many areas of study. Others may be available from government agencies or foundations focused on national needs. Specific colleges may have fellowships available from endowment funds from successful alumni or trust funds donated by deceased alumni or faculty members. These are limited in number and amounts and often targeted to very specific interests of the donor. Hence, there is stiff competition for such fellowships. Depending on the source, specific nature and terms of the fellowship, the funds the graduate student receives will be either taxable or not.

GTAs and **GRAs** are available from the college itself, and are commonly offered as competitive enticement to selected student applicants. A **GTA**-supported graduate student will be employed to assist professors by grading homework, setting up lab experiments etc. in undergraduate classes. At the doctoral level such students might actually teach a section of a multi-section course under the mentoring of the professor responsible for the course. A **GRA**-supported graduate will be employed to conduct research-related work on some aspects of a professor's research program. Ideally (and in many cases) the work is specifically applicable (indeed matched) to the student eventually completing a M.S. thesis or Doctoral dissertation requirement for the degree.

If successful in gaining a **GTA** or **GRA**, the graduate student earns a modest (but sufficient) salary and commonly, a **GTA** or **GRA** includes payment of tuition. So the cost of living burden is decreased or even eliminated. For either a **GTA** or a **GRA** the graduate student is employed by the department in which the student is pursuing the degree. For a **GTA** he or she is paid from budgeted funds of that department. For a **GRA** the student is paid from funds available from the professor's funded research grants for the particular project. In either case, the student is performing work so the income is taxable. A summary of the federal tax implications is given in **APPENDIX II**.

Many graduate students are married. Often one of them is not a student and is otherwise employed as a means of personal and educational support. It is also possible both are graduate students with **FSA** financial aid. For any **Direct PLUS Loans**, their joint income would be a factor in the amounts awarded to either one or both of them. Any **GTA**, **GRA**, **Fellowship** or other academics-based support received from non-**FSA** loan sources of either or both of them will be considered as income in making the application.

Normally it is best to accept **GTA**, **GRA**, **Fellowship** financial aid before borrowing **FSA** funds. Any gap remaining in financial burden might be borne by **FSA** Graduate Loans and, if needed, **Direct PLUS Loans**. But it is possible the amount of non-governmental support is high enough to significantly limit or even preclude **FSA** loans. So the alert is to be careful to assess the possibility of precluding any **FSA** support at all, when **FSA** loans are needed as well. It is advisable to consider this carefully and, if pertinent, discuss it with academic officials before accepting the full amount of any non-**FSA** support.

In Lesson 16 Nicole's Dad worked with her on the calculations involved in consolidating her **FSA** Undergraduate loans. In her case the **LOAN AMOUNT** for the consolidate loan was a small amount, $11873. As such it placed her in the 15-year **TERM** bracket. She also only had two loans to consolidate. In reality, many different circumstances occur. As the average student loan debt is around $28000 to $29000, it is evident that much higher **consolidated LOAN AMOUNTS** than Nicole's do occur. Let's look at an example SITUATION.

SITUATION 25

Crystal will complete her undergraduate college studies in May, 2018. She has four unsubsidized loans, one per year from 2014 to 2017. Each was first disbursed on August 1 of the applicable year and is in deferred status. She paid the ongoing interest during that period.

The **LOAN AMOUNTS** were $4144.00, $2982.00, $5029.00, and $3083.00 After paying the **ORIGINATION FEES** ($44.00, $32.00, $54.00 and $33.00, rounded), the initial **PRINCIPAL AMOUNTS** owed are $4100.00, $2950.00, $4975.00, and $3050.00 (all rounded to the nearest $). They total $15075.00. All loans are to be repaid on the **Standard** repayment plan and with a **TERM** of 10 years.

Crystal is considering applying for a **Direct Consolidation Loan**. She inquires with a potential approved lender. The lender indicates the **ANNUAL RATE OF INTEREST** is 4.25%. The **TERM** is 15 years. The **MONTHLY PAYMENT** is $113.41 and the **CUMULATIVE INTEREST** = $5338.08. Let's illustrate how the lender determined that information.

The **LOAN AMOUNT** for the consolidated loan will be the sum of the **OUTSTANDING PRINCIPAL** amounts of the past loans. Because Crystal will have paid the interest during deferred period, the **OUTSTANDING PRINCIPAL** of each past loan will equal its initial **PRINCIPAL**.

The **WEIGHTED INTEREST RATE** = $4100.00 x 4.66% + $2950.00 x 4.29% + $4975.00 x 3.76% + $3050.00 x 4.45% = 64040.00 $ x %.

The **WEIGHTED AVERAGE INTEREST RATE** = 64040.00 $ x %/$15075.00 = 4.248% = 4.25% (rounded upward).

For a **Direct Consolidation Loan**, there is no **ORIGINATION FEE** (= $0.00).

As the **LOAN AMOUNT** = **PRINCIPAL** = $15075.00 is in the $10000.00 and $19999.99 bracket, the **TERM** is set at 15 years.

MONTHLY RATE OF INTEREST = 4.25%/12 months = 0.354%/month (rounded)

$$MRATIO = 0.354/100 = 0.00345$$
$$TERM = 15 \text{ years} \times 12 \text{ months/year} = 180 \text{ months}$$
$$(MRATIO + 1)^{term} = (1 + 0.00345)^{180} = (1.00345)^{180}$$
$$= (1.00345)(1.00345)(1.00345)..... 180 \text{ times!}$$
$$= 1.89 \text{ (rounded)}$$
$$NUMERATOR = PRINCIPAL \times MRATIO \times (MRATIO + 1)^{TERM}$$
$$= 15075.00 \times 0.00345 \times 1.89 = 100.86 \text{ (rounded)}$$
$$DENOMINATOR = (MRATIO + 1)^{term} - 1 = 1.89 - 1 = 0.89$$
$$MPAYMENT = NUMERATOR/DENOMINATOR = 100.86/0.89 = \$113.33 \text{(rounded)}$$

A precisely calculated **MPAYMENT = $113.41**, the value indicated by the lender. Using precise numbers the partial flow of the loan repayment for the loan is as follows:

Loan Amount	15075						Principal = 15075.00	
Origination Rate	0.00%							
Origination Fee	0.00							
Term in Years	Annual Rate of Interest	Month	Monthly Payment	Applied to Interest	Applied to Principal		Remaining Principal	Cumulative Interest
15	4.25	1	113.41	53.39	60.02	0.00	15014.98	53.39
		2	113.41	53.18	60.23	0.00	14954.76	106.57
		12	113.41	51.01	62.40		14340.62	626.49
		24	113.41	48.31	65.10		13574.41	1221.16
		36	113.41	45.49	67.92		12775.00	1782.62
		48	113.41	42.54	70.86		11940.95	2309.43
		60	113.41	39.47	73.94		11070.74	2800.10
		130	113.41	18.71	94.70		5188.22	4855.99
		180	113.41	0.40	113.01		0.00	5338.07

SITUATION 25 – CONTINUED

At the end of the **TERM** the **CUMULATIVE INTEREST** of $5338.07 represents $5338.07/$15075.00 x 100 = 35.41% of the **LOAN AMOUNT**. So this is a costly loan. One favorable point is that it represents an average of 35.41%/15 years = 2.36% year on the declining balance. That is noticeably less than the stated **ANNUAL RATE OF INTEREST** of 4.25%.

SITUATION 25 exemplifies the detailed process for determining the outcome of a consolidated loan. But to determine the **CUMULATIVE INTEREST** requires the ability to develop the **AMORTIZATION SCHEDULE** . To eliminate that need a base loan approach like that used in prior Lessons can be used.

Consolidated-Base Loan Table

For the base loan, the **LOAN AMOUNT** is $1000.00. There is no **ORIGINATION FEE** so the

PRINCIPAL is equal to the **LOAN AMOUNT**. There is a complication when it comes to the **ANNUAL RATE OF INTEREST**. For a consolidated loan there are no previously set **ANNUAL RATES OF INTEREST**. The applicable rate for any particular set of loans being consolidated is the **WEIGHTED AVERAGE INTEREST RATE** that results for them. Here's how that was handled.

Depending on the nature (Undergraduate, Graduate or Parent), mix of individual **LOAN AMOUNTS** involved and their timing, that value (rounded upward) will range between 3.50% and 8.00%, in 0.125% increments. So the results of base consolidation loan are needed for each possibility

The author calculated the base loan costs for all of those possibilities. The following **CONSOLIDATED-BASE LOAN TABLE** provides the results. For compactness the listings are for increments of 0.25%. For the unlisted intermediate values of the **WEIGHTED AVERAGE INTEREST RATE,** you can either round to the closest listing or use interpolation. The results will be approximate but very close to the precise values from an actual **AMORTIZATION SCHEDULE**.

CONSOLIDATED-BASE LOAN TABLE						
PRINCIPAL = LOAN AMOUNT = $1,000.00	MONTHLY PAYMENT					
	TERM					
WEIGHTED AVERAGE INTEREST RATE	10 Years	12 Years	15 Years	20 Years	25 Years	30 Years
3.50	9.89	8.51	7.15	5.80	5.01	4.49
3.75	10.01	8.63	7.27	5.93	5.14	4.63
4.00	10.12	8.76	7.40	6.06	5.28	4.77
4.25	10.24	8.88	7.52	6.18	5.42	4.92
4.50	10.36	9.00	7.65	6.33	5.56	5.07
4.75	10.48	9.12	7.78	6.46	5.70	5.22
5.00	10.61	9.25	7.91	6.60	5.85	5.37
5.25	10.73	9.37	8.04	6.74	5.99	5.52
5.50	10.85	9.50	8.17	6.88	6.14	5.68
5.75	10.98	9.63	8.30	7.02	6.29	5.84
6.00	11.10	9.76	8.44	7.16	6.44	6.00
6.25	11.23	9.89	8.57	7.31	6.60	6.16
6.50	11.35	10.02	8.71	7.46	6.75	6.32
6.75	11.48	10.15	8.85	7.60	6.91	6.49
7.00	11.61	10.28	8.99	7.75	7.07	6.65
7.25	11.74	10.42	9.13	7.90	7.23	6.82
7.50	11.87	10.55	9.27	8.06	7.39	6.99
7.75	12.00	10.69	9.41	8.21	7.55	7.16
8.00	12.13	10.82	9.56	8.36	7.72	7.34
CUMULATIVE INTEREST						
	TERM					
WEIGHTED AVERAGE INTEREST RATE	10 years	12 Years	15 Years	20 Years	25 Years	30 Years
3.50	186.63	226.09	286.79	391.90	501.87	616.56
3.75	200.73	243.35	309.00	422.93	542.39	667.22

4.00	214.94	260.76	331.44	454.35	583.51	718.68
4.25	229.25	278.31	354.10	486.16	625.21	770.97
4.50	243.66	296.91	376.99	518.36	667.50	824.05
4.75	258.17	313.85	400.10	550.94	710.35	872.91
5.00	272.79	331.84	423.43	583.89	753.77	932.54
5.25	287.50	349.87	446.98	617.23	797.74	987.91
5.50	302.32	368.25	470.75	650.93	842.26	1044.04
5.75	317.23	386.67	494.74	685.00	887.32	1100.84
6.00	332.35	405.22	518.94	719.43	932.90	1158.36
6.25	347.36	423.92	543.36	754.83	979.01	1216.56
6.50	362.58	442.77	567.99	789.38	1025.62	1275.42
6.75	377.89	461.75	592.84	824.87	1072.73	1334.92
7.00	393.90	480.87	617.89	860.72	1120.34	1395.06
7.25	408.81	500.13	643.15	896.90	1168.42	1455.80
7.50	424.92	519.53	668.62	933.42	1216.97	1517.17
7.75	440.13	539.90	694.30	970.28	1265.99	1579.08
8.00	455.93	558.70	720.17	1007.46	1315.49	1641.55

Using the Consolidated Base Loan Table

SITUATION 25A

In SITUATION 25, Crystal's consolidated loan has an **ANNUAL RATE OF INTEREST** of 4.25 % and the **TERM** is 15 years.

The 4.25% value is directly listed in the **CONSOLIDATED-BASE LOAN TABLE**.

For a base consolidated **LOAN AMOUNT** of $1000.00 the tabulated **MONTHLY PAYMENT** = $7.52 and **CUMULATIVE INTEREST** = $354.10.

Crystal's actual consolidated **LOAN AMOUNT** is $15075.00 so the **SCALING FACTOR** = $15075.00/$1000.00 = 15.075. **MONTHLY PAYMENT** = 15.075 x $7.52 = $113.36 and **CUMULATIVE INTEREST** = 15.075 x $354.10 = $5338.06.

The results are essentially the same as calculated above in detail. The differences are due to round-off in the tabulated base values and subsequent calculations.

Exercise 29: Repeat SITUATION 25A with the Crystal's **PRINCIPAL AMOUNTS** *being $2075.00, $2925.00, $1750.00, and $3225.00.*

Your results should be: TERM = 12 years, WEIGHTED AVERAGE INTEREST RATE = 4.375%, SCALING FACTOR = 9.975, MONTHLY PAYMENT = $89.18, CUMULATIVE INTEREST = $2868.91 (using interpolation of listed base values = midway between results for 4.25% and 4.50%).

SITUATION 25B

The parents of Crystal in SITUATION 25 also took out **Direct PLUS Loans** at the same times as

Crystal and for the same **LOAN AMOUNTS**. All loans are to be repaid on the **Standard** repayment plan and have a **TERM** of 10 years. They also paid the ongoing interest during deferment.

For a **Direct Consolidation Loan** the **ANNUAL RATE OF INTEREST** is stated as 7.00%. The **TERM** is stated as 15 years with a **MONTHLY PAYMENT** of $135.50 and **CUMULATIVE INTEREST** of $9314.71. Before signing for the loan Crystal's parents confirm that information by calculating it themselves.

As the **LOAN AMOUNT** of $15075.00 is in between $10000.00 and $19999.99, the **TERM** is set at 15 years.

The **TOTAL WEIGHTED INTEREST RATE** = ($4100.00 x 7.21% + $2950.00 x 6.84+ $4975.00 x 6.31 + $3050.00 x 7.00) = 102481.25 $ x %. The **WEIGHTED AVERAGE INTEREST RATE** = 102481.25 $ x %/$15075.00 = 6.80% = 7.00% (rounded up).

Using the **CONSOLIDATED-BASE LOAN TABLE**:

For a base consolidated **LOAN AMOUNT** of $1000.00 the tabulated **MONTHLY PAYMENT** = $8.99 and the **CUMULATIVE INTEREST** = $617.89.

The **SCALING FACTOR** = 15.075. **MONTHLY PAYMENT** = 15.075 x $8.99 = $135.52 and **CUMULATIVE INTEREST** = 15.075 x $617.89 = $9314.69.

The **CUMULATIVE INTEREST** is $9314.69/$15075.00 x 100 = 61.79% of the **LOAN AMOUNT**. Compared to Crystal, her parents paid $9314.69 - $5338.06 = $3976.63 (74.49%) more **CUMULATIVE INTEREST**.

ASIDE: The precisely calculated **MONTHLY PAYMENT** = $135.50 and **CUMULATIVE INTEREST** = $9314.71.

Exercise 30: *Repeat SITUATION 25B for Crystal's parents' loans with initial* **PRINCIPAL** *amounts being $2075.00, $2925.00, $1750.00, and $3225.00.*

Your results should be: **WEIGHTED AVERAGE INTEREST RATE** *= 7.00%,* **TERM** *= 12 years,* **MONTHLY PAYMENT** *= $102.54,* **CUMULATIVE INTEREST** *= $4796.68.*

SITUATION 25C

Crystal of SITUATION 25 plans to begin a Master's degree in August, 2018 and complete it in two years. She expects to need a **Graduate Unsubsidized Loan** in her first year only. Assuming she will receive that loan, she estimates that after the **ORGINATION FEE** is taken out she will have a **PRINCIPAL** = $6000.00 and a **TERM** = 10 years. She uses the **ANNUAL RATE OF INTEREST** of 6.00%, the rate for the July 1, 2017- June 30, 2018. Let's examine the effects of Crystal including that loan is her eventual **Direct Consolidation Loan**.

The additional loan makes the **PRINCIPAL** = $15075.00 + $6000.00 = $21075.00. As this amount is between 20000.00 and 39999.99, the **TERM** is set at 20 years.

The **WEIGHTED INTEREST RATE** = $4100.00 x 4.66% + $2950.00 x 4.29% + $4975.00 x 3.76% + $3050.00 x 4.45% + $6000.00 x 6.00% = 100040.00 $ x %. The **WEIGHTED AVERAGE INTEREST RATE** = 100040.00 $ x %/$21075.00 = 4.747% = 4.75 = % (rounded upward).

For a **WEIGHTED AVERAGE INTEREST RATE** of 4.75% and a base consolidated **LOAN AMOUNT** of $1000.00 the tabulated **MONTHLY PAYMENT** = $9.12 and **CUMULATIVE INTEREST** = $313.85.

The **SCALING FACTOR** = 21.075. **MONTHLY PAYMENT** = 21.075 x $6.46 = $136.14 and **CUMULATIVE INTEREST** = 21.075 x $550.94 = $11611.06

This is a very costly loan. The **CUMULATIVE INTEREST** is $11611.06 /$21075.00 x 100 = 55.09% of the **LOAN AMOUNT**. However, it constitutes an average of 55.09%/20 years = 2.75% per year on the declining balance compared to the stated **ANNUAL RATE OF INTEREST** of 4.75%.

ASIDE: The precisely calculated **MONTHLY PAYMENT** = $136.14 and **CUMULATIVE INTEREST** paid is $11610.99.

Exercise 31: *Wilson has completed studies and is in a grace period. He has four **Unsubsidized Loans,** one per year from 2014 to 2017. Two are from his third and fourth year undergraduate studies and two are from graduate studies. Each was first disbursed on August 1 of the applicable year and is in deferred status. He paid the ongoing interest during that period.*

*After paying the **ORIGINATION FEES**, the **PRINCIPAL** amounts owed are $5890.00, and $6310.00 for the undergraduate loans and $12500.00 and $13500 for the graduate loans. In May 2018, he will graduate and act to consolidate them. What are the **TERM, WEIGHTED AVERAGE INTEREST RATE, MONTHLY PAYMENT** and **CUMULATIVE INTEREST**?*

*Your **partial** results should be: **WEIGHTED AVERAGE INTEREST RATE** = 5.375%; **MONTHLY PAYMENT** = $260.14, and **CUMULATIVE INTEREST** = $24221.86.*

Exercise 32: *Repeat Exercise 31, except Wilson's graduate loan **PRINCIPAL** amounts are doubled.*

*Your **partial** results should be: **TERM** = 30 years, **MONTHLY PAYMENT** = $364.56, and **CUMULATIVE INTEREST** = $67027.39.*

While a **Direct Consolidation Loan** does eliminate tracking and repayment of multiple different loans, there are both pros and cons to consolidation. The website http://studentaid.ed.gov/repay-loans/consolidation lists them. The following are the key considerations.

Loan consolidation can greatly simplify loan repayment by centralizing your loans to one bill and can lower monthly payments by giving you up to 30 years to repay your loans. You might also have access to alternative repayment plans you would not have had before, and you'll be able to switch your variable interest rate loans to a fixed interest rate.

However, if you increase the length of your repayment period, you'll also make more payments and pay more in interest. Consolidation may also cause you to lose certain borrower benefits—such as interest rate discounts, principal rebates, or some loan cancellation benefits—that are associated with your current loans. Once your loans are combined into a **Direct Consolidation Loan**, they cannot be reversed. The individual loans that were consolidated are paid off and no longer exist.

Let us examine why these alerts are a critical considerations.

SITUATION 25D

Acting wisely, Crystal in SITUATION 25C decides to compute the **CUMULATIVE INTEREST** she would pay for her original **FSA** loans if she does not consolidate them. There are five separate loans but the **TERM** is the same for all of them, namely 10 years. Let's refer to the consecutive loans as Loan 1 through Loan 5. To do each loan, the corresponding results from the applicable **BASE LOAN TABLE** (Undergraduate or Graduate) must be scaled accordingly.

From the UG- and G-BASE LOAN TABLES:

The **MONTHLY PAYMENT** amounts are $10.33, $10.15, $9.90, $10.23 and $10.98.

The **CUMULATIVE INTEREST** amounts are $250.23, $229.06, $199.15, $238.20 and $328.70.

NOTE: For the future graduate loan, she used the July 1, 2017 – June 30, 2018 loan rates.

The **SCALING FACTORS** are 4.144, 2.982, 5.029, 3.083 and 6.00.

For the actual LOAN AMOUNTS:

The **COMBINED MONTHLY PAYMENT** = 4.144 x $10.33 + 2.982 x $10.15 + 5.029 x $9.90+ 3.083 x $110.23 + 6.00 x $10.98 = $220.28 compares to the $133.19 for the consolidated loan. As expected the **MONTHLY PAYMENT** amount for the consolidated loan is significantly lower than for combined unconsolidated loans. Specifically, it is 60.5% of that amount. But the payment would last 20 years instead of 10 years.

The **COMBINED CUMULATIVE INTEREST** = 4.144 x $250.23 + 2.982 x $229.06 + 5.029 x $199.15+ 3.083 x $238.20 + 6.00 x $328.70 = $5504.13 which compares to $11611.06 for the consolidated loan. As expected the amount for the consolidated loan is enormously <u>higher</u> than for the <u>combined</u> <u>unconsolidated</u> loans. Specifically, it is 2.11 times that amount, more than two times as much.

SITUATION 25D demonstrates that consolidation can be very costly. Indeed, it can be devastating for students who have borrowed a very high combined **LOAN AMOUNT**. That is not infrequent when private colleges and graduate school enter the picture. The author strongly agrees with the statement on the FSA website, "Carefully consider whether loan consolidation is the best option for you."

Borrowers should numerically compare and weigh a **Direct Consolidation Loan** versus keeping the original loans with their shorter **TERMS**. One course of action is to begin paying all loans back as soon as the funds are disbursed, if one can afford that even if it involves parental assistance with the payments. However the parents are likely to also have their own **FSA** loans to pay. If so, they too will be tempted to consolidate and need to consider the implications as well. And given their **ANNUAL RATE OF INTEREST** is 6.41% (or 7.21%) for **FSA** loans, it's even more important. Indeed, since their **ANNUAL RATE OF INTEREST** is higher, the benefit of <u>not</u> consolidating would be somewhat more. They might also more easily afford the payments.

From the above perspective Crystal should <u>not consolidate</u> her loans. To do that, she must be able to afford the combined **MONTHLY PAYMENTS.** However, in Lesson 16 Nicole's Dad showed her how it was preferred to consolidate her loans and accelerate them by making a **MONTHLY PAYMENT** equal to that combine amount. Let' see how that works out on Crystal's case.

Accelerating Repayment of a Consolidated Loan

SITUATION 26

In SITUATION 25C Crystal had $21075.00 (after paying **ORIGINATION FEES**) in various **FSA** loans and examined consolidating them.

When she consolidates them her **TERM** is 20 years with a combined **MONTHLY PAYMENT** of $136.19. The **CUMULATIVE INTEREST** was $11610.99.

In SITUATION 25D, Crystal compared those results to treating the loans separately. Each separate loan has a **TERM** of 10 years. The combined **MONTHLY PAYMENT** is $220.28. The combined **CUMULATIVE INTEREST** is $5504.13.

As another alternative, consider Crystal accelerating repayment of the consolidated loan by paying a monthly **ADDITIONAL AMOUNT APPLIED TO PRINCIPAL** of $84.09. That makes the **TOTAL AMOUNT APPLIED TO PRINCIPAL** = $136.19+ $84.09 = $220.28. That's the same as her combined **MONTHLY PAYMENT** for the various individual loans.

The resulting partial **AMORTIZATION SCHEDULE** is:

Term in Years	Annual Rate of Interest	Month	Monthly Payment	Applied to Interest	Applied to Principal	Additional Amount Applied to Principal	PRINCIPAL 21075 OUTSTANDING PRINCIPAL	Cumulative Interest
20	4.75	1	136.19	83.42	52.77	84.09	20938.14	83.42
		2	136.19	82.88	53.31	84.09	20800.74	166.30
		12	136.19	77.34	58.85	84.09	19396.45	964.83
		48	136.19	55.50	80.69	84.09	13855.85	3354.37
		84	136.19	30.31	105.88	84.09	7468.49	4897.15
		120	136.19	1.28	134.91	84.09	104.96	5463.75
		121	136.19	0.42	135.78	84.09	-114.91	5464.17
		121	105.38	0.42	104.96	0.00	0.00	5464.17

SITUATION 26 - CONTINUED

The outcome is very interesting. Crystal pays off her accelerated consolidated loan in 120 months. That's the same timing as the 10-year **TERM** of her individual loans. In the last month the loan ends with an adjusted additional amount of $105.37. The **CUMULATIVE INTEREST** is $5464.17. That's only $39.96 less than the $5504.13 paid for the combined unconsolidated individual loans.

*Exercise 33: Calculate lines 49 and 85 for the **AMORTIZATION SCHEDULE** in SITUATION 26.*

*Your **partial** results should be:*

Term in Years	Annual Rate of Interest	Month	Monthly Payment	Applied to Interest	Applied to Principal	Additional Amount Applied to Principal	OUTSTANDING PRINCIPAL	Cumulative Interest
20	4.75	49	136.19	55.50	80.69	84.09	13855.85	3354.37
		85	136.19	29.56	106.63	84.09	7277.77	4926.71

In SITUATION 26, if the additional payment is affordable then the **CUMULATIVE INTEREST** paid is essentially the same whether Crystal pays the individual loans or consolidates and accelerates. Let's see if that is generally the outcome.

SITUATION 27

Roger is an independent student and has four undergraduate **FSA** loans. Consecutively, they were first disbursed on August 1 in years 2014-2017. For each loan, the **LOAN AMOUNT** was $10300.00 and the **TERM** was 5 years. The loans are in deferred status with ongoing interest being paid. Roger began repayment after graduating in May, 2108.

Without showing details of the scaled base loan calculations:

For the individual loans:

After **ORIGINATION FEES**, the combined **PRINCIPAL** = $10189.58 + $10189.48 + $10190.00 + $10189.89 = $40758.95.The combined **MONTHLY PAYMENT** = $190.76 + $189.01 + $186.53 + $189.73 = $756.02. When paid off the combined **CUMULATIVE INTEREST** = $1252.79 + $1150.00 + $1003.74 + $1194.39 = $4600.91.

For the consolidated loan:

The **WEGHTED AVERAGE INTEREST RATE** = 4.375%, which is midway between the 4.25% and 4.50% of the **CONSOLIDATED-BASE LOAN TAB**LE. The **PRINCIPAL** amount is near the bottom of the $40000.00 to $59999.99 **USDE TERM** bracket for 25 years. The **MONTHLY PAYMENT** = 40.76 x ($5.42 + $5.56)/2 = $223.77 ($223.67 precisely by the amortization equation). When paid off, the combined **CUMULATIVE INTEREST** = 40.76 x ($625.21 + $667.50)/2 = $26345.43 ($26341.86 precisely).

If Roger can pay $756.02 - $223.77 = $532.25 as an **ADDITIONAL AMOUNT APPLIED TO PRINCIPAL**, the **AMORTIZATION SCHEDULE** (not shown) indicates the loan is paid off in 5 years plus 1 month and the **CUMULATIVE INTEREST** = $4705.22.That's only $104.31 more than if he does not consolidate.

By either keeping his loans unconsolidated or by consolidating them and accelerating, Roger can save nearly $22000.00 in **CUMULATIVE INTEREST**. However, he must be able to afford paying $756.02 per month for 61 months.

SITUATION 27A

Assume Roger's four loans in SITUATION 27 are $15000.00 each.

Without showing details of the scaled base loan calculations:

For the unconsolidated loans the combined **PRINCIPAL** = $59357.70 The **MONTHLY PAYMENT** = $1101.00 and when paid off the combined **CUMULATIVE INTEREST** = $6700.35.

For a $59357.70 consolidated loan, the **WEGHTED AVERAGE INTEREST RATE** = 4.375%. The **PRINCIPAL** amount is near the top of the $40000.00 to $59999.99 **USDE TERM** bracket for 25-years. The **MONTHLY PAYMENT** = 59.36 x ($5.42 + $5.56)/2 = $325.88 ($325.73 precisely). When paid off, the combined **CUMULATIVE INTEREST** = 59.36 x ($625.21 + $667.50)/2 = $38367.63 (also $38361.93 precisely).

If Roger can pay $1101.00 - $325.88 = $775.12 as an **ADDITIONAL AMOUNT APPLIED TO PRINCIPAL**, the **AMORTIZATION SCHEDULE** (not shown) indicates the loan is paid off in 5 years plus 1 month and the **CUMULATIVE INTEREST** = $6853.57. That's only $153.22 more than if he does not consolidate.

Either keeping his loans unconsolidated or consolidating and accelerating, Roger can save about $32000.00 in **CUMULATIVE INTEREST**. However, he must be able to afford paying $1101.00 per month for 61 months.

NOTE: Technically, Roger has borrowed more than the **AGGREGATE LOAN AMOUNT** of $45000.00 for four years of study, and more than the $57500.00 for up to six years of study. The $45000 amount was used to force his amount to near the top of the **USDA TERM** bracket, but not spill over into the next bracket. The intent of SITUATIONS 27 and 27A was to observe the numerical findings for the individual loans versus accelerated consolidated loan at each end of the bracket. The next section expands on this investigation of the comparison.

General Applicability of the Acceleration Approach

SITUATIONS 27 and 27A also result in the **CUMULATIVE INTEREST** for the accelerated consolidated loan being only slightly different than the combined amount if the loans are not consolidated. For SITUATION 27 the consolidated loan was for a **LOAN AMOUNT** at the low end of the applicable **FSA TERM** bracket. For the SITUATION 27A the **LOAN AMOUNT** was at the high end. The caveat is that for the consolidated loan the **MONTHLY PAYMENT** + **ADDITIONAL AMOUNT APPLIED TO PRINCIPAL** was exactly equal to the combined **MONTHLY PAYMENT** for the unconsolidated loans.

The preceding suggests that the closeness in **CUMULATIVE INTEREST** might be the outcome for many, possibly all, cases that might arise. That is not known for certain unless one actually calculates the results for the specific case at hand. In the first edition of the book the author examined many cases at extreme ends of possibility and falling in each of the **FSA TERM** brackets and above the last one. In each case four loans of equal amount were first disbursed in August of each year from 2011 to 2015. The applicable **ANNUAL RATE OF INTEREST** for each period of disbursement was used, namely 6.80%, 3.86%, 4.66% and 4.29%. They were deferred with **MONTHLY INTEREST** paid. The following are selected examples at the extreme ends of the **STUDENT LOAN TERM BRACKETS**.

Loan	Loan Amount	Annual Rate of Interest	TERM in Years	Combined Monthly Payment	Combined Cumulative Interest	Combined Additional Amount Applied to Interest	Combined Cumulative Interest	Months to Payoff
Individual	2400 per loan	3.86-6.80	5	178.18	1233.65	0.00	1233.65	60
Consolidated	9600	5.00	12	87.86	3152.27	90.32	1265.51	61
Individual	4800 per loan	3.86-6.80	5	357.76	2467.29	0.00	2467.29	60
Consolidated	19200	5.00	15	150.24	8044.68	207.52	2519.38	61
Individual	25000 per loan	6.84-7.90	5	1901.22	18269.38	0.00	18269.38	60
Consolidated	100000	7.125	30	645.45	136557.75	1255.77	18375.36	61

Individual	25000 per loan	6.84-7.90	10	1117.03	38239.00	0.00	38239.00	120
Consolidated	100000	7.125	30	645.45	136557.75	471.58	38508.08	121
Individual	25000 per loan	6.84-7.90	15	866.23	60117.44	0.00	60117.44	180
Consolidated	100000	7.125	30	645.45	136557.75	220.78	60630.81	181

These additional examples appear very convincing. The accelerated consolidation loan pays off one to later than the unconsolidated loan. The **CUMULATIVE INTEREST** paid on the accelerated consolidated loan is only slightly higher than the combined amount for the unconsolidated loans. In the tabulated examples the **LOAN AMOUNT** and **TERM** were the same for all four unconsolidated loans. However, the findings were also substantiated for Roger in SITUATIONS 27 and 27A where different **LOAN AMOUNTS** were involved (for the same **TERM**). In those, the **ANNUAL RATES OF INTER**EST were also the values for the period 2014-2017.

The author has not investigated the circumstances of different **TERMS** for each loan (whether the same **LOAN AMOUNT** or not). Nor has he done it at length for the period 2014-2017. There is simply too wide a variation in possibilities which makes it too exhaustive to attempt. My sense is that the findings would still be substantiated but perhaps be a bit to moderately less close in some cases.

Despite the option to accelerate a consolidated **FSA** loan, the author still advocates caution. There is risk involved as it requires strong discipline and steadfastness in making the unforced additional payment amounts. For example, in SITUATION 27 Roger must be able to afford $756.02 per month to either keep his individual loans or consolidate and accelerate them as depicted. For the latter he will pay a required $223.77 per month and have to add $532.25 every month for 61 months.

In SITUATION 27A Roger must be able to afford $1101.00 per month to either keep his individual loans or consolidate and accelerate them as depicted. For the latter he will pay a required $325.88 per month and have to add $775.12 every month for 61 months.

I suspect that many borrowers are prone to self-defaulting on those additional payment amounts. When other monetary needs or desires arise it can became a habit to just "skip" the additional amount. On the other hand, the acceleration affords great leeway should one's income take a downturn because one is not locked into either the high combined **MONTHLY PAYMENT** of the individual unconsolidated loans or the **ADDITIONAL AMOUNT APPLIED TO PRINCIPAL** of the accelerated consolidated loan.

Regardless of the reason, if some or many or all additional amounts are skipped then the penalty is the increase in **CUMULATIVE INTEREST** and time needed to pay off the loan. For Crystal in SITUATION 26, depending on the extent of skipping additional amount, the **CUMULATIVE INTEREST** will increase from $5504.13 to an amount as high as $11610.99. The time to full payment will increase from about ten years to as many as twenty-five years. For Roger in SITUATION 27, as he skips the additional amount more and more the **CUMULATIVE INTEREST** will increase from $4600.91 to an amount as high as $29834.22. In SITUATION 27A, his **CUMULATIVE INTEREST** will increase from $6700.35 toward $38367.63.

In accelerating the consolidated **FSA** loans, SITUATIONS 27 and 27A involved making the **MONTHLY PAYMENT + ADDITIONAL AMOUNT APPLIED TO PRINCIPAL** the same as for the combined **MONTHLY PAYMENT** for the unconsolidated loans. That was done to examine that specific effect. In reality the borrower can accelerate by any additional amount he or she can afford. Also, the borrower need not consolidate all his or her loans. Some combination of those two aspects can be used to arrive at a balance of the two that has the payments and longevity fit to the financial circumstances of the borrower.

Earlier, the author mentioned his belief that the college education be a shared burden of parents and the student. If **FSA** loans are needed, both should share that commitment. If that is done the student may be only facing half the burden level of SITUATIONS described herein. That is the best way parents can assist as opposed to seeing the child face the "pay me later costs" of a possible very high **LOAN AMOUNT** on a consolidation loan with a 20-30 year **TERM**. That approach can take the **Direct Consolidation Loan** completely out of the picture, which is ideal.

You've just gotten your first **FSA** student loan award. The coming college years will bring more of them. Immediate questions arise. Can I afford to begin repayment right away? Should I defer repayment until I complete my studies and have a secure job in my field? What if I incur financial hardship and still have my loan payment staring me in my face? What if I have to skip payments? Avenues exist to handle these questions. They are best managed if considered even before the circumstances arise. If so, positive actions can result. If not addressed with fore-thought, then they can lead to the three enemies of student loans.

Enemy No. 1 – Deferment

For **FSA** loans interest is incurred from the time any funds are disbursed. Disbursements occur during the time the student is attending college. Typically, the student is unemployed and lacks income to begin repayment at the outset. Parents can assist with repayment and by borrowing **FSA** loans themselves. Nevertheless, borrowers may simply need to delay the start of repayment to a later time. To accommodate such realities, repayment of **FSA** loans can be *deferred* until the student leaves school and during a six month grace period after the student ceases to be enrolled at least half-time. A parent can also request deferment. Indeed, predominantly the author assumed a base assumption that his fictitious borrowers would defer their loans. (Nicole and her parents were one exception.) For the most part he also had a base assumption that they paid the **MONTHLY INTEREST** during deferment. Admittedly, he stated technical reasons regarding why those choices were advantageous in his writing of the many SITUATIONS.

It can be very demanding on a family's budget to make loan payments while paying many other direct and indirect expenses of their child's college costs. So deferment may be a necessity especially for parents with more than one child in college. There are monetary consequences to deferment of student loans. As they can be very costly, deferment can become student loan Enemy No. 1.

The best way to avoid this lurking enemy is to begin repayment as soon as possible. Right away is best. If that is not possible, then **FSA** allows and encourages the borrower to at least pay the ongoing interest charges on a regular basis. Typically, that would be on a monthly basis. So a choice arises, should I pay my ongoing interest or not? By paying the interest only, the borrower incurs that cost without reducing the debt. By skipping the payment of interest the borrower incurs additional monetary consequences. Let's examine both aspects.

- Interest Paid During Deferment and Grace Periods -

In Lessons 12-14, Nicole's Dad showed her approximate ways and the precise way (by **AMORTIZATION SCHEDULE**) of calculating the amount of **PRIOR CUMULATIVE INTEREST** incurred by paying **MONTHLY INTEREST** during the deferment/grace period. Using some aspects of one of his approximate approaches together with **BASE LOAN TABLES**, there is a simplified but more accurate way to do it. It involves the following steps.

For a single loan:

The **MONTHLY INTEREST** amount can be calculated as follows.

MONTHLY RATE OF INTEREST = ANNUAL RATE OF INTEREST/12

FRACTION = MONTHLY RATE OF INTEREST/100

MONTHLY INTEREST = FRACTION x OUTSTANDING PRINCIPAL

As the **MONTHLY INTEREST** is being paid on time each month, the **OUTSTANDING PRINCIPAL** will remain equal to the initial **PRINCIPAL** of the loan. So each month the **MONTHLY INTEREST** will be the same amount as given by

MONTHLY INTEREST = FRACTION x PRINCIPAL

To calculate the **PRIOR CUMULATIVE INTEREST** for any given loan, multiply the **MONTHLY INTEREST** by the applicable number of months. That is,

PRIOR CUMULATIVE INTEREST = MONTHS x MONTHLY INTEREST

If the **PRINCIPAL** is the base **LOAN AMOUNT** of $1000.00, then the **MONTHLY INTEREST** is the **SCALING FACTOR** x **BASE MONTHLY INTEREST**. Making that substitution,

PRIOR CUMULATIVE INTEREST = MONTHS x SCALING FACTOR x BASE MONTHLY INTEREST

The **BASE MONTHLY INTEREST** is taken from the applicable **BASE LOAN TABLE**.

For multiple loans:

Do the above for each loan and sum the results to get the **COMBINED PRIOR CUMULATIVE INTEREST**.

The **MONTHLY RATE OF INTEREST** and **BASE MONTHLY INTEREST** amounts for each possible Undergraduate and Parent base loan were included in earlier tables. For convenience they are repeated here.

LOAN AMOUNT =1000.00					
PERIOD OF DISBURSEMENT	**BORROWER**	**ANNUAL RATE OF INTEREST**	**MONTHLY RATE OF INTEREST**	**PRINCIPAL**	**BASE MONTHLY INTEREST**
7/1/14-6/30/15	UG	4.66%	0.3883%	989.28	3.84
7/1/15-6/30/16	UG	4.29%	0.3575%	989.27	3.54
7/1/16-6/30/17	UG	3.76%	0.3133%	989.32	3.10
7/1/17-6/30/18	UG	4.45%	0.3708%	989.31	3.67
7/1/14-6/30/15	P	7.21%	0.6008%	957.12	5.75
7/1/15-6/30/16	P	6.84%	0.5700%	957.08	5.46
7/1/16-6/30/17	P	6.31%	0.5258%	957.28	5.03
7/1/17-6/30/18	P	7.00%	0.5833%	957.24	5.58

Example:

SITUATION 28

Jonathan began a 4-year undergraduate degree in August 2014 and will complete it in May 2018. Each academic year, he and his parents each borrowed $4000.00. $2000.00 was disbursed on August 1 and on the following February 1. Each loan had a 5-year **TERM**.

The **COMBINED PRIOR CUMULATIVE INTEREST** each paid during deferment/grace period is calculated as follows.

There are eight loans. **MONTHLY INTEREST** is paid on the first loan for 51 months (45 months until graduation plus 6 months for the grace period). Each succeeding loan will involve 6 months less time than the previous loan. For each loan, the **SCALING FACTOR** = $2000.00/$1000.00 = 2.0. Here are the results.

For each loan:

PRIOR CUMULATIVE INTEREST = MONTHS x SCALING FACTOR x BASE MONTHLY INTEREST

For Jonathan's first loan: **Using the applicable BASE MONTHLY INTEREST amount from the above table,**

PRIOR CUMULATIVE INTEREST = 51 x 2.0 x 3.84 = $572.25

For all of Jonathan's loans:

COMBINED PRIOR CUMULATIVE INTEREST = 51 x 2.00 x $3.84 + 45 x 2.00 x 3.84

+ 39 x 2.00 x $3.54 + 33 x 2.00 x 3.54

$$+ \ 27 \times 2.00 \times \$3.10 + 21 \times 2.00 \times \$3.10$$

$$+ \ 15 \times 2.00 \times 3.67 + 9 \times 2.00 \times \$3.67$$

$$= \$391.68 + \$345.60 + \$276.12 + \$233.64$$

$$+ \ \$167.40 + \$130.20 + \$110.10 + \$66.06$$

$$= \$1720.80$$

For all of Jonathan's parents' loans:

COMBINED PRIOR CUMULATIVE INTEREST $= 51 \times 2.00 \times \$5.75 + 45 \times 2.00 \times 5.75$

$$+ \ 39 \times 2.00 \times \$5.46 + 33 \times 2.00 \times \$5.46$$

$$+ \ 27 \times 2.00 \times \$5.03 + 21 \times 2.00 \times \$5.03$$

$$+ \ 15 \times 2.00 \times \$5.58 + 9 \times 2.00 \times \$5.58$$

$$= \$586.50 + \$517.50 + \$425.88 + \$360.36$$

$$+ \ \$271.62 + \$211.26 + 167.40 + \$100.44$$

$$= \$2640.96$$

SITUATION 28 – CONTINUED

NOTE: As expected, the **PRIOR CUMULATIVE INTEREST** for the successive loans gets less and less. But the **COMBINED PRIOR CUMULATIVE INTEREST** amounts are very significant!

Exercise 34: Repeat *SITUATION 28 for sequential <u>yearly</u> LOAN AMOUNTS being $1000.00, $3000.00, $5000.00 and $7000.00. Each LOAN AMOUNT is distributed two equal half amounts.*

Your results should be:

For Jonathan: For the first loan the PRIOR CUMULATIVE INTEREST = $97.92, and for all eight loans the COMBINED PRIOR CUMULATIVE INTEREST = $1246.92.

For his parents: For the first loan the PRIOR CUMULATIVE INTEREST = $146.63, and for all eight loans the COMBINED PRIOR CUMULATIVE INTEREST = $1938.00.

Exercise 34A: Repeat Exercise 34 except repayment begins without a grace period.

Your partial results should be:

For Jonathan: For the first loan the **PRIOR CUMULATIVE INTEREST** *= $86.40, and all eight loans the* **COMBINED PRIOR CUMULATIVE INTEREST** *= $874.49.*

For his parents: For the first loan the **PRIOR CUMULATIVE INTEREST** *= $129.38, and all eight loans the* **COMBINED PRIOR CUMULATIVE INTEREST** *= $1561.37.*

- Interest Paid After the Deferred/Grace Period -

Once the differed/grace period is over, repayment of a loan begins. In earlier Lessons Dad used the **AMORTIZATION TABLE** to determine the amount. Alternatively, **BASE LOAN TABLES** can be used to calculate the subsequent costs.

If the **PRIOR CUMULATIVE INTEREST** has been paid, resulting the **LOAN AMOUNT** for the succeeding loan is the initial **PRINCIPAL** = initial **LOAN AMOUNT – ORIGINATION FEE**. That's because the **ORIGINATION FEE** has already been paid.

If a **BASE LOAN TABLE** is then used for that subsequent **LOAN AMOUNT**, an error occurs. That's because the **BASE LOAN TABLES** have the subtraction of an **ORIGINATION FEE** embedded in them. No subtraction should occur. To correct for that, an adjustment to values taken from them is necessary. Let's illustrate how that is done.

SITUATION 28A

Jonathan and his parents begin repayment of their loans. At the end of the grace period, each loan will have the initial **PRINCIPAL** (= $2000.00 – **ORIGINATION FEE**) as the **LOAN AMOUNT** and a 5-year **TERM**.

Consider Jonathan's first loan.

From the UG-BASE LOAN TABLE:

LOAN AMOUNT = $1000.00

ORIGINATION FEE = $10.72

PRINCIPAL = $989.28.

Based on that PRINCIPAL amount the base MONTHLY PAYMENT = $18.52 and base CUMULATIVE INTEREST = $121.63.

SITUATION 28A - CONTINUED

For the actual loan, the **ORIGINATION FEE** has been previously paid. The base values must be adjusted to reflect that. Otherwise the **ORIGINATION FEE** would be double counted.

ADJUSTED BASE MONTHLY PAYMENT = ($1000.00/$989.28) x $18.52 = $18.72

ADJUSTED BASE CUMULATIVE INTEREST = ($1000.00/$989.28) x $121.63 = $122.95

For the actual subsequent loan:

SUBSEQUENT CUMULATIVE INTEREST = SCALING FACTOR x $122.95

= 2.00 x $122.95 = $245.90

SITUATION 28A - CONTINUED

Omitting the similar calculations, for all eight of Jonathan's loans collectively here are the combined results.

COMBINED SUBSEQUENT CUMULATIVE INTEREST = $1806.10

TOTAL CUMULATIVE INTEREST = COMBINED PRIOR CUMULATIVE INTEREST + COMBINED SUBSEQUENT CUMULATIVE INTEREST

= $1720.80 + $1806.10 = $3526.90

SITUATION 28A - CONTINUED

The **COMBINED PRIOR CUMULATIVE INTEREST** amounts are only slightly less than the **COMBINED SUBSEQUENT CUMULATIVE INTEREST** amounts. That illustrates the high cost of not starting repayment upon disbursement of the loans.

For his parents' first loan:

SUBSEQUENT CUMULATIVE INTEREST = $776.12

For all eight of his parents' loans,

COMBINED SUBSEQUENT CUMULATIVE INTEREST = $2937.14

TOTAL CUMULATIVE INTEREST = COMBINED PRIOR CUMULATIVE INTEREST + COMBINED SUBSEQUENT CUMULATIVE INTEREST

= $1720.80 + $2937.14 = $4657.94
= $2640.96+ $2148.03= $2937.14

Exercise 35: *Calculate the* ***SUBSEQUENT CUMULATIVE INTEREST*** *for Jonathan's last loan.*

Your result should be: ***SUBSEQUENT CUMULATIVE INTEREST*** *= $233.43.*

- Quantifying the Effect of Not Paying Monthly Interest During the Deferred/Grace Period -

The results for Jonathan of SITUATION 28 illustrate that the **COMBINED PRIOR CUMULATIVE INTEREST** paid during possible deferment and grace periods is substantial. When estimating the **TOTAL COST** of **FSA** loans one should take into account. However, it is even more costly to skip paying that interest. It takes a special twist to do it. Let's show how that is done.

In a computerized **AMORTIZATION SCHEDULE** the **MONTHLY PAYMENT, AMOUNT APPLIED TO INTEREST** and **AMOUNT APPLIED TO OUTSTANDING PRINCIPAL** are automatically calculated each month, as if they were paid. But if the borrower makes made no payments at all, adjustments have to be made. The end result must show that the **OUTSTANDING PRINCIPAL** does not decline each month and instead the unpaid **MONTHLY INTEREST** is added to it. To illustrate that precisely, let's examine the following underlined **AMORTIZATION SCHEDULE** for Jonathan's first loan.

Loan Amount	2000.00						
Origination Fee Rate	1.072%						
Origination Fee	20.00						Principal = 1978.56
Term in Years	Annual Rate of Interest	Month	Monthly Payment	Applied to Interest	Applied to Principal	Additional Applied to Principal	Outstanding Principal
5	4.66	1	37.03	7.68	29.35	-37.03	1986.24
		2	37.03	7.71	29.32	-37.03	1993.96
		12	37.03	8.02	29.01	-37.03	2072.75
		24	37.03	8.40	28.63	-37.03	2171.42

36	37.03	8.80	28.23	-37.03	2274.80
48	37.03	9.22	27.81	-37.03	2383.09
51	37.03	9.33	27.70	-37.03	2410.96

All but one aspect is the same as for a usual **AMORTIZATION SCHEDULE** . Because they were not paid the usual schedule was adjusted to remove the monthly **AMOUNT APPLIED TO PRINCIPAL** and **AMOUNT APPLIED TO INTEREST**. That was done by entering a monthly **ADDITIONAL AMOUNT APPLIED TO PRINCIPAL** of -$37.03 (the negative of the **MONTHLY PAYMENT**). The effect is the unpaid **MONTHLY INTEREST** is being added to the **OUTSTANDING PRINCIPAL**.

For example, after Month 1, the **OUTSTANDING PRINCIPAL** = $1978.54 + $7.68 = $1986.24. In the next month **MONTHLY INTEREST** is charged on that amount. Had the prior **MONTHLY INTEREST** been paid, then the **OUTSTANDING PRINCIPAL** would be $1986.24, not $1978.56.

This continues each month. The overall consequence is the **OUTSTANDING PRINCIPAL** increases each month by the amount of the skipped **MONTHLY INTEREST**. Correctly, the unpaid interest is being cumulatively added to the debt. So "interest is being charged on unpaid interest" and the **OUTSTANDING PRINCIPAL** is "growing faster and faster." After Month 12 the **OUTSTANDING PRINCIPAL** = $2072.75, an increase of $94.20 in that 12 months. After Month 24 the **OUTSTANDING PRINCIPAL** = $2171.42, and increase of $98.66 in that next 12 months.

In Month 51 the **OUTSTANDING PRINCIPAL** has increased to $2410.96! That's $2410.96 - $1978.56 = $432.40 (about 22%) more money owed than at the start of repayment. Let's refer to that as **EXTRA PRINCIPAL**.

Omitting calculations, if the **PRIOR CUMULTIVE INTEREST** had been paid, then the repayment of $1978.56 in a 5-year repayment **TERM** would result in **SUBSEQUENT CUMULATIVE INTEREST** of $236.89. For the $2410.96, the **SUBSEQUENT CUMULATIVE INTEREST** = $288.65, $51.76 more. Let's refer to that as **EXTRA CUMULATIVE INTEREST**.

That result is for Jonathan's first loan alone. There are seven other loans involved. If their **MONTHLY INTEREST** is skipped during the deferred/grace period, then each leads to an **EXTRA PRINCIPAL** amount. After deferment ends, an **EXTRA CUMULATIVE INTEREST** amount is incurred during repayment. Of course, for the seven other subsequent loans the effect steadily diminishes because the number of months of unpaid **MONTHLY INTEREST** declines for each loan.

Let's examine Jonathan's last loan.

Omitting calculations, in Month 9 the **OUTSTANDING PRINCIPAL** has increased from $1978.62 to $2045.62. That an **EXTRA PRINCIPAL** of $67.00.

By comparison, if the **PRIOR CUMULATIVE INTEREST** had been paid, then the repayment of

$1978.62 in a 5-year period would result in **SUBSEQUENT CUMULATIVE INTEREST** of $231.93. After repaying the $2043.12 amount, the **SUBSEQUENT CUMULATIVE INTEREST** = $239.78. That implies an **EXTRA CUMULATIVE INTEREST** of $7.85.

For the other loans the **EXTRA CUMULATIVE INTEREST** amounts are each in between $7.85 and $67.00, so modest. However, they are extra costs.

For the parents, it is worse. For their first loan, the **OUTSTANDING PRINCIPAL** increases from $1914.24 to $2753.79. That's $839.55 in **EXTRA PRINCIPAL**. For their last loan it increases from $1914.48 to $2044.60. That's an **EXTRA PRINCIPAL** of $130.12. As their **ANNUAL RATES OF INTEREST** are significantly higher as well, they pay much more **EXTRA CUMULATIVE INTEREST** on each loan than Jonathan.

The best course of action would be to not use a deferment/grace period. If one can afford to start repayment immediately after disbursement of each loan, then the entire **PRIOR CUMULATIVE INTEREST** and **EXTRA CUMULATIVE INTEREST** are eliminated.

Enemy No. 2 - Forbearance

For borrowers encountering a period financial hardship (e.g. not having a job after leaving college or being hospitalized for a period of time) the **U.S.D.E.** provides an option to place a loan into forbearance. If you are in forbearance then you are allowed to skip interest payments on a **FSA** loan. But there are the above consequences. Let's examine a hypothetical (but not unrealistic) SITUATION that depicts that circumstance.

SITUATION 29

In May, 2017 Zachary completed a two-year private school program for an Associate Degree in culinary arts. He moved to a large urban city, not yet having a salaried job. The going is tough and it's a competitive time to land a professional job. He is working at odd jobs (server in a restaurant, sales clerk in a department store etc.), all part time and low paying.

Zachary has two past **FSA** loans which were first disbursed on August 1 of each academic year. Each had a **LOAN AMOUNT** $4000.00 and a 5-year **TERM**. During college he deferred his loan repayments and skipped paying **MONTHLY INTEREST**.

Upon graduating he obtained a **Direct Consolidation Loan** and entered a 6-month grace period. When it ended, due to the high cost of urban rent and city living, he requested and was approved for forbearance for up to two years. During that period he skipped paying **MONTHLY INTEREST**. After the forbearance period ends, Zachary begins to repay the consolidated loan,

The following is the trail of the consequences of his loans.

For Loan 1:

Being first disbursed on August 1, 2015, the **ANNUAL INTEREST RATE** was 4.29%. The **ORGINATION FEE RATE** was 1.073%. The **ORIGINATION FEE** = 0.01073x $4000 = $42.92 and the resulting **PRINCIPAL** = $4000.00 - $42.92 = $3957.08.

Zachary has had this loan for 27 months. The following is the adjusted **AMORTIZATION SCHEDULE** .

LOAN 1								PRINCIPAL = 3957.08	
Term in Years	Annual Rate of Interest	Month	Monthly Payment	Amount Applied to Interest	Amount Applied to Outstanding Principal	Additional Amount Applied to Outstanding Principal	Outstanding Principal	Cumulative Interest Not Paid
5	4.29	1	74.17	15.56	58.60	-74.17	3972.65	15.56
		2	74.17	15.63	58.54	-74.17	3988.27	31.19
		12	74.17	16.25	57.92	-74.17	4147.95	190.87
		24	74.17	17.04	57.13	-74.17	4348.02	390.94
		27	74.17	17.24	56.93	-74.17	4399.53	442.45

SITUATION 29 - CONTINUED

The **OUTSTANDING PRINCIPAL** is growing larger and larger. In Month 27 it has increased to $4399.53. That's an increase of $4399.53 - $3957.08 = $442.45, the amount of the **CUMULATIVE INTEREST NOT PAID**. Zachary was digging a deeper and deeper hole.

For Loan 2:

Being first disbursed on August 1, 2016, the **ANNUAL RATE OF RATE** was 3.76%. The **ORIGINATION FEE RAT**E was 1.0068%. The **ORIGINATION FEE** = 0.01068 x $4000.00 = $42.72. The resulting **PRINCIPAL** = $4000.00 - $42.72 = $3957.28.

Zachary had this loan for 15 months. Omitting the calculations, his **OUTSTANDING PRINCIPAL** increased to $4147.41. That's an increase of $190.13, the amount of **CUMULATIVE INTEREST NOT PAID.**

For Loan 1 + Loan 2 combined:

The combined **ORIGINATION FEE** = $42.92 + $42.72 = $85.64 and combined **OUTSTANDING PRINCIPAL** = $4399.53 + $4147.41= $8546.94. The combined **CUMULATIVE INTEREST NOT PAID** = $442.45 + $190.13 = $633.58.

For Loan 3 (the Direct Consolidation Loan during forbearance):

By not having to actively make any **MONTHLY PAYMENTS** on Loans 1 and 2 Zachary paid little attention to their increasing **OUTSTANDING PRINCIPALS**. For the same reason he does not notice the **PRINCIPAL** for the consolidation loan is $8546.94 compared to $7914.36 for his combined individual loans. He has not realized that he has gone backwards in debt!

Nevertheless, the **Direct Consolidation Loan** ensues. Due to the amount of **PRINCIPAL**, the loan **TERM** is 12 years. Omitting calculations, the **WEIGHTED AVERAGE INTEREST RATE** is 4.125%.

Zachary is in forbearance. For two years no **MONTHLY PAYMENTS** are made, including skipping the **MONTHLY INTEREST**. The partial adjusted **AMORTIZATION SCHEDULE** follows.

LOAN 3							PRINCIPAL = $8,546.94	
Term in Years	Annual Rate of Interest	Month	Monthly Payment	Applied to Interest	Amount Applied to Outstanding Principal	Additional Amount Applied to Outstanding Principal	Outstanding Principal	Cum. Interest Not Paid
12	4.125	1	75.35	29.38	45.97	-75.35	8576.32	29.38
		2	75.35	29.48	45.87	-75.35	8605.80	58.86
		24	75.35	31.79	43.56	-75.35	9280.65	733.71

SITUATION 29 - CONTINUED

The **ADDITIONAL AMOUNT APPLIED TO OUTSTANDING PRINCIPAL** of -$75.35 serves to cancel out automatically generated **MONTHLY PAYMENT** each month.

Month 24:

Zachary's **OUTSTANDING PRINCIPAL** has increased from $$8,546.94 to $9280.65, $733.71. That equals the **CUMULATIVE INTEREST NOT PAID** = $733.71.

For Loan 4 (the **Direct Consolidation Loan** *after forbearance):*

Via an E-mail message Zachary is informed that his period of forbearance is over and he has to start making payments. As is typical practice, the lender adjusted the loan. The adjusted loan will begin with a **PRINCIPAL** of $9280.65, a fresh 12-year **TERM** and unchanged **ANNUAL RATE OF INTEREST** of 4.125%.

Month 144:

Using the **CONSOLIDATED-BASE LOAN TABLE** with a **SCALING FACTOR** = 9.281 (rounded): By interpolation, the **MONTHLY PAYMENT** = 9.281 x ($8.76+$8.88)/2 = $81.85 and **CUMULATIVE INTEREST PAID** = 9.281 x ($260.76 + $278.31)/2 = $2501.55.

For the four Loans combined:

Prior to the **Direct Consolidation Loan** Zachary had only paid the combined **ORIGINATION FEES** (= $42.92 + $42.72 = $85.64) on Loans 1 and 2. The resulting combined **PRINCIPAL** was $3957.08 + $3957.28 = 7914.36.

When he began forbearance, that had increased to a combined **(OUTSTANDING) PRINCIPAL** of $8546.94. During forbearance Zachary paid nothing and the combined **(OUTSTANDING) PRINCIPAL** increased to $9280.65.

After forbearance Zacchary paid off Loan 4. Atop paying the $9280.65, he incurred **CUMULATIVE INTEREST** = $2501.55, a total of $11782.20. Adding in the initial **ORIGINATION FEES** he paid out a total of $11867.84 on the $8000.00 awarded. That's a **TOTAL COST** = $3867.84, about 48%.

Let's add a twist to SITUATION 29.

SITUATION 29A

Assume that at the end of forbearance, the lender does not adjust the **MONTHLY PAYMENT** for the consolidated loan. Instead it is kept at $75.35 instead of $81.85. Zachary does not realize the nuance, that it should be higher. He starts making timely **MONTHLY PAYMENTS** of $75.35.

NOTE: The **Consolidated-Base Loan Table** cannot be used in this circumstance.

The following is the resulting partial **AMORTIZATION SCHEDULE** :

LOAN 3 CONT'D							PRINCIPAL = 9280.65	
Term in Years	Annual Rate of Interest	Month	Monthly Payment	Applied to Interest	Amount Applied to Outstanding Principal	Additional Amount Applied to Outstanding Principal	Outstanding Principal	Cum. Interest Paid
12	4.25	1	75.35	31.90	43.45	0.00	9237.20	31.90
		2	75.35	31.75	43.60	0.00	9193.61	63.66
		143	75.35	4.62	70.73	0.00	1273.73	2768.13
		144	75.35	4.38	70.97	0.00	1202.76	2772.51
		160	75.35	0.37	74.98	0.00	33.46	2808.81
		161	75.35	0.12	75.23	0.00	-41.77	2808.93
		161	*33.58*	*0.12*	*33.46*	*0.00*	*0.00*	*2808.93*

SITUATION 29A - CONTINUED

NOTE: The last payment would overpay the loan by $41.77, so the **MONTHLY PAYMENT** is adjusted as shown in the italicized entries.

Month 144:

Zachary expects to be free of debt. Instead the loan is not yet paid off. He still owes $1202.76. And he already has **CUMULATIVE INTEREST PAID** = $2772.51. Zachary wonders "How could this have happened to me?" But he must make a choice. He either has to pay that amount or continue the loan for 17 more months!

If the loan is continued it takes 17 more months to pay it off. At that time the **CUMULATIVE INTEREST PAID** would have increased to $2808.93. That's $2808.93 - $2501.55 = $307.38 more than if he paid the $81.85 each month.

Having been successfully employed and saved money, Zachary wisely chooses to pay off the debt in full. He moves on having learned an important. If you have to go into deferment and/or forbearance try to at least pay the monthly **AMOUNT APPLIED TO INTEREST**. As to figuring out why this outcome happened, Zachary purchases this book and by reading it he will find out.

Alertly, the reader may have the thought that Zachary would have had to pay interest on his loans in any circumstance. Let's look into the difference between the above events and his alternative of having at least paid the **MONTHLY INTEREST** each month on all his loans.

SITUATION 30

Instead of skipping his entire **MONTHLY PAYMENT**, Zachary of SITUATION 29 pays the **MONTHLY INTEREST** part of his loans.

It should be apparent that for their entire **TERMS** Zachary's **OUTSTANDING PRINCIPAL** for each loan would remain at the initial amount. Each month his **MONTHLY INTEREST** would be the same amount.

For Loan 1:

The **MONTHLY RATE OF INTEREST** = 4.29%/12 months = 0.3575%. The **MONTHLY INTEREST** = 0.003575 x $3957.08 = $14.13 (rounded). After 27 months he would have **CUMULATIVE INTEREST PAID** = 27 x $14.13 = $381.51 (rounded).

Let's show the preceding in a partial **AMORTIZATION SCHEDULE** :

LOAN 1							PRINCIPAL 3957.08	
Term in Years	Annual Rate of Interest	Month	Monthly Payment	Applied to Interest	Amount Applied to Principal	Additional Amount Applied to Principal	Outstanding Principal	Cum. Interest Paid
5	4.29	1	73.39	14.15	59.25	-59.25	3957.08	14.15
		2	73.39	14.15	59.25	-59.25	3957.08	28.30
		27	73.39	14.15	59.25	-59.25	3957.08	382.05

SITUATION 30 - CONTINUED

Month 1:

The **MONTHLY PAYMENT** = $73.39. Only the **AMOUNT APPLIED TO INTEREST** of $14.15 is paid. To reflect that, the **ADDITIONAL AMOUNT APPLIED TO PRINCIPAL** is set to -$59.25. The effect is the **OUTSTANDING PRINCIPAL** remains at $3957.08. The **CUMULATIVE INTEREST PAID** is $14.15.

Succeeding months repeat the entries of Month 1, except the **CUMULATIVE INTEREST** incrementally increases by $14.15 each month. After Month 27, the **CUMULATIVE INTEREST PAID** = $382.05.

For Loan 2:

The **MONTHLY RATE OF INTEREST** = 3.76%/12 months = 0.3133%. So the **MONTHLY INTEREST** = 0.003133 x $3957.28 = $12.40 (rounded). After Month 15 Zachary will have **CUMULATIVE INTEREST PAID** = 15 x $12.40 = $186.00 (more precisely, $185.99).

When Zachary consolidates the loans, the combined **OUTSTANDING PRINCIPAL** = $3957.08 + $3957.28 = $7914.36.

For Loan 3 (the Direct Consolidation Loan):

The **PRINCIPAL** is $7914.36 and it results in a 12-year **TERM**. Omitting calculations, the **WEIGHTED AVERAGE INTEREST RATE** = 4.125%.

The **MONTHLY RATE OF INTEREST** = 4.125%/12 months = 0.3438%. The **MONTHLY INTEREST** = 0.003438 x $7914.36 = $27.21 (rounded). After Month 24 Zachary will have paid **CUMULATIVE INTEREST PAID** = 24 x $27.21 = $653.04 (more precisely, $652.94).

Month 24:

Forbearance ends. The **PRINCIPAL** remains $7914.36 and with a new 12-year **TERM** and **ANNUAL RATE OF INTEREST** of 4.125%. Zachary starts making full payments.

Month 144:

Using the **CONSOLIDATED-BASE LOAN TABLE** with a **SCALING FACTOR** = 7.9184 (rounded):

The **MONTHLY PAYMENT** = 7.914 x ($8.76 + $8.88)/2) = $69.80 and **CUMULATIVE INTEREST PAID** = 7.914 x ($260.76 + $278.31)/2 = $2132.74

For the three loans, Zachary had a combined **CUMULTATIVE INTEREST PAID** = $378.68 + $186.00 + $653.04 + $2132.74 = $3350.46. Adding in the **ORIGINATION FEES** of $85.64, the **TOTAL COST** = $3436.10. The **TOTAL COST** is about 43% of the $8000.00 borrowed.

Comparing SITUATIONS 29 and 30, Zachary pays $3867.84 - $3436.10 = $431.74 more **CUMULATIVE INTEREST** if he skips paying **MONTHLY INTEREST** than if he pays it. In this case, it's a very modest difference. Andi it occurs over 16 years! The reader can make his or her own decision as to which path is better.

In SITUATIONS 29, 29A and 30, the results are for $8000.00 of total borrowed money at the outset. For the same circumstances, if the **LOAN AMOUNT** is the average student **FSA** debt of about $30000.00, the results are much higher. The results prior to the consolidation loan can be proportioned by $30000.00/$8000.00 = 3.75. The results for the **DIRECT CONSOLIDATED LOAN** are more than proportionally higher. That's because for that **LOAN AMOUNT**, the **USDE TERM** bracket results in a 20-year **TERM** instead of a 12-year **TERM**. In this case, the **ANNUAL RATE OF INTEREST** was the same 4.125% whether the **MONTHLY INTEREST** was skipped or not.

The author repeated SITUATIONS 29 and 30 for that higher amount and compared the results.

SITUATION	LOAN AMOUNT	TERM	MONTHLY INTEREST	TOTAL COST	PERCENT TOTAL COST
29	8,000.00	12 years	SKIPPED	3868.14	48
30	8,000.00	12 years	NOT SKIPPED	3436.10	43
29-modified	30000.00	20 years	SKIPPED	21488.04	72
30-modified	30000.00	20 years	NOT SKIPPED	17392.08	58

As expected, for both **LOAN AMOUNTS**, when the **MONTHLY INTEREST** is not skipped, the **TOTAL COST** is less than if it is skipped. That's because in each sequential loan (Loans 1 to 4) the **PRINCIPAL** is lower than if it is not skipped.

For SITUATION 29 and SITUATION 30 the **PERCENT TOTAL COST** is 48% and 43%, respectively. For SITUATION 29-modified and SITUATION 30-modified, the **PERCENT TOTAL COST** is 72% and 58%, respectively.

The latter percentages are dramatically higher. That's primarily due to the **TERM** of the **DIRECT CONSOLIDATED LOAN** increasing from 12 years to 20 years.

The preceding SITUATIONS demonstrate that delaying the payment of **MONTHLY INTEREST** is never positive. When deferment/grace/forbearance time periods come into, it is becomes "pay me now or pay me later." Paying later always costs more. A student who completes graduate school will likely borrow significantly more **FSA** funds than one who does not. Such student will attend college for 5-10 years and could delay loan repayment for that many years then go into forbearance. For a larger **PRINCIPAL** combined with a higher **ANNUAL RATES OF INTEREST** the monetary costs paid later dramatically increase both in absolute and percentage terms. Skipping the **MONTHLY INTEREST** and then going then going into a forbearance period would result in even much more dramatic, possibly extreme, consequences.

Of course the least cost option is if Zachary had started repayment upon disbursement of the funds and not consolidated his loans. Had he done that for the $8000.00, then (omitting calculations) his **TOTAL COST** would be $920.05, or 12% . It's a lot less than $3867.84 or even $3436.10.

For the $30000.00 amount the **TOTAL COST** would be $3450.18, or also 14%. It's enormously less than $21488.04 or even $17392.08!

Enemy No. 3 – Foreclosure

Consequences exist even when the omission is permitted by the lender as is the case of deferment and forbearance of **FSA** loans. In the case of private (non-government based) loans (such as a bank personal loan for a computer), deferment and forbearance are more difficult to obtain. For private loans if **MONTHLY PAYMENTS** are skipped without approval, the property is the collateral and the lender can *foreclose* on the loan.

Foreclosure is a specific legal process in which a lender attempts to recover the **PRINCIPAL** of a loan from a borrower who has stopped making payments to the lender. It is the step of confiscating and/or forcing the sale of the asset used as the collateral for the loan. For a small item like a computer or automobile the lender might simply repossess it (hiring a bold and nasty individual to take it from you) and use a collection agency to recover any net loss of outstanding loan repayment funds.

For **FSA** loans if you are neither in deferment nor in forbearance and skip payments then you could face foreclosure. There is no tangible asset; your grades and degree cannot be taken away (even if you want some bad grades taken away). So some possible actions are the use of a collection agency and garnishing your wages and/or tax refund. The latter means legally withdrawing the debt from those payments before you receive them. And your credit rating will tumble. Interest paid on student loans qualifies as a deduction in paying federal income tax. So the **IRS** will also know about you. If you are in delinquency they will be looking for you too. They will find you. So make your **FSA** loan payments on time.

Pomp and Circumstance is being played. As Nicole walks down the aisle in single file with her college classmates, she's thinking how far she's come from being a high school kid to a being college kid and now about to be a college graduate. She's also thinking how far her parents came in making this day possible. Being called a smarty pants and then smarter pants along the way reinforces her appreciation for their caring that she reaches her full potential. Today is a big step forward in that direction. When she is walking back down this aisle, her career start will be in motion.

Nicole also thinks about the financial planning and maneuvering it took to make it possible, and in an affordable way. She may never repay that in money, but she aims to do so by being successful. That means doing well at her first job, wisely using her income and avoiding debt. Because her entry job will take her even farther away in distance she's a bit chagrin and sad. Those wonderful actual Dad face to daughter face meetings to shake out solutions to the monetary demands of taking on and handling debt will greatly lessen in frequency. She's sure there will be some, but Skype will be the more frequent setting. Somehow virtual face to face won't be quite the same as being together.

She's reached her seat. There's still a few more minutes until last student with a surname beginning with Z takes his seat. So she unfolds her Commencement program and glances down at the large white envelope inside. It's marked "To Dad – The Greatest One Ever – Thank you for getting me to this Day". She knows what's inside. She cannot wait to give it to him.

After her most recent meeting with her Dad, she had an interesting assignment in a business course. The task was to write a short paper on a topic related to financing their college education. Well, right up her alley! Then a great big, blinding light bulb came on. Though blinded she saw through it to the ideal topic. She wrote it. Now she was looking at that white envelope, recalling all that happening. She had put her paper inside. It was marked in red with an A+. And after Commencement she would be giving it to her A+ Dad.

So here's how that A+ paper goes:

Beware of Brackets – Count Every Penny in Your Student Loans

From the time I was a "little girl" my Dad has regularly taken time with me to teach me about managing debt. Like most kids, the "Dad, I need _____, can you give me the money?" plea was something I often did. The blank was one of many things kids plead for. For me it was a skateboard, to go bowling, to go skiing etc. He also taught me about "negotiation" and a "contract". I learned had to negotiate an outcome agreeable to both of us. For me it was to get what I wanted. For him it was setting conditions for which I he would give it to me. The contract was in place once he and I accepted the conditions.

I recall, way back, he gave me money for a fishing license when I agreed to give him all the fish I caught. My Dad called that the "terms of the contract" That was great, since I did not want the fish. I only wanted to meet the boy across the street who liked to fish. So I scribbled up a contract and we signed it. What I learned was to be very careful about reading anything involving debt carefully before agreeing and signing. Well, fast forward.

By the time I started college, with my Dad's guidance I knew everything about managing a credit card before I got one. He also took oodles of time to prepare me for taking out student loans and being smart about repaying them to limit interest I pay. If he had not shown me all that then I might not be here at Dream University writing this paper. But he did and so I here I am doing it.

Once I started earning money by working teen jobs and then college kid odd jobs, he taught me about filing my tax returns. This year, I filed my own tax return for the first time. That was just a few days ago. It sparked my idea for this assignment. So here it goes.

Anybody who has filed a **Federal income tax return** to the **Internal Revenue Service (IRS)** and had to pay taxes is familiar with *tax brackets*. I sure am, now. They're a bit quirky. Each tax bracket is associated with a specified Federal tax rate based on the total taxable income. As my taxable income gets higher and higher, it elevates into higher and higher tax brackets. With the exception of the first one, the tax rate for any tax bracket is not applied to my entire taxable income. In each particular tax bracket its tax rate applies to the increment of taxable income that is above a taxable income cap for the preceding bracket. That tax rate only applies until that increment of taxable income raises the total taxable income to the income cap of the particular tax bracket. Additional increments of taxable income then go into the succeeding tax brackets and are taxed on the same basis within each bracket as each comes into play. Wow, on reread that's a mouthful. It almost sounds like my Dad. Basically, if I separate my income into a series of increments then the first increment is taxed the least, the next ones are taxed more and more and the last increment is taxed the most.

The taxable income ranges of the tax brackets differ for **single individuals** vs. **married couples filing jointly**. As students are predominantly single, let's peek at those brackets. As backdrop to my main topic, I have to grind out the unpleasant details.

The **IRS** uses whole dollars (no cents) for income. For 2017 taxable income if that income is $0 to $9325 then I am in the 10% tax bracket. That means I pay a tax of 10% on it. If my taxable income is

$9326 to $37950 then I am in the 15% tax bracket. I pay a tax of 10% on the first $9325 of it and of 15% on the amount above $9325. If my taxable income is $37951 to $91900 I am in the 25% tax bracket. I pay a tax of 10% on the first $9325 of it, plus 15% on the amount above that until it reaches $37950, plus 25% on the amount above $37950. There are four higher brackets (the highest is 39.6% for a taxable income of $418400 or more), but my point is made. As my taxable income successively moves up into those higher tax brackets I am incrementally taxed more and more on my additional taxable income. The following are examples of how income tax is calculated.

If my taxable income is $11225, then I pay an income tax of 0.10 x $9325 + 0.15 x ($11225 - $9325 = $2000.00) = $932.50 + $300.00 = $1222.50 ($1233 rounded) in income tax. That's a **FRACTION** = $1233/$11225 = 0.1100; thus overall it's 11.00% tax on my total taxable income.

If my taxable income is $47450, then I pay an income tax of 0.10 x $9325 + 0.15 x ($37950 - $9325 = $28225) + 0.25 x (47450 - $37950 = $10000.00) = $932.50 + $4293.75 + $2375.00 = $7601.25 ($7601 rounded). That's a **FRACTION** = $7601/$47450 = 0.1602; thus overall it's 16.02% tax on my total taxable income.

It's kind of confusing and more than a bit tedious to do these calculations, at least for me. It must be for most people, too. I suppose that's why the **IRS** provides *tax tables* to be used instead of doing them. The tax tables (found in IRS Publication 17, available at www.irs.gov) list the tax owed for what I'll call "mini-brackets" of taxable income ranges. There are a lot of mini-brackets included. For example, for a **single individual**, if taxable income is at least $47450 but less than $47500, then the listed income tax is $7608 (the listed amount is higher than the above $7601 because it is based on the average of that range). If instead the taxable income is at least $47500 but less than $47550, then the listed income tax is $7620. These mini-brackets don't change the tax rates of the actual larger **IRS** brackets; they just do the tax calculation for you.

Notice that if I have taxable income of $47500 my income tax is $7620 - $7608 = $12 more than it is for a taxable income of $47499. That extra $1 of taxable income causes me to incur $12 additional income tax. That's a **FRACTION** = $12/$1= 12; a 1200% income tax rate on that dollar! Even though it is a small amount of money, I can imagine many people "fudging" their income to be $1 less in order to drop down by one mini-bracket. I just might think about it myself.

What's all this got to do with student loan debt? Let's see.

ASIDE: My Dad liked to use a **BOLD CAPITALIZED FONT** to emphasize important words. So in writing this paper I borrowed his way.

Direct Consolidation Loans for **Federal Student Aid** (**FSA**) also use brackets, but they are more ominous than those of the **IRS**. The **TERM** of a consolidated loan is set by the lender using specific brackets of **LOAN AMOUNT**. Let's refer them as the **STUDENT LOAN TERM BRACKETS**. I've tabulated them below.

LOAN AMOUNT	TERM
$0.00 to $7499.99	10 years
$7500.00 to $9999.99	12 years
$10000.00 to $19999.99	15 years
$20000.00 to $39999.99	20 years
$40000.00 to $59999.99	25 years
$60000.00 or more	30 years

How do these become insidious? If one is not careful, a single penny increase in the **LOAN AMOUNT** for a consolidated **FSA** loan can make a huge difference in cost. Let's examine how huge it can be.

SITUATION N1

Student 1 has consolidated $9999.99 in **FSA** loans for a 12-year **TERM**. Student 2 has consolidated $10000.00 for a 15-year **TERM**.

The **ANNUAL RATE OF INTEREST** for a consolidated loan is determined by the prorating process. For a student the value will be between the present 3.40% for undergraduate loans and $6.80% for the graduate student loans being consolidated. Let's use 5.00% for both students.

For these initial **OUTSTANDING BALANCES,** in Year 1 Student 1 would pay roughly 0.05 x $9999.99 = $499.9995 rounded to $500.00. Student 2 roughly pays 0.05 x $10000.00 $500.00 exactly. No difference in the result? So what's the problem?

The problem occurs in the long term, i.e. over the full **TERM** of the loans. The effect of the two different loan **TERMS** is dramatic. Let's see why.

The following are partial **AMORTIZATION SCHEDULE S** for each student.

Student 1						LOAN AMOUNT = 9999.99	
Term in Years	Annual Rate of Interest	Month	Monthly Payment	Amount Applied to Interest	Applied to Outstanding Balance	Outstanding Balance	Cumulative Interest
12	5.00	1	92.49	41.67	50.82	9949.17	41.67
		2	92.49	41.45	51.03	9898.13	83.12
		12	92.49	39.29	53.20	9375.95	485.83
		24	92.49	36.57	55.92	8719.98	939.73
		120	92.49	9.13	83.36	2108.18	3206.87
		144	92.49	0.38	92.11	0.00	3318.42

Student 2						LOAN AMOUNT = 10000.00	
Term in Years	Annual Rate of Interest	Month	Monthly Payment	Amount Applied to Interest	Applied to Outstanding Balance	Outstanding Balance	Cumulative Interest
15	5.00	1	79.08	41.67	37.41	9962.59	41.67
		2	79.08	41.51	37.57	9925.02	83.18
		12	79.08	39.92	39.16	9540.61	489.57
		24	79.08	37.91	41.17	9057.73	955.63
		120	79.08	17.72	61.36	4190.47	3679.99
		144	79.08	11.28	67.80	2638.54	4025.97
		180	79.08	0.33	78.75	0.00	4234.29

Over the **TERMS** of the loans, for the extra $0.01 borrowed Student 2 will pay $4234.29 - $3318.42 = $915.87 more **CUMULATIVE INTEREST** than Student 1. That's a **FRACTION** = $915.87/$0.01 = 91587; 9158700% interest on that extra penny! Over 9 million percent!

Even at <u>Month 144,</u> the difference is $4025.97 - $3318.42 = $707.55; 7075500% interest on that extra penny. Over 7 million percent!

ASIDE: For both students the actual **CUMULATIVE INTEREST** after 12 months is not the ball park estimate of $500.00. That earlier estimate assumed the debt was unchanged for that time period. It was used just to catch the reader's attention. That detail is irrelevant to the actual outcomes. The loan debt is actually declining monthly. The average debt over the 12 months is less than the full **LOAN AMOUNT.** As a result the actual interest for each student is somewhat less than $500.00.

Even if the **LOAN AMOUNTS** differed by more than $0.01, say $9900.00 vs. $10100.00, the difference in **CUMULATIVE INTEREST** is still dramatic.

Student 1						LOAN AMOUNT = 9900.00	
Term in Years	Annual Rate of Interest	Month	Monthly Payment	Amount Applied to Interest	Applied to Outstanding Balance	Outstanding Balance	Cumulative Interest
12	5.00	1	91.56	41.25	50.31	9849.69	41.25
		2	91.56	41.04	50.52	9799.16	82.29
		144	91.56	0.38	91.18	0.00	3285.24

Student 2						LOAN AMOUNT = 10100.00	
Term in Years	Annual Rate of Interest	Month	Monthly Payment	Amount Applied to Interest	Applied to Outstanding Balance	Outstanding Balance	Cumulative Interest
15	5.00	1	79.87	42.08	37.79	10062.21	42.08
		2	79.87	41.93	37.94	10024.27	84.01
		144	79.87	11.39	68.48	2664.92	4066.23
		180	79.87	0.33	79.54	0.00	4276.63

Over the **TERMS** of the loans Student 2 will pay $4276.63 - $3285.24 = $991.39 more **CUMULATIVE INTEREST** than Student 1. For the $200.00 difference in **LOAN AMOUNTS** that's a **FRACTION** = $991.39/$200.00 = 4.95; 495% interest on that extra $200.00.

SITUATION N1 involved values at the low end of the **STUDENT LOAN BRACKETS**. I also looked at the other end of the brackets.

SITUATION N2

Student 1 has consolidated $59999.99 in **FSA** loans for a 25-year **TERM**. Student 2 has consolidated $60000.00 for a 30-year **TERM**. The following are partial **AMORTIZATION SCHEDULE** S for each student.

Student 1						LOAN AMOUNT = 59999.99	
Term in Years	Annual Rate of Interest	Month	Monthly Payment	Applied to Interest	Applied to Outstanding Balance	Outstanding Balance	Cumulative Interest
25	5.00	1	350.75	250.00	100.75	59899.24	250.00
		2	350.75	249.58	101.17	59798.06	499.58
		12	350.75	245.28	105.47	58762.85	2971.90
		240	350.75	78.58	272.18	18586.70	42767.66
		300	350.75	1.46	349.30	0.00	45226.20

Student 2						LOAN AMOUNT = 60000.00	
Term in Years	Annual Rate of Interest	Month	Monthly Payment	Applied to Interest	Applied to Outstanding Balance	Outstanding Balance	Cumulative Interest
30	5.00	1	322.09	250.00	72.09	59927.91	250.00
		2	322.09	249.70	72.39	59855.51	499.70
		12	322.09	246.63	75.47	59114.78	2979.90
		240	322.09	127.34	194.75	30367.36	47669.67
		300	322.09	72.16	249.94	17067.93	53695.83
		360	322.09	1.34	320.76	0.00	55953.47

Over the **TERMS** of the loan, for the extra $0.01 borrowed Student 2 will pay $55953.47 - $45226.20 = $10727.27 more **CUMULATIVE INTEREST** than Student 1. That's a **FRACTION** = $10727.27/$0.01 = 1072727; thus 107272700% interest on that extra penny! Over 100 million percent!

Even at <u>Month 300</u>, the difference is $53695.83 – 45226.20 = $8469.63; 84,696,300% interest on that extra penny, over 80 million percent!

Even with a larger difference in the **LOAN AMOUNTS**, say $59000.00 vs. $61000.00, the difference in **CUMULATIVE INTEREST** is still dramatic.

Student 1						LOAN AMOUNT = 59000.00	
Term in Years	Annual Rate of Interest	Month	Monthly Payment	Applied to Interest	Applied to Outstanding Balance	Outstanding Balance	Cumulative Interest
25	5.00	1	344.91	245.83	99.07	58900.93	245.83
		2	344.91	245.42	99.49	58801.44	491.25
		12	344.91	241.20	103.71	57783.47	2922.37
		240	344.91	77.27	267.64	18276.93	42054.88
		300	344.91	1.43	343.48	0.00	44472.44

Student 2						LOAN AMOUNT = 61000.00	
Term in Years	Annual Rate of Interest	Month	Monthly Payment	Applied to Interest	Applied to Outstanding Balance	Outstanding Balance	Cumulative Interest
30	5.000	1	327.46	254.17	73.29	60926.71	254.17
		2	327.46	253.86	73.60	60853.11	508.03
		12	327.46	250.74	76.72	60100.03	3029.56
		240	327.46	129.46	198.00	30873.48	48464.17
		300	327.46	73.36	254.10	17352.40	54590.76
		360	327.46	1.36	326.10	0.00	56886.03

Over the **TERMS** of the loans Student 2 will pay $56886.03 - $44472.44 = $12413.59 more **CUMULATIVE INTEREST** than Student 1. For the $2000.00 difference in loan amounts that's a **FRACTION** = $12413.59/$2000.00 = 6.21; 621% interest on that extra $2000.00.

I need to point out a significant **ALERT** concerning **STUDENT LOAN TERM BRACKETS** compared to Federal income tax brackets.

Each Federal income tax bracket applies to an increment of taxable income. The tax rate of that bracket applies only to the increment of taxable income that falls within that bracket.

By contrast, consolidation of **FSA** student loans puts the entire **LOAN AMOUNT** into a single **STUDENT LOAN TERM BRACKET** and its **TERM** applies to the full **LOAN AMOUNT**. For example, if I have a consolidated **LOAN AMOUNT** of $25999.99 then it's in the **STUDENT LOAN TERM BRACKET** of $20000.00 to $39999.99. It has a **TERM** of 20 years on the entire amount. I do not have one loan for $9999.99 increment with a **TERM** of 12 years and another loan for a $16000.00 increment with a **TERM** of 15 years.

Typically a student borrows **FSA** money annually. As the loans accumulate the total amount successively approaches the caps on each of the bracket and then spills over into the next one. It is important to keep a close tally of the increasing total amount of **FSA** student loan debt. For a small increment of borrowed *later* money the resulting total amount can spill over from being just under a bracket cap into the next bracket. As a higher bracket is approaching, he/she may want to accept a little bit less money. Indeed, count every penny! A conscientious student would observe each increment of money borrowed and stop borrowing at an amount just below a palatable bracket cap.

One problem is that the **FSA** web site for loan information does not include the **STUDENT LOAN TERM** brackets! A student may not find out they exist until they have to consolidate. I only know of them because my Dad told me when we first looked into student loans. He found out by calling a student loan lender and then confirmed it by calling the **USDE**.

What else can one do to adjust the situation? It is up to you, the borrower, to take the step of informing the **USDE** that you want to consolidate loans. Then the **USDE** will inform you of an assigned "servicing lender". You do not have to consolidate all your individual loans. You can indicate any subset of them. Then the servicing lender will communicate the terms of the loan to you. That will consist of the **PRINCIPAL**, the **ANNUAL RATE OF INTEREST** and, typically based on the **STUDENT LOAN BRACKETS**, the **TERM** of the loan. Again, the borrower may not know about those **STUDENT LOAN BRACKETS** and simply assume the stated **TERM** is the only option.

This information will be conveyed electronically. You will have the option to either accept the terms or not. You will also have a contact point to call should you need additional information or clarifications. Make that call! You can indicate a desire to consolidate a different subset. Whether you consolidate all your loans or not, try to negotiate a change in the **ANNUAL RATE OF INTEREST** and/or the **TERM** of the loan. In any case, another consideration is to consider making a larger one-time payment to pay off some of the **OUTSTANDING BALANCE** to one or more of the existing loans before doing the consolidation to get the total amount owed into a lower bracket.

Maybe the **USDE** has good intentions in having the **STUDENT LOAN BRACKETS**. For a given **LOAN AMOUNT** the longer the **TERM** the lower is the **MONTHLY PAYMENT**. A graduating student about to start a job likely feels a need to spread the loan repayment out over a long **TERM** for that reason. But, he/she has to look beyond that.

My Dad honed me in on the fact that **CUMULATIVE INTEREST** paid is the vital consideration. He showed me that the longer is the **TERM** the greater is the **CUMULATIVE INTEREST**. He showed me how it is not a proportional effect. Doubling the **TERM** more than doubles the **CUMULATIVE INTEREST**. And as one moves up the **STUDENT LOAN TERM BRACKETS** it's not just the **TERM** that is increased. The **LOAN AMOUNT** has also increased. The difference in **CUMULATIVE INTEREST** for $60000 borrowed for 30 years compared to $10000 borrowed for 15 years is dramatic. I calculated it. For an **ANNUAL RATE OF INTEREST** of 5% the former is $55953. The latter is $4234.

If a student has very good creditworthiness and ability to make higher payments, the loan service might consider a request to shorten the **TERM** of the consolidated loan and/or reduce the **ANNUAL RATE OF INTEREST**. So it is worth a try at negotiating such changes and doing it verbally at the outset of deciding to do a consolidation. If a "little girl" did it for a fishing license, then an older "little girl" (and an older "little boy") can try it for student loans. Call them! Of course, if the student has graduated into a job with good to excellent salary that will help immensely.

The preceding scenarios assume the graduating student will choose to consolidate his/her loans. Vividly, I recall my Dad cautioning against it. Keeping your separate **FSA** loans unconsolidated avoids the misstep of carelessly putting all your **FSA** marbles into one basket with a loan **TERM** much longer than any of the individual loans. The collective **MONTHLY PAYMENT** amounts of the individual loans will total to a higher combined **MONTHLY PAYMENT** than for the consolidated loan but they will be paid off much sooner, at dramatically less combined **CUMULATIVE INTEREST**. In effect you take charge of the negotiation mentioned in the preceding paragraph by not having to negotiate at all. Not pursuing the consolidation option could leave you in the same cost situation as doing the consolidation loan and being successful in negotiating its terms. Just as vividly I recall my Dad also showing me how I can consolidate my loans and avoid the consequence of paying a huge amount of interest. Here's what I learned.

The **COMBINED MONTHLY PAYMENTS** the individual loans will be much higher than the **MONTHLY PAYMENT** of the consolidated loan. I can accelerate repayment of the consolidated loan by making a **MONTHLY PAYMENT** equal to those **COMBINED MONTHLY PAYMENTS**. The extra amount is an **ADDITIONAL AMOUNT APPLIED TO PRINCIPAL** and it will substantially shorten the loan repayment time. That almost invariably occurs if each of those individual loans has the same **TERM**.

Most students defer their loan repayment until after graduation. If they do, and each loan has the same **TERM,** then their repayment will be simultaneous. If they can afford the amount of their **COMBINED MONTHLY PAYMENTS** then they should consolidate their loans and accelerate them. They should pay that amount each month. The extra margin is the **AMOUNT APPLIED TO PRINCIPAL**, the acceleration. In most cases the consolidated loan will be paid off in the same time as the shorter **TERM** of the individual loans. And the lessened **CUMULATIVE INTEREST** will be about the same amount as for the **COMBINED CUMULATIVE INTEREST** of the unconsolidated loans at the end of their common **TERM**. My Dad tried tons of examples and made those observations. They led to his conclusion regarding consolidation. So it's total believable. So much so I will be doing it myself.

My Dad added mention of a safeguard aspect of accelerating the consolidated loan. Should an adequate job not come about right away or financial setbacks in income arise down the road, then one can fall back to just making the lower **MONTHLY PAYMENT**. Once recovered, return to accelerating.

With so many college students facing so much debt upon graduation, the preceding advice gotten from **MY DAD** offers a possible lifeline. If any of them need one then **MY DAD** and **I** would be grateful if you consider grabbing on to his!

Oh, by the way. My Dad still calls me his "little girl". I suppose he always will. Or with luck, when I finally outsmart him about a money matter, I will have grown up in his view. No matter, I like being his "little girl" and always will. But I do aim to outsmart him some day. Come to think of it, I sort of already did with that fishing license contract. But I want to do it with a "big girl" money matter.

Reprise

When the joyful tears in her Dad's eyes began Nicole just watched and waited. She knew when he looked up from her paper he would have gotten to the end. Then he looked up.

"My! My! Nicole. What an amazing young woman you have become. I cannot even imagine writing such a well-constructed pragmatic paper in such a sensitive way. I couldn't be any prouder of you or thankful than I am right now. Please excuse my sort of crying. It has been worth every penny and every day Mom and I spent raising you. Now you're so high I need to be on a cloud to see you. Maybe I am. And to see how you took what I've taught you about handling debt and created your own extension of it. That's just priceless. In fact it's way more. It's irreplaceable."

"So Dad, maybe this is the moment when I outsmarted you?"

"Well, I wouldn't exactly say that. It's more like showing your professor and I how especially smart you are standing on your own two feet. Or when you will be when you've come off that well deserved cloud. It's much more important to be as smart as you are than to outsmart anyone. And right now you're wearing the smartest looking pair of pants, I mean gown, I've ever seen you in."

"I see your point and agree. But I still expect to outsmart you one day, just for the fun of it."

"I'm sure you will. I'm very sure you will. But I can wait till that day comes. So let's head out now before I start bawling. I've got to find an impenetrable place to put your gift away for safe keeping. Maybe along the way we can find a place like Comic Cones, have a cone and read some lighter material."

"Fabulous, Dad, and it'll be my treat! You've spent enough on me already."

ACKNOWLEDGEMENTS

I owe the inspiration for undertaking my book series to my wife Irene and daughter Jody (now Jody Zorn). A long- time marriage and raising a child to adulthood brought first hand encounters with all the types of debt needs and challenges addressed in it. While not mirrored in my writing, those encounters were the food for thought that went into it. Collectively they led to the mental menu that outlined it.

Through that time Irene and I overcame youthful inexperience in money management matters and gradually worked toward mutual acumen and strength in managing our monetary resources. My progression is summarized in the Preface. In time Irene formed her own at-home business in interior design. That led to her increasing competence in fiscal management and accounting aspects of running it. Everything we do with our domestic money we do together. We meld our individual wish lists and priorities into a joint set, at least annually. No big decisions are made without conversation and concurrence. I am deeply thankful for her understanding and patience with the pragmatism involved in my developing and exhaustively using spreadsheet after spreadsheet after spreadsheet through the years. It's been a labor of love and I know she knows and feels that was my motivation. It helped us to live through the larger financial matters with minimal stress and not have unanticipated torpedoes hit and sink our ship. Navigating that sea led to the skills and strategies I endeavor to share with my readers.

Jody has always been and independent and energetic sort of individual. Whatever she dreams of having she finds a path to getting it. In early days, if money was involved she gathered it by hook (not crook), persuasion, bartering and wheeling and dealing in the sort of ways kids try do those things. So it took time to rein that in and redirect her toward realism in meeting monetary needs. Over time she seemed to value my insight and help in important money matters more and more. Somehow I had motived her to want to ask for, listen to and consider my advice. And lots of that came in spreadsheet form, too. She has no passion for them. She has no desire to do them. So accepting them from me was very gracious of her. More important she has grown to respect and appreciate my input and thoughts. Every call that has come from her asking my opinion was a welcomed pleasure. I love her for making those calls. They still occur and buoy my joy at being her Dad and make me feel like I did a pretty good job. The approaches and evolution that led to that outcome underpin the relationship I gave to my two characters. By doing so, my characters present a realistic example of how others might go about it. It's based on pragmatics but buoyed by a mix of inner/outer subtleties, amateur psychology, patience and humor I employed in my own actual case.

I express my deepest appreciation to my Reviewer No. 1 and Reviewer No. 2. That's how I referenced them on file tabs and in early formal messages. But each is a special person not a number. Each provided thorough, detailed mark-ups and helpful answers to questions I included with transferred material. Each merits a mini-story.

Reviewer 1: Timea ("Timi") Balogh was contracted when she was a junior-year high school student. I did that with a mix of intent and hesitation. On intent, my books are targeted for 16-year olds and onward. About a 16-year old she was, so a fit. But could a high school kid effectively review an adult's semi-technical book? I knew of her proficiency in mathematics, but gave her a brief quiz to test her actual acumen. She passed and on the payroll she went. Along the way I learned of Timi's passion for reading. It shone though in her earnest, professional reviews. She reviewed up to and including Lesson 11 (mortgage loans) of the original several manuscripts. At that time it was a behemoth (but now sub-divided). Then Timi stopped. Perhaps it was the level of material vis-à-vis her age and experience. Perhaps the boyfriend who came along was a factor too. No matter. Timi did a marvelous job. Reading her feedback one would barely know it was from a high school kid. It was exactly what I needed to know. It gave me a barometer on of how many Lessons into the planned book that a high schooler could take it. I could adjust accordingly. In appreciation, Timi became my "Timmy", the Ramen roommate with the credit card problem. That's why in the end Timmy's math prowess shone through. Timi, I thank you sincerely for the high quality of your help.

Reviewer 2: Serendipity was in play. Nicole Ehrlich was hired at the end of her first year in college. In passing, I learned of her start in a degree related to publishing. On further talk, a mention that she had left that degree program came. She saw limited future with printed news and printed writing on the decline. She was now in between, not in college, working out her next step. As I walked away my writer's light bulb came on! A brief ask, a yes, followed by a formal contract, and Nicole was on my payroll, too. That choice became the best step I made in the path leading to this book. After three plus decades of my marking up (in red) the work of my many, many college students, the red pen was in the hand of a student and turned toward my work. It had to be an interesting juxtaposition for Nicole as well. But I'd never see any reluctance or caution taken. Nicole proved to be extremely competent in the task at hand.

To me, it was clear that Nicole had been a top notch A+ student in her education related to the three R's. I could not have had my work more effectively critiqued. From the general to the nitty-gritty Nicole fired away at it. Always caring but never hesitant, she picked up everything and marked and commented thoroughly. On a few occasions we jousted and hashed out the correctness of certain unusual words. We each won a couple, perhaps. More likely, Nicole won them all. Always on target, her reviews motivated me to make most of my major changes and saw me through the first nine drafts. Whenever I wavered or tired in fix ups, she pushed me on. As it moved along the harder and harder the suggested cutting decisions became and the more and more I resisted. In the end I did virtually all of them. The book series is so much improved because of it. The student did the professor well! As appreciation for Nicole's commitment and professionalism I gave her name to my principal character. It was a late change but just felt right. Nicole and my "Nicole" arc a lot alike, but are neither twins nor clones by any means. I treasured working with both of them. I feel that someday the actual Nicole will be an author herself and a wonderful one for sure.

ASIDE: Maybe I'm the only person to who has not read the Harry Potter books? I owe the use of several contemporary Harry Potter–based items to Nicole as well. One was due to her happenstance mention that she was headed out to play a game of "quidditch". Strange it was to me, so I asked "what's that?" So she described it a bit. It sounded weird and silly to me. I wondered to myself, "College kids play this?" Then I researched it on the web and snuck the word into the next draft of another volume. When I needed a scary character, Nicole provided me the name of "Voldemort". When in need of a phrase somewhat akin to "beam me down" as in "beam me down Scottie" from Star Trek, she shared that when Harry Potter characters want to get places quickly they "disapparate". I'll add reading J. K.

Rowland's literary works to me TO DO list. Years ago, I did see one movie.

ASIDE: Oh, by the way. Presently, Nicole is majoring in Mathematics and minoring in Physics at the University of Colorado in Boulder. Fancy that, the actual Nicole is a smarty pants too.

For two plus years, essentially every other Thursday, I parked myself in the lounge at a local Marriott hotel. Cleaning people shoving me out of my home base necessitated that regimen. Numerous staff got used to the guy sitting there keypunching away at his book manuscripts. If I was a "no show" then things felt "out of place" for them. When I was there, it always felt like the "right place" for me.

Diane Curry was my regular on-duty barista. She honed in on my usual "diet Pepsi and martini glass of salty snacks" and served my occasional lunch orders. Occasionally she "comped me" my usual. Once it was when I forgot my wallet. Other times I suppose I probably looked either tired or chagrined while doing (maybe not doing) my writing.

Diane was a sounding target for some of my "thinking out loud" moments. At times, I called her over for my reading to her of sample passages, usually the intended humorous ones. Her laughter each time told me they actually were so. She got peeks at other passages and her confirmation that they fit some of her experiences helped my confidence. I will miss her welcoming tone and greetings, until I set about finalizing the next volume. I'm very thankful for her putting up with my omnipresence and letting me take up the same old seat every time.

On one "Diane is off-duty" Thursday, a college-age Lizzie Hughes was the barista. In conversation, she mentioned she was earning and saving money for graduate school because out-of-state tuition (at the local university, where I had worked) was so high. I shared that I was writing a book which included the topic of college costs and loans. I casually offered advice on how she might get financial aid including a reduction to in-state tuition as a part of it. It was one surprised and bright smile I got in return. I cannot say enough about how nice it made me feel.

Amid pauses in my writing, I overhead many lounge guest conversations on topics as varied as snowflakes. One in particular, I share.

I listened as two H&M (the clothing store) personnel representatives interviewed college kids for floor sales jobs at a newly opening site at the adjacent mall. It told me a lot about how college kids in need of part-time or full-time work in these economically stretched days respond in an interview. Overhearing the post interview appraisals was interesting as well. I chimed in with my opinion on some of the applicants. It seemed welcomed. Hopefully, they got the jobs. I couldn't avoid wondering if they had student loan debt to deal with.

ASIDE: The back of the book cover photo of the author was taken in that Marriott satellite site. The idea came when I spontaneously asked Diane to take a photo with my cell phone camera, "just for my memories". Immediately, I knew I had just gotten my book photo. Quality was great. In time she graciously understood when I returned with my professional photographer daughter and son-in-law to retake it. Close call, but bias won. Thank you to Diana. Thank you to Jody (again) and Zach Zorn of Zorn Photography in Denver, Colorado for the final photoshoot.

On a rush schedule, Jody also did the photo shoot for the front cover photo. Jody also formatted the written matter for the cover, spine and back of the book. It was deeply special to have her team with her Dad and dedicate her great talents to those key pieces of the book

Dennis Zorn (Zach's Dad and my golfing buddy) posed as the fictional Dad on the cover. Middle school student Sophia Acott (daughter of my CrossFit pal, Katherine Acott) posed as the fictional daughter. It was a fun session and I am deeply grateful to them for their willingness and courage to put wonderful faces (theirs) to my two characters. It brings them to life in a very personal way.

Some time ago, my son-in-law Zach Zorn asked my advice in regard to a student loan matter. That likely was not easy to do. Evidently, Jody and he had used forbearance at one time for their past student loans He had uncertainty and concerns about the later discovered consequences to the debt owed. After investigating the trail of each of their loans, I explained the monetary aspects leading to the consequences and how to go about adjusting for the dilemma. In light of that I later researched the topic and produced my content about forbearance in LESSON 19 Student Loan Enemies No. 1, No. 2 and No. 3. In memory of that occasion I used the name "Zachary" for my hypotetical character and his past circumstance as the food for thought behind the Situations I used. Hopefully, the great father of my first grand-child knows how much I appreciated being asked about it and for my help and advice. By way of that my readers benefit very much now, too.

There are few formal referenced publications behind this book. I simply wrote my story as the reflection of my personal experiences and growth in managing my personal debt. The few I used were internet based. Some are cited directly in the body. I augmented those with conversations with several people engaged professionally.

As related to this volume on **THE COLLEGE EXPERIENCE**:

Via phone conversation, a staff person in the Financial Aid office at Colorado State University verbally walked me through the internal sequence events and timing for developing a first-year student applicant's financial-aid package. She answered my litany of questions about the timing of the offer, handling of unknown future FSA loan costs, flow of information subsequent to acceptance etc. That conversation allowed me to be accurate about timeline details, so as to correctly incorporate them in my written content and example Situations.

Via phone conversation with a Customer Service representative for the U.S. Department of Education's FSA student loan program, I clarified many intricate aspects of the extensive federal web site content. Via that site and searches of numerous other web sites, I tediously established the historical track of the Origination Fee Rates and Annual Rates of Interest.

I conversed with an agent at my own past student loan servicer, EdFinancial Services, about the setting of the TERM vis-à-vis the loan amount for a consolidated loan amount. That led to the bracket information contained in my book. His indication was that was typical bracketing. It might or might not be the case for your specific loan servicer, but likely is so.

I chatted with a Customer Service agent for Chase for a lengthy time about the precise details of their calculation of monthly interest on a Visa revolving credit card debt. I verbally walked through one of my numerical examples with him. As a result I confirmed the correctness of my understanding and math calculations for the situation of an outstanding balance revolving from month to month. We each originating from Massachusetts long ago, an enjoyable side chat about past Boston Red Sox and Boston Celtics teams of yore ensued. I thank him for his patient help and shared memories.

Regrettably, the above contacts were not permitted to disclose a full name, so I left them general. An exception is Colorado State University for which I carelessly neglected to ask.

Monetary details of the present total costs of completing a 4-year college education used for Nicole and her Dad's walk through their assessment are realistic. I used an arbitrary sampling of actual colleges to get a flavor for the ranges involved. I glanced through numerous sites then chose six for a seeming representative range of costs. For public institutions, I closely examined Colorado State University, the University of Indiana, and the University of South Carolina. For private institutions I used Butler University, Colorado College, and the University of Evansville.

Interestingly, some college web sites provide a useful financial aid estimator. They seem to be based on FAFSA criteria and merit-based (usually termed gift-aid) criteria at the specific institution. One inputs a student applicant's geographic data (in-state or out-of-state; for the former also a zip code and high school attended) and academic GPA information etc. plus income, financial asset and federal tax data for the student and parents. Click on ENTER and a potential financial aid package results. In highlight, it is stated as estimated, not a guaranteed package etc. If you have serious intention to apply and use a college's estimator, then also inquire further before you do.

I used the University of Evansville's estimator to run through a range of data situations. That gave me a flavor for a range of outcomes; a mix of loans and granted funds (FSA, internal university, external local or state government etc.). I formulated the estimated costs and financial aid amounts used for Nicole and her Dad. I neither fudged, nor tweaked the numbers. I created a seeming typical possibility. It surprisingly unfolded as a challenging one. Then I "worked the problem" as if I had to actually solve it for my own child's need. I converted that solution into the Nicole and Dad saga. As part of that solution, I had fictitious Nicole consider attending the local college for one or two years, for lower costs. Then I had her elect to do so for one year. Nowadays, that circumstance and choice are very common. My hypothetical Nicole/Dad Situation told me why in a big way. So too for my readers, I suppose.

Late in the game, I learned of the Income Share Agreement approach to financing college costs. I added information about it to **APPENDIX IV**, The information came via a news article "A proposal for paying for higher education costs" published in the "Point/Counterpoint" section of the Fort Collins Coloradoan (May 15, 2016). It was co-written by the USA TODAY Editorial Board and Ben Miller of the Center for American Progress. Purdue University offers them. Visits to the website BackaBoilerinfo@prf.org and a phone conversation with a staff person at the Purdue Division of Financial Aid. I was unable to locate other universities with an **ISA** program but found a few private entities that offer such contracts.

I attended an informative one-hour class on the topic of self-editing taught by Molly McCowan, Lead Word Nerd, INKBOT Editing. She proved to be the referee for one of my word jousts with Nicole. Is it "Student Loans <u>Is</u> My Alma Mater" (my sense) or "Student Loans <u>Are</u> My Alma Mater" (Nicole's sense)? Nicole won. But I still wonder. Molly pointed me toward my Chicago Book of Style to confirm it. Hesitating to lose for sure, I have yet to do that.

In 2015 I attended a few selected hour-long sessions of Money Smart Week offered at Colorado State University annually. They underscored much of my understandings and offered new pieces to the puzzle. Money Smart Week was created by the Federal Reserve Bank of Chicago and thousands of its events have been conducted by local experts at libraries and campuses nationwide, evidently on-line as well.

I am immensely indebted to and appreciative of Kerrie Flanagan; my consultant, writing coach and editor for this book series. She founded (in 2007) Northern Colorado Writers, a group that supports and encourages writers of all levels and genres, and was its Director for eight years. Kerrie is also the Publisher of Hot Chocolate Press. She's an author and freelance writer and a very busy person. But you'd never know it from her calm, patient, welcoming personality and manner. When meeting with her, her at-large world seemed invisible and my little writing task was her caring focus. In content reading my near final draft of the manuscript, she spared me the many red marks I so often made on many of my graduate students theses and dissertations. So few were they, I kind of felt my writing was better than felt and at least pretty good. I am especially thankful to Kerrie for several indispensable assistances.

Initially written as a single behemoth-near anthology, Kerrie recommended splitting that monster-sized book into specific cubicles, written as separate volumes. The behemoth was also a mix of narrative-technical content and periodic dialogue. By seeming mind-reading, Kerrie drew attention to the merit of expanding the dialogue approach to a dominant presence. Those were timely things, coming as reinforcement just as I was internally pondering likewise. Albeit a retreat to a second starting point, they were wise choices.

Once taken, the dialogue path became a lot of fun and a means to speak more clearly and explain subject matter to my readers. Unknowingly to me, Kerrie helped me find the "voice" that is mine (and the Dad's) in this book. Never having written dialogue, hearing her eventual comment, "You've found your voice" was very uplifting and needed. Just as important, she gently nudged me to giving a consistent, different "voice" to Nicole. I converted myself into the youthful Nicole and that was the most fun of all. So thank you Kerrie for steering the "good ship fun" ("lollipop" has been taken by a little girl named Shirley Temple) along.

Writing a book involves a seemingly never to be ending amount of seat time and finger usage. Thankfully neither my back side, nor my bottom side, nor my knuckles wore down through 2+ years and 11 draft manuscripts.

I cannot express enough appreciation for my chair for providing me sufficient enough comfort to make it through to the book itself. As to my fingers, they're fine too. I appreciate them hanging in the entire time. I greatly appreciate my CrossFit coaches (Jorine Peterson and Justin Thompson) at Miramont Life Center for keeping my body in more than good enough shape to handle it. Some members of my class group were aware of my book project and their saying they await its outcome and book signing was a subtle but much appreciated boon to my pushing on.

My office floor merits mention. Widespread use of it as a secondary desk throughout was imperative and invaluable. My only complaints are those days I had to pick up everything for the cleaning people to vacuum it. Typically that set me back a day or two each time. Nonetheless, thank you to my office floor.

Most importantly I close with this. Writing a book is an intensive, time consuming process. This one took 2.75 years or so. Writing a book is also a mix of inspiration, labor of good will, determination, persistence, and seemingly endless revisions and refinements. The goal is to "get it right" for the readership. Writing a book also flows through frequent frustrations and setbacks. There are lots of repeated minutiae tasks: rechecking all data and math, correcting discovered mistakes, checking consistency of formats, renumbering Situations and Exercises, etc. Then interest rates and other parameters change each year. One redoes a lot of numbers and exhaustive tables. No author survives the gauntlet without periodic visible and auditory expression of desire to figuratively heave things. I was no exception.

Above all appreciations, I love my wife for her patience, understanding and ability to eventually block it out when those temperamental moments and phases came along and her caring to tell me to carry on.

Federal Student Aid Program

Federal student loans are available through the **Federal Student Aid** program of the **U.S. Department of Education** (**U.S.D.E.**). Full details about the federal government student loan programs are available at https://studentaid.ed.gov/sa/. Because the circumstances of the individuals seeking such loans vary widely, the web site is exhaustive. Financial standing of the applicant and the parents, possible independency from parents, and undergraduate degree vs. graduate degree program are just a few of the many parameters. But one must navigate them in order to be informed about the many different cubicles into which that individual might fit.

This Appendix provides basic information about the federal student loan programs. It includes information either taken directly from or condensed from the preceding web site and is sufficient for the most common circumstances. While still lengthy and dry reading, it provides a necessary base of current reference information needed by the reader. As such, it is available to be revisited by the reader whenever needed thereafter. The reader should also refer to the **U.S.D.E.** web site periodically for updated information and rules.

Application and Criteria

Students attending a four-year college or university, community college, or trade, career, or technical school are eligible for loans from the federal government. .

The student completes one application for all **FSA** programs, the **Free Application for Federal Student Aid (FAFSA)** which is available online. This is an extensive application, and among many things, it includes financial information about the student and the student's parents. The latter is applicable until the student can apply as an independent person (see the above web site for rules about that circumstance). The primary items likely needed are the applicant's Social Security Number, most recent federal income tax returns, W-2s, and other records of money earned, bank statements and records of investments (if applicable) and records of untaxed income (if applicable). For dependent children, this information is also needed from the parents.

Direct Subsidized and Direct Unsubsidized Loans are available only to undergraduate students who have demonstrated financial need. Prior to July 1, 2102 graduate and professional students could apply for them, but no longer can do so. The student's school determines the amount he or she can borrow. Except for the following limitation, the rules are essentially the same for both. For a **Direct Subsidized Loans** The **U.S. D. E.** pays the loan interest while the student is in school (at least half-time) and for a six month **grace period** after leaving school and during any approved period of **deferment** (postponement of the loan payments while you are in school or in military service). However for funds disbursed before July 1, 2014 the student owes the interest accrued during the grace period. The interest alone can be either paid as it is incurred or can be skipped. If skipped it is then added to the

PRINCIPAL or **OUTSTANDING BALANCE** of the loan.

Direct Unsubsidized Loans are only available to undergraduate, graduate and professional degree students and are not based on financial need. The student's school determines the amount that can be borrowed and considers all other financial aid the student may have or will receive. The amount that can be borrowed is based on the cost of attendance (tuition, fees, room and board, other school charges etc.) The student incurs interest during all periods of the loan, including deferments and "forbearance" (a period of financial hardship). The interest alone can be either paid as it is incurred or can be skipped. If skipped it is then added to the **PRINCIPAL** or **OUTSTANDING BALANCE** of the loan.

Direct PLUS Loans are available for parents (biological, adoptive, or in some cases, stepparent) of an undergraduate student, if a student has also applied via the **FAFSA**. They also are available for graduate/professional students who are independent of their parents. To take out a **Direct PLUS Loan** for the first time, the parents must complete a **PLUS Application** and **master promissory note (MPN)**. Unless the student's school does not allow more than one loan to be made under the same **MPN**, the parents can borrow additional **Direct PLUS Loans** on a single **MPN** for up to ten years.

Parents must not have adverse credit standing. Otherwise, if extenuating circumstances exist and a creditable endorsement is provided, they can make an application. Parents must use the loan money received only to pay for the child's education expenses at the school that is giving them the loan. Education expenses include school charges such as tuition, room and board, fees, and indirect expenses such as books, supplies, equipment, dependent child care expenses, transportation, and rental or purchase of a personal computer.

Typically the child's school will disburse the loan money by crediting it to the child's school financial account to pay tuition, fees, room, board, and other authorized charges. If the loan disbursement amount exceeds the child's school charges, the school will transfer the remaining balance to the parents to cover other educational costs. Dependent students whose parents have applied for but were unable to get a **Direct PLUS Loan** are eligible to receive additional **Direct Unsubsidized Loan** funds.

The preceding are the primary general **FSA** loan options and are covered in this Primary. Undergraduate and graduate students with demonstrated financial need can also apply for **Federal Perkins Loans**. In these loans the admitting college is the lender. **Health Profession Loans** are available through the U.S. Department of Health and Human Services and are needs-based, too. Students must be entering a health profession-related degree (medicine, veterinary medicine, etc.). Both loans are subsidized and partially funded by payments from prior borrowers. The funds available are more limited and dependent on the specific situation at any given college. Readers are referred to the colleges of interest (to them) as the best and direct source of information.

Interest Rates

Interest is incurred from the time any funds are disbursed (transmitted to the borrower). The **ANNUAL RATES OF INTEREST** for the various types of loans change every year. The rates are set based on Congressional determination and action.

For any direct subsidized or unsubsidized loan there is an **ORIGINATION FEE.** That means the borrower is charged that percent of the loan funds as a loan processing fee. In part it covers the cost associated with considering the application and handling the details of determining the awarded funds. But mainly it is because although **FSA** loans are "government loans" many of them are maintained by non-government (private) entities, banks and loan financing companies. That means they incur costs to set up the loan involved, accounting work, disburse the loan funds, receive and process payments, track repayment, and manage any changes that occur in the loan terms that may arise.

For readers of this Primer, it is assumed the rates for the July 1, 2015 – June 30, 2016 period and the past three years are pertinent. For future and older loans, the concepts and calculation procedures still apply to whatever rates were in play when those loans were disbursed.

The applicable periods and rates for a **Direct Loan** and a **Direct PLUS Loan** are as follows.

ANNUAL RATES OF INTEREST:

Loan Type	Borrower Type	Period of Disbursement			
		July 1, 2014 - June 30, 2015	July 1, 2015 - June 30, 2016	July 1, 2016 - June 30, 2017	July 1, 2017- June 30, 2018
		Annual Rate of Interest			
Direct Subsidized Loans	Undergraduate	4.66%	4.29%	3.76%	4.45%
Direct Unsubsidized Loans	Undergraduate	4.66%	4.29%	3.76%	4.45%
Direct Unsubsidized Loans	Graduate or Professional	6.21%	5.84%	5.31%	6.00%
Direct PLUS	Parent of Undergraduate	7.210%	6.840%	6.310%	7.000%
Direct PLUS	Graduate or Professional	7.210%	6.840%	6.3110%	7.000%

ORIGINATION FEES:

Loan Type	Borrower Type	Period of Disbursement			
		Oct. 1, 2014 - Sept. 30, 2015	Oct. 1, 2015 - Sept. 30, 2016	Oct. 1, 2016 - Sept. 30, 2017	Oct. 1, 2017 - Sept. 30, 2018
		Origination Fee			
Direct Subsidized Loans	Undergraduate	None	None	None	None
Direct Unsubsidized Loans	Undergraduate	1.073%	1.068%	1.069%	1.066%
Direct Unsubsidized Loans	Graduate or Professional	1.073%	1.068%	1.069%	1.066%
Direct PLUS	Parent of Undergraduate	4.292%	4.272%	4.276%	4.264%
Direct PLUS	Graduate or Professional	4.292%	4.272%	4.276%	4.264%

NOTE: For the Period of Disbursement of Oct. 2013 – Sept. 30, 2014 for Direct Unsubsidized Loans the **ORIGINATION FEE RATE** for (Undergraduates, Graduates, and Professionals) was 1.072%, For Direct PLUS Loans (Parents, Graduate, and Professional)) it was 4.288%.

NOTE: Belatedly (at the time of proofing the submitted manuscript) the **ANNUAL RATES OF INTEREST** became available for the period of July 1, 2018 – June 30, 2019. They are: Undergraduate 5.045%, Graduate or Professional 6.595%, Direct PLUS Loans (Parents, Graduate, and Professional) 7.595%). The **ORIGINATION FEE RAT**E for post Sept. 30, 2018 were not yet set by the agency.

NOTE: Purposely, in the text, the author predominately used the highest **ANNUAL RATES OF INTEREST** values listed above (from the period July 1, 2014 – June 30, 2015) of 4.66% and 6.21%, 7.21% for Undergraduate, Graduate/Professional and Direct PLUS Loans, respectively, and the corresponding **ORIGINATION FEE RATES** of 1.073%, 4.291%. All results would be somewhat higher if the new rates were known and used. The differences in results are insignificant to the outcomes and observations. The **CONSOLIDATED - BASE LOAN TABLE** is still applicable as the new rates lie within the range of listed **ANNUAL RATES OF INTEREST**

The **ORIGINATION FEE** is taken out of the loaned funds before they are disbursed, thus reducing the amount actually received. The loan is disbursed in increments over the year and the **ORIGINATION FEE** is proportionally applied to those amounts. As the funds are disbursed incrementally, the interest is charged to the ongoing **OUTSTANDING BALANCE**. Whenever payments are made the **OUTSTANDING BALANCE** will change accordingly.

Available Loan Amounts

The amount a student (or parent) can borrow is determined on an annual basis using updated **FAFSA** information. Many students don't finish their degrees on time. Due to course scheduling or retaking failed courses, the time can be longer. Many students also work and do not take a full schedule each term. Students and parents can borrow funds for a period of up to 1.5 times listed time for completion of a degree program. For a four-year Bachelor's degree that's a six-year period of time. For a two-year Associate degree that's a three-year period of time. A student is not required to finish his or her degree "on time" but there is a limit to the flexibility.

The student's school determines the loan type(s), if any, and the actual loan amounts the student is eligible to receive each academic year. The student might be awarded both subsidized and unsubsidized loans. There are limits on the amounts that a student may be eligible to receive each academic year (**Annual Loan Limits**) and the total amounts that a student may borrow for undergraduate and graduate study (**Aggregate Loan Limits**). The actual loan amount a student is eligible to receive each academic year may be less than the **Annual Loan Limit**. If the total loan amount received over the course of the student's education reaches the **Aggregate Loan Limit**, he or she is not eligible to receive additional loans. However, if the student repays some of loans to bring the outstanding loan debt below the **Aggregate Loan Limit**, he or she could then borrow again, up to the amount of remaining eligibility under the **Aggregate Loan Limit**.

The following tabulated information details the current **Annual** and **Aggregate Loan Limits** for **FSA** loans. It is taken from http://studentaid.ed.gov/types/loans/subsidized-unsubsidized.

Year	Dependent Students (except students whose parents are unable to obtain PLUS Loans)	Independent Students (and dependent undergraduate students whose parents are unable to obtain PLUS Loans)
First-Year Undergraduate Annual Loan Limit	$5,500—No more than $3,500 of this amount may be in subsidized loans.	$9,500—No more than $3,500 of this amount may be in subsidized loans.
Second-Year Undergraduate Annual Loan Limit	$6,500—No more than $4,500 of this amount may be in subsidized loans.	$10,500—No more than $4,500 of this amount may be in subsidized loans.
Third-Year and Beyond Undergraduate Annual Loan Limit	$7,500—No more than $5,500 of this amount may be in subsidized loans.	$12,500—No more than $5,500 of this amount may be in subsidized loans.
Graduate or Professional Students Annual Loan Limit	Not Applicable (all graduate and professional students are considered independent)	$20,500 (unsubsidized only)
Subsidized and Unsubsidized Aggregate Loan Limit	$31,000—No more than $23,000 of this amount may be in subsidized loans.	$57,500 for undergraduates—No more than $23,000 of this amount may be in subsidized loans. $138,500 for graduate or professional students—No more than $65,500 of this amount may be in subsidized loans. The graduate aggregate limit includes all federal loans received for undergraduate study.

Note that the limits are almost doubled for an independent student (one not dependent on parents). The higher limits also apply to dependent students whose parents are unable to get **PLUS** loans. The latter could occur due to adverse credit standing, criminal incarceration or other negative parental factors.

Graduate and professional students enrolled in certain health profession programs may receive additional **Direct Unsubsidized Loan** amounts each academic year beyond those shown above. For these students, there is also a higher **Aggregate Loan Limit** on **Direct Unsubsidized Loans**.

The available Aggregate Loan limits show that reaching the high levels of debt mentioned above is not surprising. For and undergraduate degree situation alone, the debt can reach $57500.00

For an undergraduate student, note that the **Aggregate Loan Limit** does not permit the student to borrow the maximum permissible amount of money for every year up the maximum of six allowed for a four year degree. For example, if a dependent undergraduate student uses only unsubsidized loans and borrows the maximum **Annual Loan Limit** amount for each of four years, the total he or she would borrow is $5500.00 + $6500.00 + $7500.00 + $7500.00 = $27000.00. Borrowing $4000.00 for a fifth year would take the total to $31000.00 which is at the maximum **Aggregate Loan Limit amount**. The student could not borrow any money for a sixth year of study. As one alternative, the student could instead borrow $2000.00 for each of the fifth and sixth years, half the maximum allotment for the fourth year.

If an <u>independent</u> <u>undergraduate</u> student uses only unsubsidized loans and borrows the maximum **Annual Loan Limit** amount for each of four years, the total he or she would borrow is $9500.00 + $10500.00 + $12500.00 +$12500.00 = $45000.00. Borrowing $12500.00 for a fifth year would take the total to $57500.00 which is at the maximum **Aggregate Loan Limit amount**. The student could not borrow any money for a sixth year of study. Alternatively, the student could instead borrow $6250.00 for each of the fifth and sixth years, half the maximum allotment for the fourth year.

For a <u>graduate</u> student who has borrowed the maximum of $57500.00 as an independent undergraduate student, if he or she borrowed the maximum **Annual Loan Limit** amount of $20500.00 for four years that would sum to $57500.00 + 4 x $20500.00 = $57500.00 + $81000.00 = $139500.00. That exceeds the **Aggregate Loan Limit** of $138500, by $1000. That student could only borrow $20250.00 annually, not $20500.00 (Perhaps the politicians intended $139500.00 but were not able to do the math correctly?) To earn a Master degree and a PH.D., it typically takes about five years. In that case, this student could borrow $81500.00/5 years = $16100.00 per year of graduate study.

A <u>dependent undergraduate</u> student could only borrow to an **Aggregate Loan Limit** of $31000.00 as an undergraduate. In that case, as a graduate student he or she would have $138500.00 - $31000.00= $107500.00 left to borrow for his or her graduate studies. Thus for five years the student could theoretically borrow $107500.00/5 years = $21500.00 per year which exceeds the **Annual Loan Limit** of $20500.00 per year by $1000.00 per year = $5000.00 total. Thus the actual annual amount borrowed could only be $102500.00/5 years = $21200.00 per year.

If this student had not borrowed any funds as an undergraduate, the graduate funds of $138500.00 would last $138500.00/$20500.00 per year = 6.75 years of the **Annual Loan Limit** was borrowed each year. That many years might be necessary for some doctoral degrees atop getting the Master's degree.

There are no set limits for **Direct PLUS Loans**, but <u>parents</u> may not borrow more than the cost of their child's education minus any other financial aid received, such as a **Direct Subsidized** or **Direct Unsubsidized Loan**. The child's school will determine the actual amounts the parents may borrow.

If the total loan amount one receive over the course of their education reaches the Aggregate Loan Limit, then the borrower is are not eligible to receive additional loans. However, if the borrower repays some of his/her loans to bring to reduce the outstanding loan debt to being below the **Aggregate Loan Limit**, he/she could then borrow again, up to the amount that returns the total to the **Aggregate Loan Limit.** Of course, that adds even more borrowing to the debt picture.

Clearly, a student and parents can each accumulate a substantial amount of student loan debt. If a dependent undergraduate takes six years to complete an undergraduate degree he or she may have qualified for and used up to $31000.00 in loans. If independent he or she may have qualified for and used up to $57500.00 in loans. Regardless of dependency, a graduate or professional degree student may have qualified for and used up to $138500.00 in **FSA** loans. That limit includes any loans taken out as an undergraduate student. Essentially, the $138500.00 upper range is similar to the price of buying a condominium. If the ongoing repayment and added borrowing process is in play, then the amount could be even higher maybe approaching. The annual rate of interest for undergraduate students is similar than for current home mortgage loans. The annual rates of interest for graduate students and parents are substantially higher. The **ORIGINATION FEE** for students is similar to that of many home mortgage loans. But the **ORIGINATION FEE** for parents is enormously higher. Compared to current annual rates of interest on bank savings accounts (0.05% to 0.5% being common), the **FSA** annual rates of interest for parents are stratospheric.

General Process

For new students seeking financial aid, the students first completes and submits the FAFSA to the federal government. It includes a list of institutions to which the applicant wishes to provide the information. For a timely and correct application it will take a few days to a few weeks for that to happen. Once any listed college receives the application for admission the decision on admission can take several months or more.

Once decided and if admitted, within a few weeks the student will receive a financial aid package, detailing all elements of financial aid being offered, whether **FSA** related or not. For **FSA**, the details will include maximum amounts of subsidized and unsubsidized aid available and the current applicable annual rates of interest in place and repayment options. The package applies to the first year of studies. As federal information changes, updates will be provided and posted on the college's web-site. The student can then accept part or all of the funds being offered for the first term, once he or she decides to accept and register for classes. It is logical to exhaust the any subsidized aid offered before accessing unsubsidized aid in part or entirety.

For subsequent terms (semester or quarters) that first year, the funds available for that term become updated and available once the student registers for classes. That usually occurs during a pre-registration period about two-thirds to three-quarters of the way into the first term.

For each succeeding academic and federal years the **FAFSA** must be resubmitted in advance of that year with updated information. Financial aid packages are detailed and offered at the outset of each year, once the student has registered for classes. The amounts will be based on the updated **FAFSA** data.

There will be a deadline for accepting any loans. Accepted loans can be canceled in part or in total any time before the funds are disbursed.

Repayment Options

A variety of repayment options exist and are changeable at any time. Extensive details can be found at http://studentaid.ed.gov/repay-loans/understand/plans. The most common repayment options are the **Standard** repayment plan and the **Extended** repayment plan. A **Standard** repayment plan requires a fixed monthly payment of $50.00 or more for up to ten (10) years. An **Extended** repayment plan requires at least $30000.00 of outstanding debt and can be made for up to 25 years. Either a fixed payment or graduated payment amount is available. Other available repayment plans include **Graduated, Pay as You Earn, Income Contingent** and **Income-Sensitive.** They apply to applicants who seek to lessen their **MONTHLY PAYMENT** during periods of differing conditions of financial constraint or hardship. However, the borrower must meet the applicable qualification criteria. The reader is referred to the preceding web-site for specific information.

The other options also extend the period of repayment (**TERM**) of the loan and increase the **TOTAL INTEREST** paid over that **TERM.** Clearly, placing long allowed repayment periods atop the large amount of money that can be borrowed can lead to substantial repayment costs. Borrowing $138500.00 for twenty five (25) years is an extreme that will lead to an immense amount of interest being paid for a student. For parents, their higher annual rate of interest only exacerbates the options.

Loan Consolidation

FSA loans have the characteristics of credit card debt. Each year a loan is awarded at a given level of money and established annual rate of interest. However the funds are disbursed incrementally over the year so the borrowed amount increases in steps, just like making a few periodic purchases on a credit card. As each year a new loan or new loans are requested and approved, it is similar to having multiple credit cards. Like a credit card, interest on any **FSA** loan is charged on a daily basis using the daily outstanding balance each day.

There is a wide variation of loan possibilities that can and do occur for millions of college students when they are taking on the loans. But thereafter things change. Regardless of the sequence of taking the loans and the **Annual Loan Limits** involved as the money was disbursed, in the end the student has accumulated a certain amount of borrowed money. The repayment and interest accrual then ensue for those fixed amounts within each category of loans involved for any particular borrower. For a student continuously in college, loan payments are **deferred** until he or she has completed or left college studies and passed a six month **grace period**. If subsidized **Direct Loans** are involved then the interest during that time is paid by the government. For unsubsidized **Direct Loans** and **PLUS Loans**, the interest during that time is paid by the borrower. If left paid, the interest is accumulated and added to the **PRINCIPAL** until repayment begins.

Repayment of multiple **FSA** loans is complicated. An undergraduate student could be awarded both a subsidized loan and an unsubsidized loan each year of his or her education. So an undergraduate student could end up with as many as twelve loans. A graduate student who completes a Masters and a doctoral degree could end up with five or more additional student loans. A parent could also end up with multiple loans. Each of these separate loans would have a different **TERM, ANNUAL RATE OF INTEREST**, variable vs. fixed rate and repayment schedule and may have been made by different lenders. The multiplicity of tracking loans could become a significant nuisance, even overwhelming; especially for borrowers using other than the **Standard** repayment plan.

To avoid the above loan repayment tracking headaches, within the **Direct Loan Program** a student borrower can simplify loan repayment by **consolidating** his or her loans. Parents may also consolidate multiple loans. **Consolidation** is the process by which separate loans can be combined into a single loan. As a result, the borrower begins repayment for a single loan. Consolidation is the equivalent of cutting up all credit cards and transferring all the debt to one card. Of course, that will result in the outstanding balance being the combined amounts from the various cards, which is not necessarily a good thing. But cutting up excess credit cards is always positive. There are negative aspects and risk in consolidating **FSA** loans and they can be significant. They are described and illustrated in Lessons 16 and 18.

To consolidate, the **FSA** borrower must have at least one loan that is either in a grace period or in repayment. A borrower is allowed to seek a **Direct Consolidation Loan** at any time that is the case. Complete details are available at www.loanconsolidation.ed.gov. The following are highlights of that information.

Consolidation changes the loan situation to one of a single loan. Once consolidated no more loans are to be added, so the **PRINCIPAL** set at the outset is fixed. Also, repayment is done on the basis of a **MONTHLY PAYMENT** as determined by the amortization process.

The **PRINCIPAL** for the **Direct Consolidated Loan** will be the sum of the separate loan amounts owed on the day the lender approves the application. The consolidated loan will have a new fixed annual rate of interest. The fixed rate will be the "weighted average" of the annual rates of interest on the separate loans being consolidated, rounded up to the nearest 0.125%. Weighted average means the average is based upon a proportioning that gives relative weight to each loan's annual rate of interest based upon its corresponding loan amount. The higher the loan amount the greater is the weight applied to its annual rate of interest. The result is the single interest rate will differ from that of each of the separate loans.

There is no application fee (or origination fee) for a **Direct Consolidation Loan**, and the borrower may prepay the loan at any time without penalty. The **TERM** of the consolidated loan will be new and in the range of twelve to thirty years. Typically, the **TERM** is set by the lender using specific ranges of **LOAN AMOUNT** tied to particular **TERM**s as follows.

LOAN AMOUNT	TERM
$0.00 to $7499.99	10 years
$7500.00 to $9999.99	12 years
$10000.00 to $19999.99	15 years
$20000.00 to $39999.99	20 years
$40000.00 to $59999.99	25 years
$60000.00 or more	30 years

The resulting **MONTHLY PAYMENT** amount can be either lower or higher than the total of the payments for the original separate loans, but is usually noticeable lower because the **TERM** is almost always longer. However, extension of the **TERM** caused by redoing the loan will lead to higher **CUMULATIVE INTEREST** over time. As will be illustrated subsequently, the additional interest can be and usually is substantial.

Normally, once loans are consolidated, the resulting **TERM** is <u>not</u> changeable. However, if a borrower directly contacts the lender it may be possible to negotiate a change in **TERM**. It is easier to negotiate a <u>shorter</u> **TERM** than a <u>longer</u> **TERM**. For the former it indicates a borrower has the means to make a higher payment, and if creditworthiness is acceptable, it is likely approved. For the latter it may signal an inability to afford the current payment and possible creditworthiness issues. In that circumstance a **hardship case** should be sought.

A borrower can consolidate an existing consolidation loan again if an additional **Direct Loan** is included in the consolidation. That can occur if a student returns to college for more studies. The **TERM** may or may not change when that is done. For example, if 13 years remain on a 15-year consolidated loan the thirteen years might become the **TERM** for the new **LOAN AMOUNT**. Such things are a matter of negotiation with the lender. Also when an either an **FSA** loan or a **Direct Consolidation Loan** is in **forbearance** the payments are delayed but the **TERM** is not, resulting in a <u>higher</u> **MONTHLY PAYMENT** amount when repayments are renewed. Forbearance occurs when a requested break in the repayment is accepted during temporary inability to make the monthly payments, such as inadequate income.

FSA loan borrowers can incur substantial amount of debt. **Aggregate Loan Limits** indicate the possibilities. For an undergraduate student or a parent the average **FSA** loan debt is about $28000.00. For graduate students a $40000.00-$50000.00 amount can result easily. As several to many separate loans, it is common that borrowers inevitably consider consolidation of their loans.

Some readers may wonder how Nicole's parents managed to save $50000 for her college educational costs. So let's examine various aspects of that accomplishment.

Saving for College Costs

In pure numbers the parents had about 18 years to accumulate the $50000. In simple terms they need to save $2778 per year, which is $231 per month. That assumes they began saving the year she was born. If they began say 2 years prior, the amount is $2500 per year, which is $208 per month.

Taking into account inflation, requires more involved math, namely exponents. A somewhat simpler approximate way can be used. If the rate of inflation was in play for 20 years the parents would have begun with a much lower saved amount. At www.inflationdata.com one access historical inflation rate data from 1913 forward. Using a provided calculator, I determined the <u>cumulative</u> rate of inflation from January 1999 to January 2018 was 50.86%. What that means is that $1.00 saved in January, 1999 grows to $1.51 by January 2018.

Via complex math, the annual rate of inflation was 2.19% (rounded).

ASIDE: For interested readers, here's how to calculate the 2.19%. If **ARI** is the annual rate of increase, then after 19 years the $1.00 becomes $1 \times (1 + \textbf{ARI}/100)^{19}$. And.

$$1 \times (1 + \textbf{ARI}/100)^{19} = 1.51$$

Using a calculator and trial and error values of **ARI**, the result is **ARI** = 2.19% (rounded).

To account for inflation, the parents would begin with $208 per month in January, 1999 and then increase every year to the previous monthly amount multiplied by 1.0219. The succeeding amounts (rounded) would be $208, $212, $217 and so on up to $313 in January, 2018. That is possible if the family earnings increase by that same annual rate or more. Of course, the parents will accumulate more than $50000. Omitting the (precise) calculations, the actual amount will be $61807.

NOTE: To accumulate $50000, the parents would have started with a monthly amount of only $208 x ($50000/$61807) = $168.

During that time the funds will also be gaining monthly interest. If the annual rate of interest on their savings account was steady at 1%, then (omitting the (precise) calculations) the total saved will be $67956. If instead it was invested monthly and earned a steady 3%, the total saved would be $82954. At 5% it would be $102574.

NOTE: To accumulate $50000, the parents would have started with a monthly amount of only $208 x ($50000/$67956) = $153. Or, $208 x ($50000/$82954) = $125. Or, $208 x ($50000/$$102574) = ($101)

The future annual rates of inflation are unknown. If it is assumed the above 2.19% value applies to the future 20 years in time, then the projection would lead to the same results if the initial monthly savings begin at $208. For different starting monthly amount, the outcomes would be proportional. For example, for a starting with monthly amount of $416 the accumulated savings would be doubled. The results for the interest (investment) rates would also be proportional.

For readers capable of doing (via spreadsheets) the detailed calculations omitted above different assumptions for future inflation, interest and investment rates could be tried. For projections other than 20 years, the calculator at www.inflationdata.com can be used to get the annual rate of inflation based on immediate past history for fewer or more years.

Tax Benefits for Education Costs

Presently there are numerous income tax benefits in play for helping to pay college costs. They are described in IRS Publication 970. Ways of saving money are the use of a) so called Qualified Tuition Programs, b) Tax-Free Savings Bonds, and c) Coverdell Educational Savings Account. Each can be set up well before and/or during the student's studies. Several tax deduction and tax credit possibilities also exist once the studies begin and while repaying student loans. Depending on the circumstances involved, some scholarships might also be tax free.

These tax benefits apply to studies at eligible educational institutions. Although worded differently for each in IRS Publication 970, for most of these benefit possibilities an eligible educational institution is any college, university, vocational school, or other postsecondary educational institution eligible to participate in a student aid program administered by the U.S. Department of Education. It includes virtually all accredited public, nonprofit, and proprietary (privately owned profit-making) postsecondary institutions. The educational institution should be able to tell you if it is an eligible educational institution. Certain educational institutions located outside the United States also participate in the U.S. Department of Education's Federal Student Aid (FSA) programs. Where different, mention is made below.

- Qualified Tuition Programs -

Qualified Tuition Programs (QTPs) are sometimes called 529 Savings Plans (named after Section 529 of the federal tax code). But the word "savings" is a misnomer because the program involves investing money not bank savings accounts. So simply "529 Plans" is more accurate. They are set up and maintained by the states and eligible public or private colleges, universities, vocational schools or other post-secondary educational institution. One should be knowledgeable about investing in the stock and bond markets before setting up a QTP. An introduction to the topic is included in a subsequent volume in my book series.

Typically a QTP involves investing in mutual funds managed by established financial companies. So they carry the advantages and risks of investing in the stocks or bonds included in the funds. Safer money market funds are also options. Consequently, the QTPs are more secure for long-term investing (saving). If the QTP is not directly operated by the state, then investment management fees are likely to be incurred.

The tax advantage of a QTP is no federal tax is due on withdrawals (called 'distributions") provided the money is used entirely to pay a student's qualified educational expenses of a designated beneficiary. The designated beneficiary is either a future or present student. Typically that person is either the child or grandchild of the QTP investor. But anyone can be a beneficiary, including the investor. An individual can set up multiple QTPs. For example, a parent might set one up separately for each child and for multiple grandchildren. If a loss occurs in the invested funds, the investor might be able to claim it as a tax deduction. If that arises, one should consult the IRS publications and/or your tax accountant.

Qualified expenses include tuition and required fees; course-required books, supplies and equipment; room and board (with some constraints); computers, peripheral equipment, qualified software and Internet access. The student must be enrolled at least half-time at the time of the expenses.

Plans can be set up in any state where they are available. The advantage is that the market for QTPs is competitive. If the QTP is set up in the state of residence then state tax exemptions might be available. For a state having no income tax, there would be no benefits.

There are no income restrictions on the contributor. Contributions cannot exceed the actual qualified educational expenses. Excess distribution amounts will be taxed.

- Tax-free education savings bonds -

So-called series EE bonds issued after 1989 or so-called series I bonds qualify for federal educational tax benefits if used for qualified education expenses. Bond owners must have been at least 24 years old before the bond was issued. Interest earned is federal tax free for any bonds redeemed and used for qualified expenses of the bond owner, a spouse or any dependent claimed on the bond owner's tax return.

Qualified direct expenses include only tuition and required fees. Contributions of proceeds into a QTP and a Coverdell Educational Savings Account also qualify.

The exclusion of interest from federal taxes is only available to married couples filing joint returns and to single filers. It is not available to a married person filing separately. A 100% deduction applies for a joint return adjusted gross income (AGI) less than $117250 ($781500 if single or the head of a household). The deduction phases down to zero for a joint return AGI of $147250 ($931500 if single or the head of a household). These income limits apply in the year you use bonds for educational purposes. The exclusion is claimed using IRS Form 8815.

- Coverdell Educational Savings Accounts -

For readers interested in setting up a trust or custodial account a Coverdell Educational Savings Account is applicable. They are available for a joint AGI income up to $220000 ($110000 if single or the head of a household). Due to the contribution and distribution complexities involved the reader is advised to seek professional legal as well as tax accounting advice to do so. Coordination with other tax benefit savings options also complicates the details.

- American Opportunity Credit -

For a 2017, a federal tax credit of up to $2500 per qualified student was available for each year for up to 4 years of postsecondary education, a total of $10000 per qualified student. The annual amount might also increase in forthcoming tax years. It is available during the period of studies (at least half-time for at least one academic period, e.g. one semester). Qualified expenses must occur during studies and include tuition, fees, books and course materials whether required for enrollment or not. Contributions of proceeds into a QTP also qualify.

The qualified student is you, a spouse or a dependent for whom you claim an exemption on your tax return. The credit is for the person paying the expenses of the student. These are direct subtractions from the federal tax normally owed each year. One cannot claim the deduction of for one's self if he or she is listed as a dependent on another person's tax return (such as a parent). In fact, if someone else (e.g. a former spouse) other than you, your spouse or your dependent pays the expenses for your listed dependent you get to take the tax credit.

The tax credit is computed in two increments; 100% of the first $2000 of eligible expenses, 25% of the next $2000 (0.25 x $2000 = $500). The full tax credit applies for a joint return AGI less than $160000 ($80000 if single or the head of a household). The tax credit phases down to zero for a joint return AGI of $180000 ($90000 if single or the head of a household). The credit is claimed using Form 8863 and entering the amount in the applicable location on Form 1040 (or Form 1040A).

- Lifetime Learning Credits -

For 2017, a lifetime learning credit of $2000 per student per federal tax return is available for post-secondary education and for courses taken to acquire or improve job skills. It is available for an unlimited number of tax years. The annual amount might also increase in forthcoming tax years.

The credit is available for any courses taken at an eligible educational institution. Qualified expenses must occur during studies and include tuition and other costs. Other costs are required fees, books, course materials and equipment if the expenses are required to be paid to the institution for enrollment.

The credit is for the person who paid the expenses of the eligible student. The rules regarding this are the same as for the American Opportunity Credit

The credit is computed as 20% of the first $10000 of eligible expenses. A full tax credit applies for a joint return AGI less than $112000 ($56000 if single or the head of a household). The deduction phases down to zero for a joint return AGI of $132000 ($66000 if single or the head of a household). The credit is claimed using Form 8863 and entering the amount in the applicable location on Form 1040 (or Form 1040A).

- Deduction of Interest on Student Loans -

For 2017, a federal tax deduction of up to $2500 annually was allowed for interest paid on student loans. The loans must be either from government or private lending entities. Loans obtained from a related person (parent, sibling, grandparents etc.) or from a qualified employer plan are not applicable. To be an eligible loan, the qualifications for the student, the institution and the expenses are generally the same as required for FSA student loans. The expenses must have been either incurred or paid within a reasonable time before or after you took the loans out.

The loans must have been for you, your spouse or a person who was your dependent when you took out the loan. You must be legally obligated to pay the interest. If you are the student, you cannot take the deduction if someone else (typically a parent) is claiming an exemption for you on their tax return. For dependents some exceptions to the general rules apply. For example, if your child marries later, he or she can file a joint return with a spouse and still be your dependent for this deduction. See IRS Publication 970 for other aspects. For this deduction, an eligible educational institutions also include those conduction an internship or residency program leading to a degree certificate from an institution of higher education or a hospital, or other health care facility that offers postgraduate training.,

The full tax credit applies for a joint return AGI up to $135000 ($65000 if single or the head of a household). The tax credit phases down to zero for a joint return AGI of $165000 ($80000 if single or the head of a household). The credit is by entering the amount in the applicable location on Form 1040 (or Form 1040A).

- Tuition and fees deduction -

For 2017, a federal tax deduction of up to $4000 was available for tuition and required fees paid at a qualified educational institution for an eligible student. The qualified student is either you, or a spouse, or a dependent for whom one claims an exemption on their tax return. The full tax credit applies for a tax payer who has paid the expenses. You cannot claim if another person can claim you as a dependent and take the deduction on their return, even if they don't do so.

A $4000 tax deduction applies for a joint return AGI up to $130000 ($65000 if single or the head of a household). Above that income, a $2000 deduction applies for a joint return AGI up to $160000 ($80000 if single or the head of a household). For a higher AGI no credit is allowed. The credit is claimed using Form 8917 and entering the amount in the applicable location on Form 1040 (or Form 1040A).

- Scholarships, Fellowships, Assistantships -

Scholarships are typically awarded to undergraduate students to assist them in pursuing their studies. Fellowships are awarded to assist graduate students in pursuing studies and research. Awards include monetary amounts and allowances. If awarded to a candidate for a degree at an eligible educational institution, some of these may be tax-free.

Pursuit of a bachelor's or higher degree at a college or university qualifies as candidacy. A program of training for employment in a recognized occupation is also candidacy. Students in primary or secondary school also might be awarded scholarships. That's constitutes candidacy too.

Qualified education expenses for tax-free scholarships and fellowship grants include tuition and required fees, books, supplies, and equipment that are required for the courses. Room and board (or lodging and meals), travel costs, research costs, clerical help, and non-required equipment and expenses are excluded.

Tax free awards do not have to be reported in a tax return. If the award requires services to be performed for hourly payment or salary, that income is not tax-free and must be reported. . Exceptions exist for some awards targeted to health professions.

Other qualified components are not reportable if not part of the reimbursement for services performed. Exceptions exist for some health profession targeted awards. Commonly services provided are either teaching assistance or research assistance by graduate students, Hence the awards are more commonly termed graduate teaching assistantships (GTAs) or graduate research assistantships (GRAs). Some fellowships involve payment for independent, solitary conduct of research, not assistance. Some doctoral graduate students are hired as full-or part-time instructors and conduct independent, solitary teaching.

GRAs typically include payment of the tuition. Some GRA awards include tuition reductions, e.g. to offset the difference between out-of-state and in-state tuition. Typically the GRA award pays the resulting amount. For graduate students, unless a tuition reduction is specifically included as payment for services, it is a tax-free amount. Any portion that is specifically included as payment for services must be reported as income.

Typically GTA awardees must pay their tuition (whether reduced or not) out of personal funds. That tuition is includable in the above tax benefits if the tax benefit is not limited to undergraduate students.

If you receive a tuition reduction for education below the college level (including primary, secondary, or high school), it is tax-free for specific cases. It is tax free only if a) you are an employee or b) are a retired employee or left on a disability, or c) are widow or widower of either one, or d) are a dependent spouse or child of any of the three.

- Double Benefits -

Double benefits are not allowed. One cannot claim the same education expenses for two different tax benefit options. One cannot claim any expenses already paid for by another source, such as by an employer or via a tax free scholarship or via gifts or inheritances. IRS Publication 970 also addresses treatment of certain other technicalities that might occur.

Alertness to this issue is one thing. Navigating the tax code to insure it does not happen is another thing. Those nasty, head scratching tax forms and instructions try to lead one through it successfully. With careful attention it can be done. Otherwise use of a professional accountant might enter the picture.

- State Income Taxes -

In the author's state of residence, Colorado, the following applies. The federal education tax deductions apply automatically. That's because the federal taxable income is automatically entered the base state taxable income at the outset of the state tax return form. Then certain adjustments applicable to Colorado follow. Once the state tax owed is calculated, certain state tax credits can be subtracted if applicable. There are no state education tax credits. The federal education tax credits are subtractions from the federal tax owed only. They play no role in the taxes one owes to the state. Readers likely will find similar circumstances in their applicable state of residence, but need to investigate their particular state's treatment of education costs.

What the Future Holds

The preceding tax benefits apply for federal tax rules for 2017 income. What about the future?

Anybody can predict the future. It's just they cannot do it with certainty. However, for 2018 there is some certainty known. In December 2017 a tax reform bill was passed in the Congress and became law. Little was changed in the provisions for educational tax benefits. At http://blog.getintocollege.com/new-tax-bill-passed-what-does-tax-reform-mean-for-students-and-parents/ initial effects were summarized. The 529 Plans were expanded to cover up to $10000 in K-12 expenses for each child. The Lifetime Learning Credit income limits were increased to $134000 for a joint return ($67000 for an individual). As a general point, dependent exemptions were replaced increased standard deductions and a child tax credit for children up to 17 years in age. A $500 family tax credit was added for children older than 17 and for other dependents.

In saving for college costs over the coming years, the present federal tax benefits may or may not continue. If they do, details and amounts will change over time. If they don't, it's hard to imagine alternative options won't come into play. It's hard to imagine the same would not occur regarding deductions and credits allowed at the time a future student is actually in college and the costs are being paid. What's important is to recognize some benefits will exist to offset actual costs. Then do you best to put your finger up into the wind and guesstimate in what range a percentage reduction might be. Also use resources like www.inflationdata.com to help project future costs. Then start saving for the estimated costs to the extent you can afford to do so.

Exercise 21:

YEARLY COSTS

	Year 1	Year 2	Year 3	Year 4	TOTAL	AVERAGE
Sure Thing	13500	14040	14602	15040	57181	14295
Sure Thing-R&B	24500	25480	26499	27559	104038	26010
Hoped For	40500	42120	43805	45557	171982	42995
Dream	49500	51480	53539	55681	210200	52550

YEARLY GIFT AID

0.4	Year 1	Year 2	Year 3	Year 4	TOTAL	AVERAGE
Sure Thing	5400	5616	5841	6016	22872	5718
Sure Thing-R&B	9800	10192	10600	11024	41615	10404
Hoped For	16200	16848	17522	18223	68793	17198
Dream	19800	20592	21416	22272	84080	21020

YEARLY COSTS - YEARLY GIFT AID

0.6	Year 1	Year 2	Year 3	Year 4	TOTAL	AVERAGE
Sure Thing-R&B	8100	8424	8761	9024	34309	8577
Sure Thing	14700	15288	15900	16536	62423	15606
Hoped For	24300	25272	26283	27334	103189	25797
Dream	29700	30888	32124	33408	126120	31530

YEARLY COSTS – YEARLY GIFT AID –YEARLY SAVINGS

8000	Year 1	Year 2	Year 3	Year 4	TOTAL	AVERAGE
Sure Thing-R&B	100	424	761	1024	2309	577
Sure Thing	6700	7288	7900	8536	30423	7606
Hoped For	16300	17272	18283	19334	71189	17797
Dream	21700	22888	24124	25408	94120	23530

YEARLY COSTS – YEARLY GIFT AID –YEARLY SAVINGS – YEARLY BUDGET

4800	Year 1	Year 2	Year 3	Year 4	TOTAL	AVERAGE
Sure Thing	-4700	-4376	-4039	-3776	-16891	-4223
Sure Thing-R&B	1900	2488	3100	3736	11223	2806
Hoped For	11500	12472	13483	14534	51989	12997
Dream	16900	18088	19324	20608	74920	18730

YEARLY COSTS – YEARLY SAVINGS – YEARLY BUDGET

4800	Year 1	Year 2	Year 3	Year 4	TOTAL	AVERAGE
Sure Thing	700	1240	1802	2240	5981	1495
Sure Thing-R&B	11700	12680	13699	14759	52838	13210
Hoped For	27700	29320	31005	32757	120782	30195
Dream	36700	38680	40739	42881	159000	39750

TOTAL LOAN AMOUNTS

	With Gift Aid		Without Gift Aid	
	Total	Per Year	Total	Per Year
Hoped For	51989	12997	120782	30195
Dream	74920	18730	159000	39750

HALF TOTAL LOAN AMOUNTS

	With Gift Aid		Without Gift Aid	
	Total	Per Year	Total	Per Year
Hoped For	25995	6499	60391	15098
Dream	37460	9365	79500	19875

HALF TOTAL LOAN AMOUNTS

	With Gift Aid		Without Gift Aid	
	Total	Per Year	Total	Per Year
Hoped For	25995	6499	60391	15098
Dream	37460	9365	79500	19875

ADJUSTED TOTAL LOAN AMOUNTS - NICOLE

	With Gift Aid		Without Gift Aid	
	Total	Per Year	Total	Per Year
Hoped For	25995	6499	27000	27000
Dream	27000	6750	27000	27000

ADJUSTED TOTAL LOAN AMOUNTS - PARENTS

	With Gift Aid		Without Gift Aid	
	Total	Per Year	Total	Per Year
Hoped For	25994	6499	93782	23445
Dream	47920	11980	132000	33000

UNDER-GRADUATE			STANDARD REPAYMENT		EXTENDED REPAYMANT		
DISBURSED 7/1/14-6/30/15	ANNUAL RATE OF INTEREST 4.66%	TERM	5 Years	10 Years	15 Years	20 Years	25 Years
LOAN AMOUNT	ORIGINATION FEE (RATE = 1.072%)	PRINCIPAL	MONTHLY PAYMENT				
1000	10.72	989.28	18.52	10.33	7.65	6.34	5.59
25995	279	25716	481	269	199	165	145
27000	289	26711	500	279	207	171	151
LOAN AMOUNT	ORIGINATION FEE (RATE = 1.072%)	PRINCIPAL	YEARLY AMOUNT				
1000	10.72	989.27	222	124	92	76	67
25995	279	25716	5777	3222	2386	1978	1744
27000	402	37058	6000	3347	2479	2054	1811
LOAN AMOUNT	ORIGINATION FEE (RATE = 1.072%)	PRINCIPAL	CUMULATIVE INTEREST				
1000	10.73	989.27	122	250	388	533	687
25995	279	25716	3162	6505	10074	13865	17869
27000	289		3284	6756	10464	14401	18560
PERCENT CUMULATIVE INTEREST			12	25	39	53	69

APPROXIMATE YEARLY INTEREST = AVG. LOAN AMOUNT x 4.66/100

HF = $6499 x 4.66/100 x 4 = $1211 (rounded)   D = $6750 x 4.66/100 x 4 = $1258 (rounded)

APPROXIMATE CUMULATIVE INTEREST

HF = 1211 x 2.75 = $3331   D = $1258 x 2.75 = $4800

Exercise 22:

YEARLY COSTS

	Year 1	Year 2	Year 3	Year 4	TOTAL	AVERAGE
Sure Thing	13500	14040	14602	15040	57181	14295
Hoped For	0	42120	43805	45557	171982	42995
Dream	0	51480	53539	55681	210200	52550

YEARLY GIFT AID

0.4	Year 1	Year 2	Year 3	Year 4	TOTAL	AVERAGE
Sure Thing	5400	5616	5841	6016	22872	5718
Hoped For	0	16848	17522	18223	68793	17198
Dream	0	20592	21416	22272	84080	21020

YEARLY COSTS - YEARLY GIFT AID

0.60000	Year 1	Year 2	Year 3	Year 4	TOTAL	AVERAGE
Sure Thing	8100	8424	8761	9024	34309	8577
Hoped For	0	25272	26283	27334	78889	25797
Dream	0	30888	32124	33408	96420	31530

YEARLY COSTS – YEARLY GIFT AID –YEARLY SAVINGS

13967	Year 1	Year 2	Year 3	Year 4	TOTAL	AVERAGE
Hoped For	0	11305	12316	13367	36988	9247
Dream	0	16921	18157	19441	54519	13630

YEARLY COSTS – YEARLY GIFT AID –YEARLY SAVINGS – YEARLY BUDGET

6400	Year 1	Year 2	Year 3	Year 4	TOTAL	AVERAGE
Hoped For	0	4905	5916	6967	17788	4447
Dream	0	10521	11757	13041	35319	8830

TOTAL LOAN AMOUNTS

	With Gift Aid	
	Total	Per Year
Hoped For	17788	4447
Dream	35319	8830

UNDERGRADUATE LOAN AMOUNTS

	With Gift Aid	
	Total	Per Year
Hoped For	8894	2224
Dream	17659	4415

UNDER - GRADUATE			STANDARD REPAYMENT		EXTENDED REPAYMANT		
DISBURSED 7/1/14-6/30/15	ANNUAL RATE OF INTEREST 4.66%	TERM	5 Years	10 Years	15 Years	20 Years	25 Years
LOAN AMOUNT	ORIGINATION FEE (RATE = 1.072%)	PRINCIPAL	MONTHLY PAYMENT				
1000	10.72	989.28	18.52	10.33	7.65	6.34	5.59
8894	95	8799	165	92	68	56	50
17569	188	17381	325	181	134	111	98
LOAN AMOUNT	ORIGINATION FEE (RATE = 1.072%)	PRINCIPAL	YEARLY AMOUNT				
1000	10.72	989.27	222	124	92	76	67
8894	95	8799	1977	1103	816	677	597
17569	188	17380	3905	2178	1613	1337	1179
LOAN AMOUNT	ORIGINATION FEE (RATE = 1.072%)	PRINCIPAL	CUMULATIVE INTEREST				
1000	10.73	989.27	122	250	388	533	687
8894	95	8799	1977	1103	816	677	597
17569	188	17380	3905	2178	1613	1337	1179
PERCENT CUMULATIVE INTEREST			12	25	39	53	69

Exercise 23:

YEARLY COSTS - YEARLY GIFT AID

0.6	Year 1	Year 2	Year 3	Year 4	TOTAL	AVERAGE
Sure Thing-R&B	8100	8424	8761	9024	34309	8577
Hoped For	0	0	26283	27334	53617	25797
Dream	0	0	32124	33408	65532	31530

YEARLY COSTS – YEARLY GIFT AID –YEARLY SAVINGS

11192	Year 1	Year 2	Year 3	Year 4	TOTAL	AVERAGE
Hoped For	0	0	15091	16142	31233	7808
Dream	0	0	20932	22216	43148	10787

YEARLY COSTS – YEARLY GIFT AID –YEARLY SAVINGS – YEARLY BUDGET

9600	Year 1	Year 2	Year 3	Year 4	TOTAL	AVERAGE
Hoped For	0	0	5491	6542	12033	3008
Dream	0	0	11332	12616	23948	5987

UNDER - GRADUATE			STANDARD REPAYMENT		EXTENDED REPAYMANT		
DISBURSED 7/1/14-6/30/15	ANNUAL RATE OF INTEREST 4.66%	TERM	5 Years	10 Years	15 Years	20 Years	25 Years
LOAN AMOUNT	ORIGINATION FEE (RATE = 1.072%)	PRINCIPAL	MONTHLY PAYMENT				
1000	10.72	989.28	18.52	10.33	7.65	6.34	5.59
6017	65	5952	111	62	46	38	34
11974	128	11846	222	124	92	76	67
LOAN AMOUNT	ORIGINATION FEE (RATE = 1.072%)	PRINCIPAL	YEARLY AMOUNT				
1000	10.72	989.27	222	124	92	76	67
6017	65	5952	1337	746	552	458	404
11974	128	11846	2661	1484	1099	911	803
LOAN AMOUNT	ORIGINATION FEE (RATE = 1.072%)	PRINCIPAL	CUMULATIVE INTEREST				
1000	10.73	989.27	122	250	388	533	687
6017	65	5952	732	1506	2332	3209	4136
11974	128	11846	1456	2996	4641	6387	8231
PERCENT CUMULATIVE INTEREST			12	25	39	53	69

APPENDIX IV: Afterthoughts

Attacking Your FSA Student Loan Debt

Student loan debt is of major significance to college graduates. For young people entering post college life and one day envisioning purchasing a residence the impact hits home soon. When applying for a normal loan, for example for an automobile or perhaps for the purchase of a condo, the impact is the possible inability to qualify for those loans.

In evaluating loan applications the main factors the lender considers are the borrower's ability to afford the loan and dependability of repaying it entirely. That is not done by a willy-nilly approach. Lenders look at the existing debt to income ratio of the applicant, value of assets, collateral etc. Graduated students at a typical age of the early twenties likely have minimal personal assets and little to offer in collateral. So the first factor is mostly in play. On the debt side, the student loans are likely the only debt but a big one. On the income side, upon graduation the undergraduate student may or may not have a job. If the recent graduate does have a job it may be in an underpaying part-time expedient job. That set of circumstances leads to inability to qualify for other loans. Basically, the applicant cannot demonstrate either present ability or near to intermediate term dependability to repay the desired loan.

In simple math terms student loan debt reduces the amount one can borrow for other needs by that amount. Take the average **FSA** debt of about $30000. If a graduate could otherwise qualify for an automobile loan of $40000 he or she would only qualify for a $10000 loan. So you end up buying a used car instead of that fancy new one. If you have a good job and might otherwise qualify for a $150000 home mortgage loan, then that amount would drop to $120000. You end up buying an older existing condo rather than a brand spanking new one. Take a graduate with an **FSA** debt nearing the higher end, say $100000 with a 30-year **TERM**. That may hinder qualifying for other loans for a long time.

Anecdotally, the preceding has become more and more evident. Many young people are marrying later than past generations, purchasing a home significantly later, renting condos rather than owning, living at home with parents to an older age.

On the other side of the coin, students who minimize or avoid **FSA** debt and find career oriented employment do not encounter such tightened constraints. Using advance preparation and careful, strategic approaches Nicole and her Dad worked out a highly manageable game plan for affordably repaying their **FSA** loan debts. Following their game plan or a similar one is the best step. However that is not a reality for many borrowers. Tens of millions of people carry student loan debt. The number of them falling behind on repayment or totally defaulting is on the rise. So what is one to do if you are on the bad side of the coin?

It's a pretty tight knot and no quick solution is possible. For a young person entering college I have offered Lessons about: awareness and precautions about the **FSA** loan process; paying interest during deferment; using the consolidation option effectively; forbearance during a hardship status; and hopefully sharing the **FSA** borrowing by a combination of student and Parent loans.

Now, I offer what I would do if I was a recent graduate, single and with **FSA** loan debt.

1- Consolidate my loans and accelerate repayment by paying make a **MONTHLY PAYMENT** equal same total amount as would have to be paid for the unconsolidated loans.

2- Live at home until I get a suitably paying job near to or in my degreed profession.

3- During that period find any job that provides me income, so I can provide enough take home pay to meet my monthly **FSA** loan repayments and pay some rent to my parents.

4- Suggest that my parents use the rent money to help pay off their own **FSA** loans, if any exist. They might just reply "Use it toward your own loans." as we can cover our own closely controlled expenses.

5- If it is not possible to cover all my expenses, use forbearance but at least pay the monthly interest on time to avoid adding to my **FSA** debt. Pay as much more than that as I can afford.

6- Recognize that while in college I had relatively low base financial needs. Keep them that way until I find suitable career employment and as long a while after that as practical.

7- If possible, once I find suitable career employment stay at home a bit longer and keep my other expenditures close to those relatively low base financial needs. Strive to use ½ of take home pay toward **FSA** loans. Doing so will substantially accelerate paying off my **FSA** debt. In many cases it will quickly eliminate an average **FSA** loan debt.

8- Complete a mock loan application for an automobile and a mock loan application for a home mortgage for target loan amounts envisioned as my realistic needs. Use real data on personal financial status. Informally visit a loan officer to converse about my general creditworthiness, extent of loan amounts for which I presently qualify. Inquire about the necessary amount of **FSA** debt reduction and/or income increase to be able to qualify for each target loan amount.

9- In negotiating a salary/benefits package from the professional employer, ask my employer to consider committing a monthly amount of benefit pay to my **FSA** loan debt. It's similar to the employer paying part or all of the employee's health insurance or other benefits. Discuss that idea after a salary level is nearly negotiated. Then suggest it be reduced for that purpose, equally at most or possibly a bit less. Doing that lessens payments for income taxes and other withholdings. The employer night agree but tie it in some way to longevity at the firm. That's a fair step.

10- Do not apply for optional additional loans even if I have to drive a bit of a jalopy and retain a college level constrained daily expenditure until my **FSA** debt is sufficiently paid off to allow me to qualify for the full loan amount I need.

11- With a suitable job in hand, as soon as pragmatically possible begin increasing the **MONTHLY PAYMENT** on my consolidated **FSA** loan to accelerate repayment. Increase it as much as possible, and keep doing so as much as my income permits.

Presently, auto and mortgage loan interest rates are very low. They likely won't stay that way much longer. Each increase in loan rates translates to an increase in the **MONTHLY PAYMENT** needed for the loan, consequently decreasing the **LOAN AMOUNT** for which you could qualify. Act promptly to pursue and complete the above strategies as soon as possible. While not as vital as carrying on life's basic essentials, that focus should be among your highest priorities if the not the top of that "To Do" list.

Income Share Accounts

Recently, an alternative to **FSA** student loans has arisen. It's termed an **Income Share Account (ISA)** and works differently than a loan. It's a contract. The college commits (allocates) an agreed amount of funds to the student. The student agrees to later exchange a portion of his/her post-graduation income as repayment. The amount of funds is determined by request of the student, reflecting his/her assessment of the personal need.

At Purdue University, a <u>minimum</u> amount of $5000 is applicable. A maximum (cap) exists, too. The cap amount depends upon the student's existing student loan situation and prior **ISA** commitments. There is no effect on any non-loan grants, scholarships etc. he/she might have in place. The maximum **ISA** amount allowed will be such that a student's combined financial aid from all sources does not exceed his/her Cost of Attendance (a terminology specific to Purdue University).

The student agrees to a certain amount of allocated money. But he/she is neither committed to repay that specific amount of money nor to pay any interest. Instead, he/she agrees to pay the university a percentage of his/her subsequent annual job income over an agreed number of years. The percentage and number of years vary among students. More or less they reflect the average earning potential of the student's major. For example, on average, a civil engineering graduate will earn more than a history graduate etc. Each will have different **ISA** conditions set. The Purdue University web site provides a Boiler Comparison Tool to generally assess the cost of an **ISA** by discipline.

For a Spring 2018 graduate in Civil Engineering, the results are as follows. For $32000 allocated, the percentage is 9.70% for 96 months (8 years). The average entry salary is $54000 ($4500/month) and rises 3.80% annually. The **MONTHLY PAYMENT** begins at $439 and ends at $592. The total repayment is $49493. That's a cost of $17493, about 52% of the allocated funds. For a **FSA Direct PLUS loan** (7.00%, 10 years) the calculator gives a **MONTHLY PAYMENT** of $418 and total repayment is $50107. For a private loan (9.5%, 10 years) it gives a **MONTHLY PAYMENT** of $457 total repayment is $54803.

NOTE: For the alternative loans, it is unclear whether the Purdue calculator uses $32000 as the **PRINCIPAL** before or after an **ORIGINATION FEE**. Using amortization, for a **FSA Direct PLUS** loan (7.00%, 10 years, **LOAN AMOUNT** = $33425, **ORIGINATION FEE** = 4.264%, **PRINCIPAL** =$32000) the author calculated a **MONTHLY PAYMENT** of $372 and total repayment is $52426. For a private loan (9.5%, 10 years, **LOAN AMOUNT** = $33425, **ORIGINATION FEE** = 4.264%,) he calculated a **MONTHLY PAYMENT** of $414 and a total repayment of $52558.

For a like graduate in History the results are as follows. The Purdue calculator gives $32000 allocated and the percentage is 12.54% for 112 months (9.33 years). The average entry salary is $37000 ($3083/month) and rises 3.80% annually. The **MONTHLY PAYMENT** begins at $383 and ends at $555. The total repayment is $51189. That's a loan cost of $14612, about 58% of the allocated funds. For a **FSA Direct PLUS** loan and a private loan the total repayment is same as for the civil engineering student.

NOTE: The above comparison shows the much lower paid history major has to make much higher

MONTHLY PAYMENTS in order to pay off the same allocation. That is illogical and more demanding. That history major likely would have to contract a smaller allocation and/or a longer contract repayment period.

Apparently, the student would repay the university an amount close to what he/she would pay (including interest) with an **FSA Direct PLUS** loan for a **LOAN AMOUNT** equal to the **ISA** allocated amount. In effect the total repaid on the **ISA** option is similar to that of an **FSA Parent loan**. However, since in the **ISA** program there is no actual interest paid (in the technical financial sense) being paid, then there is no federal tax deduction for that sizable portion of the repaid amount. Combined with the high total cost, the **ISA** option is unfavorable. A student should pursue available regular **FSA Undergraduate** loans first. If additional funds are needed, then the **ISA** option could be considered. The following caveat is play, too.

The aim of the university is to get its allocated money back, at least the amount initially committed to the student and in a reasonable timing. The aim of the student is to be able to do so affordably. But there is risk involved to each party. The more the student actually earns the more money he/she will repay. Technically, it could far exceed the initially implied amount. That is controlled by the university placing a cap on the total amount to be repaid. The less the student actually earns, the less he/she will repay. That is to the student's benefit. Technically it can be far below the initially implied amount. Further, there is minimum income level (lower limit) in place, below which the student will not have to repay anything.

Students can use a 6-month grace period after graduation. For student's pursuing advanced studies (graduate school) repayment is delayed during that time.

PREFACE TO BOOK 2: THE CAR FINANCING EXPERIENCE

Formally borrowing money for the first and navigating the unfamiliar territory can be a daunting experience. Indeed, for some it represents a scary challenge. I know. As a young adult, I experienced a bit of it first-hand. In fact, "experienced" is a misnomer. There was little to no prior experience. There were only the first "encounters" with the need to borrow money.

Being wary or afraid of debt can be overcome. As my life moved along, the hard knocks came and went. Learning from my mistakes gradually brought competence and confidence. More passage of time and professional budget management responsibilities at my job further honed my skills and sharpened my strategic capabilities. As a husband, I evolved to having effective techniques and tools to keep the domestic finances in good stead. I figured out how to wisely borrow money and repay it efficiently. As a team, my wife and I manage financial resources attentively and together. We never argue about money, we jointly plan for its utilization.

As a parent, I faced the challenge of teaching my daughter to achieve similar progressions. After all, like many teens, she simply had no interest in learning about money; let alone from her parent. It took time, patience and craftiness. And it took about ten years, from the time she was sweet sixteen to her burgeoning adulthood at twenty-five years old. That quarter-century old daughter was now welcoming, asking for and using my experienced guidance. As she aged another decade or so, there was more to share and for bigger needs. Being able to communicate was a boon to helping out when asked to do so.

With helpful guidance, competent advice and increasing experience with debt matters, a young teen can become increasingly more knowledgeable and comfortable about borrowing money. But you have to make contact first. "Earth to Mars?" "Parent to Teen?" Often, parents are stymied with initiating money management guidance with their adolescent kids. I want to help them start the negotiations. More so, I want to help them mimic my mode of attack and path to progress and eventual success.

DEBT is a Four-Letter Word - *But it Need Not Be!* is an ongoing series of books focused on helping young people learn how to handle newfound debt needs. Each volume covers different aspects of debt needs and issues that occur as a young person grows from about the age of 16 to the age of 35 or so. **THE CAR FINANCING EXPERIENCE** is the second sequential book in the series.

In the first volume, subtitled **THE COLLEGE EXPERIENCE**, the reader walked along as fictionalized high school junior Nicole began considering her interest in pursuing a college degree. The path eventually led to the day she walked down the aisle at her college Commencement. Tagging along was her fictionalized Dad who guided her through the financial aspects of paying for the costs of that education. Nicole graduated with her debt due to the costs of college successfully managed. In between a lot happened and the reader saw the details of all of it.

Nicole's walk began with her enthusiastic, teenaged plea for a credit card. Because some of her high school friends had gotten one, she just had to have one too. She mentioned it to her Dad. "Some of my older friends in the senior class came back this year with a credit card. They were pretty proud, almost bragging about it. I never thought about it but now I'm sort of envious of them. We've never talked about credit cards, so I don't know anything about them. I guess I'll eventually need one, so can you explain them to me? Then maybe I can get one, too?"

Being very anxious to "get one", Nicole presumptively asked her Dad, "How does someone get a credit card? How can I get one?"

While seemingly an episode apart from anything related to college, to her Dad his daughter's inquiry stirred inner thoughts that one day, not far from then, Nicole would be in college and indeed need a credit card. In time she was there and had one, but not until then.

Dad's passage through the inevitable worries about his teenage kid having a credit card, the risks of having one, to her actually getting one was a small part of a larger picture. Initially it was credit cards, later it became student loans. He had a heartfelt desire for Nicole to be accepted into an academic program at a college that best fits her career endeavor. But those costs had to be within the family's financial means. And there was an overarching monetary aspect on his mind. He wanted to teach his teen growing to college graduate age how to effectively handle debt needs. The reader saw in depth how that was accomplished; the calculation procedures, the calculations themselves, the analysis of different options, the decisions made, and the logic and strategies behind the decisions.

Equally important, the reader observed the non-monetary aspects of how Nicole's Dad interacted with her. It was done softly, but no helicopter was involved in doing it. As each monetary task came along, it was addressed together. Dad developed numerical information needed, but made sure Nicole was learning how he calculated it. He implemented careful, detailed analysis of the information and made sure Nicole understood his thinking. In every subsequent step, a strategy was involved before it was taken. Prerequisite to each step was Dad's quizzing of Nicole's understanding of the options and implications. As decisions followed, they moved further along the path, taking each step side-by-side.

How her Dad went about teaching Nicole was as important to observe as the tangible, nitty-gritty monetary items he shared. The reader watched him building a more and more comfortable relationship as he moved his daughter along an invisible parallel path. It led from his understandable initial hand-holding to Nicole's increased self-reliance in handling personal debt.

Nicole and her Dad navigate through her independent need for a credit card for ongoing college expenses, financing her college dreams, considering graduate school, and planning for post-graduation repayment of student loans. Now, Nicole has graduated college and will move further along that path. Nicole and her Dad will proceed through the next stage of her/their development. She will begin to navigate through what the author terms the "post-college experience". So will the reader. **THE CAR FINANCING EXPERIENCE** volume covers the first segment of that path.

In **THE CAR FINANCING EXPERIENCE** and subsequent volumes the reader continues to walk along as Nicole encounters new debt needs. She's just graduated college. Now her path will wind toward and through common post-college debt situations. Increasing complexity and monetary magnitude of the debts ensue. A need for a new car moves into her forefront. Later, purchasing a first condo arises. Further along, moving up to single family residence advances from her horizon. Her Dad will still be accompanying her. His caring teaching approach continues, but with a more mature and independent

Nicole walking aside him.

In **THE CAR FINANCING EXPERIENCE** Nicole faces a challenge not uncommon to young college graduates. Ever since her sweet sixteen year-old birthday, she's been driving a parent-provided, low-cost car. Now she needs to replace that long-used, undependable car. And, for the first time, she has to do it herself. As in **THE COLLEGE EXPERIENCE**, her Dad shares his informed, strategic borrowing strategies based on his own experiences and approaches. Together they use them to carefully make important decisions and take vital borrowing steps. In the end, adult Nicole has become more self-reliant and takes those steps alone.

The motivation and approach to each volume of the **DEBT is a Four-Letter Word - *But it Need Not Be!*** book series are kept consistent. For my new readers, the preceding *PREFACE TO VOLUME 1* **(THE COLLEGE EXPERIENCE***)* shares those aspects in detail.

Ideally, the new reader should consider first reading **THE COLLEGE EXPERIENCE***,* but it is not absolutely necessary. While **DEBT is a Four-Letter Word - *But It Need Not Be!*** is a sequential book series, this second volume can be read as a standalone book. To enable that, a few base, generic monetary topics presented in the first volume are covered in condensed lengths.

While continuing Nicole's journey, the material in **THE CAR FINANCING EXPERIENCE** is applicable to anyone wanting to learn more about the car purchasing, car loan, car leasing and car brokering processes. The pros and cons to purchasing a car compared to leasing one are illustrated. Also, purchasing a leased car after the lease ends involves significant overall cost considerations. The author details how to determine those and make a financial decision about that option. Equally valuable, the reader will learn how to monetarily project and compare the option of purchasing a car outright to leasing the same car and purchasing it when the lease ends. Armed with that knowledge, an informed choice can be made before acting on either one.

The author also covers basic aspects about car insurance needed for a purchased car. Critical aspects of insurance needs for a leased car are also detailed. He also covers the financial implications of a leased car either being stolen or being damaged beyond repair in an accident before the lease ends.

DEBT is a Four-Letter Word - *But It Need Not Be*! is written in narrative, non-fiction style. It shares the hypothetical, but realistic, evolving fiscal development of a daughter as her Dad teaches her in depth skills in wisely taking on debt. As her abilities for wise decision-making, timely borrowing and effective repayment of debt grow, so does the maturity of their relationship. Nicole's not so secret desire is to, one day, outsmart her Dad. I invite you to the peak in and see how close she comes to achieving that. You can drive along at your own pace and have fun!

Open your mind, sharpen your pencils again and let the **LESSONS** on **THE CAR FINANCING EXPERIENCE** begin!